MALCOLM X
THE FBI FILE

MALCOLM X
THE FBI FILE

CLAYBORNE CARSON
INTRODUCTION BY SPIKE LEE
EDITED BY DAVID GALLEN

Carroll & Graf Publishers, Inc.
New York

First Carroll & Graf edition 1991
Second Printing 1992

Carroll & Graf Publishers, Inc.
260 Fifth Avenue
New York, NY 10001

Library of Congress Cataloging-in-Publication Data

Carson, Clayborne, 1944–
    Malcolm X : the FBI file / commentary by Clayborne Carson ;
introduction by Spike Lee ; edited by David Gallen. — 1st Carroll &
Graf ed.
        p.   cm.
    Includes bibliographical references and index.
    ISBN 0-88184-751-8 : $23.95. — ISBN 0-88184-758-5 (pbk.) : $12.95
    1. X, Malcolm, 1925–1965. 2. Afro-Americans—Biography. 3. Black
Muslims—Biography. 4. United States. Federal Bureau of Investigation
—History. I. Gallen, David. II. United States. Federal Bureau of
Investigation. III. Title.
BP223.Z8L5794   1991
320.5'4'092—dc20   91-26697
                                                                 CIP

Manufactured in the United States of America

For my son, David Malcolm Carson

ACKNOWLEDGEMENTS

The publisher gratefully acknowledges permissions to reprint from the following:

Amsterdam News, for excerpts throughout.

Barry Gray and WOR Radio, for interview June 8, 1964.

William Kunstler, for WMCA Radio interview June 8, 1964.

Irv Kupcinet, for WBKB Television interview January 30, 1965.

Los Angeles Herald Dispatch, for excerpts throughout.

New York Post, for "Malcolm X to Elijah: Let's End the Fighting," June 26, 1964. © 1964 by New York Post Company, Inc.

The New York Times, for "Malcolm X Seeks U.N. Negro Debate," August 13, 1964. © 1964 by The New York Times Company, Inc.

Omaha World-Herald, for "Malcolm X's Talk June 30," June 15, 1964; "Malcolm X's Talk Tonight," June 30, 1964; "Malcolm X Declares Anything Whites Can Do Blacks Can Do Better," by Duane Snodgrass, July 1, 1964.

Pittsburgh Courier, for excerpts throughout.

Mike Wallace, for WNTA Television interviews in "The Hate That Hate Produced," July 13–17, 1959.

Washington Post Company, Inc., for excerpts from *New York Herald Tribune*, April 26, 1964, and June 16, 1964. © 1964 by New York Herald Tribune, Inc. All rights reserved.

Westinghouse Broadcasting Company and WBZ Radio (Boston), for interview on "The Bob Kennedy Show," March 24, 1964.

WMAL Radio, for interview February 2, 1963.

WUST Radio, for interview May 12, 1963.

CONTENTS

INTRODUCTION

When I was growing up one of my favorite shows on television was *THE FBI* (Righter of the Wronged, Protector of the Weak). I liked how Efrem Zimbalist, Jr., the FBI Big Cheese, every week outguessed, outsmarted and outmaneuvered crooks, Communists, thieves, murderers, to uphold truth, justice and the American way. I know I couldn't have been the only one who watched it; the man himself, J. Edgar Hoover, loved it also. Back in those days I was young and believed the FBI, CIA and the police were the good guys; they were righteous. Over time, I found out, like many others, this isn't the case at all, except in television and the movies.

One can safely say the Federal Bureau of Investigation has never been a friend to African-Americans. As far back as Marcus Garvey and A. Phillip Randolph the Bureau has more than kept its watchful eye on black leaders trying to uplift their people.

I was fascinated reading this book. At the same time, though, I found it frightening. We all live in a wicked country where the government can and will do anything to keep people in check.

I might add that I see the FBI, CIA and the police departments around this country as one and the same. They are all in cahoots and along with the Nation of Islam they all played a part in the assassination of Malcolm X. Who else? King? Both Kennedys? Evers? Hampton? The list goes on and on.

J. Edgar Hoover was a known racist and he did all he could and more to stop any movement by or on behalf of blacks, all under the guise of protecting democracy.

This book chronicles the growth in the evolution of Malcolm from his early "white man is the devil" days to his later, more developed world outlook right before he was killed. One can see that the Bureau and agencies like it cannot work successfully without informants. They had plants around Malcolm at the highest levels of all his organizations: The Nation of Islam, Muslim Mosque, Inc., and the Organization of Afro-American Unity. To me, that's the sad part. Malcolm was sold out. A house nigger turned him into Massa just like one did Nat Turner and countless others. It's also ironic that Brother Gene, one of Malcolm's bodyguards who gave him mouth-to-mouth resuscitation seconds after he'd been shot down and was dying, also proved to be a police informant. The Bureau knew Malcolm's every move, knew he was being hunted down, but stood back and let him and Elijah fight it out in public (a dispute which they encouraged no doubt).

I'm still surprised they even let these papers out. Turn that around and wonder what was destroyed: What documents will we never know about?

It's 1991 and the Federal Bureau of Investigation we know from television and *Mississippi Burning* are far, far from reality. Fortunately, there are books like this that combat these Walt Disney/John Wayne bogus images. The Bureau, however, would make THE GREAT AMERICAN GANGSTER MOVIE.

—Spike Lee

Part I
Malcolm and the
American State

Malcolm and the American State

For maximum effectiveness of the Counterintelligence Program, and to prevent wasted effort, long-range goals are being set.

1. Prevent the coalition of militant black nationalist groups. In unity there is strength; a truism that is no less valid for all its triteness. An effective coalition of black nationalist groups might be the first step toward a real "Mau" in America, the beginning of a true black revolution.

2. Prevent the rise of a "messiah" who could unify, and electrify, the militant black nationalist movement. Malcolm X might have been such a "messiah"; he is the martyr of the movement today. Martin Luther King, Stokely Carmichael and Elijah Muhammad all aspire to this position. Elijah Muhammad is less of a threat because of his age. King could be a very real contender for this position should he abandon his supposed "obedience" to "white, liberal doctrines" (nonviolence) and embrace black nationalism. . . .
—FBI memorandum, March 4, 1968.

Malcolm X's political and historical significance increased after his assassination. His public statements as a minister and political leader reached mainly a black urban audience while millions of every race read his posthumously published autobiography and speeches. He gained prominence as a caustic critic of civil rights leaders, but by the end of his life his evolving ideas had converged with the militant racial consciousness stimulated by the civil rights protest movement. During his public career, he was affiliated with one of the smaller African-American religious groups and never participated in the major national meetings of black leaders; yet he is remembered as one of the most influential political leaders of modern times. To some admirers he became

an icon—a heroic, almost mythological, figure whose arousing
orations have become indisputable political wisdom. To detrac-
tors he remains a dangerous symbol of black separatism and
anti-white demagoguery. One of the most widely discussed and
controversial African-American leaders of this century, Malcolm
remains insufficiently understood, the subject of remarkably little
serious biographical and historical research.

This edition of Malcolm X's FBI surveillance file seeks to re-
tify a particularly serious deficiency in previous writings on Malcolm—that is, the failure to study him within the context of
American racial politics during the 1950s and 1960s. The surveillance reports document Malcolm's life from his final years in
prison during the early 1950s through the time of his assassination in February 1965. They trace Malcolm's movement from the
narrowly religious perspective of the Nation of Islam toward a
broader Pan-Africanist worldview. The file illuminates his religious and political world suggesting the extent to which his ideas
and activities were perceived as threatening to the American
state. When examined in the context of the FBI's overall surveillance of black militancy, Malcolm's FBI file clarifies his role in
modern African-American politics.

Although some writings about Malcolm X have referred to the
FBI file, most biographical accounts have not placed him within
the framework of national or international politics. Instead, Malcolm has usually been portrayed as an exceptional individual
whose unique experiences inspired his distinctive ideas, as a person affecting African-American politics rather than being affected by the constantly changing political environment.[1] Even
Malcolm's relationships and activities within the Nation of Islam
remained shrouded in rumor and mystery, despite the crucial
role that organization played in Malcolm's ideological development.

Moreover, research regarding Malcolm remains largely unin-
formed by the outpouring of scholarly studies of his main ideological competitor, Martin Luther King, Jr. Although King, like
Malcolm, was a remarkable orator, recent writings on him have
placed King within the wider framework of African-American
political and religious history.[2] Similarly broadly focused studies

are needed in order to understand Malcolm's evolving role in a multifaceted African-American freedom struggle that shaped his ideas even as he influenced its direction. Malcolm and King were articulate advocates of distinctive philosophies and political strategies, but neither leader's historical significance can be equated solely with the emotive power of his words. Both Malcolm and King sought to provide guidance for a mass struggle that generated its own ideas and leaders. Rather than simply followers of Malcolm or King, the activists, organizers, and community leaders who constituted the grass roots of the freedom struggle magnified both leaders' political impact.

Instead of extensive research based on sources produced at the time, popular and scholarly understanding of Malcolm X derives largely from published texts of his speeches and from *The Autobiography of Malcolm X,* a vivid and enlightening, yet undocumented, narrative prepared by Alex Haley. Haley shaped his subject's recollections into a moving account of Malcolm's transformation from abused child to ward to criminal to religious proselytizer to radical Pan-Africanist. The autobiography is an American literary classic that has enriched the lives of many readers. It elicits empathy, revealing the world through its narrator's eyes, but it is less successful as social and political history. Malcolm's political ideas become conclusions drawn solely from his personal experiences. His changing attitudes toward whites becomes the central focus of the narrative, while his political influences, contacts, and activities are reduced to subthemes. All serious study of Malcolm X must begin with the *Autobiography;* unfortunately, many works on him do not extend beyond the biographical and historical information provided by Malcolm himself.[3]

1. Social Origins of Malcolm's Nationalism

Like most autobiographies, Malcolm's account of his life was intended to explain how he came to enlightenment and fulfillment, but his narrative is incomplete and misleading. Malcolm's early experiences limited his subsequent political choices but do not explain them. Malcolm's conversion to Elijah Muhammad's doctrines was a rejection rather than a culmination of his previous life. He repudiated the Christian teachings of his childhood and affiliated with a religious organization he had never previously encountered. He insisted that the major national civil rights groups and their middle-class leaders did not represent needs of the black masses, but, before joining the Nation of Islam, he had never been affiliated with any African-American advancement organization. Despite his fervent advocacy of racial unity and institutional development, he was, ironically, an outsider with respect to the most important African-American institutions. His life was spent mainly as an angry, though insightful, critic, hurling challenges from the margins of black institutional life. With some justification, he saw himself as a leader uniquely capable of arousing discontented African Americans that leaders such as Martin Luther King, Jr., could not reach. During most of his life, however, his status as an outsider prevented him from having the type of impact on the direction of African-American politics that he would achieve as a marbyr.

Malcolm's black nationalism derived, ironically, from his exclusion from the African-American social and cultural mainstream. Although his parents, Louise and Earl Little, were organizers for Marcus Garvey's Universal Negro Improvement Association (UNIA), his childhood experiences did not connect him to the enduring institutions of black life. Rather than memories of a nurturing African-American household, Malcolm's autobiography emphasized the white forces that destroyed his family. He remembered racist whites forcing his family to move from Omaha, Nebraska, where he was born in 1925, to Milwaukee, then to Lansing, Michigan, and finally to a home outside East Lansing. Malcolm gives few indications that he was involved as a child in African-American social life. Malcolm remembered his father as an embittered itinerant preacher who, despite his Garveyite sympathies, displayed and infused Malcolm with ambivalent racial attitudes. "I actually believe that as anti-white as my father was," Malcolm surmised, "he was subconsciously so afflicted with the white man's brainwashing of Negroes that he inclined to favor the light ones, and I was his lightest child." Watching his father deliver sermons, Malcolm was "confused

and amazed" by his emotional preaching and acquired "very little respect for most people who represented religion." Taken to
UNIA meetings by his father, Malcolm was unmoved by the
message of racial pride. "My image of Africa, at that time, was of
naked savages, cannibals, monkeys and tigers and steaming jun-
gles." Malcolm felt that his mother treated him more harshly
than his siblings because his light complexion stirred memories of
her own mixed-race ancestry. Neither of Malcolm's parents were
able to shelter him or provide him with dependable resources to
deal with the racism of the surrounding world. When Earl Little
was killed in 1931, six-year-old Malcolm believed rumors that
"the white Black Legion had finally gotten him."[4] Afterwards,
Malcolm's family life rapidly deteriorated. His mother resented
her dependence on welfare assistance. As she progressively lost
her sanity, Malcolm became more and more incorrigible. At the
age of thirteen, Malcolm was removed from his family entirely
and sent to reform school.

In contrast to Malcolm's experience of a disintegrating family
life and social marginalization, Martin Luther King, Jr., his prin-
ciple ideological adversary, spent his childhood within a stable,
nurturing African-American family and community.[5] "My parents have always lived together very intimately, and I can hardly
remember a time that they ever argued," King once recalled.
Growing up in the house his grandfather, A. D. Williams, had
purchased two decades before King's birth in 1929, the family's
roots in the Atlanta black community extended to the 1890s,
when Williams had become pastor of Ebenezer Baptist church.
After Williams's death in 1931, Martin Luther King, Sr. became
Ebenezer's Pastor. The church became King, Jr.'s "second
home"; Sunday School was where he met his best friends and
developed "the capacity for getting along with people." Although
he, like Malcolm, came to dislike the emotionalism of black religious practice, he developed a lifelong attachment to the black
Baptist church and an enduring admiration for his father's "no-
ble example."[6] King and his family developed strong ties to
Atlanta's black institutions, including businesses, civil rights organizations, and colleges such as Morehouse and Spelman. While
Malcolm's family experienced economic hardship during the De-

pression years, King "never experienced the feeling of not having the basic necessities of life." Both Malcolm and King acquired antielitist attitudes during their childhoods, but the former resented middle-class blacks while the latter acquired a sense of noblesse oblige.⁵ As a teenager, Malcolm ended his schooling after the eighth grade when he was discouraged from aspiring to be a professional.⁶ King completed doctoral studies and saw education as a route to personal success and a career of service to the black community.

Both Malcolm and King recalled having anti-white attitudes during their formative years, but white people occupied a much more central place for Malcolm as a young man than for King, who had little contact with whites as a youth. Malcolm's evolving attitudes toward whites were complex and volatile, serving as the underlying theme of his autobiography. As a child, his mother took him to meetings of white Seventh Day Adventists, whom Malcolm recalled as "the friendliest white people I had ever seen."⁷ His account of his youth includes both descriptions of encounters with white racism and indications of his own ambivalent feelings toward whites. Often the only black in his class, he refrained from participating in school social life. He admitted nevertheless that he secretly "went for some of the white girls, and some of them went for me, too." Elected president of his eighth grade school class, he concedes that he was proud: "In fact, by then, I didn't really have much feeling about being a Negro, because I was trying so hard, in every way I could, to be white."⁸ After moving to Boston in 1941, Malcolm soon straightened his hair in order to look more "white," and brushed off a black, middle-class woman named Laura in order to pursue his white lover.⁴ King, for his part, reacted to a childhood rejection by a white friend by determining to "hate every white person" and thereafter had little social contact with whites until his college years.⁹ Spending his formative years as part of an African-American elite, he resented white racial prejudice but was rarely personally affected by it. His racial identity most often brought him rewards rather than punishments.

Unsurprisingly, therefore, Malcolm's conversion to the Islamic teachings of Elijah Muhammad involved a rejection of his past that would have been inconceivable for King. While in prison for robbery, Malcolm repudiated his earlier life and symbolized his rebirth in the Nation of Islam by abandoning his surname. He joined an organization that had not been part of his environment as a youth and acquired a new past through the racial mythology of the Nation. Malcolm's acceptance of the idea that he was a member of the Lost-Found Nation of Islam in North America made his previous life—and indeed all the postenslavement experiences of African-Americans—only a negative reference point for his new identity. For Malcolm, black adherence to Christianity simply reflected the fact that African-Americans had been brainwashed and separated from their true history. During his adult life, Malcolm would increase his knowledge of the African-American historical literature, but he also popularized the historical myths of Elijah Muhammad, which replaced the complexities of African-American history with tales of the "Asian Black Nation" and "the tribe of Shabazz."[10] Unlike the main African-American Christian churches, the Nation of Islam did not have deep historical roots in the African-American experience, and its development was largely isolated from that of other black religious institutions. Malcolm learned from Elijah Muhammad that African-American history was not a long struggle toward freedom but simply the final stage of the decline of the "Black Man," who had once ruled the earth. The Nation's version of the past was not based on historical research, but it appealed to blacks such as Malcolm who did not identify with the black Christian churches that were more rooted in African-American history.

In contrast to Malcolm's negation of his past, King placed great importance on his family's deep roots in the Baptist church and the Atlanta black community. King's great-grandfather, grandfather, and father had been Baptist ministers. He saw African-American history and the history of his own family as a successful climb from enslavement to freedom and from poverty to affluence. King's adult life as a religious leader was built upon the foundation of his childhood experiences and his ties to the African-American Baptist church and to black leadership networks. While Malcolm became a critical outsider urging blacks to reject mainstream institutions, King became a critical insider seeking to transform those institutions.

Malcolm's and King's strengths and limitations as leaders were related to their ability to mobilize African-American institutions on behalf of the racial goals they sought. Malcolm's political evolution demonstrates the extent to which black nationalism had become marginalized since its nineteenth-century heyday. While nineteenth-century nationalists Martin Delany and Alexander Crummell were products of mainstream black institutions, Marcus Garvey and Elijah Muhammad were outsiders—the former an alien who came to the United States only as an adult, the latter a Muslim in a Christian-dominated culture. Garvey was able to gain a massive following and build an institutional base in the United States despite the opposition of mainstream leaders, but he could never supplant them or their institutions. Elijah Muhammad similarly attacked the "so-called Negro" leaders and attracted a sizable following; yet he could never effectively challenge the dominance of the national civil rights groups.

Only toward the end of his life did Malcolm begin to move beyond his role as a representative of Elijah Muhammad. As he became restive under Muhammad's cautious leadership, he strengthened his ties with black activists who were affiliated with the major black churches and civil rights groups. He continued to criticize the national civil rights leaders, but he recognized that the civil rights movement contained militant factions with which he could work. Malcolm continued to call himself a black nationalist, but the term was no longer sufficient to describe his ideology. Advocacy of the goal of establishing a black-controlled nation no longer detracted from the achievement of goals that were more attainable in the short term. After his break with the Nation of Islam in 1964, Malcolm defined black nationalism as black control of the political and economic life of black communities, as racial pride and self-reliance. Malcolm also insisted that he was "giving a new interpretation to the civil-rights struggle, an interpretation that will enable [black nationalists] to come into it, take part in it."[11]

Malcolm's new interpretation was consistent with the evolving ideas of many of the militant activists who had participated in the civil rights struggle, because it suggested a strategy that was in accord with their own experiences. Just as nationalism was an insufficient term to describe ideas that are only tenuously connected with the long-term goal of establishing a black nation, so too was integrationism inadequate to describe the increasingly far-reaching objectives of the activists who spearheaded the civil rights protests of the 1960s. By the time of Malcolm's break with Elijah Muhammad, many of these activists saw themselves as participants in a freedom struggle seeking rights that extended beyond civil rights legislation or even the rights guaranteed by the United States Constitution. Such activists also recognized that future black progress would require the transformation of the African-American institutions that had made possible previous gains. Rather than simply a movement toward the assimilation of white cultural values, the struggle was becoming by 1964 a movement toward the political, economic, and cultural transformation of white and black America.

Many black leaders of the mid-1960s continued to insist that black nationalism and integrationism represented mutual exclusive, antagonistic ideologies, but Malcolm and King were among those who began to recognize the limitations of their perspectives. Malcolm, even more than King, was willing to modify his views in order to bridge the nationalist-integrationist ideological conflict. As he did so, his black nationalism became less strident but also more potent. The FBI closely observed the shift in his ideological orientation and increasingly saw him an important element in an upsurge of racial militancy.

2. Malcolm and the FBI

Malcolm X's affiliation with Elijah Muhammad attracted the attention of the FBI, but during the 1950s and early 1960s, the federal government did not view the Nation of Islam or black nationalists in general as major threats to national security. Instead, during the Cold War era, leftist internal subversion was the nation's major concern. Malcolm's advocacy of racial separatism and his anti-white public statements alarmed many white Americans who became aware of them, but, until the late 1950s, most government officials who knew of him considered him a minor cult figure. Even during the early 1960s, Malcolm's black nationalist rhetoric did not cause much concern among whites, because it was not seen as an major element within African-American politics. As late as 1966, a *Newsweek* opinion survey indicated that most blacks supported the civil rights organizations and their leaders, and only five percent of the respondents indicated approval of black nationalism. A similarly small proportion of blacks expressed positive opinions about the "Black Muslims" and Elijah Muhammad. The large proportion of "not sure" responses regarding the Nation of Islam reflected wide-spread uncertainty among blacks regarding its policies.[12] After a decade of civil rights protests, black militancy was still commonly defined as approval for confrontational tactics rather than separatists strategies. In 1967, when the FBI officially extended its Counterintelligence Program (COINTELPRO) beyond leftist organizations to include "Black Nationalist-Hate Groups," the Nation of Islam was targeted but so too were King and the Southern Christian Leadership Conference.[13] The FBI's increasing concern about black nationalist agitation was clearly a result of the increasing militancy, during the first half of the 1960s, of blacks who were not black nationalists. Malcolm's significance as a subversive threat reflected his gradual movement from the margins of African-American politics toward active support for militant grass roots activism.

Nevertheless, under the leadership of J. Edgar Hoover, the FBI had exhibited intense hostility to all forms of African-American militancy, including the politically inert black nationalism of the 1950s. Indeed, David Garrow, in his study of the FBI's vendetta against King, has argued that the Bureau's essential "social role has been not to attack critics, Communists, blacks, or leftists per se, but to repress all perceived threats to the dominant, status-quo-oriented political culture."[14] Hoover's intense racism, however, insured that he would use his power with special vigor against black militancy. Hoover's career in the Justice Department began during the era of "New Negro" militancy after World War I, and, as an official of the General Intelligence Division and the Bureau of Investigation, he soon became involved in counterintelligence efforts aimed at Marcus Garvey and A. Philip Randolph.[15] As head of the FBI, he intensified the Bureau's program of domestic surveillance during the 1930s and 1940s. During this period, the United States government became far more concerned about communist subversion than about waning black nationalist activism and the FBI's continuing interest in the minuscule Nation of Islam was largely a result of the group's opposition to military service. This surveillance did not result from a belief among most government officials that the Nation was subversive but from the determination of Hoover to maintain surveillance of a large number of suspect groups, even without explicit authority from his nominal superiors in the Justice Department.

During the early years of Malcolm's ministry the federal government's policies toward the Nation of Islam were inconsistent. While Hoover and other Bureau officials saw the group as one of many which advocated black militancy, other officials of the Justice Department were not convinced that the Muslims posed a serious threat. The 1975 Church Committee hearings on intelligence activities revealed extended discussions between the FBI and Justice Department officials regarding the Nation of Islam. According to testimony before the committee, the Bureau suggested in 1952 that the Muslims be added to the Attorney General's list of subversive organizations. The Department of Justice concluded the following year that the Nation of Islam would not be prosecuted under the anticommunist Smith Act but decided that "the group would under certain circumstances represent a serious threat to our national security." In 1954, government officials decided against prosecuting the Nation for conspiracy to violate the Selective Service Act. Afterwards, the Justice Department approved continuing wiretap surveillance of Elijah Muhammad while also responding inconclusively to the FBI's requests for advice on whether Muslim activists should remain on the Security Index. In 1959, Hoover's nominal superiors refused to support his request to prosecute the NOI or place it on the Attorney General's list of subversive organizations. The following year, the Justice Department advised Hoover that Black

Muslims could not be automatically barred from government employment but gave the FBI authority to continue its investigation of the Nation of Islam. During the 1960s, Justice Department officials continued to questioned whether Elijah Muhammad's prophesies actually constituted national security threats even while refraining from ordering the FBI to discontinue its investigation. Without explicit instructions from Justice Department officials, the FBI continued to compile information on the Muslims until after the death of Elijah Muhammad.[16]

During his public life Malcolm gradually shifted his nationalist perspective from Elijah Muhammad's politically inert racial separatism towards a Pan-African perspective that brought him closer to the increasingly militant African-American political mainstream. While a loyal spokesperson for Elijah Muhammad, he had advocated a form of nationalism that aroused the emotions of blacks and the fears of whites. The FBI reports of his early speeches mentioned his apocalyptic predictions of race wars and divine retribution, but Justice Department officials were more perplexed than worried by Malcolm's vague metaphors and religious prophecies that communicated anti-white sentiments without explicitly calling for racial confrontations. An FBI report of Malcolm's speeches at New York's Temple No. 7 offers an example of the kind of apocalyptic prophecies that excited black audiences while not provoking white authorities:

LITTLE told this group that there was a space ship 40 miles up which was built by the wise men of the East and in this space ship there are a number of smaller space ships and each one is loaded with bombs. LITTLE stated that when ELIJAH [MUHAMMAD] of Chicago, Illinois, gives the word these ships will descend on the United States, bomb it and destroy all the "white devils." According to LITTLE these bombs will destroy all the "devils" in the United States and that all the Muslims in good standing will be spared.[17]

When FBI agents interviewed Malcolm a few months after this speech, they described him as "uncooperative" but nevertheless willing to reassure them that "Muslims are peaceful and they do not have guns and ammunition and they do not even carry knives." Malcolm insisted that he had "never been a member of the Communist Party" and that the NOI did not "teach hatred." When questioned about the War of Armageddon, Malcolm reportedly "remarked that the Bible states this will be when God destroys the devil."[18]

Malcolm sought to separate himself from leftist subversion and civil rights agitation, which were more immediate government concerns than was black nationalism. Malcolm's initial hostility toward the expanding civil rights protest movement at times extended beyond verbal attacks to include opportunistic overtures to the white opponents of civil rights. As had Marcus Garvey during the 1920s, Malcolm represented the Nation of Islam in a meeting with the Ku Klux Klan representatives, seeking to arrange an accommodation based on mutual support for racial segregation. According to the FBI's report of the meeting, which occurred in Georgia on January 28, 1961, Malcolm solicited the Klan's help with Muslim plans to separate from the United States. After his break with Elijah Muhammad, Malcolm expressed his shame over participating in the meeting, revealing that it resulted in a tacit agreement between the NOI and the Klan. "From that day onward the Klan never interfered with the Black Muslim movement in the South."[19]

During the late 1950s and early 1960s, Malcolm X's speeches often suggested that the federal government was worried about the threat posed by the Nation of Islam, but such comments overstated the government's concern. When compared to the extensive FBI investigation of King, the file on Malcolm contains few indications that the FBI ever devoted much effort to combating his influence until after his break with Elijah Muhammad. Even then, the FBI did not understand the nature of the threat posed by either Malcolm X or Elijah Muhammad, nor did it develop a coherent program to combat black nationalist agitation until after Malcolm's death. Instead, during the first half of the 1960s, the FBI was primarily concerned with the possibility that communists, rather than black nationalists, might gain control over the African-American freedom movement.

While investigating Malcolm and the Nation of Islam, the FBI rarely made them the targets of its aggressive and often illegal counterintelligence activities. When Hoover officially established the COINTELPRO in 1956, its initial goal was to disrupt the activities of the Communist Party, USA, which had long been the target of aggressive FBI tactics, including extensive recruitment of informers and efforts to exacerbate factionalism. COINTELPRO was later expanded to include such targets as the Socialist Workers Party, the Puerto Rican independence movement, and even the Ku Klux Klan. Although isolated COINTELPRO activities were undoubtedly directed against Malcolm and the Nation of Islam, only in 1967, two years after Malcolm's death, did Hoover include the Nation of Islam as a COINTELPRO target. Elijah Muhammad was mentioned among "extremists" who warranted special attention. An August 25 memorandum to field offices announced:

The purpose of this new counterintelligence endeavor is to expose, disrupt, misdirect, discredit, or otherwise neutralize the activities of black nationalist, hate-type organizations and groupings, their leadership, spokesmen, membership, and supporters. . . .[20]

3. Politicization of Nationalism

As Malcolm became increasingly successful as a minister of the Nation of Islam, he also began to recognize the political limitations of his religious message. During the first decade of his ministry, his political perspective had been shaped by the apolitical, religious orientation of the Nation of Islam. He was always careful to acknowledge that he was speaking on behalf of Elijah Muhammad and sought to distance himself from black radicalism. This was not only a reflection of his subordinate status in the Nation but also of his belief that religious conversion to Muhammad's form of Islam offered a better route to racial advancement than the strategies of social reform within the American political system. Malcolm's account of his formative experiences mentioned few contacts with political ideas, whether conventional or radical. He had only a passing awareness of the extensive leftist activities that took place while he was in New York during the 1940s. Although Malcolm's autobiography mentions in passing rent-raising parties where activists sold the Communist newspaper *Daily Worker,* and proclaimed the Communist Party as "the only political party that ever ran a black man for the Vice Presidency of the United States," Malcolm describes himself as unaffected by left activism: "to my sterile mind in those early days, it didn't mean much."[21] Even Malcolm's 1950 statement that he had "always been a Communist" should be seen primarily as an outgrowth of Malcolm's effort during World War II to convince selective service officials that he was unfit for the military. The 1952 visit Malcolm reportedly received in prison from a member of the Crispus Attucks Club of the American Youth for Democracy may suggest a latent openness to radicalism, but he was undoubtedly sincere, if not totally accurate, when he told FBI interviewers in 1955 that he had "never been a member of the Communist Party or the American Youth for Democracy" and claimed not "to have known anyone who was associated with it."[22]

Malcolm's primary function as a Muslim minister was not to advocate a political program but to present Elijah Muhammad's religious ideas and recruit new members for the Nation. As a devoted follower of Elijah Muhammad, he saw civil rights leaders primarily as unworthy competitors to the person he proclaimed "the greatest Living Emancipator and Truth Bearer that the world has ever known."[23] Nevertheless, even as he verbally attacked white "devils" and "brainwashed" integrationist leaders, his effort to expand his audience eventually brought him into direct contact with civil rights activists. Despite his insistence that the Nation of Islam truly represented the black masses, the upsurge of Southern civil rights protests forced Malcolm to reassess his relationship to the Southern black struggle. For the most part, the most visible manifestations of mass militancy among blacks during the early 1960s were guided by representatives of the civil rights organizations that had been the targets of Malcolm's verbal barbs against integrationism. Malcolm's nationalism did not supplant the civil rights activism of the early 1960s. Instead, his mature thought represented a convergence of his earlier ideas and those that emerged from sustained black protest movements. The "Black Power" rhetoric of the period after Malcolm's death owed much to his influence, but the new African-American racial consciousness also resulted from internal changes in the civil rights protest movement—particularly the increasing involvement of poor and working-class blacks and the growing emphasis on economic and political empowerment. As the Southern civil rights movement became a broadly focused, national freedom struggle, a new militant racial consciousness became evident among grass roots activists, even among those who had little awareness of Malcolm X. Organizers and activists who were involved in the grass roots mobilizations of 1963 and 1964 increasingly saw the ideas of Malcolm X as consistent with the conclusions drawn from their own movement experiences.

Malcolm X, for his part, not only attracted increasing support from grass roots activists but also moved toward their confrontational tactics and away from Elijah Muhammad's tactical accommodationism in anticipation of Allah's eventual retribution. Although he was the Nation of Islam's most effective proselytizer during the decade before his death, Malcolm increasingly recognized the insufficiency of the Nation's religious and racial separatism as a means of achieving African-American advancement. He saw that his own early criticisms of the civil rights protest movement had overstated the Nation of Islam's credentials as a force for social change and understated the potential of grassroots activists in the civil rights movement to become such a force. Malcolm abandoned his position as a dissenter affiliated with a small religious group in order to forge closer relations with black activists who had successfully mobilized mass protest movements. While remaining critical of cautious mainstream civil rights leaders, he acknowledged the success of some of these leaders in pushing the civil rights movement toward greater militancy.

During the late 1950s, in the aftermath of the Montgomery, Alabama, bus boycott, Malcolm and Elijah Muhammad reacted ambivalently to the emergence of King as a nationally known civil rights leader. According to a 1958 FBI report, Malcolm, apparently seeking to distance his organization from civil rights activism while securing the release of two jailed Muslims in Alabama, referred to King as a "traitor" "who is being used by the White man."[24] As Lewis V. Baldwin has demonstrated, these verbal attacks against King did not prevent Malcolm from seeking a dialogue with King and other civil rights leaders.[25] In 1960, for example, Malcolm wrote to King, Roy Wilkins of the NAACP, and other leaders to invite each as "spokesman and fellow-leader of our people" to attend and, if they wished, to speak at an "Education Rally" in New York. Malcolm explained that by participating, civil rights leaders could hear Elijah Muhammad and then "make a more intelligent appraisal of his teachings, his methods and his programs."[26] Malcolm recognized that King had little to gain from attending the Muslim-sponsored rally, but the appeal for dialogue was a consistent theme in Malcolm's speeches, even as he became more and more caustic in his attacks on civil rights leaders.

While King continued to ignore numerous invitations from the Nation of Islam, Malcolm was occasionally successful in his efforts to interact with civil rights leaders directly. During late 1961 and early 1962, for example, he participated in a series of debates with Bayard Rustin at Howard University and the University of Chicago on the topic "Integration or Separation." He also took part in similar debates with Edward Warren, president of the Los Angeles NAACP.[27] Malcolm occasionally offered his support to non-Muslim protest activities. During 1962, he addressed Harlem rallies on behalf of unionized hospital workers. On one occasion, he joined black labor leader A. Philip Randolph on the podium and applauded the struggle of black and Spanish-speaking workers as part of a larger "fight for human rights and human dignity."[28] Later in the year, he joined a Harlem rally to protest police brutality, pointing out the inconsistency of blacks being asked to fight against the nation's enemies abroad while turning the other cheek at home.[29] Malcolm also apparently was invited to speak in Birmingham in the midst of the spring 1963 demonstrations. On another occasion, he attended a rally to protest the 1963 murder of four black girls in a Birmingham church bombing. Although rally organizer Jackie Robinson tried to keep him from speaking, audience members called for Malcolm and created a ruckus until he came to the platform and quieted them.[30]

Writing in August 1963 to King and other civil rights leaders, Malcolm adopted a conciliatory tone, noting that the nation's "racial crisis" demanded immediate steps "by those who have genuine concern before the racial powder keg explodes." Malcolm argued that if Kennedy and Khrushchev could negotiate agreements, "it is a disgrace for Negro leaders not to be able to submerge our 'minor' differences in order to seek a common solution to a common problem posed by a *Common Enemy.*" He assured the civil rights leaders that, if they attended a Muslim-sponsored rally in Harlem, he would "guarantee order and courtesy for all speakers."[31]

As Malcolm's outreach activities brought him into contact with grass roots activities throughout the nation, his dissatisfaction with Elijah Muhammad's policies increased. In his autobiography, he noted his conviction "that our Nation of Islam could be an even greater force in the American black man's overall struggle—if we engaged in more *action.*" He explained that he privately believed that the Nation should alter its "general non-engagement policy" and that "militantly disciplined Muslims" should participate in mass protests.

> It could be heard increasingly in the Negro communities: "Those Muslims *talk* tough, but they never *do* anything, unless somebody bothers Muslims." I moved around among outsiders more than most other Muslim officials. I felt the very real potentiality that, considering the mercurial moods of the black masses, this labeling of Muslims as "talk only" could see us, powerful as we were, one day suddenly separated from the Negroes' front-line struggle.[32]

Malcolm recounted that his effort to politicize his Muslim ministry was already in progress during 1963. His disillusionment with Elijah Muhammad after learning of his infidelities had made him less comfortable stressing the moral teachings of the Nation. "If anyone had noticed," he asserted, "I spoke less and less of religion" and instead "taught social doctrine . . . current

events, and politics. I stayed wholly off the subject of morality."[33]
Furthermore, he became increasingly restive at having to restrict
his public statements because of the resentments of other Muslim
officials. He recalled resenting having to refuse interviews during
1963 and having to restrain his comments on contemporary issues of concern to blacks.

> When a high-power-rifle slug tore through the back of
> NAACP Field Secretary Medgar Evers in Mississippi, I
> wanted to say the blunt truths that need to be said. When a
> bomb was exploded in a Negro Christian church in Birming-
> ham, Alabama, snuffing out the lives of those four beautiful
> little black girls, I made comments—but not what should
> have been said about the climate of hate that the American
> white man was generating and nourishing.[34]

While suppressing such sentiments, Malcolm maintained his
public stance of hostility toward national civil rights leaders.
During the summer of 1963, after the major civil rights groups
announced plans for a Washington March for Jobs and Freedom,
Malcolm followed Elijah Muhammad's instructions not to cooperate with the civil rights groups sponsoring the event. An FBI
report noted that he warned NOI members that the march was
likely to end in a bloodbath and that they would be expelled if
they participated.[35] Malcolm's personal feelings about the march
were probably more restrained. Because the Nation of Islam was
coincidentally holding its annual convention during the week of
the march, Malcolm was able to observe the demonstration,
which attracted over 200,000 participants. Talking with reporters
at the Statler Hilton, which serve as headquarters for march organizers, he remarked, "I am not condemning or criticizing the
March, but it won't solve the problems of black people." In the
Autobiography he acknowledged widespread black support for
the march, explaining that he opposed national civil rights leaders. He spoke more positively of grass roots advocates of militant
action who "envisioned thousands of black brothers converging
together upon Washington—to lie down in the streets, on airport
runways, on government lawns—demanding of the Congress and

the White House some concrete civil rights action."[36] Speaking in
November at a Northern Negro Leadership Conference in Detroit, Malcolm accused the leadership of subverting the initial
grass roots enthusiasm for the march. "They joined it, became a
part of it, took it over," he charged. "And as they took it over, it
lost its militancy. It ceased to be angry, it ceased to be hot, it
ceased to be uncompromising."[37]

Although Malcolm's sharp criticisms of the "Big Six" civil
rights leaders drew the most attention from his audience, the
"Message to the Grass Roots" marked a major turning point in
his political orientation. The address was delivered at a conference called by the Reverend Albert B. Cleage as part of an effort
to create a "Freedom Now" political party. Simply by attending
the gathering, Malcolm implied that he was willing to ally himself with non-Muslim militants. "What you and I need to do is
learn to forget our differences," he advised. "You don't catch hell
because you're a Baptist, and you don't catch hell because you're
a Methodist." Malcolm criticized the nonviolent tactics of the
"Negro revolution," insisting that the "black revolution" would
involve bloodshed; but he also indicated a degree of respect for
the militancy that had been displayed by local movements, such
as those in Cambridge, Maryland, and Danville, Virginia. "The
Negroes were out there in the streets," Malcolm proclaimed.

> They were talking about how they were going to march on
> Washington. . . . That they were going to march on Wash-
> ington, march on the Senate, march on the White House,
> march on the Congress, and tie it up, bring it to a halt, not
> let the government proceed. They even said they were going
> out to the airport and lay down on the runway and not let
> any airplanes land. I'm telling you what they said. . . .
> That was the black revolution.[38]

Malcolm's implicit support for civil rights militancy could not
become explicit as long as he remained in the Nation of Islam.
He realized that Elijah Muhammad had little sympathy for any
form of militancy that assumed that racial advancement could
come through reform of the American political system. Once he

decided to break with Elijah Muhammad, however, Malcolm's support for grass roots militancy opened the way for a concerted effort to inject himself into the African-American freedom struggle. On March 8, 1964, when he officially announced his departure from the Nation of Islam, Malcolm stated that he was "prepared to cooperate in local civil rights actions in the South and elsewhere. . . ." He insisted that he was not abandoning his black nationalist objectives but merely acknowledging that racial reforms were worthy immediate goals. "Good education, housing and jobs are imperatives for the Negroes, and I shall support them in their fight to win these objectives, but I shall tell the Negroes that while these are necessary, they cannot solve the main Negro problem."

Although NAACP executive director Roy Wilkins responded coolly to Malcolm's overtures, other civil rights leaders reacted more favorably. Cecil Moore of the NAACP commented, "There's always room for more in the civil rights struggle. So, we welcome Malcolm X into the field."[39] King remained ambivalent about establishing ties with one of the harshest critics of his nonviolent strategy. On March 26, 1964, the two men met briefly when King was at the U. S. Capital to testify on the pending civil rights legislation. Malcolm, clearly pleased by his success in finally having a direct encounter with King, grinned broadly as he shook hands with the smiling King, as the two posed for a photographer. A few months later, a King associate, probably acting with King's approval, sought Malcolm's help in obtaining a United Nations declaration on behalf of African-American rights. A proposed meeting of the two leaders never took place.[40] Despite Malcolm's break with Elijah Muhammad, the gulf that had developed between him and King could not be readily bridged. When King recalled the Washington encounter, he acknowledged that Malcolm was "very articulate" but remained disturbed by Malcolm's "demagogic oratory," particularly his call for armed self-defense by blacks. King warned, "And in his litany of articulating the despair of the Negro without offering any positive, creative alternative, I feel that Malcolm has done himself and our people a great disservice."[41]

In his autobiography, Malcolm describes his trip to Mecca, in the spring of 1964, as a crucial turning point in the development of his worldview. His dramatic account of the resulting "radical alteration" of his racial outlook probably belies the more gradual maturation of his political outlook. Indeed, the suddenness of the transformation in Malcolm's perspective while abroad suggest that his experiences in Arab and African nations strengthened inclinations that had been suppressed during his years in the Nation of Islam. This explains Malcolm's sudden responsiveness to positive interracial contacts that previously would not have countered his ingrained skepticism. While in Lagos, Nigeria, he enthusiastically reported the warm reception he had received while abroad. He made public his new views regarding whites by referring to Islamic teachings that his previous international travels and extensive readings would certainly have brought to his attention. He claimed that a book he had read on the way to Jedda had made him "more open-minded." He had become convinced that the Koran was against violations of the human rights of individuals of all religions. "Islam is a religion which concerns itself with the human rights of all mankind, despite race, color, or creed. It recognizes all (everyone) as part of one Human Family."[42]

After returning to the United States, Malcolm (now calling himself El-Hajj Malik El-Shabazz Al-Sabban), established the Organization of Afro-American Unity to unite African Americans "around a non-religious and non-sectarian constructive program for Human Rights." Writing to invite Roy Wilkins to an OAAU meeting in June 1964, Malcolm described the new organization as an effort to "transcend all superficial, man made divisions between the Afro-American people of this country who are working for Human Rights" and assured Wilkins that the OAAU "would in no way compete with already existing successful organizations."[43] Although Malcolm's earlier criticisms made it difficult for him to improve relations with King, he increasingly recognized that the civil rights movement contained varied ideological tendencies. Still hostile to activism that he defined as integrationist and pacifistic, Malcolm began to express more positive attitudes toward the grass roots leaders and organizers of a mass movement that was becoming increasingly concerned with goals beyond civil rights.

During the last year of his life, Malcolm's political trajectory merged with that of many young activists in the Student Nonviolent Coordinating Committee (SNCC), the most militant of the black protest groups active in the South. SNCC workers' intense full-time involvement in Southern black struggles placed them in the vanguard of the ideological transformation that would soon fracture the national civil rights coalition. Stokely Carmichael, for example, was initially skeptical about Malcolm's views when he first encountered him at Howard University, but by 1964 he was among the SNCC workers questioning the idealistic interracialism that had once been dominant in the group.[44]

A turning point in Malcolm's relations with SNCC came unexpectedly during his second 1964 tour of Africa. SNCC chairman John Lewis and staff member Donald Harris crossed paths with Malcolm in Kenya on October 18. The two had been in Ghana soon after Malcolm had departed and were told of the "fantastic impressions" Malcolm had made during his visit. "Because of this, very often peoples' first attitude or impression of us was one of skepticism and distrust," Lewis and Harris reported. "Among the first days we were in Accra someone said, " 'Look, you guys might be really doing something—I don't know, but if you are to the right of Malcolm, you might as well start packing right now 'cause no one'll listen to you.' " Africans in Ghana and other places they visited, the SNCC workers discovered, wanted to know what was SNCC's relationship with the Organization of Afro-American Unity. "In every country he was known and served as the main criteria for categorizing other Afro-Americans and their political views." Lewis and Harris were pleasantly surprised, therefore, when Malcolm arrived at their Nairobi hotel, and they used the chance encounter to begin extended discussions.

We spent the rest of that day and evening as well as a good part of the following day talking with Malcolm about the nature of each of our trips. At that point [Malcolm] had been to eleven countries, talking with eleven heads of state and had addressed the parliaments in the majority of these countries. Although he was very tired he planned to visit five more countries. He felt that the presence of SNCC in Africa was very important and that this was a significant and crucial aspect of the "human rights struggle" that the American civil rights groups had too long neglected. He pointed out (and our experience bears him correct) that the African leaders and people are strongly behind the Freedom Movement in this country; that they are willing to do all they can to support, encourage and sustain the Movement, but they will not tolerate factionalism and support particular groups or organizations within the Movement as a whole. It was with this in mind that he formed his Organization of Afro-American Unity.

Discussion also centered around Malcolm's proposed plan to bring the case of the Afro-American before the General Assembly of the United Nations and hold the United States in violation of the Human Rights Charter. The question was at that time (and ultimately was evident) that support from the civil rights voices in this country was not forthcoming and the American black community was too plinted [sic] to attempt such a move without looking like [complete] asses and embarrassing [our] most valuable allies. We departed with Malcolm giving us some contacts and the hope that there would be greater communication between the [OAAU] and SNCC.[45]

On November 24, 1964, Malcolm returned to the United States with renewed determination to establish continuing contacts with activists in SNCC and other groups. At a November 29 OAAU rally at Harlem's Audubon Ballroom, Malcolm agreed with local activist Jesse Gray's suggestion that mercenaries should be sent to Mississippi rather than to the Congo. He continued to emphasize the need to link the African-American freedom struggle with freedom struggles throughout the world. "You waste your time when you talk to this man, just you and him."[46] On December 20, Fannie Lou Hamer, a SNCC worker and former congressional candidate of the Mississippi Freedom Democratic Party (MFDP) shared a Harlem platform with Malcolm, who suggested that his role in the black struggle was to strengthen the hand of nonviolent groups by demonstrating to whites that more violent alternatives existed. "We *need* a Mau Mau," he announced. "If they don't want to deal with the Mississippi Freedom Democratic Party, then we'll give them something else to deal with. If they don't want to deal with the Student Nonviolent Committee, then we have to give them an alternative."[47] After hearing Hamer speak, Malcolm immediately invited her and the SNCC Freedom Singers to be honored guests at an OAAU meeting, where he clarified his position regarding civil rights. Despite having once doubted whether African Americans were United States citizens, he argued that blacks should register to vote as independents. After Hamer spoke, Malcolm told his followers, "I want Mrs. Hamer to know that anything we can do to help them in Mississippi, we're at their disposal." At the end of December, Malcolm met with a SNCC-sponsored group of youngsters from McComb, Mississippi, and told them, "we here in the Organization of Afro-American Unity are with the struggle in Mississippi one thousand per cent. We're with the efforts to register our people in Mississippi to vote one thousand per cent. But we do not go along with anybody telling us to help nonviolently."[48]

Early in 1965, Malcolm met with a group of civil rights leaders in a gathering organized by Juanita Poitier, the wife of actor Sidney Poitier. Labor leader A. Philip Randolph, Whitney Young of the Urban League, Dorothy Height of the National Council of Negro Women, and actor Ossie Davis were among those who attended. Davis recalled that the group "spent that day discussing Malcolm's philosophy, the mistakes he made, what he wanted to do now, and how he could get on board the people's struggle that was taking place."[49]

Malcolm's most direct involvement in the Southern black struggle occurred a few weeks before his death. On Wednesday evening, February 3, 1965, he addressed several thousand Tuskegee Institute students, and the following Thursday morning, he spoke to student activists at Brown's Chapel A.M.E. Church in Selma, Alabama. SCLC staff member Andrew Young recalled that, in order to lessen its impact on the audience, Malcolm's talk was "sandwiched between" those of two other SCLC staffers, James Bevel and Fred Shuttlesworth. Coretta Scott King, who arrived at the Chapel shortly after Malcolm's speech, recalled that Young sought her help in steering the students back toward nonviolence. She later wrote that Malcolm reassured her that, by coming to Selma, he intended to assist her husband's work, commenting, "If the white people realize what the alternative is, perhaps they will be more willing to hear Dr. King."[50] An FBI report of the speech noted that Malcolm called upon President Johnson to "order a full scale investigation of the Ku Klux Klan" but that he did not threaten action by his followers. The FBI report commented:

[Malcolm] further stated that no one at the church, or any Negro in Selma involved in the demonstrations, had done nothing they would not have done if he had never appeared in Selma. He apparently made this statement due to press statements that his presence in Selma had embarrassed other civil rights leaders.[51]

Malcolm was unsuccessful in his attempt to meet with King while in Selma, but such a meeting with King undoubtedly would have occurred if Malcolm had lived.

Shortly after leaving Selma, Malcolm embarked on his final foreign visit. On February 8, he addressed the First Congress of the Council of African Organizations. When he flew to Paris to deliver another talk, French authorities barred his entry, calling him an "undesirable" likely to "trouble the public order." Forced to return to London after a few hours of questioning in the Orly Airport transit lounge, Malcolm reacted to the French action in a conversation with Afro-Cuban nationalist Carlos Moore. "I was surprised . . . since I thought if there was any country in Europe that was liberal in its approach to things, France was it, so I was shocked when I got there and couldn't land." He blamed the American government, suggesting that France had "become a satellite of Washington, D. C."[52]

Soon after his return to the United States, Malcolm's house

was firebombed. He attributed the act to his enemies in the Nation of Islam. While the identity of the arsonist was never determined, Malcolm's public criticisms of Elijah Muhammad had unquestionably made him a target for Muslim zealots. During December, Fruit of Islam Captain Raymond Sharrieff had sent an open telegram to Malcolm officially warning him that "the Nation of Islam shall no longer tolerate your scandalizing the name of our leader and teacher, the Honorable Elijah Muhammad, regardless of where such scandalizing has been."[53] Minister Louis X (later Louis Farrakkan), once Malcolm's protégé, also attacked his former friend in strong terms. "IS Malcolm bold enough to return and face the music . . . ? Would he like to face Mr. Muhammad?" Louis X wrote in *Muhammad Speaks*. Describing Malcolm as "the target of the dissatisfaction of both his own followers (which are very few) and the followers of Muhammad," Louis X condemned Malcolm for his efforts to establish ties with civil rights groups:

He had blasted the white man and the NAACP for 9 or 10 years. He had preached the truth, as revealed to Muhammad by Allah: that the white race was a race of devils. . . . Malcolm now pleads to the white man that he had learned they were not devils, by seeing so-called white Muslims in Mecca. . . .

Malcolm was doomed, according to the article. "The die is set, and Malcolm shall not escape, especially after such evil, foolish talk about his benefactor (Elijah Muhammad). . . . Such a man as Malcolm is worthy of death, and would have met with death if it had not been for Muhammad's confidence in Allah for victory over the enemies."[54]

Malcolm's assassination on February 21, 1965, ended his efforts to establish an alliance between his nationalist followers and the militant offspring of the civil rights movement. Deprived of Malcolm's leadership, African-American politics remained divided into hostile, warring camps. After Malcolm's death, the divisions were evident even among militant blacks who saw themselves as his ideological descendants. On one side were nationalists who resolutely refused to participate in efforts to achieve black advancement through struggle within the American political system. On the other were radical activists who sought to mobilize African-Americans for confrontational politics while placing little emphasis on the cultural and psychological transformation that would foster effective black political action.

4. Malcolm's Ambiguous Political Legacy

Assassinated while still at an early stage of his development as an independent political leader, Malcolm X became, after his death, a historical influence on the black struggles. Deprived of the opportunity to continue refining his ideas, he left a body of thought, mostly in the form of speeches, to be developed and reinterpreted by others. His death came on the eve of a turbulent era of African-American politics that made his words prophetic. During 1966 and 1967, the debate over the Black Power slogan brought many of his still controversial ideas into the black political mainstream. Nevertheless, Malcolm's ideological descendants disputed the nature of his political legacy and selectively borrowed from it. "Cultural nationalists" saw the "Old Malcolm"— before his break with the Nation of Islam—as their spiritual mentor, while "revolutionary nationalists" were inspired by the "New Malcolm" of 1964 and 1965. Malcolm, himself, was unable to offer guidance to the black activists who transformed his ideas into Black Power politics. The contradictory tendencies in Malcolm's life paralleled the bitter and sometimes deadly intra-black conflicts of the late 1960s. Indeed, Malcolm became one of the first victims of those internecine battles.

The FBI's interest in Malcolm did not end with his death. Instead, the Bureau's efforts to combat the new forms of racial militancy became more ruthless in the post-Malcolm era. Aware of the threat that Malcolm might have posed if he had succeeded in unifying the black militant community, the FBI attempted to exacerbate conflicts among the various factions that identified themselves with Malcolm's ideas. The FBI's COINTELPRO against so-called "black nationalist-hate groups," which had begun in August 1967, sought to forestall a black nationalist coalition that would lead to "a true black revolution." In the view of FBI leaders, the danger posed by Malcolm X was not simply that he was a black nationalist but that he had been a potential " 'messiah' who could unify, and electrify, the militant black nationalist movement." Malcolm clearly would have been targeted for COINTELPRO's "dirty tricks" if he had not been assassinated. The FBI's treatment of black nationalists became more hostile as they followed Malcolm's lead in abandoning separatist strategies that did not involve confrontations with white authorities.[55]

By the end of the 1960s, the federal government had developed a policy toward black militancy that clearly distinguished between groups and leaders that were considered potential threats and those that were not. The criterion for inclusion on the list of COINTELPRO targets was not advocacy of racial separatism; black political groups and leaders were treated as worthy of aggressive counterintelligence projects according to the extent to which they sought to undermine capitalism and to mobilize mass confrontations with government authorities. Thus, despite his integrationist sentiments, King remained a major target of the FBI until his death. Conversely, the FBI did not target the Congress of Racial Equality (CORE), which, despite the black separatist leadership of Roy Innis, established ties with the Nixon administration.

By associating himself with the upsurge in nonnationalist activism of the 1963–1965 period, Malcolm helped to transform African-American nationalism into something it had not been since the Garvey era—that is, a movement that was taken seriously as a threat by the United States government. Although the FBI had long been interested in the Nation of Islam, only after Malcolm's break with the group did the FBI shift the focus of its covert programs from anticommunism to efforts to undermine black nationalist militancy. The reasons for this shift included both the rise of urban racial violence and the increasing involvement of nationalists in mass activism. By 1967, the Bureau had recruited an army of more than three thousand informants in black communities with BLACKPRO and other informant programs. When the counterintelligence program was revised, during August 1967, to target so-called "Black Nationalist-Hate Groups," the Nation of Islam was included among the groups to receive the FBI's "intensified attention." Yet, according to Kenneth O'Reilly's comprehensive study of the FBI's efforts against black militancy, during the 1967–1968 period most local offices no longer considered the Nation of Islam a major threat.[56]

Indeed, in March 1968, when FBI field offices were directed to identify targets for new COINTELPRO efforts, the emphasis was on potential rather than existing threats posed by black nationalist leaders and organizations. A memorandum written to W. C. Sullivan stressed the need to "prevent the *coalition* of militant black nationalist groups." SNCC leader Stokely Carmichael was identified as a militant with "the necessary charisma" to become the "messiah" who might have unified the "militant black nationalist movement." Ultimately, the California-based Black Panther Party became the primary target of the FBI's COINTELPRO projects. The Panthers, with their emphasis on armed self-defense and militant (though not anti-white) rhetoric, were clearly the political offspring of Malcolm's last years.

Had Malcolm lived, he might have moderated the destructive ideological conflicts that made black militants so vulnerable to the FBI's "dirty tricks." During the last year of his life, he abandoned a form of black nationalism that limited itself to criticisms of integrationist leaders while failing to offer serious alternatives to civil rights activism. Rather than standing apart from racial reform movements, he associated himself with the most militant elements in those movements. He began to emphasize those aspects of the black nationalist tradition that were consistent with the objectives of those seeking racial reforms within the American political system. Instead of viewing the development of black-controlled institutions as inconsistent with the insistence on equitable government policies with regard to blacks, he saw each as contributing to the other. Although Malcolm's own emphasis on the need for blacks to defend themselves paved the way for the rhetorical excesses of later Black Power militants, his increasing respect for the activists who used nonviolent tactics aggressively might have encouraged other black nationalists to appreciate the need for a broad range of tactics in a sustained mass struggle. As a respected black nationalist, he may have been able to prevent the intellectual—and sometimes physical warfare —that broke out between "cultural nationalists" and "revolutionary nationalists" and that divided SNCC, CORE, and the Black Panthers. Rather than encouraging verbal warfare between nationalists and integrationists, by the time of his death Malcolm was already urging black nationalists to see themselves as building upon the civil rights organizing of the early sixties.

Although Malcolm undoubtedly would have exerted a major influence in the transformation of African-American politics during the last half of the 1960s, we can only speculate about the direction black politics might have taken if both Malcolm and King had had the opportunity to discuss and refine their political views. King criticized the Black Power slogan as counterproductive, but he refused to condemn Stokely Carmichael and other former civil rights workers who became Black Power proponents. Deeply rooted in African-American religion and closely connected with African-American institutions, King came to recognize the importance of explicit appeals to racial pride, even as he continued to condemn anti-white rhetoric and to reject separatist ideologies. In his last book, *Where Do We Go from Here: Chaos or Community*, King defended Black Power "in its broad and positive meaning" as "a call to black people to amass the political and economic strength to achieve their legitimate goals." He acknowledged the value of the slogan as "a psychological call to manhood." He condemned the "tendency to ignore the Negro's contribution to American life and strip him of his personhood." King argued, "To offset this cultural homicide, the Negro must rise up with an affirmation of his own Olympian manhood. Any movement for the Negro's freedom that overlooks this necessity is only waiting to be buried. As long as the mind is enslaved the body can never be free."[57] Coretta Scott King has insisted that "Martin firmly agreed with certain aspects of the program that Malcolm X advocated," particularly the need for racial pride and black access to power. She surmised that "at some point the two would have come closer together and would have been a very strong force in the total struggle for liberation and self-determination of black people in our society."[58]

African-American politics of the period after King's death would have been strengthened by the ideological convergence hinted in Malcolm's last speeches and King's last writings. As the most respected and well-known advocate of black nationalism, Malcolm might have been a strong voice against forms of black nationalism that lead to cultural atavism, cultism, opportunism, or other forms of regressive politics. Similarly, King would certainly have spoken against civil rights leadership that refrained from using aggressive, nonviolent tactics against racial oppression. Both would have pushed the African-American freedom struggle toward greater attention to the problems of the black poor. Both would have stressed the international dimensions of the struggle for social justice. They would have remained controversial leaders and the targets of the repressive agencies of the American state, but their courage and experience as leaders would have made them valuable sources of advice for the black activists who followed them.

Malcolm X's life provides many useful insights for today. The most useful of these is that all ideologies, even black nationalism, can retard as well as foster black unity and mass militancy. During his life, he had the courage to affiliate with a small group outside the African-American mainstream; he also had the courage to break his ties with that group when he determined that more effective political institutions were needed. He argued against allowing the political skepticism of black nationalists to turn into political apathy or pessimism. The present era of African-American politics requires the wisdom of the nationalist tradition as a necessary corrective to civil rights reform efforts that are overly cautious or fail to appreciate African-American cultural distinctiveness. The development of African-American institutions under black leadership is a necessary component of any effort to achieve significant reforms in the United States, but such institutions are strengthened when African Americans are accorded fair treatment as United States citizens.

For too long, African-American politics has been divided by a false dichotomy. Nationalism and integrationism are inadequate terms to describe the vast range of political insights that have been outgrowths of past struggles. Debates over the use of violence are unproductive without a recognition that all effective political movements combine elements of persuasion and coercion. Malcolm X's intellectual legacy can be fully appreciated only when it is seen as part of the larger legacy of the African-American freedom struggles of the 1950s and 1960s.

1. Although a definitive biographical of Malcolm has not yet been written, useful biographical information can be found in C. Eric Lincoln, *Black Muslims in America* (Boston: Beacon Press, 1961); Louis Lomax, *When the Word Is Given* (Cleveland: World Publishing, 1963); Peter Goldman, *Death and Life of Malcolm X* (Urbana, Ill.: University of Illinois Press, 1979); George Breitman, *Last Year of Malcolm X: The Evolution of a Revolutionary* (New York: Merit, 1967). Eugene Wolfenstein, *The Victims of Democracy: Malcolm X and the Black Revolution* (Berkeley: University of California Press, 1981) and Bruce Perry, *Malcolm X: The Life of a Man Who Changed Black America* (New York: Station Hill, 1991) provided interesting, though controversial, psychological insights.

2. See, for example, David J. Garrow, *Bearing the Cross: Martin Luther King and the Southern Christian Leadership Conference* (New York: William Morrow, 1966); Taylor Branch, *Parting the Waters: America in the King Years, 1954–63* (New York: Simon and Schuster, 1988); and Clayborne Carson, "Reconstructing the King Legacy: Scholars and National Myths," in Peter J. Albert and Ronald Hoffman, eds., *We Shall Overcome: Martin Luther King, Jr., and the Black Freedom Struggle* (New York: Pantheon Books, 1990).

3. Perry's recent controversial study is exceptional in this regard, but the reliability of this work cannot be determined until its sources —particularly transcripts of interviews with Malcolm's associates —are made available to other researchers.

4. Malcolm X, with Alex Haley, *Autobiography of Malcolm X* (New York: Ballantine Books, 1965), pp. 4, 5, 7, 10.

5. Although my conclusions depart from his, the following discussion has been influenced by James H. Cone's insightful comparative study *Martin & Malcolm & America* (Maryknoll, New York: Orbis Books, 1991).

6. Quotations from Martin Luther King, Jr., "Autobiography of Religious Development," unpublished papers written at Crozer Theological Seminar, November 1950.

7. Malcolm X, with Alex Haley, *Autobiography,* p. 17.

8. Malcolm X, with Alex Haley, *Autobiography,* p. 31. Malcolm asserts that he was elected president of his seventh-grade class, but Perry convincing argues that he must have been in the eighth grade at the time. See *Malcolm,* p. 37.

9. King, "Autobiography."

10. C. Eric Lincoln, *The Black Muslims in America* (Boston: Beacon Press, 1961), p. 75. The Nation of Islam's mythology of racial origins generally saw black identity within the context of a broader African-Asian identity. Malcolm's initial image of the Messiah W. D. Fard was not of a black man but of a "light-brown-skinned" person with "an Asiatic cast of countenance." See Malcolm X, with Alex Haley, *Autobiography,* p. 186. Malcolm often expressed an identification with Asian nations, particularly nations such as Japan, Korea, and Vietnam that were engaged in wars against the United States.

11. See, for example, Malcolm's discussion of black nationalism in "The Ballot or the Bullet," in George Breitman, *Malcolm X Speaks: Selected Speeches and Statements* (New York: Merit, 1965), pp. 23–44.

12. See William Brink and Louis Harris, *Black and White: A Study of U. S. Racial Attitudes Today* (New York: Simon and Schuster, 1967), pp. 248, 254, 260.

13. See Director, FBI, to SAC, Albany, March 4, 1968, reprinted in Ward Churchill and Jim Vander Wall, *The COINTELPRO Papers: Documents from the FBI's Secret Wars Against Domestic Dissent* (Boston: South End Press, 1990), pp. 108–111.

14. David J. Garrow, *The FBI and Martin Luther King, Jr.: From 'Solo' to Memphis* (New York: W. W. Norton, 1981), pp. 208–209.

15. See, for example, Hoover to Frank Burke, August 12, 1919, in Robert A. Hill, ed., *Marcus Garvey and the Universal Negro Improvement Association Papers,* vol. 1 (Berkeley: University of California, 1983), pp. 479–480.

16. See United States Senate, Hearings before the Select Committee to Study Governmental Operations with Respect to Intelligence Activities, vol. 6, Federal Bureau of Investigation, testimony of Frederick A. O. Schwarz, Jr., November 18, 1975, p. 37–39. In 1960, Walter Yeagley, of the Justice Departments Internal Security Division told Hoover that the Nation of Islam should not be designated as a subversive group because its rhetoric was "more calculated and designed to arouse hatred and antipathy against the white race as a race, rather than against the Government. There is evidence of language which speaks of the destruction of America, but is couched more in terms of prophecy and prediction, often referring to the 'War of Armageddon," than in terms of incitement to action." See Exhibit 27 in Hearings, vol. 6, p. 428. See also David J. Garrow, *FBI and Martin Luther King, Jr.,* p. 154.

17. FBI, New York, 105-8999, January 28, 1955.

18. FBI, New York, 105-8999, January 28, 1955.

19. Bruce Perry, ed., *Malcolm X: The Last Speeches* (New York: Pathfinder, 1989), p. 123.

20. Director, FBI, to SAC, Albany, August 25, 1967. According to David J. Garrow, the FBI "played assorted COINTEL tricks on the [Nation of Islam] as early as the late 1950s." See *FBI and Martin Luther King, Jr.,* p. 154.

21. Malcolm X, with Alex Haley, *Autobiography,* p. 76.

22. FBI, January 28, 1955.

23. FBI, 04/30/58, Part II, section 3.

24. See FBI, April 30, 1958, in part II, section 2.

25. Lewis V. Baldwin, "A Reassessment of the Relationship between Malcolm X and Martin Luther King, Jr.," *Western Journal of Black Studies* 13 (1989): p. 104.

26. Malcolm X to King, July 21, 1960.

27. See FBI reports; Clayborne Carson, *In Struggle: SNCC and the Black Awakening of the 1960s* (Cambridge: Harvard University Press, 1981), p. 103; Henry Hampton and Steve Fayer, *Voices of Freedom,* p. 249.

28. *Muhammad Speaks,* July 31, 1962, and January 31, 1963.

29. *Muhammad Speaks,* September 15, 1962.

30. Perry, *Malcolm,* p. 210; Hampton and Fayer, *Voice of Freedom,* p. 256.

31. Letter sent to King, Roy Wilkins, Gardner C. Taylor, Adam Clayton Powell, James Farmer, Whitney Young, A. Philip Randolph, Ralph Bunche, Joseph H. Jackson, and James Forman, August 1, 1963, in Malcolm X 1960–1965 folder, NAACP Papers, Group III, Box A227, Library of Congress.

32. Malcolm X, with Alex Haley, *Autobiography,* p. 289.

33. Malcolm X, with Alex Haley, *Autobiography,* pp. 294. According to Bruce Perry, Malcolm, as early as 1959, "unsuccessfully tried to secure Elijah Muhammad's permission to boycott Harlem stores that refused to hire or promote black employees. The same year, the Messenger made Malcolm apologize for organizing a protest demonstration in nearby Newark. Malcolm kept pressing Mr. Muhammad for permission to engage in demonstrations. The Messenger instructed him not to raise the subject again." See *Malcolm,* p. 211.

34. Malcolm X, with Alex Haley, *Autobiography,* pp. 293.

35. FBI, November 15, 1963.

36. Quoted in Thomas Gentile, *March on Washington: August 28, 1963* (Washington: New Day Publications, 1983), p. 162; Malcolm X, with Alex Haley, *Autobiography of Malcolm X,* p. 278.

37. Malcolm X, "Message to the Grass Roots," in George Breitman, ed., *Malcolm X Speaks: Selected Speeches and Statements* (New York: Merit Publishers, 1965), p. 16.

38. Breitman, ed., *Malcolm X Speaks,* p. 14.

39. Quoted in *Philadelphia Inquirer,* March 14, 1964.

40. FBI 105-8999-1-25a, June 27, 1964 (telephone log); see discussion in James H. Cone, *Martin & Malcolm & America,* p. 207.

41. King quoted in *Playboy* interview, reprinted in James Melvin Washington, *A Testament of Hope: The Essential Writings of Martin Luther King, Jr.* (San Francisco: Harper & Row, 1986), pp. 364–365.

42. Press release in Malcolm X Folder in NAACP Papers, Group III, Box A227, Library of Congress.

43. Malcolm X to Roy Wilkins, June 24, 1964. In a May 15, 1964, letter to Wilkins, James Shabazz, secretary of Muslim Mosque, Inc., assured Wilkins that Malcolm would not "attack any person or organization that is engaged in the struggle" and asked "forgiveness for the unkind things that he has said in the past." See Malcolm X Folder in NAACP Papers, Group III, Box A227, Library of Congress.

44. See Clayborne Carson, *In Struggle,* pp. 100, 144, and *passim.*

45. *John Lewis and Donald Harris, "The Trip," report submitted December 14, 1964, cited in Carson, In Struggle,* p. 135.

46. Breitman, ed., *Malcolm X Speaks,* p. 97.

47. Breitman, ed., *Malcolm X Speaks,* p. 115.

48. Breitman, *Malcolm X Speaks,* p. 152.

49. Hampton and Fayer, *Voices of Freedom,* p. 260.

50. Coretta Scott King, *My Life with Martin Luther King, Jr.,* p. 256. Coretta King also remarked that by the time of Malcolm's assassination her husband came to believe that "Malcolm X was a brilliant young man who had been misdirected. They had talked together on occasion and had discussed their philosophies in a friendly way" (p. 258). See also account in James H. Cone, *Martin & Malcolm & America,* p. 209.

51. FBI Mobile, 44-557, February 4, 1965. See also Carson, *In Struggle,* p. 135.

52. "Malcolm X Barred by French Security," *New York Times,* February 10, 1965; Malcolm quoted in taped conversation with Carlos Moore, February 9, 1965, reprinted in John Henrik Clark, *Malcolm X: The Man and His Times* (Trenton, New Jersey: Africa World Press, 1990), p. 205.

53. "Nation of Islam Warns Malcolm X," *The Crusader,* quoted in FBI, November 25, 1964.

54. Minister Louis X, "Boston Minister Tells of Malcolm—Muhammad's Biggest Hypocrite," *Muhammad Speaks,* December 4, 1964.

55. Director, FBI, to SAC, Albany, March 4, 1968.

56. See memorandum from FBI Director to SAC, Albany, August 25, 1967, reprinted in Churchill and Wall, *The COINTELPRO Papers,* pp. 92–93; Kenneth O'Reilly, *"Racial Matters": The FBI's Secret File on Black America, 1960–1972* (New York: Free Press, 1989), p. 277–278.

57. Martin Luther King, Jr., *Where Do We Go from Here: Chaos or Community?* (Boston: Beacon Press, 1967), p. 43.

58. Coretta Scott King, *My Life with Martin Luther King,* pp. 256 –257; and Coretta Scott King, quoted in Hampton and Fayer, *Voice of Freedom,* p. 264.

Part II
Chronology

Chronology

The date in brackets following an entry in the chronology refers to the date of the FBI report or memorandum in which the information appears. In those few instances where the information is from a document in the FBI file but is not attached to an FBI report or memorandum, the date refers to the report or memorandum that immediately precedes it.

May 10, 1919	Earl Little, a Baptist preacher from Georgia, marries Louise in Montreal; couple moves to Philadelphia, Pennsylvania.
1922 or 1923	Earl and Louise move with their three small children to Omaha, Nebraska.
1924	According to *Autobiography,* "Ku Klux Klan riders" warn family to leave town because whites will not tolerate Earl Little's UNIA (United Negro Improvement Association) "back to Africa" preachings.
May 19, 1925	Malcolm Little born at University Hospital in Omaha, Nebraska [FBI 1/28/55].
December 1926	Little family moves to Milwaukee, Wisconsin.
May 27, 1927	UNIA newspaper *Negro World* identifies Earl Little as leader of UNIA chapter in Indiana Harbor (East Chicago), Indiana.
January 1928	Littles buy a house in Lansing, Michigan; Earl continues to preach.
November 7, 1929	House burns to the ground; family unharmed.

December 1929	Earl Little builds a new home for family on outskirts of East Lansing, Michigan.
1930	In Detroit, followers of W. D. Fard establish the first Temple of Islam.
January 1931	Malcolm Little enrolls in kindergarten at Pleasant Grove Elementary School.
September 28, 1931	Earl Little is run over by a streetcar and dies; Malcolm hears rumor that his father was murdered by the Black Legion, a local white supremacist group.
January 9, 1939	Louise suffers a nervous breakdown and is declared legally insane; committed to the state mental hospital at Kalamazoo.
Spring 1939	Malcolm Little tells his favorite teacher that he wants to become a lawyer; he is told, "That's no realistic goal for a nigger."
August 1939	Social worker recommends that Malcolm be placed in a juvenile home; Judge John McClellan concurs.
Summer 1940	Visits sister Ella in Boston, Massachusetts.
1940–1941	Lives in various foster homes in the Lansing area.
February 1941	Returns to Boston; works at a variety of jobs—shoe shining, dishwashing, soda-jerking, and for New Haven Railroad—and becomes involved in Boston's criminal underworld.
December 1942	Moves back to Michigan and lives in Flint for about two months.
March 1943	Moves to New York and works for New Haven Railroad.
Spring 1943	Fired from railroad job; he becomes a waiter at Small's Paradise in New York.
June 1, 1943	Registers at Local Board 59 of New York City [FBI 1/28/55].
October 25, 1943	U.S. Army finds Malcolm Little men-

	tally disqualified for military service because of "psychopathic personality inadequate, sexual perversion, psychiatric rejection" [FBI 1/28/55].
October 1943	Works on railroad occasionally; thrives as "Big Red," pushing dope, playing the numbers, peddling bootleg whiskey, and hustling.
July 1944	Works (under the name Jack Carlton) as a bar entertainer at a New York nightclub called The Lobster Pond.
October 1944	Returns to Boston and works as a packer in Sears Roebuck warehouse in Brookline; quits after three weeks.
November 30, 1944	Indicted for larceny; receives three-month suspended sentence and is placed on probation for one year [FBI 5/4/53].
December 4, 1944	U.S. Army classifies Malcolm Little 4F [FBI 1/28/55].
January 1945	Back in Michigan after New York holiday stint, works at various jobs, including waiter at nightclub.
August 1945	Returns to Harlem.
December 1945	Embarks on Christmas stealing spree in Boston with friend Bea, her sister Joyce Caragulian, Sonny Brown, Kora Marderosian, and Jarvis.
January 12, 1946	Arrested in Boston jewelry store while trying to reclaim stolen watch he had left for repair.
January 15, 1946	Indicted for carrying firearms [FBI 5/4/53].
January 16, 1946	Indicted for larceny and breaking and entering [FBI 5/4/53].
February 27, 1946	Begins serving prison term at Charlestown Prison [FBI 5/4/53].
March 1946	Begins reading program in prison library.

January 1947	Transferred to Concord Reformatory.
1947–48	Converts to the teachings of the Honorable Elijah Muhammad (EM).
March 1948	Transferred to Norfolk Prison Colony and gains access to excellent library.
January 29, 1950	Mails letter warning: "The time has come for the devils to be destroyed" [FBI 5/4/53].
March 23, 1950	Transferred back to Charlestown State Prison.
June 29, 1950	Mails letter claiming: "I have always been a Communist" [FBI 5/4/53].
January 9, 1951	Mails letter stating his desire to "replace the seeds of hate and revenge which [he] has sown . . . with the Seed of Love and Justice" [FBI 5/4/53].
May 29, 1951	Parole denied; remains at Charlestown Prison [FBI 5/4/53].
January 1952	Member of Crispus Attucks Club of the American Youth for Democracy (AYD) visits Malcolm Little in prison [FBI 5/4/53].
August 7, 1952	Paroled from state prison [FBI 5/4/53].
August 8, 1952	Travels to Detroit, where he works as a furniture salesman at a store managed by his brother, Wilfred.
August 31, 1952	Travels to Chicago with members of Detroit Temple No. 1 to hear the Honorable Elijah Muhammad speak. Later that month he receives his X from the NOI (Nation of Islam).
September 23, 1952	Confidential informant provides FBI with three letters written by MX [FBI 5/4/53].
January 1953	Leaves furniture store for job on Ford Motor Company's Lincoln-Mercury Division assembly line.
February–June 1953	Attends various NOI meetings [FBI 3/16/54].

June 1953	Named assistant minister of Detroit Temple No. 1; quits auto plant job.
Fall 1953	Becomes first minister of Boston Temple No. 11.
January 1954	Attends meetings of New York Temple No. 7 [FBI 9/7/54].
January 8, 1954	Speaks at Boston NOI Temple meeting [FBI 9/7/54].
February 1954	Serves as tour leader for New York Temple No. 7 during NOI Convention in Chicago [FBI 9/7/54].
March 1954	Becomes minister of Philadelphia Temple No. 12; attends numerous NOI meetings in Philadelphia [FBI 11/18/53].
June 1954	Becomes minister of New York Temple No. 7.
January 10, 1955	In FBI interview, MX states that he resides in Queens, New York, denies being a teacher or minister of the Temple, and denies affiliation or membership in Philadelphia, Detroit, and Boston Temples [FBI 1/28/55].
May 1, 1955	Holds NOI meeting in Lansing, Michigan [FBI 1/31/56].
July 8, 1955	Tells audience at Philadelphia Temple meeting that the FBI will visit and try to intimidate them [FBI 1/31/56].
November 11, 1955	Identified as official minister of the NOI Temple No. 12 in Philadelphia [FBI 4/23/57].
1955	According to *Autobiography,* MX first hears rumors of EM adultery.
February 26, 1956	Arranges transportation for NOI members to go to Chicago for "Savior's Day" [FBI 1/28/55].
August 25–26, 1956	Lectures to over two hundred NOI members at the first Southern Goodwill

Tour of the Brotherhood of Islam in Atlanta, Georgia [FBI 4/23/57].

1956
Betty Sanders joins New York Temple No. 7; renamed Sister Betty X.

April 14, 1957
After NOI member Hinton Johnson is beaten by police and jailed, contingent of Muslims from Temple No. 7 gathers outside the 123rd Street police station. MX demands that Johnson be taken to a hospital and then sends the NOI members home.

July 18, 1957
Los Angeles Herald-Dispatch carries article captioned "Young Moslem Leader Explains The Doctrine of Mohammedanism." MX begins "God's Angry Men" column in *Herald-Dispatch* this week [FBI 4/40/58].

September 1957
Serves as minister of NOI Temple in Detroit, Michigan [FBI 4/30/58].

October 30, 1957
Hospitalized in New York due to "heart attack" [FBI 4/30/58].

November 1957
Wilfred Little, brother of MX, states that MX has recovered from his "heart attack" [FBI 4/30/58].

November 9, 1957
Pittsburgh Courier reports MX announcement that Hinton Johnson is filing a one-million-dollar suit against the officers who beat and arrested him in April.

November 28, 1957
Los Angeles Herald-Dispatch carries article captioned "Malcolm X Speaks at Elks Hall Wed. Night" [FBI 4/30/58].

December 1957
Tells EM of his plan to marry Sister Betty X.

January 12, 1958
From Detroit, MX telephones Sister Betty in New York with a marriage proposal; two days later they are married in Lansing.

January 19, 1958
The newlyweds drive back to New York

and reside in three rooms of a two-family flat in East Elmhurst, Queens.

May 20, 1958 — FBI observes MX with EM in Chicago [FBI 11/19/58].

May 21, 1958 — Attends funeral of Marie Muhammed, mother of EM, in Chicago [FBI 11/19/58].

July 2, 1958 — FBI designates MX as a "key figure" [FBI 7/2/58].

October 29, 1958 — Speaks at NOI meeting in Philadelphia [FBI 5/19/59].

November 1958 — First child, Attilah, is born

February 8, 1959 — Speaks at NOI meeting in New York [FBI 5/19/59].

February 11, 1959 — Speaks at NOI meeting in Buffalo, New York [FBI 5/19/59].

February 15, 1959 — Speaks at NOI Temple No. 18 in Cleveland [FBI 5/19/59].

March 22, 1959 — At New York NOI meeting, asks if any FBI representatives, cops, or detectives are present [FBI 5/19/59].

March 29, 1959 — Tells New York NOI meeting that Negroes should sit and wait without violence because the white man will destroy himself [FBI 5/19/59].

April 23, 1959 — *Los Angeles Herald-Dispatch* publishes article captioned "Malcolm X calls for Bandung Conference of Negro Leaders" [FBI 11/17/59].

April 24, 1959 — States at New York NOI meeting that a Jew "is one of the worst of the devils" [FBI 11/17/59].

May 3, 1959 — Speaks at New York NOI meeting [FBI 11/17/59].

May 27, 1959 — Passport issued to Malcolm Little, also known as Malik El-Shabazz.

July 5, 1959 — Announced at New York NOI meeting that MX has left for Holland. Travels from there to Egypt, Mecca, Iran, Syria, and Ghana as EM's ambassador [FBI 11/17/59].

July 13, 1959   FBI learns from NOI member in New York that MX has met with Nasser of Egypt while in Africa [FBI airtel 7/13/59].

July 13–17, 1959 WTNA-TV Channel 13 in New York, airs five-part report by Mike Wallace entitled "The Hate That Hate Produced" [FBI 5/19/59].

July 26, 1959   At Saint Nicholas Arena in New York, MX speaks about recent trip to the Middle East prior to speech by EM; states that he became ill during the visit and was unable to go to Mecca [FBI 11/17/59].

August 24, 1959   Tells joint meeting of the FOI (Fruit of Islam) and MGT (Muslim Girls' Training) of Temple No. 7 that "the FBI would want to know everything so they hire these stool pigeons to start trouble" [FBI 11/17/59].

August 25, 1959   Speaks at NOI meeting in New York [FBI 11/17/59].

Sep 9, 1959   At New York NOI meeting, reads a letter the KKK (Ku Klux Klan) sent to the New York Police Commissioner [FBI 11/17/59].

Sep 16, 1959   Narrates movies of recent trip abroad at NOI meeting at Temple No. 25 in Newark, New Jersey [FBI 11/17/59].

August 22, 1959   In "Pulse of the Public" column, New York Amsterdam News carries letter written by MX from Khartoum, Sudan [FBI 11/17/59].

March 3, 1960   Debates William M. James on WMCA radio show called "Pro and Con"; the

	topic is: "Is Black Supremacy the Answer?" [FBI 11/17/59].
March 23, 1960	Speaks at NOI meeting in New York [FBI 5/17/60].
July 1960	Family moves to a seven-room house at 23–11 97th Street in East Elmhurst, Queens.
August–October 1960	According to FBI informants, allegedly forms nucleus of followers within NOI to take over after Elijah Muhammad's death; plans to run for public office "to obtain power for himself" [FBI 11/17/60].
September 21, 1960	Claims to have spoken recently with Fidel Castro for thirty minutes at the Hotel Theresa in Harlem [FBI 11/17/60].
December 1960	Says U.S. revolution is starting in Harlem and expresses admiration for Lenin and Stalin; predicts that Africans will be free with the assistance of the Russian army [FBI 11/17/60].
December 25, 1960	Second daughter, Qubilah, is born.
January 28, 1961	Meets with Ku Klux Klan officials to solicit aid in obtaining land [FBI 11/17/60].
February 20, 1961	Says NOI was not behind recent demonstrations at United Nations over the death of former Prime Minister Patrice Lumumba of the Congo [FBI 11/17/60].
March 24, 1961	Debates Walter Carrington of the NAACP (National Association for the Advancement of Colored People) at Harvard Law School forum entitled "The American Negro: Problems and Solutions" [FBI 11/17/60].
September–October 1961	Visits Los Angeles [FBI 11/17/61].

October 16, 1961   Appears on NBC television program "Open Mind" with Morroe Berger, Kenneth B. Clark, Richard Haley, and Constance B. Motley, with moderator Eric P. Goldman. The topic is "Where is the American Negro Headed?"

November 21, 1961   Dr. Harry Rivlin, acting president of City College of New York, announces that he has no objection to the Eugene V. Debs Club inviting MX to speak on campus.

December 1961   EM returns from tour of Muslim countries and issues directive that NOI temples shall now be called mosques.

January 1962   Delivers speech blasting Negro leadership to an overflowing crowd in Homes Hall at Los Angeles City College.

February 15–16, 1962   In Chicago, debates Bayard Rustin on the topic "Integration or Separation for the Black Man?"

March 11, 1962   *New York Journal American* reports that civil rights leaders James Farmer and Whitney Young downgrade the influence of MX upon the Negro community and the overall civil rights struggle.

April 27, 1962   NOI member Ronald Stokes dies in police shooting; MX attempts to rally Negroes to protest killing [FBI 11/16/62].

May 1, 1962   Attends a New York symposium sponsored by the Committee to Aid the Monroe Defendants.

May 5, 1962   Conducts funeral services for Stokes [FBI 11/16/62].

May 10, 1962   *Los Angeles Herald-Dispatch* reports that more than two thousand people attend the funeral of Ronald Stokes; also covers MX press conference concerning the shooting [FBI 11/16/62].

May 17, 1962   Tells *Los Angeles Herald-Dispatch* that

	Stokes's death was "murder in cold blood" [FBI 11/16/62].
May 20, 1962	Speaks at protest rally at Park Manor Auditorium. Claims that socialists, communists, and liberals are joining to get rid of the common enemy with white skin [FBI 11/16/62].
June 6, 1962	*Los Angeles Herald-Examiner* reports on a tape recording of an NOI meeting in which MX states that a recent plane crash in Paris was Allah's way of executing justice upon those responsible for the lynching of Stokes [FBI 11/16/62].
September 15, 1962	Delivers impromtu address at outdoor rally in Harlem to protest police brutality.
November 26, 1962	Dora McDonald, secretary to Martin Luther King, Jr., informs MX that King refuses to debate him because "he has always considered his work in a positive action framework rather than engaging in consistent negative debate."
December 1962	Delivers speech entitled "Black Man's History" at Mosque No. 7.
1962	Rumors of EM's adultery cause numerous Muslims to leave Chicago Mosque No. 2; MX talks to three of EM's former secretaries, all of whom have had children by EM. MX learns that EM's son Herbert has been instructing "Muhammad Speaks" writers to feature MX as little as possible.
January 1, 1963	Speaks at New York Mosque No. 7 dinner program, "A Night with the FOI," which includes music, exhibits, drills, and special demonstrations by the FOI.
January 30, 1963	Speaks at Hi-Fi Country Club in Charlotte, North Carolina [FBI 3/13/63].
February–April 1963	Feelings of resentment and animosity

	develop between MX and EM's family [FBI 11/16/62].
February 3, 1963	In an interview at WMAL in Washington, D.C., MX states that EM does not advocate overthrow of the government. Says FBI goes beyond its duty in "religious suppression" of Muslims [FBI airtel 2/04/63].
February 4, 1963	States during WMAL program that "the FBI spends twenty-four hours a day infiltrating or trying to infiltrate Muslims" [FBI 2/04/63].
February 26, 1963	Takes control of NOI Convention in Chicago. FBI claims that EM's family resents MX's alleged statements against EM and his family and his attempts to advise the family [FBI 11/16/62].
March 10, 1963	Returns to New York from Chicago on orders from EM. [FBI 11/16/62].
April 1963	Flies to Phoenix, Arizona, to meet with EM at EM's home
April–October 1963	Serves as Interim Minister of the NOI in Washington, D.C. [FBI 11/15/63].
May 1963	Writes apologetic letter to EM telling him they should work together and not be divided [FBI 11/15/63].
May 1963	Interviewed by James Baldwin on television.
May 12, 1963	Speaks to audience of four hundred at radio station WUST in Washington, D.C. May 13 *Washington Post* carries article entitled "400 Hear Malcolm X Speak Here" [FBI 5/13/63].
	Interviewed by WUST in Washington, D.C., between 1:00 and 1:30 P.M. on the program "Focus" [FBI 5/12/63?].
May 17, 1963	*New York Times* reports that MX attacks President Kennedy for the way he

	dealt with the Birmingham crisis [FBI 11/15/63].
May 25, 1963	*New York Amsterdam News* reports that MX attacks Martin Luther King, Jackie Robinson, and Floyd Patterson as unwitting tools of white liberals [FBI 11/15/63].
June 7, 1963	Blasts Los Angeles Mayor Sam Yorty in "Muhammad Speaks" article and charges Los Angeles with operating a "Ku Klux Klan police force" that uses Gestapo tactics against the black community and Muslim religious groups.
June 13, 1963	EM instructs MX not to assist the NAACP or any other Negro organization in civil rights demonstrations [FBI 11/15/63].
June 1963	Adam Clayton Powell invites MX to speak at Abyssinian Baptist Church; delivers speech entitled "The Black Revolution."
August 17, 1963	Announces at NOI Bazaar in Boston Arena that EM and the NOI are not supporting or participating in the March on Washington [FBI 11/15/63].
August 19, 1963	Informs audience at FOI meeting at Mosque Number No. 7 in New York that NOI members who participate in March on Washington will be given ninety days to leave the mosque [FBI 11/15/63].
August 26, 1963	Replaced as head of NOI in Philadelphia [FBI 11/15/63].
August 27, 1963	Tells a reporter that "well, whatever black folks do, maybe I don't agree with it, but I'm going to be there [at the March on Washington], brother, 'cause that's where I belong."
August 28, 1963	Attends March on Washington as a criti-

cal observer; comments that he can't understand why Negroes should become so excited about a demonstration "run by whites in front of a statue of a president who has been dead for a hundred years and who didn't like us when he was alive."

September 1963   Speaks at rally organized by Jackie Robinson.

Fall 1963   Delivers speech in Philadelphia entitled "The Old Negro and the New Negro."

November 7, 1963   Speaks at the City College of New York.

November 10, 1963   Delivers "A Message from the Grass Roots" in Detroit at the Northern Negro Grass Roots Leadership Conference.

November 22, 1963   President Kennedy assassinated in Dallas, Texas.

December 1, 1963   States at NOI rally in New York that JFK "never foresaw that the chickens would come home to roost so soon," despite a directive from Elijah Muhammad that no Muslim minister comment on the assassination [FBI 12/6/63].

December 4, 1963   EM suspends MX from NOI for commenting on the death of President Kennedy [FBI 12/6/63].

January 2, 1964   EM, MX, and two unnamed individuals have a conversation during which they speak at length about recent developments [FBI 1/23/64].

January 6, 1964   Summoned to Phoenix for a secret preliminary hearing with Elijah Muhammad, John Ali, and Raymond Sharrieff; rumors circulate in Harlem that Malcolm has been not only suspended but also "isolated," which means that all Muslims are forbidden to speak to him.

January 14, 1964   Meets with Alex Haley (writer for *Read-*

er's Digest) at the International Hotel outside Kennedy Airport.

January 15, 1964
During visit with Cassius Clay at his fight camp in Miami, MX tells sports reporters that he will be reinstated with the NOI in ninety days, although he believes the case to be otherwise.

January 21, 1964
Returns to New York from week's vacation with family at Cassius Clay's home in Miami, Florida: Does not attend dinner sponsored by the FOI and MGT of Mosque No. 7 in New York; relaxes in Queens and works on a book about NOI [FBI airtel 1/21/64]. Has not publicly engaged in any NOI activity since being suspended by EM from NOI.

February 4, 1964
States that Bayard Rustin is "nothing but a homosexual" [FBI 2/5/64].

In Queens, New York, refuses comment on his suspension from the NOI but says it was his own fault and he is not bitter toward EM. Believes that so-called Negro leaders are incompetent to lead Negroes; affirms that he would have no objection to being contacted by the FBI regarding demonstrations or public affairs contemplated by the NOI [FBI 2/5/64].

February 10, 1964
Rift between MX and EM appears to be widening [FBI 2/10/64].

February 27, 1964
Allegedly leaves Hampton House in Miami but intends to return in March; says, "If you think Cassius Clay was loud, wait until I start talking in March" [FBI airtel 3/3/64].

February 1964
Former assistant to Malcolm at Mosque No. 7 informs him that he has been asked by a mosque official to wire MX's car with a bomb.

March 6, 1964   Summons issued to MX for speeding on Triborough Bridge [FBI 5/19/64].

March 8, 1964   *New York Times* carries article entitled "Malcolm X Splits With Muhammed." MX plans to create "black nationalist party" and will cooperate with local civil rights actions in order to heighten political consciousness of Negroes.

March 9, 1964   Meeting between MX, E. Grant, and J. Warden to discuss incorporation of MMI (Muslim Mosque, Incorporated).

Informant reports that EM has ordered MX to surrender his home and car, both of which are owned by the NOI [FBI airtel 3/12/64].

Appears on "The World At Ten" from 10:00–10:30 P.M.on WNDT Channel 13 in New York; talks about split with EM [FBI 3/11/64].

March 10, 1964   NOI member sends letter to MX requesting that he return all NOI property, including his home at 23–11 97th Street, East Elmhurst, Queens.

Tells *Ebony* magazine that Black Muslim leaders have "got to kill me. They can't afford to let me live. . . . I know where the bodies are buried. And if they press me, I'll exhume some."

NOI sends MX certified letter requesting that he and his family vacate the premises at 23–11 97th Street in East Elmhurst because the house was purchased and is owned by Muslim mosque No. 7.

March 11, 1964   Sends telegram to EM stating that actions are necessary because of pressures from within NOI; MX also releases copy of telegram to the press.

March 12, 1964   Calls 11:00 A.M. press conference at

Park Sheraton Hotel, at which he issues copy of his March 8 statement and his March 11 telegram to EM.

Holds press conference in Tapestry Suite of Park Sheraton Hotel, New York; audience of sixty hears MX read a prepared statement and a telegram he sent to EM on March 11; announces a restricted meeting at 8:30 P.M. on March 15 at the George Washington Carver Club in New York [FBI 3/13/64].

March 16, 1964	Certificate of incorporation is filed for MMI. Appears in court and pleads not guilty for speeding violation [FBI teletype 5/19/64].
March 18, 1964	Speaks at Leverett House, Harvard University, according to March 19 report by informant [FBI 4/3/64].
March 23, 1964	Sends six followers to meet with leaders of EM's mosque in New York [FBI 3/27/64].
March 24, 1964	Speaks on "Bob Kennedy Show" on WBZ, Boston, from 6:30 –8:00 P.M.; subject is "Negro—Separation and Supremacy" (according to March 25 informant's report; clarifies statement concerning death of President Kennedy [FBI 4/3/64].
March 26, 1964	Meets Martin Luther King, Jr. face-to-face for the first and only time after King news conference at U.S. Capitol.
April 3, 1964	Delivers speech, "The Ballot or the Bullet," at Cleveland symposium sponsored by CORE (Congress of Racial Equality).
April 4, 1964	EM tells The New Crusader that MX's failure to maintain silence during his suspension forced EM to extend the suspension.

April 8, 1964   NOI files eviction proceedings against
                         MX; MX answers them on April 13;
                         hearing is set for April 17 but is post-
                         poned twice, first until May 26 and then
                         until June 3.

                         Delivers speech at a Militant Labor Fo-
                         rum in New York.

April 12, 1964   Announces at MMI rally that he is pre-
                         paring for a three-week African tour, ex-
                         pecting to leave on April 16 [FBI tele-
                         type 4/14/64].

                         Delivers "Ballots or Bullets" speech in
                         Detroit.

April 13–May 21,   Travels abroad.
1964

April 13, 1964   Answers a hearing set for April 17; hear-
                         ing postponed until May 26, then until
                         June 3, and again until June 15.

                         Leaves for Cairo, Egypt [FBI 1/20/65].

                         Departs JFK International Airport in
                         New York at 7:00 P.M.under alias Malik
                         El-Shabazz, according to informant's re-
                         port; flies on one-way ticket to Frank-
                         furt, Cairo, Jedda, Cairo [FBI teletype
                         4/14/64].

April 20, 1964   After pilgrimage to Mecca, MX writes
                         letter stating that many white people he
                         met during his pilgrimage displayed a
                         spirit of unity and brotherhood that pro-
                         vided him with a new, positive insight
                         into race relations; in Islam, he now
                         feels, lies the power to overcome racial
                         antagonism and to obliterate it from the
                         heart of white America. May 8 *New
                         York Times* reports on a letter written by
                         Malcolm while in Africa; article caption
                         reads: "Malcolm X Pleased by White
                         Attitude on Trip to Mecca" [FBI 1/20/
                         65].

April 21–30, 1964	Prince Faisal, ruler of Arabia, honors MX as guest of the state.
April 30, 1964	Flies to Beirut; speaks at Sudanese Cultural Center on shortcomings and failures of American civil rights movement.
May 2–6, 1964	Flies back to Cairo and takes train to Alexandria, Egypt, where he boards airplane to Nigeria.
May 6–10, 1964	In Lagos, featured on Nigerian radio and television programs.
May 8, 1964	Sponsored by the National Union of Nigerian Students, MX speaks to an enthusiastic audience of approximately five hundred students at the University of Ibadan [FBI 1/20/65].
May 10, 1964	Flies to Accra, Ghana, invited by the Marxist Forum, a new student organization at the University of Ghana [FBI 1/20/65].
May 13, 1964	Delivers lecture entitled "Will Africa Ignite America's Racial Powder Keg?" at the University of Ghana [FBI 1/20/65].
May 14, 1964	Addresses Ghanian parliament.
May 15, 1964	Meets Ghanian President Kwame Nkrumah and describes meeting as his highest single honor, not only in Ghana but in all of Africa; that afternoon addresses two hundred students at the Kwame Nkrumah Ideological Institute in Winneba.
May 17, 1964	Encounters Cassius Clay at Hotel in Accra. Meeting is awkward because of Clay's continued loyalty to EM.
May 17–18, 1964	Flies to Dakar, Senegal, then to Morocco.
May 19, 1964	Thirty-ninth birthday; arrives in Algiers. Warrant issued for his arrest at 12:30 P.M. for failing to appear at May 19 trial

for a speeding summons [FBI teletype 5/19/64].

May 21, 1964   Arrives at New York's Kennedy International Airport at 4:25 P.M. aboard Pan Am flight from Paris, France [FBI 5/22/64].

May 22, 1964   *New York Times* article appears titled "Malcolm Says He Is Backed Abroad" [FBI 5/22/64].

May 23, 1964   Debates Louis Lomax on "The Negro Revolt," during which MX states that he has somewhat changed his mind regarding the white man [FBI 1/20/65].

Appears on "Kup's Show" on Channel 7 in Chicago; states that many whites want to help the struggle of the Negro [FBI 1/20/65].

May 29, 1964   Speaks at Militant Labor Forum symposium.

June 4, 1964   Radio station WDAS in Philadelphia, Pennsylvania, interviews MX regarding his break with the NOI.

June 7, 1964   MMI sponsors public rally at Audubon Ballroom in New York. In answer to a question from the audience, Malcolm states that EM is the father of six illegitimate children.

June 8, 1964   Indicates to CBS that six women are involved in EM's scandal [FBI 1/20/65].

On the "Barry Gray Show" at 11:40 P.M. on radio station WMCA in New York, states that he makes no distinction between Governor Wallace of Alabama and President Johnson [FBI 6/9/64].

June 9, 1964   On "Mike Wallace News Program" at 11:00 P.M. states that there are some good white people [FBI 1/20/64].

June 12, 1964   Anonymous caller at 1:40 P.M. says that

MX will be "bumped off" [FBI 1/20/65].

Interviewed on WEEI (Boston) radio program, "Conversation for Peace," from 2:40 to 5:00 P.M.; states that he broke with the NOI because of moral problem; he also speaks about EM's illegitimate children [FBI 1/20/65].

Speaks on WMEX (Boston) radio program from 10:00 P.M. to 1:00 A.M. [FBI 1/20/65].

June 15, 1964	NOI eviction trial against MX ends at 1:30 P.M.; ten MMI and fifty NOI members are present, but no incidents occur; MX does not request police protection [FBI teletype 6/16/64].
June 16, 1964	*New York Herald Tribune* reports that MX is under protection of police and bodyguards because of anonymous telephone threats to wire service and newspaper that he would be shot if he appeared in court for his eviction trial; nevertheless, MX testifies at Queens County Civil Court.
	Eviction trial ends at 1:30 P.M.; judge reserves sentence [FBI coded teletype 6/16/64].
June 21, 1964	At MMI rally, MX calls Civil Rights Bill a "farce" and mentions emergence of a new group, the Organization of Afro-American Unity [FBI 1/20/65].
June 25, 1964	On Bob Kennedy's WBZ (Boston) radio show "Contact," MX states that struggle for civil rights is struggle for human rights [FBI 1/20/65].
June 26, 1964	*New York Post* publishes open letter from MX to EM calling for an end to hostilities between them.
June 28, 1964	MX announces formation of OAAU.

June 30, 1964

Wires Martin Luther King, Jr. and Student Nonviolent Coordinating Committee (SNCC) about the Saint Augustine attacks; offers assistance on behalf of civil rights movement; states that "on King's word" he would send some brothers to give the KKK "a taste of its own medicine" [FBI 1/20/65].

Speaks in Omaha, Nebraska, with "considerable tolerance toward other Negro rights groups"; *Omaha World-Herald* reports on establishment of the OAAU, an organization committed to doing "whatever is necessary to bring the Negro struggle from the level of civil rights to the level of human rights."

July 3, 1964

Reports to police a possible case of assault and battery on him by two black men at 11:30 P.M. in front of his house in East Elmhurst. Police guard his home until 4:00 P.M. the following day; On July 5, four black men with knives approach him in front of his house as he steps into his car [FBI 1/20/65].

July 4, 1964

Panel discussion on WLIB in New York.

July 5, 1964

Orders to kill MX come through from Chicago. MX informed that he can take NOI to court if he wishes [FBI 1/20/65].

July 6, 1964

Using the name Malik El-Shabazz, MX purchases one-way ticket to Cairo via London for departure on July 9 [FBI 1/20/65].

July 7, 1964

Reports to police in New York that an attempt on his life was made that day [FBI 1/20/65].

July 9, 1964

Leaves for Cairo [FBI 11/25/65].

July 17, 1964

Attends African Summit Conference in Cairo as representative of OAAU. Appeals to delegates of the thirty-four African nations to bring the cause of black people in the United States before the United Nations. Distributes a press release on OAAU letterhead on behalf of twenty-two million Afro Americans in the United States [FBI 9/17/64].

July 20, 1964 — Calls someone (a woman) from Cairo; says he will continue to travel [FBI teletype 7/21/64].

July 1964 — Interviewed in Cairo.

August 4, 1964 — At a banquet in Alexandria, Egypt, addresses more than six hundred Muslim students representing seventy-three different African and Asian countries [FBI teletype 8/7/64].

August 21, 1964 — Attends the second African Summit Conference in Cairo.

September 1, 1964 — Confidential source visits Alex Haley regarding book Haley just finished on MX [FBI 1/20/65].

In eviction suit brought by NOI against MX, civil court judge Maurice Wahl orders MX to vacate the $16,200 house he is occupying at 23–11 97th Street in East Elmhurst by January 31, 1965.

September 2, 1964 — Assistant Attorney General Yeagley requests that Hoover investigate MX's actions to see whether they violate the Logan Act [FBI letter 9/2/64].

September 12, 1964 — First edition of MX autobiography published in *Saturday Evening Post.*

September 28, 1964 — Yeagley informs FBI that if MMI is receiving funds from Arab or African governments, it will have to register under the Foreign Agents Registration Act [1/20/65].

October 3, 1964 — Addresses five to six hundred students in Addis Ababa [FBI 1/20/65].

October 16, 1964   Attorney General Lefkowitz requests
                      that Yeagley use contacts in U.S. gov-
                      ernment to locate MX so he can testify
                      in a New York NOI trial.

October 18, 1964   Flies from Dar es Salaam to Kenya with
                      Kenyan President Jomo Kenyatta and
                      Ugandan Milton Obote [FBI 1/20/65].

October 29, 1964   Visits Lagos and observes that factional-
                      ism is a major problem in Africa [FBI
                      1/20/65].

October 1964–No-   By mid-October MX has visited eleven
vember 1964   countries, talked with eleven heads of
                      state, and addressed most of their parlia-
                      ments; will continue his tour of Africa
                      for another five weeks "to better ac-
                      quaint himself with the problems facing
                      the continent," as he says in a speech in
                      Lagos.

November 13, 1964   Leaves Conakry, French West Africa
                      [FBI 1/20/65].

November 24, 1964   Returns to New York at 6:41 P.M.;
                      greeted by sixty MMI and OAAU mem-
                      bers [FBI 1/20/65].

November 28, 1964   Panel discussion on WMCA in New
                      York about crisis in the Congo.

November 29, 1964   Remarks at OAAU reception that he
                      will travel to London and Oxford [FBI
                      1/20/65].

November 30, 1964   Leaves for London [FBI 1/20/65].

December 1964   Fourth daughter, Amiliah, is born.

December 3, 1964   Debates at Oxford University; defends
                      use of extremism and "any means neces-
                      sary to bring about freedom" [FBI 1/
                      20/65].

December 7, 1964   In Chicago, Captain Raymond Sharrieff
                      of NOI issues threat to MX [FBI 12/15/
                      64].

December 12, 1964   Speaks at HARYOU (Harlem Youth

Opportunities Unlimited)-ACT Forum in Harlem.

December 13, 1964 — Five hundred people attend OAAU public meeting, at which MX speaks about Congo situation [FBI 1/20/65].

December 16, 1964 — Speaks at Harvard Law School forum.

December 20, 1964 — At OAAU rally at Audubon, MX speaks on African natural resources [FBI 1/20/65].

At Harlem rally, supports Mississippi Freedom Democratic Party.

December 28, 1964 — On the "Les Crane Television Show" in New York, MX advocates armed self-defense [FBI 1/20/65].

January 1, 1965 — Urges young people to "think for yourself" in speech at the Hotel Theresa in Harlem to a SNCC-sponsored group of high school students from McComb, Mississippi.

January 7, 1965 — Delivers speech at a Militant Labor Forum in New York.

January 12, 1965 — Registers at Hilton Hotel in New York under alias M. Khalil [FBI 1/20/65].

January 18, 1965 — Interview with Jack Barnes and Barry Sheppard, leaders of the Young Socialist Alliance (YSA); MX will approve final text before it appears in the March/April issue of *Young Socialist*.

January 19, 1965 — Pierre Berton interviews MX on his television show in Toronto.

January 24, 1965 — Speaks about Afro-American history at OAAU rally.

January 28, 1965 — Flies to Los Angeles and meets with attorney Gladys Towles Root and two former NOI secretaries who are filing paternity suits against EM.

Radio interview with Harry Ring on WBAI in New York.

January 29, 1965	Testifies before Illinois Attorney General, who is investigating NOI activities.
January 30, 1965	In Chicago, records "Kup's Show," which airs early the next morning [FBI airtel 2/4/65].
February 4, 1965	Travels to Selma, Alabama, where the SCLC (Southern Christian Leadership Conference) is involved in a campaign for blacks' voting rights; speaks at Brown's Chapel AME Church.
February 5, 1965	Leaves for London at 8:11 P.M., with a ticket for Paris, Geneva, and back to New York [FBI 2/9/65].
February 8, 1965	Addresses the First Congress of the Council of African Organizations in London.
February 9, 1965	French authorities bar MX from entering the country to speak; he is forced to return to London.
February 11, 1965	Delivers speech entitled "The oppressed masses of the world cry out for action against the common oppressor" at the London School of Economics.
February 13, 1965	Flies back to New York.
February 14, 1965	MX's house in East Elmhurst, Queens, firebombed at 2:46 A.M. [FBI 2/16/65].
	Leaves for Detroit at 9:30 A.M. [FBI 2/16/65].
	Registers at Statler Hilton Hotel in Detroit at 11:30 A.M. [FBI airtel 2/17/65].
	Interviewed by WYXZ-TV at 4:00 P.M. [FBI airtel 2/17/65].
	Speaks at first annual Dignity Projection and Scholarship Award ceremony [FBI 2/17/65].
	Speaks at Detroit rally.
February 15, 1965	Six hundred people attend OAAU rally from 8:15 –10:15 P.M. at Audubon Ballroom; Benjamin X opens; MX speaks of

February 14 firebombing and NOI conspiracy with KKK [FBI 2/16/65].

February 18, 1965   Evicted from home at 9:00 A.M.; moves belongings at 1:00 P.M. [FBI teletype 2/18/65].

Last formal talk given at Columbia University.

Last on-air appearance on WINS in New York.

February 20, 1965   In telephone conversation with Alex Haley, MX says, "The more I keep thinking about this thing, the things that have been happening lately, I'm not at all sure it's the Muslims. I know what they can do, and what they can't, and they can't do some of the stuff recently going on."

After OAAU business meeting, friend and associate Earl Grant invites MX to spend the night in the Grant household; MX replies, "You have a family. . . . I don't want anyone hurt on my account. I always knew it would end like this."

February 21, 1965   MX shot several times at 3:10 P.M. while delivering speech at an OAAU meeting in Audubon Ballroom; Thomas Hagan (Talmage Hayer) arrested outside and charged with homicide; Reuben X charged with felonious assault on Hayer and possession of a deadly weapon; MX pronounced DOA at Vanderbilt Clinic, Presbyterian Hospital.

Martin Luther King, Jr. sends telegram to Betty Shabazz, expressing his sadness over "the shocking and tragic assassination of your husband. While we did not always see eye to eye on methods to solve the race problem, I always had a deep affection for Malcolm and felt that he had a great ability to put his finger on the existence and the root of the problem. He was an eloquent spokesman for his point of view and no one can honestly doubt that Malcolm had a great concern for the problems we face as a race. . . ."

At 10:15 P.M. a confidential witness provides FBI with a .45-caliber automatic pistol used in the shooting [FBI 3/12/65].

February 22, 1965   EM denies that he or the NOI had anything to do with a slaying. In an interview on Chicago radio station WVON, he states his "shock and surprise" at the murder.

February 23, 1965   James Farmer, CORE Director states that MX murder was "a political act, with international implications" [FBI teletype 2/24/65].

February 24, 1965   Muhammad Ali asserts that he will not go into hiding because of fears of reprisal in the aftermath of MX's assassination.

February 25, 1965   FBI removes MX from its Security Index.

February 26, 1965   Norman 3X Butler arrested at 3:00 A.M. for the murder of MX; three witnesses place him at Audubon Ballroom. [FBI 3/12/65].

February 27, 1965   9:20 A.M. MX's body moved from Unity Funeral Home to Faith Temple Church.

9:50 A.M. services begin; Ossie Davis speaks.

11:10 A.M. procession to Ferncliff Cemetery, Hartsdale.

11:35 A.M. arrive at cemetery.

12:45 P.M. graveside service concludes [FBI 2/28/65].

Witness identifies Hayer and Butler as two of the assassins [FBI 3/12/65].

March 1, 1965 — Betty Shabazz meets with New York police detectives investigating the assassination.

March 5, 1965 — Jack Barnes of the Young Socialist Alliance gives speech in tribute to MX as "an authentic voice of the forces of the American revolution" at a memorial meeting organized by the Militant Labor Forum in New York.

March 8, 1965 — Witness tells New York police that he saw Hayer shoot MX while Butler and Johnson were present; he also saw Thomas 15X Johnson run out the side exit after the shooting [FBI 3/12/65].

March 10, 1965 — New York County Grand Jury indicts Hayer, 22, Butler, 26, and Johnson, 29, for murder [FBI 3/12/65].

Because MMI members all have the same "clear-cut" story, investigators shift their search toward "officials of the MMI" [FBI 3/12/65].

March 25, 1965 — FBI report indicates that Robert 35X and Charles 26X, on guard at the Audubon, left their posts, an act in violation of both NOI and MMI rules.

May 20, 1965 — Reuben X Francis fails to appear in court in connection with felonious assault charge [FBI letter from Baumgartner to Sullivan 8/25/65].

August 20, 1965 — FBI reports that Reuben X Francis has fled to Mexico.

November 5, 1965 — *New York Times* heralds publication of *The Autobiography of Malcolm X,* written with Alex Haley, as "an eloquent statement."

1965 — Betty Shabazz gives birth to twin daughters, Malaak and Malikah.

January 12, 1966   Trial for MX shooting begins [FBI 2/8/66].

February 3–4, 1966   Courtroom cleared so confidential witness can testify that he turned gun in to FBI [FBI 2/9/66].

February 8, 1966   SAC Donald E. Roney of New York office says that an SA would testify on February 9 and, if necessary, produce the FD 302 indicating receipt of the gun [FBI 2/8/66].

February 9, 1966   SA testifies and produces the FD 302 [FBI 2/9/66].

February 16, 1966   SA gives Assistant District Attorney Dermody three photos, including Hayer in karate uniform, to prove that Hayer was in NOI [FBI 2/25/66].

February 21, 1966   Ballistics expert links cartridges in Hayer's possession with the .45 used to kill MX [FBI 2/25/66].

February 24, 1966   Dermody describes photographer Durant's testimony as "frosting on the cake." Durant indicated that Hayer belonged to Newark chapter of NOI [FBI 2/25/66].

March 2, 1966   Hayer testifies that he and three others were hired to kill MX, and that Butler and Johnson are innocent [FBI teletype 3/3/66].

March 3–4, 1966   Johnson and his wife testify that Johnson was not at the Audubon [FBI 3/7/66].

March 11, 1966   Hayer, Butler, and Johnson convicted of murder in the first degree [FBI teletype 3/11/66].

April 14, 1966   Judge Charles Marks sentences Hayer, Butler, and Johnson to life imprisonment [FBI airtel 4/14/66].

May 29, 1980   Congressman W. Hughes of New Jersey writes FBI Director Webster and asks

	that he look into the assassination of MX.
June 20, 1980	Assistant Director Revell writes to Hughes to explain that the FBI has no new information.

Part III
The FBI File

Although the FBI under the leadership of J. Edgar Hoover was consistently hostile toward African-American militancy, the federal government's policies toward the Nation of Islam were inconsistent. The FBI's surveillance of Elijah Muhammad and his followers prior to the 1960s did not result from a widely shared perception among government officials that the Nation of Islam was subversive. Instead, it resulted from the determination of Hoover and other FBI officials to continue surveillance even without explicit authority. The Nation's potential as a stimulus for revolutionary and seditious activities became evident to the FBI mainly as a result of the increasing prominence of Malcolm X and the increasing militancy and scale of black protests.

While Hoover and other Bureau officials saw the group as one of many types of subversive black militancy, other officials of the Justice Department were not convinced that the Muslims represented a serious threat. The 1975 Church Committee hearings on intelligence activities included a summary of the discussions between the FBI and Justice Department officials regarding the Nation of Islam. In 1952, the Bureau suggested adding the Muslims to the Attorney General's list of subversive organizations, and the following year the Department of Justice concluded that the Nation of Islam would not be prosecuted under the anti-communist Smith Act but decided that "the group would under certain circumstances represent a serious threat to our national security." In 1954, the Justice Department decided against prosecuting the Nation for conspiracy to violate the Selective Service Act. In 1955, the Justice officials responded inconclusively to the FBI's request for advice on whether Muslim activists should remain on the Security Index. In 1959, the Department indicated to Hoover that it did not support prosecution of the Nation or designation on the Attorney General's list. In 1960, according to testimony before the Church Committee, the Department advised that the group was not subversive as defined by the employee security program. However, the FBI was requested to continue its investigation of the group.

Hoover noted on the bottom of that memorandum, after he received it, that Justice was "just stalling."

During the 1960s, Justice Department officials questioned whether Elijah Muhammad's prophesies constitute subversive threats but did not request that the FBI discontinue its investigation of the Nation of Islam. Without explicit instructions from Justice Department officials, the FBI continued to compile information on the Muslims until after the death of Elijah Muhammad.[1]

The following documents are selected from the large body of FBI records that refer to Malcolm X. They have been edited to eliminate repetitive material and some material from non-FBI sources, such as newspaper articles on Malcolm X. The Bureau opened its file on Malcolm X shortly after his release from prison in March, 1953 and in 1958 designated him "a key figure" as a result of his increasing national visibility. Even after his assassination, the Bureau continued to refer to Malcolm in its reports, especially after 1966, when the Bureau broadened the focus of its COINTELPRO from leftist organizations to include "Black nationalist-hate groups."

The file is divided into 19 sections, chronologically arranged. Included in the reports are Malcolm's personal correspondence, reports of speeches and sermons, and transcripts of radio and television interviews.

Before releasing this file, the Federal Bureau of Investigation deleted numerous passages in accordance with exemptions allowed under the Freedom of Information Act. The specific reasons for many deleted passages are indicated by the references to subsections of Title 5, United States Code, Section 552. Thus, deleted sections with the following references were withheld because they were deemed to meet the following criteria:

b2 —related solely to the internal personnel rules and practices of an agency.

b7 —(c) could reasonably be expected to constitute an unwarranted invasion of personal privacy.

—(d) could reasonably be expected to disclose the identity · of a confidential source, including a State, local, or foreign agency or authority or any private institution which furnished information on a confidential basis, and, in the case of a record or information compiled by a criminal law enforcement authority in the course of a criminal investigation, or by an agency conducted a lawful national security intelligence investigation, information furnished by a confidential source.[2]

1. United States Senate, Hearings before the Select Committee to Study Governmental Operations with Respect to Intelligence Activities, v. 6, Federal Bureau of Investigation, testimony of Frederick A. O. Schwarz, Jr., November 18, 1975, p. 37–39.

2. From "Explanation of Exemptions" obtained from the FBI's public reading room.

SECTION 1

May 4, 1953–January 28, 1955

REPORTS: 1. May 4, 1953. Boston
          2. March 16, 1954. Detroit
          3. September 7, 1954. New York
          4. November 18, 1954. Philadelphia
          5. January 28, 1955. New York

Suspecting that Malcolm X had communist sympathies, the FBI began its surveillance of him in 1953. The Bureau apparently became concerned about Malcolm because of a June 1950 letter, in which Malcolm stated that he had "always been a Communist." The first two reports reprinted below are labeled "Security Matter-C," but the FBI file increasingly focuses on Malcolm's affiliation with the Nation of Islam (NOI) rather than the possibility of leftist political activity.

In addition to background information—aliases, prison record, places of residence, and employment—the reports in this section describe Malcolm's attitudes during the initial period of his affiliation with the Nation of Islam (NOI). Particularly interesting are three letters that a confidential source gave the FBI, the last of which might be the letter addressed to that confidential source. This apologetic note, written in January 1951, may have been part of an effort by Malcolm to convince a corrections officer that he should be granted parole later that year. However, this wish was denied, and Malcolm had to wait until 1952.

As the file continues, the FBI reports reflect Malcolm's increasing prominence in the Nation of Islam by detailing events of early 1954, when he was "traveling about the United States making contacts with the various Temples of the Muslim Cult of

Islam" (MCI). The September 7 report indicates that during January and February of 1954, Malcolm increased his speaking appearances at Temple No. 7 in New York City, calling for "greater hatred on the part of the cult towards the white race." The November 18 report shows that Malcolm had by this time established his residence in New York City and had begun to deliver speeches at Temple No. 7 with stronger political content. His autobiography indicates that he was officially the Minister of Temple No. 11 in Boston early in 1954 but had moved to Philadelphia's Temple No. 12 in March. The FBI could not keep up with these rapid changes, but the file does corroborate Malcolm's autobiographical account of his becoming Minister of New York City's Temple No. 7 by the summer of 1954.

The final report of this section contains more background on Malcolm, the NOI (MCI) and the Fruit of Islam (FOI), the all-male, military guard unit of the NOI. The report concludes with an account of one of only two interviews which the FBI conducted with Malcolm. In it, he admitted membership in New York's Temple No. 7 but not in any other Temples. He spoke about Elijah Muhammad and the Muslim movement but "was very uncooperative" by refusing to elaborate on the infrastructure of the NOI.

SUBJECT   MALCOLM X LITTLE
FILE NO.   100-399321
              Section 1
              Serials 1–17

FEDERAL BUREAU OF INVESTIGATION

This case originated at: Detroit
Report made at: Boston
Date when made: 5/4/53
Period for which made: 3/20;4/1,3,6/53
Report made by: SA [BUREAU DELETION] b7C
Title: MALCOLM K. LITTLE, was Malachi Shabazz;
"Rhythm Red" Little; "Detroit Red" Little; Jack Carlton
Character of case: Security Matter-C; Security Matter-MCI

SYNOPSIS OF FACTS:

Subject resides at 4336 Williams Street, Inkster, Michigan.
Subject claimed in June, 1950, that he was a Communist and
during September, 1952, he indicated membership in the Muslim
Cult of Islam.

DETAILS:

This investigation was predicated upon information received
from [BUREAU DELETION] Norfolk, Massachusetts, to the

effect that the Subject [BUREAU DELETION] had written two letters that included comments on Communism.

I. BACKGROUND

Birth

[BUREAU DELETION] the Subject was born May 19, 1925, in Omaha, Nebraska, and is a citizen by virtue of his birth.

Employment

Information received from Boston Informant [BUREAU DELETION] of known reliability, reflects the Subject is presently unemployed.

Residence

[BUREAU DELETION] Subject resides at the home of his brother at 4336 Williams Street, Inkster, Michigan.

Military Service

[BUREAU DELETION] Massachusetts State Prison, Charlestown, Massachusetts, advised Subject's Selective Service status had been verified by prison authorities during the late 1940s and information obtained from Selective Service records reflected Subject was registered with Local Board No. 59, New York, New York, and classified 4-F.

Status of Health

Information received from [BUREAU DELETION] reflects Subject is under a doctor's care at the present time. The nature or extent of his illness is not known.

Criminal

[BUREAU DELETION] Subject was sentenced to serve 8 to 10 years on a charge of breaking and entering in the nighttime and that he began this sentence February 27, 1946. [BUREAU DELETION] Subject was eligible for parole May 29, 1951, but was denied parole at that time.

On September 23, 1953 [BUREAU DELETION] Norfolk Prison Colony, Massachusetts, stated Subject is a former inmate and had been paroled in care of Michigan parole authorities on August 7, 1952.

The following record was obtained from [BUREAU DELETION] Massachusetts State Board of Probation, Boston, Massachusetts, the central repository for all arrest records in the Commonwealth of Massachusetts:

Date	Offense	Court	Disposition
11/30/44	Larceny	Roxbury	3 months House of Correction SS 11/30/45-Filed
1/15/46	Carrying firearms	Roxbury	M.R.ss 1/15/47-Filed
1/16/46	Breaking & Enter. Larceny	Quincy	1/2-Grand Jury
2/27/46	Breaking & Enter. Larceny	Middlesex Superior	8–10 years. State
2/27/46	Breaking & Enter. Larceny	Middlesex Superior	8–10 yrs. State Pris
2/27/46	" " " " " " "	" " " "	
2/27/46	Conspiracy, Break. and Entering	Middlesex Superior	Filed
4/10/46	B & E., Larceny	Norfolk	6–8 years SP conc.
3/7/46	B & E., Larceny	Newton	Dismissed
8/7/52	Paroled 4 5/4/53	State Prison	

Credit

The records of the Credit Bureau [BUREAU DELETION] contained no reference to Subject.

II. COMMUNIST PARTY ACTIVITIES

The Communist Party has been cited by the Attorney General of the United States as coming within the purview of Executive Order 9835.

[BUREAU DELETION] several excerpts from letters written by Subject. [BUREAU DELETION] these excerpts were not quotes but rather notes jotted down [BUREAU DELETION] on the contents of these letters.

On June 29, 1950, the Subject mailed a letter.

Editors Note. *The file indicates that an unidentified source copied out sentences from this letter. In one of them Malcolm states that he has always been a Communist. In World War II, Malcolm says, he attempted to enlist in the Japanese Army, with the result that he will now never be drafted into the U.S. Army. He adds that it's not difficult to convince anyone that he's crazy since everyone has always said he was anyway.*

In January, 1952 [BUREAU DELETION] Subject had been visited by [BUREAU DELETION] a member of the Crispus Attucks Club of the American Youth for Democracy. The AYD has been cited by the Attorney General of the United States as coming within the purview of Executive Order 9835.

There is no further information concerning the Subject's Communist activities in Boston.

MUSLIM CULT OF ISLAM

[BUREAU DELETION] the Muslim Cult of Islam, which is also known as the Allah Temple of Islam, is a religious cult whose members regard Allah as their supreme being and claim to be the direct descendants of the original race on earth. The members fanatically follow the teachings of Allah as interpreted by ELIJAH MUHAMMAD, the "true prophet of Allah" entitled titular head of the Muslim Cult of Islam in the United States, and believe that any civil law which conflicts with the Muslim law should be disobeyed. The members disavow their allegiance to the United States and pledge their allegiance only to Allah and do not consider it their duty to register for Selective Service or to serve in the United States Armed Forces as they cannot serve two masters. According to the teachings of ELIJAH MUHAMMAD and the cult's ministers, the members of a minority race in the United States are not citizens of this country but are merely slaves of this country and will continue to be slaves until they free themselves by destroying non-Muslims and Christianity in the "War of Armageddon."

[BUREAU DELETION] the cult teaches that the Korean War is a futile effort by the United States to prevent the coming Asiatic conquest of the world and the defeat of the United States in Korea is a prelude to the "resurrection" when North America and Great Britain will be doomed and the original man, led by Allah, will reign supreme.

[BUREAU DELETION] the following information taken from another letter of Subject of January 29, 1950:

It is better to be jailed by the devil for serving Allah than it is to be allowed by the devil to walk free. The black man has been enslaved. The time is coming for the devils to be destroyed.

On September 23, 1952, [BUREAU DELETION] provided SA [BUREAU DELETION] with three letters, one of which is addressed to him.

Editor's Note. *Of the three letters included in the file, the first two are written by Malcolm as Salaam Alaikum in the name of Allah and His Messenger, Elijah Muhammad; they are signed "Your Brother, Malachi Shabazz." The names of the correspondents in both cases have been deleted by the FBI.*

"This is the Day of Choosing (Separation)," Malcolm announces in the first letter, which he closes with a motto: "Each One teach One!!!"

In the second letter, "Stick close to the Muslims," Malcolm admonishes, and risk ridicule, for it is "better to be laughed at and be safe from the storm [like Noah], than to be caught in the storm just because you didn't want to be laughed at."

The third letter, more personal in tone, is dated January 9, 1951. In it Malcolm apologizes to his correspondent, whose name has been deleted by the bureau, for past disruptive behavior "while under your jurisdiction." Having asserted that "from here on in my words shall be of Love and Justice," he concludes with this statement of his sincerity: "You have al-

*ways spoke frankly to me, and treated me with squareness
. . . so how could I ever be any other way except square and
frank with you?" The letter is signed Malcolm K. Little.*

[BUREAU DELETION] Muslims known to him either shave
their hair or wear goatees.

According to records [BUREAU DELETION] the Subject
wears chin whiskers.

DESCRIPTION

The following description of the Subject was obtained from the
records [BUREAU DELETION]

Name	MALCOLM K. LITTLE, was Malachi Shabazz; "Rhythm Red"; "Detroit Red"; Jack Carlton
Date of Birth	May 19, 1925 Omaha, Nebraska
Race	Negro-mulatto
Sex	Male
Residence	4336 Williams Street Inkster, Michigan
Height	6' 3½"
Weight	180 lbs.
Build	Slender
Hair	Black
Eyes	Brown
Complexion	Light
Scars & Marks	1" scar from right eye to nose; ½" scar below left elbow
Peculiarities	Confirmed user of marijuana; wears chin whiskers and mustache
Employment	Cut Rate Department Store 8940 Oakland Avenue Inkster, Michigan (Presently unemployed)
Marital Status	Single
Nationality	American
FBI No.	4282299

Social Secu-   No. 376 16 3427
rity

————— • • —————

FEDERAL BUREAU OF INVESTIGATION

This case originated at: Detroit, Michigan
Report made at: Detroit, Michigan
Date when made: 3/16/54
Period for which made: 2/5,8,9,10,11,23,24/54
Report made by: SA [BUREAU DELETION] b7C

Title: CHANGED:
MALCOLM K. LITTLE, was Malachi Shabazz; "Rhythm
Red"; "Detroit Red"; Jack Carlton; Malcolm X Little
Character of case: Security Matter-C; Security Matter-MCI

SUMMARY REPORT:

Subject presently traveling about United States making contacts with various temples of the Muslim Cult of Islam. Receives
mail at 18887 Keystone, Detroit, Michigan. Subject, [BUREAU
DELETION] wrote letters indicating he was a Communist. [BU-
REAU DELETION] Subject wrote letters indicating membership in Muslim Cult of Islam. Subject reported in attendance at
various Muslim Cult of Islam meetings in Detroit from February,
1953 to June, 1953. Criminal record and description set out.

The title of this case is being marked changed to include the
alias *Malcolm X Little,* by which name the Subject is known in
the Muslim Cult of Islam.

————— • • —————

FEDERAL BUREAU OF INVESTIGATION

This case originated at: Philadelphia
Report made at: New York
Date when made: 9/7/54
Period for which made: 8/24,25,27/54

Report made by: SA [BUREAU DELETION] b7C
Title: MALCOLM K. LITTLE, was Brother Malcolm X
Character of case: Security Matter-MCI

SYNOPSIS OF FACTS:

[BUREAU DELETION] the subject attended meetings of the MCI, Temple No. 7, NYC, during January, 1954. [BUREAU DELETION] subject was a tour leader for the NYC Temple No. 7 at the Chicago Convention of the Cult in February, 1954. [BUREAU DELETION] subject was in attendance at Temple No. 7 and was enthusiastically going over the teachings of the cult. [BUREAU DELETION] the subject has openly spoken against the "white devils" and has encouraged greater hatred on the part of the cult towards the white race. [BUREAU DELETION] that the subject resides in Philadelphia and rents a room at 2535 Humphrey Street, East Elmhurst, Queens, New York when he is in the city.

DETAILS:

Brother MALCOLM LITTLE of the Cult's Temple at Boston, Massachusetts was a guest speaker at the Muslim Cult of Islam (MCI) meeting on January 8, 1954. [BUREAU DELETION] the subject had suggested that all members start a recruitment of younger members to go to the future meetings of the MCI.

[BUREAU DELETION] MALCOLM LITTLE was in attendance at the New York Temple quite regularly and [BUREAU DELETION] MALCOLM LITTLE is going over the teachings of the Muslim Cult from the beginning. [BUREAU DELETION] the subject was very enthusiastic about discussing any basic or elementary lessons with the Muslim members in an attempt to influence the Negroes in their interest about their faith.

[BUREAU DELETION] the new minister for Temple No. 7 is an individual known as MALCOLM.

[BUREAU DELETION] MALCOLM X had stated that he had recently been transferred from the Philadelphia area to replace the former minister who had traveled from Washington to handle the duties of the minister in the New York area. He advised that MALCOLM X appeared to be more educated than other members of the cult and was a very convincing speaker. He advised that during the course of some of the subject's talks, he had openly spoken against the "white devils" and had encouraged greater hatred on the part of the cult towards the white race.

[BUREAU DELETION] during one of the sermons given by MALCOLM X, he told the audience that he had once served in a federal penitentiary and stated that he was quite proud of the fact that he was chosen to serve time in the federal penitentiary for his beliefs in the Muslim doctrine. [BUREAU DELETION] the subject had encouraged the members to deem it an honor and a privilege to be called upon by the prophet to spend time in the federal penitentiary because of their religious beliefs.

FEDERAL BUREAU OF INVESTIGATION

This case originated at: New York
Report made at: Philadelphia
Date when made: 11/18/54
Period for which made: 10/12,21,29;11/3,4,8,10/54
Report made by: SA [BUREAU DELETION] b7C
Title: MALCOLM K. LITTLE, was
Character of case: Security Matter-MCI

SYNOPSIS OF FACTS:

Subject resides at 2535 Humphrey Street, East Elmhurst, New York. [BUREAU DELETION] Minister of MCI Temple at Philadelphia and New York; has made numerous speeches at MCI meetings indicating a knowledge of the aims and purposes of the MCI; attended numerous meetings of MCI at Philadelphia during period March, 1954, to present. Description set forth.

[BUREAU DELETION] the subject spoke at a meeting of the MCI [BUREAU DELETION] and stated that Genghis Khan and Attila the Hun and many others had started to remove the devil before the devil's time was up. LITTLE explained to his audience that the war now taking shape is a race war and in this race war women, children, and old men will be killed. In any other kind of war, either political or economic, the destruction of all members of a particular group is not necessary because a person's political and economic beliefs can be changed. In the case of a race war, however, no such change can be effected and it is necessary, therefore, to kill the children of the opposing races as well as the adults.

The subject spoke at a meeting of the MCI [BUREAU DELE-TION] and stated that he was being followed by the FBI and had been questioned by them because they are frantic to stop the teaching of Islam. LITTLE stated that there is nothing that the FBI could do to stop the spreading of the message that the white man is the devil and the black man is God. [BUREAU DELE-TION]

Speeches made indicating understanding
of the aims and purposes of the MCI
The subject spoke at a meeting of the MCI [BUREAU DELE-TION] and stated that the black man in the East is "kicking out" the white man and soon the white man will be kicked out of Europe and the only place he will be able to go is North America where he will be destroyed.
[BUREAU DELETION]
[BUREAU DELETION] the subject spoke at a meeting of the MCI [BUREAU DELETION] and told those assembled that the only thing the white man will let the Negro own is a saloon or a church and if the Negro does not get drunk in the saloon, he can get drunk in the Christian church. According to LITTLE, the Christian preachers are getting paid to deceive the black man by teaching him what the devil (white man) wants him to learn. LITTLE stated that the white man knows that if the black man in North America learned about Islam, then it would be time for the white man to be destroyed.
[BUREAU DELETION]
The subject was present at a meeting of the MCI [BUREAU DELETION] and told those assembled that not only ELIJAH

MUHAMMAD teaches that this government is going to be destroyed but also teaches that all white people all over the earth are going to be destroyed. According to LITTLE, the War of Armageddon is starting in the East and America knows that the Bible prophecy is being fulfilled and they are the lost children of the so-called American Negro. LITTLE stated that the white man knows that he is going to be destroyed and that is why he keeps watch over the American black man.

[BUREAU DELETION] the subject spoke at a meeting of the MCI [BUREAU DELETION] and told those assembled that the ministers of Christianity teach many fallacious theories and tell many lies and are the hirelings of the white man and do his bidding. According to MALCOLM, the King James version of the Bible was an interpretation made by King James in order to continue the devil in power and is false.

[BUREAU DELETION]
[BUREAU DELETION] the subject spoke at a meeting of the MCI [BUREAU DELETION] and stated that nowhere else than in the Temple of Islam is it told that the white man is the devil and that nowhere else is it told that the black man is the God of the earth and the only supreme being. In addition, LITTLE advised that the white man was allotted six hundred years to rule and that time came to an end in 1914. Ever since that time the white man has been having trouble, yet there are many colored people who still love the white man and will be destroyed with him because they love him so. According to the subject, the Mau Mau in Kenya, South Africa, had to first kill many of their black brothers who insisted on protecting their white enslavers, and this too will happen in North America.

FEDERAL BUREAU OF INVESTIGATION

This case originated at: New York
Report made at: New York
Date when made: 1/28/55

Period for which made: 11/3,4,8,18,19,22,23,29;12/
                       1,3,6,9,13,20,23,27,28,/54;1/
                       3,10,11,14,17,21/55
Report made by: SA [BUREAU DELETION] b7C
Title: MALCOLM K. LITTLE, was
Character of case: Security Matter-MCI

DETAILS:

   [BUREAU DELETION]

BACKGROUND
Birth
   [BUREAU DELETION] of the Bureau of Vital Statistics,
Douglas County, Health Department, 1201 South 42nd Street,
Omaha, Nebraska, made available file A39357 which reflects that
MALCOLM LITTLE was born at the University Hospital,
Omaha, Nebraska on May 19, 1925. The parents were listed as
EARLY LITTLE, who was born in the State of Georgia, and
LOUISE NORTON LITTLE, who was born in the West Indies.
Both parents, as well as the subject, were listed as of the Negro
race and at the time of the birth were listed as residing at 3448
Pinkney Street, Omaha, Nebraska.
Education
   [BUREAU DELETION] the subject had indicated he had
eight years in an elementary school and had three years of high
school as of July 15, 1943.

Service in the Armed Forces
   [BUREAU DELETION] MALCOLM LITTLE had registered at Local Board 59 of New York City on June 1, 1943 while
residing at 2460 Seventh Avenue, Apartment 31, New York City.
[BUREAU DELETION] on October 25, 1943 the subject was
found mentally disqualified for military service for the following
reasons: psychopathic personality inadequate, sexual perversion,
psychiatric rejection. Subject was classified 4F on December 4,
1944.

Residence

On January 10, 1955 the subject stated he resides at 25–35 Humphrey Street, East Elmhurst, Queens, New York, at the home of CURTIS and SUSIE KENNER.

Employment

[BUREAU DELETION] the subject was a full-time minister of the New York Temple No. 7 of the Muslim Cult of Islam (MCI) at New York City and at Philadelphia, Pennsylvania.

[BUREAU DELETION] the subject is a minister of the MCI Temple No. 7, 102 West 116th Street, New York City, and was devoting his full time to the MCI.

Information Concerning the Muslim Cult of Islam (MCI)

[BUREAU DELETION] the MCI, also known as the Temple of Islam and the Allah Temple of Islam, is an organization composed entirely of Negroes, which was reportedly organized around 1930 in Detroit, Michigan. The national leader and founder is ELIJAH MUHAMMAD, who claims to have been sent by ALLAH, the supreme being, to lead the Negroes out of slavery in the United States.

Members fanatically follow the alleged teachings of ALLAH, as interpreted by MUHAMMAD, and disavow allegiance to the United States. Members pledge allegiance only to ALLAH and Islam and believe any civil law which conflicts with Muslim law should be disobeyed. The Cult teaches that members of the dark-skinned race cannot be considered citizens of the United States since they are in slavery in this country, and, therefore, must free themselves by destroying non-Muslims and Christianity in the "War of Armageddon." For this purpose, the Cult has a military branch called the Fruit of Islam (FOI) composed of all-male, able-bodied members, who participate in military drill and judo training.

Members of the Cult also believe that they are directly related to all Asiatic races, and any conflict involving any Asiatic nation and a Western nation is considered a part of the War of Armageddon, in which the Asiatic nation will be victorious.

Meetings and Speeches Made by the Subject at
MCI Meetings, Temple No. 7, Which is Presently
Located at 102 West 116th Street, New York City
[BUREAU DELETION] at a meeting of the MCI Temple No.
7, New York City, [BUREAU DELETION] the Minister MAL-
COLM LITTLE was the main speaker. LITTLE spoke on the
lines of racial hatred, always referring to the white race as being
"the white devils." LITTLE compared President EISEN-
HOWER to Pharaoh of Egypt in the biblical days and compared
ELIJAH MUHAMMAD of Chicago, Illinois, as to Moses. He
stated that ELIJAH MUHAMMAD is going to lead the "black
race" out of slavery in the United States as Moses did the "Jews"
in Egypt. LITTLE stated that President EISENHOWER is nothing more than a Pharaoh of the United States and is keeping the
"black man" in slavery in the United States. LITTLE stated that
the Muslims do not allow any "white devils" in this temple. They
just allow their own kind to meet and that the Muslim Temple is
only for Negroes.

[BUREAU DELETION] MALCOLM LITTLE was the principal speaker at a MCI meeting at Temple No. 7 [BUREAU
DELETION]. LITTLE spoke about the white race being the
"devil." LITTLE claimed that the "white devils" from foreign
countries could just walk into the United States and automatically become citizens but the "black men" could be born in the
United States and are not treated as citizens.

[BUREAU DELETION] MALCOLM claimed that he had
first heard of Islam while he was in jail. LITTLE stated he had
studied in jail and had been teaching Islam since his release.
LITTLE made statements that the United States Constitution
does not protect the "black man" and now they, referring to the
United States government, are passing the "civil rights bill"
which will not help the "black man" either.

[BUREAU DELETION] MALCOLM LITTLE was the main
speaker at the MCI meeting. [BUREAU DELETION] that LIT-
TLE spoke about the "white man" as being the "devil" and made

statements that the United States government could pass a bill overnight but cannot even pass a "civil rights bill" in years. LITTLE claimed that all the "white devils" are being chased out of Asia by the "black man" and that they are all coming to the United States.

LITTLE told this group that there was a space ship forty miles up which was built by the wise men of the East and in this space ship there are a number of smaller space ships and each one is loaded with bombs. LITTLE stated that when ELIJAH MUHAMMAD of Chicago, Illinois, gives the word these ships will descend on the United States, bomb it and destroy all the "white devils." According to LITTLE these bombs will destroy all the "devils" in the United States and that all the Muslims in good standing will be spared. LITTLE claimed that their Prophet ELIJAH MUHAMMAD was sent to the United States twenty years ago to save the "black people."

[BUREAU DELETION] the Minister MALCOLM LITTLE was the main speaker at [BUREAU DELETION] of Temple No. 7 [BUREAU DELETION] and that LITTLE's talk was of the usual nature of hatred of the white race. [BUREAU DELETION] that LITTLE had a clipping from the *Daily News,* a New York daily newspaper, which had headlines in regard to the jailing of eleven fliers by the Chinese. [BUREAU DELETION] LITTLE held up this article for the entire group to see and stated that the "Chinese Reds are not Communists but are black people." LITTLE stated that Red China has told all the "white devils" to get out. LITTLE stated that the world is waking up and that all the "black nations" are rising and running the "devil" out. LITTLE compared the black man in the United States to JOSEPH of the Bible being sold into slavery by his brothers.

[BUREAU DELETION] Minister MALCOLM LITTLE was the speaker at the meeting of Temple No. 7 [BUREAU DELETION] LITTLE spoke along the lines of the so-called religious aspects of the Cult and made comparisons of the "black man's" accomplishments and the evils of the "white devils." LITTLE exhibited a newspaper clipping from the *Washington Post* which contained an article by a Professor O'CONNOR. LITTLE explained that this article by O'CONNOR reflected that Jesus Christ was a black man and LITTLE explained to the group that all the prophets in the past had been black men and that there never had been white prophets.

[BUREAU DELETION] MALCOLM LITTLE was the principal speaker at the meeting [BUREAU DELETION] at which time LITTLE expounded upon the origin of the white race, stating that it was created by YACOB and it took six thousand years to create the "white devil." LITTLE stated this was obtained by breeding the white-skinned and yellow-skinned races and that when the black-skinned babies were born they were killed off and it took six thousand years to accomplish the creation of the present-day "white devil."

During this meeting LITTLE explained that the guards of the Temple are soldiers in the army and that when the war is started these guards are duty-bound to see all churches are destroyed. LITTLE made the statement that they would chop your head off too if you do not believe in the teachings of Islam. LITTLE stated that the members are "fools" if they put on the uniform of the "white devil's army."

LITTLE stated, however, he was not telling them not to do so, [BUREAU DELETION] it was indicated from the theme of LITTLE's talk that it would not be along the Muslim lines for an individual to serve in the armed forces of the United States.

[BUREAU DELETION] in regards to the overthrow of the government, MALCOLM LITTLE had made statements to the effect that it was expected that the Negro race would be the rulers of the world and it had been indicated that the white man's rule in the United States would end with the year 1955. [BUREAU DELETION] they continuously referred to the Battle of Armageddon and that it had been explained that this Battle would be between the "black man" and the "white man."

Meetings and Speeches Made by Subject at the
"Temple of Islam" 1643 North Bailey Street,
Philadelphia, Pennsylvania

[BUREAU DELETION] MALCOLM LITTLE, the Minister
of the New York Temple and the Philadelphia Temple was in
charge of the meeting [BUREAU DELETION]. LITTLE expounded on the transportation arrangements for the members of
the Cult to go to Chicago, Illinois, on February 26, 1955, which
is the Muslim holiday known as "Savior's Day." LITTLE also
welcomed new members at this meeting and appointed an assistant minister to preside in LITTLE's absence.

[BUREAU DELETION] the Minister MALCOLM LITTLE
was the speaker at the [BUREAU DELETION] meeting [BU-
REAU DELETION]. MALCOLM spoke along the usual tirade,
but in a more violent manner than usual. MALCOLM's speech
reflected the theme that the destruction of the "devil" or white
man is imminent and that the black people all over the world are
conscious of this fact. MALCOLM presented two newspaper articles to prove that this is a time of change and that the War of
Armageddon when the Gods are to destroy the devil is here.
MALCOLM also related to the group that you will be sent to
Korea and Japan and all over the world to fight to help the
"devil" to stay in power but that there is no power that can save
him as it is the will of Allah that he must be destroyed in accordance with his word.

[BUREAU DELETION] MALCOLM LITTLE spoke at the
meeting [BUREAU DELETION]at Philadelphia Temple. [BU-
REAU DELETION] LITTLE related the Muslim teachings in
regard to slave traders and the Negro as a slave in the United
States. LITTLE also related alleged mistreatment of Negroes in
the United States by the white race.

[BUREAU DELETION] the Minister MALCOLM was a
speaker at a meeting [BUREAU DELETION] at the Philadelphia Temple. MALCOLM expounded on the white race being
the "devil" and claims to be teaching the truth about the "black
man" in the United States. MALCOLM stated that ELIJAH
MUHAMMAD is standing up in this wicked government, refer-

ring to the United States government, and telling you the truth that has been hidden from you so long.

——————— • •———————

Interview of MALCOLM LITTLE on
January 10, 1955

In an interview on January 10, 1955, MALCOLM LITTLE advised SAs [BUREAU DELETION] and [BUREAU DELETION] that he resides at 25–35 Humphrey Street, East Elmhurst, Queens, New York, at the home of CURTIS and SUSIE KENNER.

The subject readily admitted membership in the MCI Temple No. 7, New York City, but would not admit that he was the minister or teacher of Temple No. 7, New York City. Subject would not admit that he was affiliated with the MCI Temple in Philadelphia, Pennsylvania, nor would he admit membership in the Detroit and Boston Temples.

The subject was uncooperative in this interview. He refused to furnish any information concerning the officers, names of members, to furnish doctrines or beliefs of the MCI or family background data on himself.

The subject stated that he believes in all the teachings of ELIJAH MUHAMMAD of Chicago, Illinois, and that ELIJAH MUHAMMAD was his leader and that he considered ELIJAH MUHAMMAD superior to all. Subject considered the "Nation of Islam" higher and greater than the United States government. He claimed that Allah is God, the supreme being, and that ELIJAH MUHAMMAD is the greatest prophet of all, being the last and greatest Apostle.

When questioned concerning alleged teachings or racial hatred of the MCI, he stated they do not teach hatred but the truth, that the "black man" has been enslaved in the United States by the "white man" and that no one could dispute it. LITTLE stated that the "black man" has died for the "white man" all over the world. He described the "black man" who respects the United States government as "Uncle Tom" in that they have considered the white man and his government first and placed themselves in a secondary position.

When subject was questioned concerning whether he would serve in the United States armed forces and if he would defend the United States against an attacking enemy he would not answer. He stated that no one could look in the future so he contended that he would not know what he would do if the above events would happen. The subject would not answer as to whether he considered himself a citizen of the United States.

When asked if he considered the MCI a government as well as a religion the subject would not answer. When asked if he considered himself and the Negro race in slavery in the United States by the white man, the subject remarked that you would have to only read the history books in the library to know that they are in slavery.

When he was questioned concerning the War of Armageddon, he remarked that the Bible states this will be when God destroys the devil. When asked how the MCI was going to participate in this war, he would not answer. When asked what the FOI and military training was for, he stated this was to teach the members to be upright and righteous. Subject claimed that Muslims are peaceful and they do not have guns and ammunition and they do not even carry knives.

The subject did, however, admit that during World War II he had admired the Japanese people and soldiers and that he would have liked to join the Japanese Army at that time. The subject claims to have never been a member of the Communist Party or the American Youth for Democracy or to have known anyone who was associated with it.

The American Youth for Democracy and the Communist Party have been designated by the Attorney General of the United States pursuant to Executive Order 10450.

SECTION 2

January 31, 1956–April 23, 1957

REPORTS: 1. January 31, 1956. New York
2. April 23, 1957. New York.

The two reports in this section reflect Malcolm's speaking activities in Chicago, Detroit, and Philadelphia during 1955 and 1956. At this point, the FBI believed that Malcolm was the No. 2 or No. 3 man in NOI, and that he represented Elijah Muhammad in Atlanta on August 26, 1956.

His speeches are militant and metaphorical, containing numerous prophetic warnings and references to the white man as "the devil." In Philadelphia, Malcolm delivered a scathing indictment in his customary angry manner:

Who hung this man on this tree? Your white Christian brother. Who raped your mother and stood her up in the market while they felt her body to see if she was a good breeder and then sold her away from her family. The white man brags about these things in the library. He has made you so blind that you sit and read this and say, "Oh, that's about people years ago." They are still hanging black men on trees.

Malcolm expresses awareness of government infiltration of the NOI and gives members explicit instructions on how to deal with FBI agents. In the first report, he is quoted as telling a group of followers "that they would be visited by the . . . FBI, but that was only an effort to intimidate them. . . ." Malcolm spoke ex-

tensively about government infiltration during this period and
warned that Allah would soon put "the devil's watchdogs in here
. . . into our hands." The section concludes with an intercepted
letter that Malcolm wrote to someone in the NOI.

SUBJECT   MALCOLM X LITTLE

FILE NO.   100-399321

                 Section 2

               Serials 18–20

FEDERAL BUREAU OF INVESTIGATION

This case originated at: New York
Report made at: New York
Date when made: 1/31/56
Period for which made: 12/1,6,14,15,21/55;1/3–6,10,13,16/56
Report made by: SA [BUREAU DELETION] b7C
Title: MALCOLM LITTLE, was
Character of case: Security Matter-MCI

SYNOPSIS OF FACTS:

   [BUREAU DELETION] subject stated he is minister of MCI
Temples in New York, Philadelphia, Boston and Springfield.
[BUREAU DELETION] subject as minister makes rules, selects
officers and plans temple activities. Subject, [BUREAU DELE-
TION] advised he is teaching in Hartford, Conn. Subject held
MCI meeting in Lansing, Michigan, about 5/1/55.

   ACTIVITY IN PHILADELPHIA, PENNSYLVANIA
   [BUREAU DELETION] at a meeting held by the Philadelphia Temple of the MCI. [BUREAU DELETION] the subject
was the principal speaker.

Editor's note. *A long extract from Malcolm's speech, perhaps verbatim, follows at this point in the file. His topic is subversion.*

"Black men all over the planet are subversive," Malcolm announces, and whom they are subverting is the "devil"—the devil being the man who has raped a black woman or lynched a black man, the man who would deprive blacks of their culture and history and religion, the man who would deceive black people in all things. This man, this devil, is white, and his government wicked. The white man and his evil government, however, will be destroyed in the last days—and so will the black men who choose to follow him, according to Malcolm. The time of Armageddon is now.

Advocating separatism from all the "white devils," Malcolm allows for no exceptions. He asserts that in the Bible God makes it clear that none of them, neither Jews nor Gentiles, are in any way good and that all of them, Gentiles and Jews alike, "are looked upon the same by the all-wise Allah." And all of them will be destroyed by Allah.

Malcolm also mentions the FBI in the course of his remarks. The Bureau's black informants and agents who follow him "all over the country" and report back to the "great white father what we say here" can be viewed only as traitors, for they stand against their own people. Soon, though, they will be delivered into the hands of the Muslims and, says Malcolm, "we are going to chop your head right off."

Among other of Malcolm's concerns regarding the Philadelphia temple are the disunity among the sisters, who seems to prefer bickering to their mission, and the MGT (Muslim Girls Training), both its leadership and its ranks ("I want you to buy scales and weigh the members on Monday and Thursday. Those who are overweight will be given two weeks to lose ten pounds or will be given time out"). He also objects to unemployment, as a brother who can't help himself can't help the temple either. Nor does he take kindly to any criticism voiced by brothers or sisters against Malcolm X.

[BUREAU DELETION] At the meeting, the subject spoke and stated that the things that are happening in the world today are the result of colored peoples all over the world telling the white man to get out. He related how this has happened in China, Japan, Iran, Egypt and all over the planet earth, where the white man has no business. He stated, "There are only two kinds of people, the white and the black, so if you are not white you must be black."

He told the group that in Masonry every step of wisdom they give is paid for dearly, but in the Temple of Islam it is all a free gift, and in Masonry you are forbidden to relate anything you learn even to your own son or daughter or wife, whatever the case may be, while in Islam you are required to tell all of your brothers and sisters and give them what Allah has given you.

He stated that they "had been taught to go around the world and fight for their name, but not to cross the street to defend a brother or sister."

[BUREAU DELETION] LITTLE related how even in the South, as bad as things were, they respected the black man, he dared to face them unafraid. He told how his father had been lynched in the persecution suffered by his people at the hands of a common enemy.

[BUREAU DELETION] at a meeting of the MCI Temple No. 12, Philadelphia, Pennsylvania, [BUREAU DELETION] the subject was the principal speaker.

Editor's note. *In the extract, perhaps verbatim, from the remarks on this occasion Malcolm exhorts the assembly to follow the teachings of Elijah Muhammad and thus "to hear the truth." To heed what Muhammad teaches, according to Malcolm, is to know that "the white man is the only devil in existence"—a devil that neither can nor would better the conditions of black people in America, for he is the very devil responsible for the unjust and iniquitous conditions under which blacks now live their daily lives. ("If you were citizens of this country," Malcolm points out later, "they would not have to sign bills for your rights.")*

Slavery is not history, nor do its injustices belong to the past, Malcolm posits. Black women are still being raped and black men hanged on trees. For too long black people have had their minds numbed by white devils preaching a white Christian religion in white Christian churches. The time has come to leave that church and enter the temple of Islam, there to be awakened out of "mental death." Elijah Muhammad, the one true prophet of Islam, will deliver his followers from the destruction soon to be visited upon the planet, when, as Malcolm describes it, "the God Almighty rains the fire down on North America." Then all the white devils—and all those blacks who worship with them in their churches—will be destroyed. And the black man shall rule as "the god of the universe."

Malcolm concludes with a statement regarding "some of the devil's watchdogs," i.e. FBI informants, present at this meeting of the MCI Temple No. 12: "A black man who can come in here and sit under these teachings will only suffer death for spying against his own people."

[BUREAU DELETION] a chicken dinner was held by the Philadelphia Temple of the MCI. [BUREAU DELETION] the subject attended this function.

[BUREAU DELETION] a meeting of the MCI was held by the Philadelphia Temple. [BUREAU DELETION] that at this meeting the subject made the principal address in which he related to them how Temple No. 12 is growing faster than any other temple in the United States.

He stated that Brother GEORGE is doing a good job and that the Messenger is pleased with the way things are going and for them to keep up the good work. He told them that he was not inclined to do much teaching that night as both of the brothers who had gone before him had taught them enough Islam to see them through the hereafter.

He put the subject on the board as "Why?" and "Feel?" He then proceeded to explain that there were no other people who had undergone the treatment that we had suffered at the hands of an enemy as cruel and vicious as this devil, and yet was always ready to defend him and show love for him. The question is "Why Feel?"

As he explained, "there was no one who could love someone who had treated them as the white man has treated you and I, but a fool."

He told the group that there was an informer in the group, and that it was the worst in the nation because they knew what he had said in the temple almost before he got back to New York, but that he did not fear for he knew that if they heard his teaching long enough they must turn against the devil for the biggest fool must eventually learn who is his enemy.

He talked on Masonic symbolism, explaining the degrees between the points of the stars, and that in Islam they have the knowledge of the entire 360 degrees in lieu of the 33 degrees of Masonry. He told that they taught immediately who the God is and that you could not learn this until you reached the top of the Masonic order. He told them, too, that it was all free, but that the Mason paid for each step.

[BUREAU DELETION] at a MCI meeting [BUREAU DELETION] the subject told the group that the Negro in the United States "loved" the white man in spite of all he had done to them only because they feared him.

He asked them why they did not go to Girard College, which is in the northern part of the country. He stated that when they are told of lynching and persecutions experienced by their people, they state that it is done down South, but he explained that Girard College is in the northern part of the United States yet they are excluded because they are "too black."

He then told the audience that there is no difference between the North and the South, only their methods are different.

He stated that stool pigeons, who have the nerve to come to the temple, listen to the teachings and tell the white man, will not be harmed by them (the Muslims), but that Allah will kill them; they are not playing with just a man, but with the work of God.

He stated that police who come in the temples have their guns and blackjacks checked at the door. Once they have heard the teachings they could never be the same. He advised them "not to tell their 'chiefs' for they already know what we teach here."

[BUREAU DELETION] LITTLE went on to state that Muslims respect their women and demand that everyone else respect them. He related how eleven Muslims went to jail because the train conductor touched one of their women and when the officers came into their car with guns, the brothers took them from them. He stated that the Muslims are peaceful people, but they will die for their women and demand that their women keep "straight."

He claimed that the black man has been controlled by fear and that he went around the world to fight for the white man, but refused to go across the street to defend his rights or protect even his mother.

He stated that he was not speaking against the government, but stated that the white man "lynched us, raped our women, segregated us and discriminated against us." He claimed that this was done by the white man and he cannot deny it, and that this is not against the government.

MALCOLM told the group to obey the law and keep out of controversy with the "devils," as they would try to provoke them into trouble.

[BUREAU DELETION] at a meeting held by the Philadelphia Temple of the MCI on July 8, 1955, MALCOLM LITTLE told the group that the Temple of Islam is the only place in the "wilderness of North America" that the "black man and black woman" hear the truth about themselves.

He told them that it was stated in the Bible that the truth will make you free, but since they were in mental bondage and did not know anything about themselves, they could not have the truth. However, thanks to Allah and his Messenger, the truth has come and they are now receiving freedom, justice and equality. . . .

[BUREAU DELETION] LITTLE stated that the men who have the advantages of the teachings of the temple respect their women. He told the women that the men they were able to attract by the display of their bodies were as common as the dog we see chasing the other dog in the streets.

He called upon them to clean themselves up and look to the

guidance of ELIJAH MUHAMMAD, of whom it is spoken in the Bible would come in the last days to redeem the last people. He called them fools who would sit and listen to the teaching of Islam and then still refuse to act on their own. . . .

He told them that they would be visited by the Federal Bureau of Investigation (FBI), but that this was only an effort to intimidate them and make them fear to come and hear anything about themselves.

[BUREAU DELETION] the subject made the following remarks to a meeting of the Philadelphia Temple of the MCI.

Editor's note. *"Charity begins at home," quotes Malcolm at the beginning of the extract included in the file at this point. But, he adds, too many black people have been so long "mentally dead" that they have been blind to the significance of the familiar maxim and deaf to the teachings of Elijah Muhammad.*

Malcolm argues that the charity of black people has been misplaced ever since they were brought to Jamestown, Virginia, "in the year 1555." For four hundred years, then, says Malcolm, they have been fighting for the enemy they should be fighting against—an enemy who preaches white supremacy, who rapes black women, hangs black men, tortures black children. The enemy is the white man, and the white man the devil soon to be "wiped off the planet earth." Thus comes Malcolm's admonition regarding charity to this enemy: "Do not have love in your heart for this man because he is about to be destroyed and if you love him, you will be destroyed along with him."

Armageddon, according to Malcolm, has already begun. Already the white devils are being destroyed by the Most High in hurricanes and floods. Their boats are sinking, Malcolm tells his audience; their cars are crashing, their airplanes are falling out of the sky. They are dying of cancers more deadly than any diseases ever before known. Only the followers of Elijah Muhammad, the true messenger of Allah, will be led out of destruction and returned to their home in the East "where they will rule the planet." For, Malcolm tells them, "you are descendants of the moon people and are from the tribe of Shabazz."

[BUREAU DELETION] LITTLE was the principal speaker of the evening and devoted his lecture to the praising of ELIJAH MUHAMMAD and a lesson on the background of the Muslim movement.

[BUREAU DELETION] LITTLE stated that it would be advisable for all members of the temple to donate at least three percent of their weekly salary to the organization, which monies would be turned over to the prophet ELIJAH MUHAMMAD in Chicago for safekeeping.

[BUREAU DELETION] that MALCOLM LITTLE made the following remarks at a meeting of the MCI held in Philadelphia, Pennsylvania.

Editor's note. *Malcolm addresses the subject of black women in this particular extract in the FBI file. Black women who wear dresses cut "so low you can see [their] knees" and who laugh at their more modest sisters arouse Malcolm's anger and despair, for such women belong to the devil's kind. Indeed, the devil is using them to trick, tempt and mislead black men, just as he used a woman to deceive Adam. Nor is it inapt, as Malcolm sees it, that the Statue of Liberty is a woman, because she, like so many of the sisters who have fallen into a miserable state, promises her people the freedom to act as indecently as they please. Not until all "the lost-found sisters" awaken to the teaching of Elijah Muhammad will the nation of Islam be complete, for only then will all the black brothers be fully free of such black women's evil influence and able finally to save themselves.*

At this point, one of the sisters, evidently taking offense at Malcolm's remarks, gets up and starts to walk out of the temple. Malcolm's words follow her as he calls upon the congregation to observe her; he scorns her "hair [of], five different shades" and warns her of her peril in imitating white devils at a time when Allah is preparing to remove "this wicked people" from the very face of the earth.

Imitation, in Malcolm's view, ensures bondage; for imitation of white people by blacks is premised—falsely—on the superiority of whites to blacks. Denying their own esteem, such blacks wear "mental chains"; they are bound in thought as well as deed to their white oppressor. Paradoxically, they act and think more like slaves than did their forefathers whose hands and feet may in fact have been manacled but whose minds were free. Not atypically, Malcolm then prophesies doom for the white oppressor ("Why do you think [Muslims] call the last day Judgment Day and the devils call it doomsday?") and salvation for all the black brothers and sisters who have heeded the call of Elijah Muhammad, for they are the true "gods of the planet earth and children of Almighty God."

[BUREAU DELETION] the following remarks were made at a meeting of the MCI at Philadelphia [BUREAU DELETION] by the subject.

Editor's note. *"We have a black body with a white head," Malcolm tells his audience in the Bureau extract of his remarks on this occasion. Black people's habits, all of them, "good and bad, belong to the white man," Malcolm continues; so do their customs—because black people have been dispossessed of their birthright and their culture. From their forefathers blacks have learned only what the white man allowed them to teach, and from the white man himself they have learned only "slavery, suffering and death and his dying religion." This white man's Christian religion teaches blacks that their Savior died for them two thousand years ago; but, for all their churchgoing and praying, blacks have not been saved, and they have yet to know "any freedom, justice or equality." What Malcolm would have his people realize, then, is that the time has come for them to end their years of bondage and suffering under the yoke of a white man's religion, for what's good for whites has not in any way proved to be good for blacks. He would awaken them to the truth that shall make them truly free, the truth offered them here and now by Islam in the teachings of Elijah Muhammad. The white man's day—the day of their slavemaster and enemy—is ending; the future lies with Elijah and in Islam salvation for the blacks.*

[BUREAU DELETION] subject's lecture before a meeting of the MCI held at Philadelphia [BUREAU DELETION]

He stated that there were twenty-four scientists in the east that were responsible for the operation of the universe and that they were spoken of in the Bible as the twenty-four olders, that they had determined that the time allotted to the present rulers of the world had expired and that because of the evil they had created in the world they too must be destroyed. The black man, who has been their victim, must first be given a chance to save himself.

Then the speaker told them that Allah had come to earth himself and that he was a man and he pointed out that since it was stated that he had talked to MOSES face-to-face, that he must have had a face and if that was so, he must have had a body, so he must have been a man. He stated the head of the twenty-four olders wrote history before it happened, that he was the supreme being and that he had taught ELIJAH MUHAMMAD that he might be the door by which the black man and woman could be saved.

ACTIVITY IN BOSTON, MASSACHUSETTS

[BUREAU DELETION] LITTLE was the principal speaker at a meeting of the Boston Temple [BUREAU DELETION]. At the meeting [BUREAU DELETION] LITTLE gave warning to those who the FBI might visit and cautioned them not to talk to government agents about Islam, but to state briefly that Islam is a religion of peace and beyond that it should not be discussed.

He advised that should a FBI agent "visit your home, request his identification, hold it in your hand for quite a while, then return it to the agent telling him that you do not wish to discuss your religion."

FEDERAL BUREAU OF INVESTIGATION

Reporting Office: New York
Office of Origin: New York
Date when made: 4/23/57
Period for which made: 5/11,15,18,19,22,25,28/56
Report made by: [BUREAU DELETION] b7C
Title: MALCOLM K. LITTLE, was
Malcolm X; Malcolm X Little
Character of case: Security Matter-NOI

SYNOPSIS:

[BUREAU DELETION] subject is official minister of NOI Temple No. 12, Philadelphia, Pa. [BUREAU DELETION] subject continues to be minister of NOI Temple No. 7, NYC. [BUREAU DELETION] believes LITTLE is No. 2 or No. 3 man in NOI. Activities of subject in various United States cities set forth. Subject resides at 25–46 99th Street, Elmhurst, New York, and has no employment other than duties in NOI.

POSITIONS HELD BY MALCOLM LITTLE

[BUREAU DELETION] as of November 11, 1955, MAL-COLM LITTLE was the official Minister of Nation of Islam (NOI), Temple No. 12, Philadelphia, Pennsylvania, and of the Fruit of Islam (FOI) of this temple.

[BUREAU DELETION] that the first southern Goodwill Tour of the Brotherhood of Islam was held on Saturday evening, August 25, 1956, and all day Sunday, August 26, 1956, in Atlanta, Georgia. He advised that approximately two hundred or more members of the Nation of Islam from over ten cities attended this meeting. He advised that ELIJAH MUHAMMAD, leader of the Nation of Islam, did not attend this meeting but was represented by MALCOLM X of New York City [BUREAU DELETION].

[BUREAU DELETION] MUHAMMAD never intended to appear in Atlanta, inasmuch as all activities were well planned

and proceeded like clockwork under the direction of MAL-
COLM.

[BUREAU DELETION] MALCOLM X is the Minister of
New York City Temple No. 7 of the organization and was introduced by the Minister of the Atlanta Temple to deliver the main
lecture of the meeting.

ACTIVITIES OF MALCOLM LITTLE IN
CHICAGO, ILLINOIS

[BUREAU DELETION] at a meeting of the NOI held during
the annual NOI Convention in Chicago, [BUREAU DELE-
TION] Brother MALCOLM was one of the main speakers. [BU-
REAU DELETION] MALCOLM told those in attendance that
the Muslim women should look around them and find out what
the women from other temples are saying and wearing, in order
that they might get ideas and find out what is going on. He also
said that there has never been a man who stood up, taught his
people what this man (ELIJAH MUHAMMAD) has taught in
another man's government. He told them that the prophet will
not forsake them and the Almighty God ALLAH will destroy
America in the near future.

[BUREAU DELETION] at a meeting of the Fruit of Islam
(FOI), Temple No. 2, Chicago, Illinois, held at the Temple of
Islam, 5335 South Greenwood Avenue, Chicago, [BUREAU
DELETION] the subject was introduced and congratulated
ISIAH, Minister of the Baltimore Temple of the NOI, for the
inspiring talk he had delivered that evening.

The subject stated that there had recently been a meeting of
the National Association for the Advancement of Colored People
in New York City, which was attended by over twenty thousand
persons, who listened to Mrs. ELEANOR ROOSEVELT. LIT-
TLE stated that Mrs. ROOSEVELT told those present at the
meeting that there are many more dark people in the world than
white and it was time for Americans to wake up to this fact.
LITTLE also declared that TALLULAH BANKHEAD also
spoke at this rally on the deplorable treatment and persecution of
the colored race in the South, especially in the State of Alabama.

LITTLE told the group that this government (United States

government) sends troops all over the world to protect the rights of smaller nations, but refuses to send troops into the South to protect the rights of black Americans. He stated that the only solution to the race problem in America was ELIJAH MUHAM-MAD.

[BUREAU DELETION] Minister MALCOLM of New York City spoke at a meeting of the Chicago Temple of the NOI. . . .

LITTLE called upon the American Negro to form his own government in the United States and told the congregation that southern white men had murdered the Negro's father and raped the Negro's mother. He stated that at this time there were two steps set forth by ELIJAH MUHAMMAD separating the Negro from the white man. The first step was for the Negro to drop the white man's name and the second step was for the Negro to drop the white man's religion, Christianity. LITTLE went on to advise that he first met ELIJAH MUHAMMAD in prison and embraced MUHAMMAD's teachings while serving a ten-year sentence. He related that as a Christian he had committed various wicked acts, but since he had become a Muslim, he had lived a new and religious life.

[BUREAU DELETION] MALCOLM of New York City addressed a meeting of the NOI, Temple No. 2, Chicago, Illinois [BUREAU DELETION]. LITTLE told the audience that ELIJAH MUHAMMAD had been sent to the United States by AL-LAH to lead the black man out of the wilderness of North America and that the white man's rule in North America was fast coming to an end as witnessed by the unrest and confusion in other parts of the world.

[BUREAU DELETION] LITTLE, in his speech, ridiculed the teachings of the Bible, especially life after death. He stated that statements in the Bible were inserted by the white man to hold the black man in slavery and as long as the black man wears the white man's name, he is the white man's property. [BUREAU DELETION] that LITTLE continued to speak along these lines for three hours.

ACTIVITIES OF MALCOLM LITTLE IN
DETROIT, MICHIGAN

[BUREAU DELETION] a regular meeting of Detroit, Michigan Temple No. 1 [BUREAU DELETION]. He stated that the guest speaker was MALCOLM LITTLE, Minister of Temple No. 7, New York City. By selecting several words and combining various roots in a manner to produce words or combinations of words, attempted to prove that the government of America was evil.

To illustrate this point, LITTLE used two words: demon "which means devil" and "krasy," which according to LITTLE is Greek and means government. LITTLE dropped the letter "n" from the word demon thereby producing "demo." He then indicated that the Greek letter "k" is represented in English by the letter "c." Therefore, the Greek word "krasy" becomes "crasy" when translated into English. By combining the two words, demo and crasy, he produced the word democracy.

[BUREAU DELETION] LITTLE then added "his syllogistic reasoning" and stated that the word meant devil government.

[BUREAU DELETION] he then continued to pursue the Muslim line of reasoning which states that all white people are devils and their government is a devil government. LITTLE said that this is why the United States is identified with the concept of democracy more than any Caucasian civilization.

ACTIVITIES OF MALCOLM LITTLE IN
PHILADELPHIA, PENNSYLVANIA

[BUREAU DELETION] at a meeting of the Philadelphia Temple of the NOI on [BUREAU DELETION], LITTLE told the group, "The black man will rule North America before the end of 1956 with the help of ALLAH and lost-found brothers if they would all pull together under the leadership of ELIJAH MUHAMMAD."

[BUREAU DELETION] LITTLE spoke at a meeting of the Philadelphia Temple [BUREAU DELETION]. He told the audience that all through history, time was the deciding factor in many events and the Bible has been rewritten to confuse the

Negro in the past; it is written in past tense so that things that are happening here and now would appear to have happened many years ago. He said the Bible tells the story of a lost people and their restoration and this story is the story of the so-called Negro, which is so jumbled that only the supreme wisdom could untangle it. He stated that no one was ever robbed as completely as the so-called Negro because even the Indian, who is robbed of his country by the white man, had his own name and language. However, the so-called Negro has nothing that was originally his.

Editor's Note. *Section 2 of the file on Malcolm X concludes with a letter written by him as Salaam Alaikum to an NOI brother whose name has been deleted by the FBI. In it Malcolm exults in the "great day" in which they are living: "A New World Order is in the making," he writes, "and it is up to us to prepare ourselves that we may be qualified to take our rightful place in it." He speaks of their teaching as "the Flame of Islam . . . sweeping across the land," a flame that has set "cities like Atlanta, Montgomery, Birmingham . . . on FIRE." He exhorts his correspondent to continue to prepare himself, to study hard and to train his mind, for, as he concludes, "ISLAM IS ON THE MARCH."*

SECTION 3

REPORT: April 30, 1958. New York

The report in this section was prepared by the FBI's New York office and covers the period from February through April 1958. A confidential source advised the FBI that Malcolm had suffered a heart attack in October 1957, but according to his brother Wilfred, he had recovered.

The report describes Malcolm's activities in Albany, Boston, Chicago, Detroit, Los Angeles, and New York. In Chicago, Malcolm allegedly denounced Dr. King at an NOI Temple No. 2 speech. In Detroit, Malcolm claimed that President Eisenhower and Governor Faubus were public enemies but private friends in a conspiracy to deter the enforcement of the Supreme Court decision in Brown vs. Topeka Board of Education.

Also included is an interview with Malcolm in the July 18, 1957, issue of the *Los Angeles Herald Dispatch,* an article crediting Malcolm with the growth of NOI membership in Detroit, and a *Pittsburgh Courier* article reporting a million-dollar lawsuit instigated by the NOI for the April 14, 1957, beating of NOI member Johnson X by New York police. Malcolm's autobiography includes an account of the beating:

> The crowd was big, and angry, behind the Muslims in front of Harlem Hospital. Harlem's black people were long since sick and tired of police brutality. And they never had seen any organization of black men take a firm stand as we were . . . and for the first time the black man, woman, and child in the streets was discussing "those Muslims." (p.234)

The section concludes with newspaper articles written by Malcolm himself deriding the tendency of oppressed people to praise leaders after they are dead instead of while they are still alive. Citing the examples of Moses, Jesus, and Marcus Garvey, he cautions people of color against making the same mistake with Elijah Muhammad.

SUBJECT   MALCOLM X LITTLE

FILE NO.   100-399321

Section 3

Serials 21–22

FEDERAL BUREAU OF INVESTIGATION

Reporting Office: New York
Office of Origin: New York
Date: 4/30/58
Investigative Period: 2/17,26;3/5,6,11;4/1–4,7,8,10,11,14,19/58
Report made by: [BUREAU DELETION] b7C
Title: MALCOLM LITTLE, was: Malcolm Shabazz; Malcolm
    X.; Minister Malcolm; Brother Malcolm
Character of case: Security Matter-NOI

SYNOPSIS

Activities of MALCOLM LITTLE in various cities throughout the United States set forth. [BUREAU DELETION] LIT-
TLE continues to hold post of Minister of NOI Temple No. 7,
NYC, but travels throughout the United States, handling problems for NOI leader ELIJAH MUHAMMAD of Chicago, Illinois. [BUREAU DELETION] subject acted as Minister of Detroit, Michigan, Temple of NOI during September, 1957.
LITTLE confined to hospital in New York City for "heart attack" during October, 1957. [BUREAU DELETION] that WIL-
FRED LITTLE, brother of MALCOLM LITTLE, during No-

vember, 1957, stated that MALCOLM LITTLE recovered from heart attack. LITTLE continues to reside 25–46 99th Street, Elmhurst, New York.

ACTIVITY IN ALBANY, NEW YORK

[BUREAU DELETION] advised that MALCOLM LITTLE attended a meeting of the NOI held by the Albany Temple on [BUREAU DELETION] . . .

. . . LITTLE stated that for years the black man has waited for Jesus to return, but he would not return and the white race themselves did not believe in the hereafter promised by Christianity. As proof MALCOLM referred to the incident of the recent sickness of President EISENHOWER and stated that the newspapers carried articles saying that EISENHOWER did not wish to receive the hereafter promised by Christianity but instead called for the doctor to save his life.

ACTIVITY IN BOSTON, MASSACHUSETTS

[BUREAU DELETION] that the Boston Temple of the NOI held a meeting in Boston, Massachusetts on [BUREAU DELETION] 1957, and that an individual introduced as brother MALCOLM, Minister of the New York Temple, was the main speaker.

. . . He stated that Negroes have died for this country (United States) and yet we are not citizens; we have worked for this country and we are not citizens. LITTLE stated that a few weeks ago, "they" wrote to "IKE" and asked him to come and help them "and what did he do, he had to go play golf."

[BUREAU DELETION] that LITTLE stated "a Jew is in the White House, Jews in the State House, the Jews run the country. You and I can't go into a white hotel down South, but a Jew can."

ACTIVITY IN CHICAGO, ILLINOIS

[BUREAU DELETION] advised that a meeting of the NOI Temple No. 2, Chicago, Illinois, was held on [BUREAU DELETION] 1957, and that MALCOLM LITTLE was one of the speakers. . . .

[BUREAU DELETION] went on to state that in his speech
LITTLE said that every leader (president) that has been voted
into office has promised to help the Negro people, but these
promises were just lies and no president has done anything for
the Negro people. He stated that ALLAH is now with them and
he is going to destroy all of the white race and the time is now.

[BUREAU DELETION] stated that LITTLE claimed he had
recently been in Mobile, Alabama, checking on an incident in
which two Muslims had been attacked by white policemen. LIT-
TLE stated that he had talked with the judge in this case who
told him that the two Muslims would be released and everything
would be alright because they are followers of Islam. LITTLE
went on to criticize the Reverend MARTIN LUTHER KING as
a traitor to the Negro people who is being used by the white man
to further the white man's aims. He stated that everything the
Negro people do today benefits the white race only and the white
race provides the Negro with all types of destructive weapons but
does not provide him with anything constructive.

ACTIVITY IN DETROIT, MICHIGAN

[BUREAU DELETION] 1957, advised that at a meeting of
the Detroit NOI Temple on [BUREAU DELETION] 1957,
MALCOLM LITTLE said "IKE" (President EISENHOWER)
and FAUBUS (Governor of Arkansas) are laughing at the Negroes. Publicly they pretend to be angry with each other, but
behind closed doors, they behave like close friends. IKE has no
love for the so-called Negro and pretends to be acting in their
behalf now, but that is because he and North America do not
have any choice. . . .

No white person loves a black man. It is against his nature.
Many white men have pretended to love the so-called Negro. You think ABRAHAM LINCOLN loved the Negro.

(MALCOLM read from a book but he never gave the title or
author. The passages he read purportedly were quotes from LIN-
COLN. He stated there was no hope for the black man in America. It also stated LINCOLN was much disturbed by the pres-

ence of black folks in the country and he suggested they go back to Africa because they could never achieve an equal status here.)

EISENHOWER has a caddy he calls "Cemetery." The name is quite appropriate because that Negro is mentally dead.

MALCOLM said America has not seen anything yet. He said when ELIJAH gets through there won't be anything left of this government.

The *Pittsburgh Courier,* on November 2, 1957, carried an article captioned, "Detroit Moslems Continue Growth," which read as follows:

Messenger Elijah Muhammad, the spiritual leader of America's fastest-growing group of Moslem converts, and considered even by many non-Moslems to be the most outspoken, uncompromising black leader ever to appear among Negroes of America, sent his fiery New York minister, Malcolm X, to represent him in Detroit.

And since his arrival here, things have really begun to hum in the Moslem World.

One of Muhammad's most devoted followers, Malcolm X is 32 years old, a six-foot three-inch, 195-pound bachelor, who devotes 24 hours daily to spreading Muhammad's messages among the Negroes of America, and organizing his followers into well-disciplined, fearless warriors for Allah.

Malcolm X has made certain organizational changes since he came, principal of which was the shifting of Minister Lemuel, who headed the Detroit Branch of Muhammad's Temple, 5401 John C. Lodge, to a temple in Cincinnati, Ohio.

Detroiters say they have never seen anything like the Moslem growth here since the days of Marcus Garvey. During the past two months, the Detroit Moslems have tripled their membership and attendance. No figures were divulged in keeping with Moslem policy.

They purchased the property at the John C. Lodge address, and it will contain a school for the purpose of private tutoring of Moslem children. The zealous followers of Muhammad have been busily cleaning and renovating the temple, and preparing better facilities for their rapidly expanding University of Islam.

A lot of credit for this amazing growth must go to Muhammad's principal lieutenants, such as Malcolm X.

ACTIVITY AT LOS ANGELES, CALIFORNIA

The *Los Angeles Herald Dispatch,* July 18, 1957 edition, carried an article captioned "Young Moslem Leader Explains The Doctrine of Muhammadanism," which read as follows:

"Islam is a flaming fire sweeping across the entire Dark World today," said young, militant Moslem leader Malcolm X, in an exclusive interview with the Los Angeles Herald Dispatch New York correspondent today. Mr. X discussed one of the most talked about and the most controversial religions in Harlem. The doctrine preached and followed by the disciples of Elijah Muhammad of Chicago, whose local followers worship in the Muhammad Temple of Islam No. 7, 102 West 116th Street.

The *Herald Dispatch,* in an effort to answer some of the questions for our readers regarding the Islamic or Moslem faith, assigned this reporter to interview the fiery young leader, the Reverend Mr. Malcolm X, whose column, "God's Angry Men" begins in the *Herald Dispatch* this week.

Q. When was your organization founded in the United States?

A. The first Temple of Islam was founded by Almighty God Allah himself, July 4, 1930, in Detroit, Michigan.

Q.   How many members of your faith are there in the United
     States today?
A.   Only Allah himself knows the exact number of Moslems
     in America who are following Messenger Elijah Muham-
     mad, but everyone does know that this number is fast-
     growing, and that Messenger Muhammad has declared
     that he will never cease teaching this Great Message until
     all of his people here have heard it (whether they accept it
     or reject it is not up to him). His job is to deliver the
     message.
Q.   Are there any white people among the followers of
     Muhammad?
A.   There has never been, is not now, and never will be even
     one white person allowed among Messenger Muhammad's
     followers. Space here is not sufficient to tell why, but in
     the future we do hope to make the reason clear.
Q.   What is the specific religious philosophy of the Islam
     faith?
A.   Messenger Muhammad teaches us to love for our brother
     what we love for ourselves, but that we must first know
     who our brother is, and who is not our brother.
Q.   Does your faith approve of marriage? If so, does it permit
     more than one wife?
A.   Family life is the backbone of Islam. A righteous wife and
     children is one of Allah's greatest blessing to man. Fol-
     lowers of Messenger Elijah Muhammad are allowed only
     one wife.
Q.   What is the objection of your faith to eating pork?
A.   Pork is filthy, diseased and germ-laden meat, with worms
     that are forever reproducing. This meat is even con-
     demned by the Scriptures of both the Christians and the
     Jews, but again space is insufficient to explain the scien-
     tific reasons why we who are Moslems, following Messen-
     ger Muhammad, do not eat it.
Q.   Does your faith have churches located throughout the
     United States?
A.   Messenger Muhammad's followers, known as the Nation

of Islam, have temples throughout America—North,
South, East and West.

Q. Are members of the faith baptized or is some other ritual
conducted when a person is accepted into the faith?

A. Members are not baptized with water as Christians are,
but are baptized with wisdom, knowledge and understanding, and are thereby saved from the sinful grave of mental
bondage and ignorance.

Q. Please give some information of Mr. Muhammad, your
leader.

A. Messenger Muhammed has suffered persecution ever since
he was missioned to teach this message to the enslaved so-
called Negroes of America. He has suffered not only from
attack by the slavemaster, but also from many of our own
kind who do not want to face the facts and be told the
truth concerning our condition here in the slavemaster's
net.

Q. Was he born in the United States?

A. Messenger Muhammad was born in the cotton fields of
Georgia.

Q. Where did he attend school?

A. His schooling was so limited that there is no record of it,
but his present work is sufficient proof that he has now
been schooled by almighty Allah himself.

Q. Is he married?

A. His wife, one of his most ardent followers, is Sister Clara
Muhammad.

Q. Does he have children?

A. He has six sons and two daughters, all of whom are devout Moslems and obedient followers of their father.

Q. Does he make his home in Chicago?

A. His home is now in Chicago, 4827 Woodlawn Avenue,
where whoever wishes to write him is free to do so. He
generally teaches every Sunday at the temple there which
is at 5335 South Greenwood.

Q. Are there any churches or temples of the faith in New
York?

A. His followers in New York worship at Muhammad's Tem-

ple of Islam No. 7, located at 102 West 116th Street, 3rd
floor, corner of Lenox. Meetings are 2 P.M. every Sunday,
and 8 P.M. on Wednesdays and Fridays. No one is allowed
entrance who has alcohol on his breath, and no one with
knives or weapons of other sorts.

The *Los Angeles Herald Dispatch,* November 28, 1957 edition,
carried an article captioned "Malcolm X Speaks at Elks Hall
Weds. Night," which read as follows:

In this connection, he declared, Negroes must come to a
realization of the importance and power of the Negro Press,
must take to heart the old adage that "the pen is mightier
than the sword." He pointed out that when the white press
recently sought to destroy one of New York's highest Negro
officials, it was only the Negro press who came to his defense
and beat back the attack. "It was the Negro press in Harlem," he declared, "that shot back 'factual bullets,' enabling
Harlemites to see what the white press was trying to do. By
digging up the facts and exposing the hidden motives of the
biased white press, the Negro press was able to shatter the
conspiracy, and prevent the people of Harlem from being
misled by the lies of the white press."
    He warned that without a powerful and militant Negro
press, the white press could deceive the Negro people with
"its powerful, well-loaded, propaganda guns," and its slan-
ders of Negro officials. "The Negro people would be wise,"
he added, "to keep this weapon (the Negro press) in good
condition, strong, well-loaded, independent, alert and
ready."

ACTIVITY AT NEW YORK CITY
The *Pittsburgh Courier,* November 9, 1957 edition, carried an
article captioned "Moslems Announce Million Dollar New York
Suit," which reads as follows:

NEW YORK. Echoes of a near-riot involving members of the Moslem sect of Prophet Elijah Muhammad and New York City police were revived here when Malcolm X announced that a million-dollar suit was being filed against local patrolmen.

Mr. Malcolm X announced that the suit was being filed by one Johnson X who was said to have been beaten into insensibility by arresting officers.

The suit, according to Malcolm X, was filed after a General Sessions Court decision ruled for the dismissal of all charges against Johnson X, who had been accused of felonious assault.

Johnson X was defended by Atty. Edward M. Jacko, along with three other individuals, two of whom were given suspended sentences and the third an acquittal.

One of the men who received a suspended sentence, Lloyd Young, is suing for $50,000 in damages from the beating allegedly inflicted on him by officers, said Malcolm X. The acquitted man, Frank Lee X, a Temple of Islam member, is seeking $75,000 in damages, Malcolm X announced.

According to Malcolm X, Johnson X is accusing officers with false arrest, false imprisonment, malicious and criminal prosecution among sundry other charges.

Malcolm X said, "Johnson X, who suffered severe and permanent brain injuries, had to undergo four major brain operations performed by Dr. Thomas W. Matthews, director of neurosurgery at the Coney Island Hospital.

A sizeable silver plate had to be inserted in Johnson's head to replace a major portion of the bone which the police had destroyed in their savage battering of his skull. He will be permanently disabled, scarred and crippled for life, and he should be amply and adequately compensated."

The ruckus involving Johnson X occurred last May when police moved in on a disturbance between a man named Reece V. Poe and an unknown woman. When police began beating Poe, Johnson X intervened and a near riot resulted.

NEWSPAPER ARTICLES WRITTEN BY
MALCOLM LITTLE

February 6, 1958

The GREAT CURSE of history is when we fail to learn or profit from the mistakes of those who have passed on before us.

Now that the Honorable Marcus Garvey is dead, many of us are making the very same mistake as the people of history . . . recognizing his glorious works among us TOO LATE. It seems that we too, like the people in the days of Moses and Jesus, are too busy paying tribute to the dead to recognize, receive and follow THE LIVING.

According to history, the Jews had been looking for an EMANCIPATOR, but when one of their own kind (Moses) came to them they immediately rejected and rebelled against him. Moses spoke of one "even greater than I" who was yet to come after him, but these same Jews who waited for Moses to die before accepting him as their EMANCIPATOR were so busy worshipping and paying tribute to this dead Moses that when Jesus came who looked like the fulfillment of Moses' prediction, they rejected the LIVING ONE and lynched him on the cross (according to their own history of it).

This Jesus who preached in Palestine, which is on the Arabian Peninsula, also predicted the coming of one in the last days who would be yet "even greater than I," but when a man named Muhammad came to these very same Semitic people preaching the NAKED TRUTH, according to history, they too rejected him and constantly plotted to murder him. Just like the other peoples of history, they were too busy following and paying tribute to some "dead leader" of the past to see, receive and follow the LIVING LEADER of the present.

Muhammad himself spoke of one who was yet to come who would be yet greater than he.

February 13, 1958

But history teaches us that it is difficult for a downtrodden people to accept LIVING LEADERS. The downtrodden have usually been so thoroughly robbed, deceived and BRAINWASHED (well indoctrinated) by their masters that their ignorant and superstitious minds seem incapable of seeing that a GREAT MAN has come to help them until after that man is dead and gone. Thus, the downtrodden always end up idolizing and paying tribute after he is dead, to the very same one whom they reject, condemn and persecute while he is living.

Will we never learn from the foolish mistakes of others? HISTORY REPEATS ITSELF: thus its historic WARNINGS should keep us on guard today.

The late Mr. Garvey came into this country awakening the downtrodden so-called Negroes to the importance of SELF, and trying to instill a Black Nationalistic spirit into us, but most of us were busy worshipping the "dead leaders" of the past, and some of us were IGNORANTLY waiting for these "dead leaders" to return from the grave, therefore we rejected the late Mr. Garvey and helped our white Christian slavemasters plot his downfall.

Now that Mr. Garvey is dead, again HISTORY REPEATS ITSELF. Many who were Mr. Garvey's greatest enemies are today his strongest advocates and defenders.

Tribute is still being paid to a DEAD Moses. Worship is being wasted on a DEAD Jesus. Millions honor a DEAD Muhammad. And, many respect and revere a DEAD Mr. Garvey.

All of these "followers" are seemingly sincere and are supposed to be intelligent. Yet, all are so busy whooping and hollering over THE DEAD, like others in history they are failing to see the greatest LIVING EMANCIPATOR and TRUTH BEARER that the world has ever known, who is right here in America today in the person of the Honorable ELIJAH MUHAMMAD.

This is the one whom Moses, Jesus and Muhammad all spoke of who would be here in America in the "last days" of the "white world" with a Divine Message of NAKED TRUTH which would give "life" (ISLAM) back to the long lost so-called Negroes, set us FREE from the clutches of our enemies and restore us back among Our Own Kind.

Did not Mr. Garvey declare that a "greater than he" was coming to carry Mr. Garvey's uncompleted work into completion? Must we who were faithful followers of the late Mr. Garvey make the same mistake of the others in history, and wait until after this great man, Messenger ELIJAH MUHAMMAD, is gone before we too recognize him fearlessly and uncompromisingly by his works that HE IS FOR US?

Why must we always worship DEAD men? Why must we always follow DEAD leaders? It is because our ignorance has slowed our thinking ability so much that our minds can't keep up with events, and by the time we realize what is happening the EMANCIPATOR is here and gone before we are mentally capable of recognizing him.

We should show forth greater wisdom TODAY. Let us forget the DEAD past and start concentrating all efforts on the LIVING PRESENT. "Let the DEAD bury the DEAD."

SECTION 4

July 15, 1958–July 21, 1959

This section begins with a July 2, 1958, FBI approval of a recommendation from the New York office that Malcolm be designated as "a key figure." This designation meant that the FBI would keep "up-to-date Security Index cards on him separately," an indication that the Bureau considered the Nation of Islam to be at least a potential threat to the nation's internal security.

The new designation reflected Malcolm's increasing visibility as a Muslim spokesperson and the FBI's awareness of Malcolm's growing involvement in international politics. A July 13 memorandum informed FBI Director J. Edgar Hoover that Malcolm met with Premier Gamal Abdel Nasser of Egypt to set up talks between Nasser and Elijah Muhammad. Two other memos, dated July 16 and 21, contain the "substantially verbatim account" of parts one and three of Mike Wallace's "The Hate That Hate Produced," which aired during the week of July 13–17, 1959. The text was sent to the Detroit Bureau "in view of the fact that NOI parochial schools in Chicago and Detroit were mentioned." Part one contains Louis Lomax's interview with Malcolm and part three contains an interview with NAACP leader Roy Wilkins, who claimed not to know who Elijah Muhammad was, even though Wallace showed pictures of Wilkins conversing with Malcolm X.

For the first time, the FBI includes speculations that Malcolm might want to succeed Elijah. Reporting on speeches in Chicago and Los Angeles, the FBI's informant suggests that older members were "somewhat resentful" of Malcolm's "extremely violent teachings and statements." Another informant explains that Malcolm desires a separate nation for the NOI within the United States, possibly California, where the NOI might buy land.

SUBJECT   MALCOLM X LITTLE
FILE NO.   100-399321
                   Section 4
                  Serials 23-33

OFFICE MEMORANDUM

UNITED STATES GOVERNMENT

TO   :   DIRECTOR, FBI (100-399321)
            DATE: 7/2/58
FROM   :   SAC, NEW YORK (105-8999)
SUBJECT: MALCOLM LITTLE
            SM-NOI

ReBulet 5/20/58, which states that in view of LITTLE's increasing activities in the affairs of the NOI on a national level, the
Bureau desires that the NYO consider him for designation as a
key figure.

The NYO after due consideration believes that LITTLE
should be designated a key figure in view of his extensive activity
as Minister of Temple No. 7, 102 West 116th Street, New York
City.

It is noted that Temple No. 7 has approximately three to four
hundred members and that in his capacity as minister, LITTLE
is the leader of Temple No. 7.

In addition, LITTLE travels to various temples throughout

the United States and at meetings of these temples has made numerous speeches which are violent in nature wherein he attacks the United States and the white race.

UACB, the NYO is designating LITTLE a key figure and is placing this case in a pending inactive status.

The NYO will continue to follow LITTLE's activities and will submit a report within six months from the date of reBulet.

———————• •———————

SAC, New York (105-8999)   July 15, 1958
Director, FBI (100-399321)
MALCOLM LITTLE
INTERNAL SECURITY - NOI
    Reurlet 7/2/58.

The Bureau agrees with your designation of Little as a key figure. You will be furnished up-to-date Security Index cards on him separately.

Inasmuch as Little has been designated a key figure, you should obtain and forward to the Bureau a current photograph of him as well as suitable handwriting specimens.

You should carefully review that part of Section 87D of the Manual of Instructions relating to key figures.

———————• •———————

FEDERAL BUREAU OF INVESTIGATION

Reporting Office: New York
Office of Origin: New York
Date: 11/19/58
Investigative Period: 10/1–3,9–24,28–31;11/3–5/58
Report made by: [BUREAU DELETION]
Title: MALCOLM K. LITTLE, was
Character of case: Internal Security - NOI

SYNOPSIS:

    MALCOLM LITTLE is Minister of Temple No. 7 of the Nation of Islam (NOI) in New York City, and is considered one of the national leaders of the NOI. He travels extensively to various parts of the United States engaging in NOI work. [BUREAU DELETION] subject may aspire to replace ELIJAH MUHAMMAD as NOI leader. NOI activities, including meetings attended and pertinent portions of speeches made by subject, set forth. Subject resides at 25–46 99th Street, East Elmhurst, Queens, New York.

At Chicago, Illinois

Subject was observed by Special Agents of the FBI on May 20, 1958, in the company of ELIJAH MUHAMMAD in Chicago, Illinois.

[BUREAU DELETION] that subject was present in Chicago at the funeral of MARIE MUHAMMAD, mother of ELIJAH MUHAMMAD, which was held May 21, 1958.

[BUREAU DELETION] advised that on [BUREAU DELETION] subject was present at the University of Islam in Chicago.

[BUREAU DELETION] that subject attended a meeting of the NOI on [BUREAU DELETION] at MUHAMMAD's Temple No. 2, 5335 South Greenwood Avenue.

At this meeting MALCOLM stated that the so-called Negro was looking and searching for a modern-day MOSES to lead them, and intimated that ELIJAH MUHAMMAD is this modern-day MOSES. Subject stated that under the flag of Islam the so-called Negroes would receive freedom, justice and equality. He stated that the Christian Bible had been written by the "Christian slavemaster" to keep the so-called Negroes in slavery. He stated that if the so-called Negro does not stop following the "white devil," the so-called Negro will be destroyed.

At Los Angeles, California

[BUREAU DELETION] that MALCOLM X was speaker at a NOI meeting [BUREAU DELETION] at Normandie Hall. . . .

MALCOLM stated that ELIJAH MUHAMMAD was a lenient man, and that if it were left to his followers like himself, MALCOLM, they would take the heads off of every white man.

[BUREAU DELETION] that there appeared to be a feeling

among a number of the older members of the NOI that MAL-
COLM X was going to do more harm than good, as they were
somewhat resentful and would not accept his extremely violent
teachings and statements, and that they felt that MALCOLM X
is too inflammatory and too drastic.

MALCOLM pointed to the Muslim flag and then at the
United States flag, and stated, "Which one of these do you think
will survive the War of Armageddon? I don't say who will survive or when. To win means to defeat your opponent. To survive
is to be still left after completely destroying or obliterating your
opponent. There will be no survivors among the losers." [BU-
REAU DELETION] MALCOLM pointed to the Muslim flag
after stating, "Come over to this and live." He then pointed to
the American flag, and stated, "because this and Christianity will
be destroyed."

[BUREAU DELETION] that subject was speaker at a NOI
meeting on [BUREAU DELETION] at Normandie Hall.
Among his remarks, subject stated as follows; "Who is our enemy?" At this point MALCOLM pointed at the United States
flag and said, "This represents our enemy. As you know this is all
we ever got from it. . . ." He then pointed to a picture of a
Negro hanging from a tree.

[BUREAU DELETION] that based on the speeches of MAL-
COLM, it seems apparent that MALCOLM believes that the
United States government should give the Negro people a state.
[BUREAU DELETION] that MALCOLM apparently believes
that this would happen in the foreseeable future in about ten to
fifteen years. For example, MALCOLM has explained that ELI-
JAH MUHAMMAD has told him he does not want his state to
be where it is too cold nor too hot, nor where there is no water
outlet to an ocean or gulf. MALCOLM pointed out that California fits this description, and that the farm to be purchased by the
NOI may be bought in California. MALCOLM explained that
once you have a foothold you can expand and absorb until the

entire state is yours, and that this is what ELIJAH MUHAM-
MAD would do.

———————. •———————

UNITED STATES DEPARTMENT OF JUSTICE
FEDERAL BUREAU OF INVESTIGATION

Report of: SA [BUREAU DELETION] b7C
Office: NEW YORK
Date: 19 MAY 1959
File Number: New York 105-8999   Bureau file 100-399321
Title: MALCOLM K. LITTLE
Character: INTERNAL SECURITY-NOI

Synopsis:

MALCOLM LITTLE is Minister of Temple No. 7 of the
NOI in New York City, and is considered one of the national leaders of the NOI. Information regarding his importance and position in the NOI set forth. LITTLE has traveled considerably throughout the United States on NOI
business. Information regarding LITTLE's visits to various
NOI temples set forth. LITTLE has made numerous
speeches setting forth the teachings and doctrines of the
NOI, pertinent portions of which are set out. LITTLE resides at 25–46 99th Street, East Elmhurst, Queens, New
York.

NOI ACTIVITY AND STATEMENTS MADE
BY SUBJECT
In Buffalo, New York
On February 12, 1959, [BUREAU DELETION] stated that a
meeting of the MTI in Buffalo, New York, was held February 11,
1959, at the above address. [BUREAU DELETION] stated
MALCOLM X was the speaker and he spoke as follows:

The Messenger wants everyone to do something for himself and to stop waiting for the white man to do everything for the Negro. He urged those in attendance to develop businesses so that the Negro could become self-dependent. He urged the followers of ELIJAH MUHAMMAD not to break any of the white man's laws, pointing out that these laws must be obeyed. He stated that the Messenger did not want his followers to break any laws of the white race. The black man and the black woman should not mix with the white race because the white race is the enemy.

The above was verified in substance on February 19, 1959 by [BUREAU DELETION].

At Cleveland, Ohio
On February 18, 1959, [BUREAU DELETION] furnished information concerning a meeting of the MTI No. 18, held February 15, 1959, at 11005 Ashbury Avenue. [BUREAU DELETION] stated MALCOLM X from New York spoke as follows:

The so-called Negroes are so lazy that they are willing to suffer anything rather than go to work. When we find a brother who is lazy we put him out of the brotherhood. Laziness in Islam is a sin. Any man that does not work in Islam is no good.

At Philadelphia, Pennsylvania
On November 3, 1958, [BUREAU DELETION] furnished information concerning a meeting of the NOI in Philadelphia held October 29, 1958. [BUREAU DELETION] stated that MALCOLM LITTLE was the speaker and spoke as follows.

Editor's note. *"The so-called Negro is so hard-hearted, so in love with his enemy [that] he does not even know who is his enemy," the file quotes Malcolm as saying before announcing the subject of his sermon, which is "why"—why it is that black Americans so love their enemy when "every other black*

*race on earth [is] trying to separate [itself] from the white
race." He then points out that most blacks define civil rights
as the right to intermarry, particularly the right of black men
to marry white women—a line of reasoning that prompts
Malcolm to ask why blacks in America are so much against
their own kind. Malcolm continues, according to the file, by
saying that the time for white people has expired and that
America is doomed, that all white people and also all the so-
called Negroes who love them are doomed. "Join into your
own kind," he tells his audience, "and reclaim that which
belongs to you—the whole universe."*

The above information was verified in substance on November
3, 1958, by [BUREAU DELETION]

At New York, New York
On February 9, 1959, [BUREAU DELETION] furnished in-
formation concerning a meeting of the NOI in New York on
February 8, 1959. [BUREAU DELETION] stated that MAL-
COLM X spoke as follows:

Self preservation is the first law of nature, preservation of
family and preservation of people as a race.
The wars of 1914 and the Second World War have weak-
ened the white race. God bless Japan for bombing Pearl
Harbor. We should thank them. The only way Japan was
conquered was through the atom bomb. The third and last
war is the fight between the darker nations and the white
race.

On March 26, 1959, [BUREAU DELETION] furnished information concerning a meeting of the NOI in New York on March
22, 1959. [BUREAU DELETION] stated Minister MALCOLM
asked if there were any representatives from the FBI or any
detectives or cops present. [BUREAU DELETION] stated a
member of the police force identified himself. MALCOLM welcomed him and stated that he wished more would come and visit
the temple. MALCOLM also stated that the officer should report

that they are law abiding people and they do not teach their
people to love "white folks." MALCOLM further stated "man
you should arrest them." We were kidnapped. We were not
brought here on the Queen Mary or the Mayflower.

The above information was verified in substance on March 23,
1959, by [BUREAU DELETION]

On March 31, 1959, [BUREAU DELETION] furnished information concerning a NOI meeting held in New York March 29,
1959.

[BUREAU DELETION] stated Minister MALCOLM spoke
and stated the sooner the so-called American Negro realized that
what is wrong with us is not the color of our skin or the texture
of our hair, but rather the condition of our minds and take steps
to rectify this condition, the sooner we can have a race of which
to be proud. MALCOLM stated that the Negroes should sit and
wait without violence because the white man will destroy himself.

This document contains neither recommendations nor
conclusions of any kind. It is the property of the FBI, and is
a loan to your agency; it and/or its contents are not to be
distributed outside your agency.

———————. .———————

FBI

Date: 7/13/59

Transmit the following in _____ PLAIN TEXT _____
Via ____ AIRTEL ____ _____

TO: DIRECTOR, FBI (25-330971)
FROM: SAC, NEW YORK (105-7809)
SUBJECT: NATION OF ISLAM
             IS-NOI
             (OO: CG)

On 7/13/59, [BUREAU DELETION] advised that he learned from a member of NOI, NYC, that MALCOLM X LITTLE was in Africa and had an audience with NASSER of Egypt. This audience was to set up meeting between NASSER and ELIJAH MUHAMMAD. [BUREAU DELETION] didn't know source of member's info.

[BUREAU DELETION] also learned from above member that NOI, NYC, planning "major boycotts" of stores in Harlem, NYC, to get better jobs for Negroes.

———————. •———————

OFFICE MEMORANDUM

UNITED STATES GOVERNMENT

TO : DIRECTOR, FBI (25-330971)
DATE: 7/16/59
FROM : SAC, NEW YORK (105-7809) (412)
SUBJECT: NATION OF ISLAM
IS-NOI
(OO: CHICAGO)
ReNYairtel, 7/14/59

As the Bureau has been advised, MIKE WALLACE on his News Beat show on WNTA-TV, Channel 13, New York, 6:30 P.M.-7:00 P.M., during the week of 7/13–17/59, is showing a five-part report which he calls "The Hate That Hate Produced."

The following is a substantially verbatim account of the first part of this report which was shown on 7/13/59.

Copies of this letter are designated for Detroit in view of the fact that NOI parochial schools in Chicago and Detroit were mentioned.

WALLACE: Tonight we begin a five-part series which we call "The Hate that Hate Produced," a story of the rise of Black Racism, of a call for black supremacy among a growing segment of American Negroes. While city officials, state agencies, white liberals and sober-minded Negroes stand idly by, a group of Negro dissenters are taking to street corner stepladders, church pulpits, sports arenas and ballroom platforms across the nation to preach the gospel of hate that would set off a federal investigation if it were to be preached by southern whites. What are they saying? Listen—

"I charge the white man with being the greatest liar on earth. I charge the white man with being the greatest drunkard on earth. I charge the white man with being the greatest . . . on earth. Yet the Bible forbids it. I charge the white man with being the greatest gambler on earth. I charge the white man, ladies and gentlemen of the jury, with being the greatest murderer on earth. I charge the white man with being the greatest . . . on earth. I charge the white man with being the greatest adulterer on earth. I charge the white man with being the greatest deceiver on earth. I charge the white man with being the greatest troublemaker on earth. So therefore ladies and gentlemen of the jury I ask you to bring back a verdict of guilty as charged."

WALLACE: The indictment you've just heard is being told over and over again in most of the major cities across the country. This charge comes at the climax of a morality play called *The Trial.* The plot, indeed the message of the play, is that the white man has been put on trial for his sins against the black man. He has been found guilty. The sentence is death. The play is sponsored, produced by a Negro religious group who call themselves the Muslims. They use a good deal of the paraphernalia of the traditional religion of Islam. But they are fervently disavowed by orthodox Moslems. Negro American Muslims are the most powerful of the black supremacist group. They claim a membership of a quarter of a million Negroes and our search indicates that for every so-called card carrying black supremacist there are perhaps ten fellow travelers. Their doctrine is being taught in fifty cities across the nation. Let no one underestimate the Muslims. They have their own parochial schools like this one in Chicago where Muslim children are taught to hate the white man. Even the clothes they wear are anti-white man, anti-American like these two Negro children going to school. Wherever they go the Muslims withdraw from the life of the community. They have their own stores, supermarkets, barber shops, restaurants. Here you see a progressive modern air-conditioned Muslim department store on Chicago's South side. Their story of hatred is carried in many Negro newspapers. Here you see their Minister MALCOLM X proudly displaying five of the biggest Negro papers in America. Papers published in Los Angeles, New York, Pittsburgh, Detroit and Newark, and Negro politicians, regardless of their private beliefs, respectfully listen when the leaders of the black supremacy movement speak. Here you see Borough President HULAN JACK shaking hands with ELIJAH MUHAMMAD, who is the leader of the Muslims, and here you see NAACP Director ROY WILKINS greeting Minister MALCOLM, the heir apparent to ELIJAH MUHAMMAD. Four or five times a year the Muslims assemble in one of America's major cities to hear their leader, ELIJAH MUHAMMAD. Here you see them arriving at Washington's Uline Arena for a meeting held only five weeks ago. Every devout Muslim attends these rallies, for sometime between now and 1970 and at just such a rally as this, the

Muslims expect that ELIJAH will sound the
death knell of the white man. Every precaution is
taken to protect their leader. As you will shortly
see, the Muslims, men and women both, submit
to a complete search before entering the meeting
hall. Some ten thousand persons attended the
rally that you see here, all of them searched like
this man. This began almost three hours before
the meeting started. They are waiting now for
ELIJAH MUHAMMAD, founder and spiritual
leader of their group. And here he comes. He is
actually ELIJAH POOLE of Georgia. During
World War II, MUHAMMAD was arrested and
charged with sedition and draft dodging. The
Department of Justice finally dropped the charge
that he advocated defeat of the white democracy
and victory for the colored Japanese, but
MUHAMMAD and his followers did serve time
in the federal penitentiary for refusing to register
for the draft.

But of more interest to New Yorkers is Minister
MALCOLM X, the Muslims' New York Minister, who you will shortly see. This is a remarkable man, a man who by his own admission to
"News Beat" was once a procurer and a dope
peddler. He served time for robbery in the Massachusetts State Penitentiary. Now he is a
changed man. He will not smoke or drink. He
will not even eat in a restaurant that houses a
tavern. He told "News Beat" that his life
changed when the Muslim faith taught him no
longer to be ashamed of being a black man. Reporter LOUIS LOMAX asks Minister MAL-
COLM X to further explain MUHAMMAD's
teachings. The conversation you will hear took
place as LOMAX and Minister MALCOLM X

were discussing the teachings of ELIJAH MUHAMMAD.

LOMAX: Mr. ELIJAH MUHAMMAD teaches that his faith, the Islamic faith, is for the black man. The black man is good. He also uses the Old Testament incident of the serpent in Adam and Eve in the Garden of Eden, and he sets up the proposition there that this is the great battle between good and evil and he uses the phrase "devil" and he uses it almost interchangeably and synonymously with the word *snake*. Now what does he mean there?

MALCOLM: Well, number one he teaches us that this individual was a real serpent.

LOMAX: It was not a real serpent.

MALCOLM: That one in the garden.

LOMAX: What was it?

MALCOLM: But as you know the Bible is written in symbols, parables, and this serpent or snake is the symbol that is used to hide the real identity of the one that this actually was.

LOMAX: Well, who was it?

MALCOLM: The white man.

LOMAX: I want to call your attention, Mr. MALCOLM, to one paragraph in this column. He says, and I quote him, "that only people born of Allah are the black nation of whom the so-called American Negroes are descendants."

MALCOLM: Yes.

LOMAX: Now, is this your standard teaching?

MALCOLM: Yes. He teaches us that the black man by nature is divine.

LOMAX: Now, does this mean that the white man by nature is evil?

MALCOLM: By nature he is other than divine.

LOMAX: Well, does this mean that he is evil. Can he do good?

MALCOLM: By nature he is evil.

LOMAX: He cannot do good?

MALCOLM: History is best qualified to reward all research and we don't have any historic example where we have found that they collectively for the people have done good.

LOMAX: Minister MALCOLM, you now, in Chicago and Detroit, have universities of Islam, have you not?

MALCOLM: Yes, sir, in Detroit and Chicago.

LOMAX: And you take your parishioners, you take children from the kindergarten ages and you train them right through high school. Is this true?

MALCOLM: Yes, sir, from the age of four up.

LOMAX: And you have a certified parochial school operating in Chicago?

MALCOLM: In Chicago.

LOMAX: And in Detroit?

MALCOLM: And in Detroit.

LOMAX: And kids come to your school in lieu of going to what we call regular day school?

MALCOLM: Yes, sir.

LOMAX: What do you teach them there?

MALCOLM: We teach them the same things that they would be taught ordinarily in school minus the Little Black Sambo story, and things that were taught to you and me when we were growing up to breed an inferiority complex in us.

LOMAX: Do you teach them what you just said to me that the white man is somewhat evil?

MALCOLM: You can go to any small Muslim child and ask him where is hell or who is the devil and he wouldn't tell you that hell is down in the ground or that the devil is something invisible that you can't see. He'll tell you hell is right where he has been catching it and he'll tell you the one who is responsible for him having received this hell is the devil.

LOMAX: And he will say that this devil is the white man?
MALCOLM: Yes.

———————• •———————

OFFICE MEMORANDUM

UNITED STATES GOVERNMENT

TO   :   DIRECTOR, FBI (25-330971)
               DATE: 7/21/59
FROM   :   SAC, NEW YORK (105-7809)
SUBJECT: NATION OF ISLAM
               IS-NOI
               Remyairtel 7/16/59

The following is a substantially verbatim account of Part
Three of "The Hate That Hate Produced." Part Three was
shown on 7/15/59 on the MIKE WALLACE "News Beat" show
on Station WNTA-TV, New York.

WALLACE: Tonight we take a look at the impact of the black
             supremacist movements upon the power struc-
             ture of the New York Negro community. Not
             infrequently, when the Harlem leaders gather,
             JAMES R. LAWSON and Minister MALCOLM
             X are there. JAMES LAWSON is President of
             the United African Nationalist Movement. He is
             a man who said that ROY WILKINS is an "Un-
             cle Tom." He calls ARTHUR SPINGARN,
             President of the NAACP, a Zionist Jew. He calls
             United Nations Under Secretary RALPH
             BUNCH the "George Washington of Israel."
             Minister MALCOLM X is the leader of the New
             York Muslims. They are the purveyors of the
             doctrine that the white man is evil by nature,

that he is incapable of doing good, that he must be destroyed; and when these black supremacists hold their major meetings such politicians as ADAM CLAYTON POWELL and HULAN JACK and City Councilman EARL BROWN are not infrequently there. Here you see City Councilman EARL BROWN addressing a Muslim rally. He is at the podium. Note Minister MALCOLM X and Muslim leader ELIJAH MUHAMMAD in the background. Manhattan Borough President HULAN JACK was at that meeting and here you see him, his back, shaking hands with ELIJAH MUHAMMAD. It should be made very clear that none of these men, EARL BROWN, HULAN JACK, ADAM POWELL, is a black nationalist or Muslim; but they are politicians, leaders of mass movements, and they need votes and so sometimes they find it necessary to rub shoulders with the black supremacists.

On May 18 of last year, New York woke up to this news story:

HULAN JACK, the Negro who had been elected to the highest municipal office ever occupied by a man of his race in this nation's history had been booed off a Harlem street corner by members of his own race. Clearly something was afoot in Harlem. No one seemed to know quite what.

"News Beat" reporter LOUIS LOMAX covered that story. LOU, what were the facts behind that story?

LOMAX: To capsule it, MIKE, the Muslims were miffed with HULAN JACK because he had not attended some rallies that were held in Harlem; they organized the booing session. Minister

MALCOLM X gave the signal by walking through a tavern door, and the booing began.

WALLACE: The booing session took place at a NAACP meeting, didn't it?

LOMAX: That is correct. They were celebrating the anniversary of the Supreme Court decision desegregating schools.

WALLACE: And the Muslims organized the booing?

LOMAX: Yes, they did. The booing signal was when MALCOLM X walked through the tavern door, and once the booing began, many non-Muslims joined in the well-organized spontaneous demonstration.

WALLACE: Well then, what did HULAN JACK do to bolster his popularity in Harlem as a result of this booing incident?

LOMAX: Well, I do not want to make any unwarranted conclusions, but the records show that within a week or two HULAN JACK hired a Negro public relations man. A month and a half later he welcomed Mr. ELIJAH MUHAMMAD, the leader of the Muslims, to New York.

WALLACE: Well, what do you say?

LOMAX: Just this. That there was unrest in the Negro community, that HULAN JACK was very unpopular, and that the Muslims were those who expressed this sentiment.

WALLACE: And he wooed the Muslims?

LOMAX: Yes.

WALLACE: That was the story, that is the story that the headlines failed to tell. . . .

WALLACE: Let us take a closer look at this man—a closer look at this man called brilliant by Congressman ADAM POWELL. This man, MALCOLM X, who preached a vesper service in ADAM POWELL's church. There he is with the glasses.

MALCOLM X, by his own admission to "News Beat," is a former dope peddler and pro-curer, an ex-convict who served time for theft in Michigan and Massachusetts prisons. He is a changed man now, he says, because ELIJAH MUHAMMAD's personal brand of Islam taught him no longer to be ashamed of being a black man. So it becomes evident that the responsible leaders of the Negro community are fully aware of the activities and teachings of the black supremacists.

But what about the NAACP? This organization is dedicated to the elimination of all racism, black and white. What does it know about the drive for black supremacy? Reporter LOMAX asked NAACP Executive Secretary ROY WILKINS what is the attitude of his organization toward the black supremacists and this is what ROY WILKINS said:

LOMAX: Mr. WILKINS, you said that you are not aware of any of these street corner meetings and what they have been saying.

WILKINS: Oh, I'm aware of the meetings, but all I said was that I haven't stood around on street corners and listened to any speeches.

LOMAX: Has the NAACP ever taken any kind of action against these people or have you ever raised the question of whether they should be on the street corner or whether they should be allowed to say these kinds of things?

WILKINS: Oh no. We believe in free speech. If they want to speak on street corners that is up to them.

LOMAX: Let me move on to something else. Several Negro newspapers, specifically the *Pittsburgh Courier* and the *Los Angeles Herald Dispatch,* carry a column written by one Mr. ELIJAH MUHAM-

MAD in which he advances the thesis that white men are devils and snakes.

WILKINS: Certainly.

LOMAX: And that they are the evil doers that are synonymous with evil and should be destroyed. Are you aware of this column and the Muslim movement in general which Mr. MUHAMMAD heads?

WILKINS: I do not read the *Los Angeles Herald Dispatch* at all and I must say that in reading the *Pittsburgh Courier* I have never read a column by Mr. who?

LOMAX: ELIJAH MUHAMMAD.

WILKINS: ELIJAH MUHAMMAD? No, no.

LOMAX: You have never seen his column?

WILKINS: I have seen the name, but I have never been induced to read it.

WALLACE: We found it incredible that ROY WILKINS was unaware of the existence of ELIJAH MUHAMMAD. Every other responsible Negro leader in the city knows about the Muslims, about ELIJAH MUHAMMAD, and about Minister MALCOLM X, who is the New York leader of the Muslims, the heir apparent to ELIJAH MUHAMMAD, the man who ADAM CLAYTON POWELL called "brilliant."

Then our research staff unearthed these picture.

Here you see ROY WILKINS conversing with MALCOLM X. That is ROY WILKINS in profile and MALCOLM X just behind him to his right. And here you see the two men shaking hands. Now maybe Mr. WILKINS does not know ELIJAH MUHAMMAD, maybe he does not know that the Muslims have parochial schools where they teach the youngsters that the white man is evil by nature and must be destroyed; maybe Mr. WILKINS does not know that there are about two hundred fifty thousand

of these people in the United States; maybe he
does not know that the members of the black
nationalist movement have taken to street corners in New York to preach hatred of the white
man; to call ELEANOR ROOSEVELT, for instance, the "African white goddess." Maybe he
does not know all these things, but I think he
should. As leader of the NAACP, he not only
should know these things, but he and his col-
leagues should begin to do something about it.
The truth is that Negro leaders do know about
these hate merchants. They have been aware of
the Muslims and of the black nationalists for
some years now; they have tried in effect to ignore them, to sweep them under the rug.

We call this series "The Hate That Hate Produced" because it is our conviction that the hate
that we have been learning about is the hatred
that a minority of Negroes are returning for the
hate the majority of Negroes have received.

Senator HUBERT HUMPHREY told the
NAACP fiftieth-anniversary convention today
that the Negro people are to be congratulated for
returning love for hate, but here we are seeing
tragic evidence, frightening evidence, that some
Negroes are returning hate for hate. The white
community must accept a good deal of the blame
for the indignities the Negroes have suffered. The
white community must admit its share of the
blame and take corrective action. But the Negro
community is not blameless. They and all of their
responsible leaders must move quickly to root
out the hatemongers in their midst.

SECTION 5

November 17, 1959–March 3, 1960

REPORTS: 1. November 17, 1959. New York
2. March 3, 1960. Text of "Pro and Con" (report not available)
3. May 17, 1960. New York

The November 17 report summarizes Malcolm's July 1959 trip to the Middle East and Africa as Elijah Muhammad's ambassador. The report begins with a *Los Angeles Herald Dispatch* article from April 1959 in which Malcolm called for a Bandung Conference of Negro leaders and branded "the entire white race as 'devils' and as a common enemy of all dark mankind." The report continues with excerpts from Malcolm's speeches from 1959 in which he takes a much less violent and aggressive stance than in previous years. The change appears to be confined to strategy and tactics and does not show a transformation of ideology. For example, on April 24 in New York City, Malcolm reportedly stated, "We must not teach hatred of the white man when introducing Islam to friends and relations. . . . In the future we will emphasize unity of the black man for economic, financial and moral betterment."

His trip abroad is detailed, with the report stating that he did not go to Mecca because he became ill. A letter from Malcolm, written while in Khartoum and published in the *Amsterdam News* on Aug. 22, 1959, insisted that Africans judge the sincerity of America's offers of assistance by U.S. treatment of its own blacks. Changes in Malcolm's strategy are even more evident after his July trip. On August 25, he reportedly instructed each NOI member in New York to "conduct himself as a true Muslim.

They should talk to no one on the outside and should be courteous to everyone."

The next report contains statements Malcolm made during an interview with William Kunstler on the radio program "Pro and Con." Malcolm defends the NOI against attacks from white liberals and "Negro leaders."

Excerpted from the May 17 report are an informant's notes from a New York speech of March 23, 1960, at which Malcolm spoke approvingly of blacks misleading the white man into believing that they love him.

SUBJECT   MALCOLM X LITTLE
FILE NO.   100-399321
                     Section 5
                  Serials 34-40

UNITED STATES DEPARTMENT OF JUSTICE
FEDERAL BUREAU OF INVESTIGATION

Report of: SA [BUREAU DELETION] b7C
Date: 11/17/59   Office: New York
File Number: New York 105-8999   Bureau: 100-399321
Title: MALCOLM K. LITTLE
Character: INTERNAL SECURITY - NOI

Synopsis:

MALCOLM LITTLE is the Minister of NOI temple No. 7, NYC, and resides at 25-46 99th St. East Elmhurst, Queens, NYC. He travels extensively throughout the U.S. visiting and speaking at various NOI temples. He is considered one of the national leaders of the NOI. In July, 1959, LITTLE took a trip to the Middle East and Africa as ELIJAH MUHAMMAD's ambassador. Portions of speeches by subject indicating teachings and doctrine of NOI set forth.

NOI ACTIVITY AND STATEMENTS MADE BY SUBJECT

The *Los Angeles Herald Dispatch* of April 23, 1959, carried an article captioned "MALCOLM X calls for Bandung Conference of Negro Leaders." This article referred to the above celebration on April 15, 1959, and related that

Mr. X had been preceded by many prominent speakers, including Manhattan Borough President HULAN JACK, and His Excellency CHARLES T. O. KING, ambassador of Liberia to the United Nations, State Senator JAMES WATSON, historian J. A. ROGERS, JOHN YOUNG III, and hosts of others.

Many of the celebrities ducked for cover as the popular, outspoken Moslem leader, pointing his finger into the CBS television cameras, branded the entire white race as "devils" and as a common enemy of all dark mankind. The biggest surprise came from the crowd, enthusiastically stomping and roaring its approval, with such thunderous applause that several times during his speech Mr. X had to hold up his hands and beg them to allow him to continue.

He pointed out that if the people in Africa are getting their freedom, then 20 million blacks here in America, instead of shouting hallelujah over what is happening 9,000 miles from America, "should study the methods used by our darker brothers in Africa and Asia to get their freedom."

"It has been since the Bandung Conference that all dark people of the earth have been striding toward freedom," stated MALCOLM X, "but there are 20 million blacks here in America yet suffering the worst form of enslavement . . . mental bondage, mentally blinded by the white man, unable now to see that America is the citadel of white colonialism, the bulwark of white imperialism . . . the slavemaster of slavemasters."

Mr. X explained that the first step at Bandung was to agree that all dark people were suffering a common misery at the hands of a common enemy. "Call him Belgian, call him Frenchman, call him Englishman, colonialist, imperialist, or European . . . but they have one thing in common: ALL ARE WHITE MEN! Only after agreeing who the common enemy is could our darker Brothers unite against him and make faster strides toward freedom.

"At Bandung they had to agree that as long as they remained divided a handful of whites would continue to rule them. But once our African Asian Brothers put their religious and political differences into the background, their unity has since been sufficient force to break the bonds of colonialism, imperialism, Europeanism . . . which are all only diplomatic terms for the same thing, WHITE SUPREMACY.

"Twenty million blacks in America are also kept divided and ruled by the same white man. Harlem has the largest concentration of blacks on earth, but Harlem is torn with so many divisions that the African Nationalist Leader is brought to America by our own white slavemaster . . . and because of our disunity the largest concentration of blacks on earth is bypassed by this African leader.

"If these Harlem 'leaders' are sincere, then let us put aside all petty differences of religion and politics, and hold a Bandung Conference in Harlem. We must come together and hear each other before we can agree. We must agree before we can unite. We must unite before we can effectively face our enemy . . . and the enemy must first be recognized by all of us as a common enemy to all of us before we can put forth a united effort against him for the welfare of all our downtrodden people."

Portions of Mr. X's speech, shown on the CBS ROBERT TROUT News Saturday, have caused great comment among Negroes.

[BUREAU DELETION] at a NOI meeting held April 24, 1959 [in New York City], MALCOLM X spoke as follows:

We must not teach hatred of the white man when introducing Islam to friends and relations. More people would embrace Islam if the white man was not talked against. In the future we will emphasize unity of the black man for economic, financial and moral betterment.

[BUREAU DELETION] a question was asked if a Jew is a member of the white race and is he among the devils. [BUREAU DELETION] MALCOLM answered as follows:

He is one of the worst of the devils. He does more to take advantage of the so-called black people than any other and yet poses as being a friend to the black people. He owns businesses in the black belts of major cities, pays low wages, and charges high prices. . . .

The subject's attendance at this meeting was verified on April 27, 1959. [BUREAU DELETION]

[BUREAU DELETION] at a NOI meeting held in New York on May 3, 1959, MALCOLM X spoke as follows:

Islam does not teach hate. The black man in Islam has so much love in his heart for other black men that there is no room for love of the white man. . . . Laws are made for the colored man. We should believe in the law "Eye for an eye, tooth for a tooth." If one black man is lynched another white man (adult or baby) should be killed even if in another state. If this were done the laws would be enforced tomorrow.

[BUREAU DELETION] on August 24, 1959, the FOI and MGT of Temple No. 7 held a joint meeting at which Minister MALCOLM spoke [in part] as follows:

Stool pigeons are only misguided brothers. It is nothing new that the FBI would want to know about the Muslims because they know everything, so they hire these stool pigeons to start trouble among the brothers and sisters. The stool pigeons should tell them that Mr. MUHAMMAD is teaching the truth and that they will not accept any more money.

[BUREAU DELETION] that at a NOI meeting held August 25, 1959, in New York, Minister MALCOLM spoke and advised that in view of all the adverse popularity of Muslims today, everyone should conduct himself as a true Muslim. They should talk to no one on the outside and should be courteous to everyone. They should not get into arguments with anyone and should be submissive as the worst is yet to come.

[BUREAU DELETION] that at a NOI meeting held in New York, September 9, 1959, Minister MALCOLM read a copy of a letter that was sent to the New York City Police Commissioner by the Ku Klux Klan (KKK). Minister MALCOLM stated that such a letter should have been made public by the Commissioner but this one had been kept quiet for a reason. Minister MALCOLM said that the KKK said that they have Negro pimps in our temple to make disturbances and to cause misunderstanding among our followers. He said that many times the FBI would hire stool pigeons and then turn right around and tell "us" who the stool pigeons are. [BUREAU DELETION] Minister MALCOLM stated that the Messenger has been teaching his followers to be law abiding, upright, respectable and to have love for their brothers.

The KKK has been designated by the Attorney General of the UNITED STATES pursuant to Executive Order 10450.

[BUREAU DELETION] at a NOI meeting of Temple No. 25, Newark, on September 16, 1959, MALCOLM LITTLE from New York was present. [BUREAU DELETION] MALCOLM showed movies of his recent trip abroad and at the same time narrated the movies. MALCOLM told the audience in his narration that this is what we have to go home to. If the devil doesn't want to give us some land here then we can go back home.

MISCELLANEOUS NOI ACTIVITY
Trip Abroad

On July 27, 1959, the file of MALCOLM LITTLE at the Passport Office, Department of State, was reviewed and disclosed the following information:

Passport number 1595569 was issued to MALCOLM LITTLE, known as Malik El-Shabazz, on May 27, 1959. This passport was marked "not valid" for travel in the following areas under control of authorities with which the United States does not have diplomatic relations: Albania, Hungary and those portions of China, Korea and Viet-Nam under communist control.

Regarding his travel plans, LITTLE stated that he intended to depart from the United States at the Port of New York City on June 5, 1959, via air transportation, for a proposed length of stay abroad of two weeks in order to visit the United Kingdom, Germany, Italy, Greece, United Arab Republic, Saudi Arabia, Sudan, Lebanon, Turkey, and "others" for the purpose of attending the annual sacred Moslem Pilgrimage Rites at the Holy City of Mecca (Saudi Arabia) being held from June 9, 1959, to June 16, 1959.

LITTLE answered "no" to questions in the application asking: "Are you now a member of the Communist Party?" and "Have you ever been a member of the Communist Party?"

The Communist Party, United States of America, has been designated by the Attorney General of the United States pursuant to Executive Order 10450.

[BUREAU DELETION] at the July 5, 1959, NOI meeting in New York, it was announced that Minister MALCOLM left by plane Friday for Holland. From there he would go to Egypt, Mecca, Iran, Syria and Ghana. He was going as ELIJAH MUHAMMAD's ambassador to "feel out" the land before ELIJAH MUHAMMAD goes.

An article appeared in the *New York Amsterdam News*, a weekly newspaper published in New York, of July 11, 1959, page 18, column 3, entitled "Malcolm X Off to Tour Middle East." This article is as follows:

Messenger ELIJAH MUHAMMAD, internationally recognized spiritual head of the fastest growing group of Moslems in the Western Hemisphere, sent his New York Minister, MALCOLM X, also known as Malik El-Shabazz, to the Middle East last Friday from International Airport.

While abroad, MALCOLM X plans to tour several African-Asian countries, including the Holy City Mecca and Medina in Arabia, and also Jerusalem.

The Moslem Minister plans to return to New York in time for the visit of Messenger ELIJAH MUHAMMAD in New York at St. Nicholas Arena on Sunday, July 26.

[BUREAU DELETION] ELIJAH MUHAMMAD, national leader of the NOI, appeared at the St. Nicholas Arena, New York City on July 26, 1959.

[BUREAU DELETION] prior to the speech by ELIJAH MUHAMMAD, Minister MALCOLM X of the NOI Temple No. 7, New York City, spoke. Among his other remarks, MALCOLM X told of his recent trip to the Far [*sic*] East.

MALCOLM X stated that he had just returned from the Far [*sic*] East. He stated he did not speak with Nasser but saw him. He stated that he was well accepted by Muslims and that the Muslims in Egypt and Africa are blacker than he. He stated he was well entertained and squired around due to the fact that he was a Muslim. He stated he was taken on a cruise in a boat in forbidden territory. [BUREAU DELETION] he did not furnish more details concerning this.

[BUREAU DELETION] MALCOLM X stated that in Egypt, he became very ill and as a result was not able to go to Mecca.

[BUREAU DELETION] LITTLE stated that he could have gone to Mecca but he felt he should return to New York for the visit by ELIJAH MUHAMMAD.

Concerning subject's trip abroad, it is noted that in the *New York Amsterdam News* issue of August 22, 1959, under the column "Pulse of the Public," page 10, column 5, a letter appeared signed by MALCOLM X, Khartoum, Sudan. This letter reflected that racial troubles in New York occupied prominent space on the front pages in Africa yesterday. The letter reflected that Africans seem more concerned with the plight of their brothers in America than their own conditions in Africa. Africans considered America's treatment of black Americans a good yardstick by which they can measure the sincerity of America's offer of assistance.

This document contains neither recommendations nor conclusions of any kind. It is the property of the FBI, and is a loan to your agency; it and/or its contents are not to be distributed outside your agency.

- - - · · - - -

NATION OF ISLAM
Recording of Radio Program
"Pro and Con"
Over Station WMCA on Thursday
(3/3/60), 10:35 P.M. to 11:00 P.M.

Pro and Con, giving you both sides of a current dispute. Tonight's controversy: Is Black Supremacy The Answer? Yes, says MALCOLM X, the New York Muslim minister. No, says Reverend WILLIAM M. JAMES, pastor of the Metropolitan Community Methodist Church in Harlem.

Now here to put your questions to both speakers is WILLIAM KUNSTLER, Professor of Law, New York Law School—Mr. KUNSTLER.

WILLIAM KUNSTLER: Nineteen sixty may well prove to be a year of decision for the American Negro. At this very moment the

United States Senate is bogged
down by a southern filibuster designed to prevent the passage of legislation protecting the Negroes' voting rights. In several southern
states, Negro students are refusing
to leave stores or restaurants that
will not serve them because of their
color. The day before yesterday, a
thousand Negroes marched on the
first capitol of the confederacy in
Montgomery, Alabama, in a protest
against segregation. One group,
known as the Muslims, has rejected
the gradualism advocated by the
NAACP and the Urban League and
is stridently proclaiming that a
white man's heaven is a black man's
hell. Its members have been called
racists and rabble-rousers by their
opponents. But even their most severe critics have to admit that the
Muslims are growing rap-
idly. Tonight we have with us
MALCOLM X, the Muslim's New
York minister, who feels that the
Negro must take his destiny in his
own hands. Opposing him is Reverend WILLIAM M. JAMES, pastor
of Harlem's Metropolitan Community Methodist Church, who rejects
Mr. X's thesis in favor of love and
tolerance among all peoples. Let's
turn first to Mr. X. Mr. X, before
we start our discussion tonight on
racial extremism in Harlem, would
you mind explaining for me the

MALCOLM X:

meaning of your name, which is the letter X.

Yes, sir, Mr. KUNSTLER. As you know, during slavery time, the slavemasters named most of the so-called Negroes in America. Mr. ELIJAH MUHAMMAD teaches us that the last names that they have are slave names and after coming into the knowledge of Islam, we who follow Mr. MUHAMMAD use X. We replace the name of our slavemasters with X, and some people would say that it doesn't make any difference, but there have been many cases of dark people in the South going to apply for rooms in a hotel and upon saying that their names were SMITH or JONES or JOHNSON or something like that, they were barred. Whereas, the same dark people who would use the names MUHAMMAD or HUS-SAN or SHARIEFF, they would not run into the same JIM CROW practices as those who didn't have that type name. So a name does make a difference and since we've been disconnected from that Eastern culture for so long that we don't know the names we originally had, we use X today until we're made familiar or until we are qualified to be accepted back among our people in the East.

WILLIAM KUNSTLER:

Well, Mr. X, getting to the point at hand, ROY WILKINS, the Executive Director of the NAACP, has

MALCOLM X:

described your Temple of Islam as being no better than the Ku Klux Klan. You think this is an adequate comment on his part?

Well, sir, I believe that ROY WILKINS is actually too intelligent to have made that statement and I find it hard to believe that he really said it. Plus, on the MIKE WALLACE show, during the summary Mr. WILKINS expressed ignorance of Mr. MUHAMMAD and his followers. I wonder then how he could so suddenly become an authority on us and how he can now find himself in a position to judge us, unless he's been doing some research since then, or perhaps he's just expressing opinions about that which he knows nothing, or he's parroting what he has been told to say or paid to say by those who have control over him. At any rate, I will challenge ROY WILKINS at any time, anywhere and under any conditions to a public debate concerning his charges that we who follow the Muslim faith are no better or are no different than the Ku Klux Klan, especially when there are over six hundred million Muslims on this earth that stretch from the China seas to the shores of West Africa and here in America. Mr. ELIJAH MUHAMMAD, who is our leader and teacher, has just returned from a tour of the Muslim countries of Africa and Asia where he visited the holy cities of Mecca and Medina in Arabia and was warmly received. I very much doubt if Mr. WILKINS was familiar with Mr. MUHAMMAD and his program, that he would make such charges and if he is familiar, I doubt that he made those charges.

WILLIAM KUNSTLER: Well, Mr. X, one point that might have led to those charges was contained in the January 25th issue of the *New York Times,* and it reads as follows: Like Mr. MUHAMMAD, MALCOLM X describes the white race as made up of quote inhuman devils whose very nature is to lie, cheat, steal, deceive, hate and murder black mankind end quote. And then you go on to say, as the *Times* reporter says, that an avenging Allah will soon wipe out the white devils. You think this is a fair commentary on whites in general, notwithstanding there might have been individual grievances?

MALCOLM X: Well, sir, I think that you'll say that where racial extremism is concerned, first you take the word *extremism* itself means exactly what it says. When a person is a racial extremist, to me he's extreme in his desire and in his love and in his devotion to his race. Taking it from that angle, it's not a crime to be a racial extremist. Catholics say that the Catholic church is the only church and the only way to get to heaven is through the Catholic

Church. Baptists say that no one can go to heaven unless they're baptized. And Jews themselves for thousands of years have taught that they alone are God's chosen people and that he would some day come and place them and them alone in the promised land. And now, despite this, the Catholics have never been accused of advocating Catholic supremacy, the Christians aren't accused of advocating Christian supremacy and the Jews are not accused of advocating Jewish supremacy, nor are they accused of teaching race hatred. And also, the same Christian Bible that they go by is loaded or laced with promises that non-Christians will be destroyed in a fiery death someday by God himself, and based upon that I find it difficult for Catholics and Christians to accuse us of teaching or advocating any kind of racial supremacy or racial hatred, because their own history and their own teachings are filled with it, if you're going to classify it as such.

WILLIAM KUNSTLER: Mr. X, on the subject of religion, the *Times* also quoted one of Mr. MUHAMMAD's pamphlets as criticizing Christianity as quote religion organized and backed by the devil for the purpose of making slaves of black mankind end quote, and then referred to the Bible as the poison book.

MALCOLM X: Yes, sir, anything you take that affects you so much so that it makes you absolutely helpless, can easily be classified as poison, and we find that the so-called Negroes here in America today are in a miserable or pitiful condition, namely because of the type of conception they've gotten of religion from getting the wrong understanding of the Bible. They actually try and practice turning the other cheek toward people who have used them. They practice loving their enemies. They practice praying for those who spitefully use them, and anytime a person believes in a teaching like that and practices it, it doesn't make them an intelligent person or man, it makes him a fool and a coward and when Mr. MUHAMMAD says that the Bible is a poison book, he doesn't condemn the book as such but he condemns the condition that the reading of it has placed the Negroes here in America in.

WILLIAM KUNSTLER: Mr. X, LESTER GRANGER, of the National Urban League, claims that the Temple of Islam can only become important in a time of crisis, like the present. Do you think you are a temporary movement to fill a need that is raised by a crisis?

MALCOLM X: Well, sir, if we are only a temporary movement, then LESTER GRANGER and Mr. WILKINS and the press that's raising so much to-do about us are wasting their time. If we're temporary, all they

have to do is sit back and wait until
we collapse. As it says in one part of
the Bible, I think it was Gameleo
[*sic*], he advised the people don't
touch that group because if they're
not with God, as they say, they'll
come to naught, but if they are with
God and God is behind them, be
careful how you deal with them because you might find yourself in opposition against God.

WILLIAM KUNSTLER: Mr. X, some of the leaders in Harlem, and I'm referring now particu-
larly to Dr. JAMES H. ROBIN-
SON of the Presbyterian Church of
the Master, have called you a hate
group, and Dr. ROBINSON said
hate groups are dangerous because
they can set off a spark end quote.
Do you think that you would classify yourself as a hate group?

MALCOLM X: Well, sir, number one, the charge
isn't so surprising, because, I'm
sorry to say, but it's true, many Negro preachers, religious leaders,
know absolutely nothing about the
origin of their own denominations,
the origin and history of Christianity, and they know much less about
the religions of the East and especially the religions of Africa and
Asia. Muslims are not a hate group,
we're not bitter toward the white
man, in fact I believe that we Muslims who follow Mr. ELIJAH
MUHAMMAD get along better
with white people than the same
Christian Negroes who go to Rever-

WILLIAM KUNSTLER:

MALCOLM X:

end ROBINSON's church, who profess to love white people. In fact, most white people recognize us Muslims and respect us for what we are just as we respect them. We recognize the white man and respect him for what he is and this mutual understanding of each other provides the more sensible climate for whatever relationship or activity must take place between us. They don't have any trouble out of us, we don't have any trouble out of them. But aren't you, Mr. X, aping the plantation philosophy that has in one sense given rise to your movement, by your own feeling that a Negro should buy black, for example, and do nothing with whites at all, as, for example, when Premier TOURE was here last November, the President of the new African republic of Guinea. When he was here, there was a movement to remove from the dais a white representative of the State Department, I believe a white woman interpreter for him. Don't you think you're reversing and doing the same thing as the southerners have done with Negroes for generations?

Sir, to my knowledge, there was not a Muslim who follows the Honorable ELIJAH MUHAMMAD at that reception at the YMCA given for President SEKOU TOURE. We knew nothing about it and we had nothing to do with it, and the way it was reported in the paper it was twisted to make it look like we were involved. But we had nothing to do with it. We don't participate in actions like that, we don't do anything to embarrass people.

WILLIAM KUNSTLER: Yet, if I can interrupt you for a moment, further, you, at your own meetings banned white reporters and white guests.

MALCOLM X: Well, sir, then that too should be understood. As you know, last year, I think it was sometime in May, we had a trial out in Queens, Long Island, a police brutality case, at which time our homes were shot up, the police shot at our women, at children and at our babies and threatened to throw my wife, who was pregnant at that time, down the back stairs because she wasn't moving fast enough for them. This trial lasted for three weeks in the Queens County Court and it was worse than a Mississippi courtroom, in so far as justice was concerned. And at that time the nine white dailies in New York didn't send one reporter out there to cover it, they weren't interested in the truth or in justice for Negroes but, rather, that which they can twist and use against us. They want to cry about the injustices in Mississippi, but they want to divert the attention of what's going on here in New York to hide their own faults. And I say again, sir, where was Mr. WILKINS? The

Jews had their MOSES, the Christians had their Jesus and the Arabs had their MUHAMMAD, we here in America today have our MOSES and our MUHAMMAD in the person of the Honorable ELIJAH MUHAMMAD.

WILLIAM KUNSTLER: Thank you Mr. X. Now we'll talk to Reverend WILLIAM M. JAMES, who rejects your nationalism and feels that Negroes will benefit more from cooperation with the white race than by going it alone.

UNITED STATES DEPARTMENT OF JUSTICE
FEDERAL BUREAU OF INVESTIGATION

Report of: [BUREAU DELETION] b7C   Office: New York, New York
Date: 5/17/60
File Number: New York 105-8999   Bureau: 100-399321
Title: MALCOLM K. LITTLE]
Character: INTERNAL SECURITY - NOI

Synopsis:

MALCOLM K. LITTLE is the Minister of NOI Temple No. 7, New York, and resides at 23-11 96th Street, East Elmhurst, Queens, New York. He travels extensively throughout the U.S. visiting and speaking at various NOI temples. He is considered one of the national leaders of the NOI. Portions of speeches by the subject indicating teachings and doctrine of the NOI are set forth.

[BUREAU DELETION] the subject attended an NOI meeting on March 23, 1960, at 102 West 116th Street, New York City.

[BUREAU DELETION] MALCOLM LITTLE made the following comments at this meeting:

He would not tell anyone to be a conscientious objector because the stool pigeons would go right out and tell the snake that he said it and it would be said that his teachings were subversive. He could only say that "he" would be a conscientious objector. . . .

[He said] this country is made up of refugees. The Pilgrims [and] Puritans were refugees. George Washington was a traitor. Refugees are still coming in and [taking] jobs. Only the bad people come in. People from the Far East, Indians, Asiatics, etc. don't come to this hell. America is hell. . . . Eisenhower is the chief warden, Nixon his deputy and [then Mayor of New York Robert F.] Wagner a "screw."

[He said further that] when a man marries a woman, he gives her his name [and] she gives up her own, [just] as [the] white man [did when he] brought black [men] to this country and gave [them] his name. The name shows ownership. When a woman is through with a man, she divorces him and takes back her maiden name. In Islam, the black man denounces his slave name and takes the unknown X. [which] means "out of," "away," "unknown," "from."

[He told them] a Muslim . . . grins up at the white man—"butters him up"—[is] very respectful; [doesn't] let him know what [he's] thinking. Says, "You're good"—to himself, [he] adds, "when you're dead." . . .

[He said] there will be two white photographers in restaurant tonight. [They are] not allowed in temple; [they] will be taking pictures. Be nice to them [he said]. [They] will be served good meal, served first. Warden always gives the doomed man the best last meal. Might be their last meal.

SECTION 6

June 1, 1960–April 6, 1961

REPORTS: 1. June 1, 1960. SAC, New York to Director
2. November 17, 1960. New York
3. February 21, 1961. New York
4. April 6, 1961. SAC, Boston to Director
5. May 17, 1961. New York

Section 6 contains information about Malcolm's activities in 1960 and 1961, relating speeches, meetings, and possible Communist activity. Malcolm's September 1960 visit with Cuban leader Fidel Castro in New York appears in the file. In addition, the Bureau continues to outline anti-white statements made at NOI meetings, and details possible areas of tension between Malcolm and Elijah Muhammad. For example, it reports an informant's statement that Malcolm planned to take over control of the NOI upon Elijah's death. Another informant predicted that Malcolm would run for U.S. Congress, "in order to obtain power for himself."

Malcolm noted in his autobiography that he heard many negative remarks concerning his aspirations.

As far back as 1961 . . . it was being said that "Minister Malcolm is trying to take over the Nation," it was being said that I was "taking credit" for Mr. Muhammad's teaching, it was being said that I was trying to "build an empire" for myself. (p.290)

Malcolm's personal power apparently did command attention. At a Harvard speech on March 24, 1961, an FBI agent noted

Malcolm's phenomenal control over his followers by reporting that NOI members in the audience only applauded Malcolm's debate opponent when Malcolm himself applauded.

Malcolm also mentions this event in his autobiography, but in a different context. While at the Harvard Law School Forum he by chance looked out a window that, he realized, faced in the same direction as the apartment house in which he used to hide out when he was a burglar. Suddenly aware of "how deeply the religion of Islam had reached down into the mud to lift [him] up, to save [him] from what [he] inevitably would have been: a dead criminal in a grave, or, if still alive, a flint-hard, bitter, thirty-seven-year-old convict in some penitentiary, or insane asylum," he vowed to Allah in that moment that he "never would forget that any wings [he] wore had been put on by the religion of Islam." (p.287)

The FBI includes important information about NOI relationships with other organizations. The NOI had attempted to solicit aid from the Ku Klux Klan and the American Nazi Party in order to attain its goal of forming a separate nation within the United States. The Bureau reports Malcolm's January 1961 meeting with Ku Klux Klan officials. FBI memos would refer to this meeting again shortly before Malcolm's death in 1965, when Malcolm began to indict the NOI for its past alliances, which he stated were not in the best interests of black people.

SAC, New York (105-7809)   June 1, 1960
Director, FBI (25-330971)
NATION OF ISLAM
INTERNAL SECURITY - NOI
Rerep SA [BUREAU DELETION] dated 5/17/60, at New York
captioned "Malcolm K. Little."

[BUREAU DELETION] a movie was shown which "was
about FBI intelligence, how they work with the local police, and
their training, and their lab." Bufiles are negative concerning previous receipt of this information.

From the description in rerep, the film allegedly shown
strongly resembles *A Day With The FBI,* which is an eighteen-
minute color film dealing basically with the working of the FBI
Laboratory, its cooperation with local law enforcement agencies,
and illustrates science in crime detection. A copy of this film has
been previously furnished your office.

Promptly review the files of your office [BUREAU DELE-
TION]. If this film was charged out or loaned to someone outside
the Bureau that individual should be interviewed to determine
where the film was [BUREAU DELETION] and whether this
film was loaned by that individual to another, or otherwise out of
his possession. In tracing this film back to an individual or indi-

viduals beyond the one to whom the film was charged out or loaned, same should be interviewed unless the files of your office contain information which would make such an interview inadvisable. If such is the case, notify the Bureau, setting forth the facts why you deem the interview inadvisable and submit your recommendations whether the Bureau should or should not grant authority for such an interview. You should also advise the Bureau the steps taken by your office to develop complete identification of this film [BUREAU DELETION]. In the event you took no action and it is now determined the film is identical with the Bureau's film, explanation of all personnel involved should be obtained and submitted to the Bureau, together with your recommendation for administrative action.

———————— • •————————

UNITED STATES DEPARTMENT OF JUSTICE
Federal Bureau of Investigation

Report of: [BUREAU DELETION] b7C
Date: 11/17/60   Office: New York, New York
File Number: New York 105-8999 Bureau File No: 100-399321
Title: MALCOLM K. LITTLE
Character: INTERNAL SECURITY-NOI

Synopsis:

Subject resides 23-11 97th St., East Elmhurst, Queens, NY, is the Minister of NOI Temple No. 7, NYC, and is considered one of the national leaders of the NOI. He travels extensively throughout the U.S. on NOI business and information regarding his attendance and participation in NOI affairs is set out, along with portions of his speeches and speeches by another in his presence, that indicates the teachings and directions of the NOI. One source believes subject desires to take over the NOI on death of ELIJAH MUHAMMAD and that he also is considering running for public office, possibly U.S. Congress. Subject contacted Cuban Premier FIDEL CASTRO while latter in NYC, during September, 1960, to attend the UN General Assembly.

Comments by MALCOLM LITTLE:
At New York, New York

[BUREAU DELETION] advised that at the NOI meeting held on May 15, 1960, subject was the speaker and he stated that the future of the black man in North America is to become the leader of the world, and this is nothing new since the black man is the true leader. According to the informant, subject further stated that "the whole earth belongs to the black man. The white man on the earth is only a passing fancy. . . . The black man can live without the white man but the white man cannot live without the black man. . . . We, the black men of the world, created the white man and we will also kill him. . . . We must destroy him for only in this way can there be peace on earth."

According to [BUREAU DELETION] subject further stated that there are no good white people on the face of the earth and that when the time comes to kill all of the white devils, all of our black brothers and sisters who think that there are some good ones will die right along with them.

[BUREAU DELETION] advised that at the NOI meeting held on June 5, 1960, the subject was the speaker and he stated that we must have some land of our own so that we can deal with other nations around the world, since Mr. MUHAMMAD has an agreement with every black nation all over the world. Subject also stated that if you have something that is not doing you any good then get rid of it and with this, according to source, subject threw the Holy Bible on the floor and said "that's where it belongs."

NOI and Political Aspirations
of MALCOLM LITTLE

[BUREAU DELETION] advised in August, and again in October, 1960, that from personal contact and conversation with subject it is his impression that subject is attempting to form a nucleus of followers within the NOI in order to take over the

NOI on the death of ELIJAH MUHAMMAD, although subject continues to openly refer to MUHAMMAD's son, WALLACE, as the logical successor.

During the same period, [BUREAU DELETION] also stated that in his opinion, subject is considering running for public office in Harlem, possibly for the United States Congress, in order to obtain power for himself.

Subject's Contact with Cuban Premier
FIDEL CASTRO, at New York, New York,
September, 1960
[BUREAU DELETION]

[BUREAU DELETION] advised on September 21, 1960, that in conversation with subject on that date, subject stated that he had visited with CASTRO for approximately thirty minutes in his Hotel Theresa room. The source advised that LITTLE stated that during his visit he told CASTRO, in reference to CASTRO himself, that usually when one sees a man whom the United States is against, there is something good in that man. To this CASTRO replied that only the people in power in the United States are against him, not the masses. LITTLE further expressed the opinion that any man who represented such a small country that would stand up and challenge a country as large as the United States must be sincere.

[BUREAU DELETION] further stated that LITTLE denied that the meeting with CASTRO was prearranged and LITTLE further stated that the NOI was not allied with CASTRO or with any foreign power on earth. LITTLE stated that the NOI was allied with God in whom they believe, hence, they cannot be affiliated with Communism since it is atheistic.

[BUREAU DELETION] stated that in explaining his reason for the visit, LITTLE stated that he was on a committee which was formed to meet and greet any of the African delegates to the United Nations when they came to Harlem, and when he heard that CASTRO had moved to a hotel in Harlem, he felt that as a representative of this committee he should greet CASTRO. LITTLE also stated he was the only member of the committee available at the time of the visit, hence, he went to the meeting with

CASTRO accompanied by three NOI members and two members of the Negro press.

This document contains neither recommendations nor conclusions of any kind. It is the property of the FBI, and is a loan to your agency; it and/or its contents are not to be distributed outside your agency.

_____. ._____

UNITED STATES DEPARTMENT OF JUSTICE
FEDERAL BUREAU OF INVESTIGATION

New York, New York
February 21, 1961
Re: Nation of Islam
Internal Security - NOI

A confidential source, who has furnished reliable information in the past, advised on [BUREAU DELETION] 1961, that Malcolm X Little, Minister of Nation of Islam (NOI) Temple No. 7, New York, New York, stated on February 20, 1961, that he and the NOI are very upset over the fact that the NOI has been accused of being behind the recent demonstrations at the United Nations over the death of former Prime Minister Patrice Lumumba of the Congo, when in fact they had absolutely nothing to do with them. Malcolm X stated that this publicity, which has ruined the good name of the NOI, has appeared in numerous United States and foreign newspapers which he himself has reviewed. Malcolm X claimed that this false accusation is based on a false statement attributing the demonstrations to the NOI by New York City Police Commissioner Stephen Kennedy and that the NOI plans some retaliatory action unless an apology is forthcoming from Commissioner Kennedy and a retraction is printed in the newspapers.

This source advised that Malcolm X did not say what retaliatory action would be taken by the NOI, but that this action would be decided upon at the forthcoming NOI Convention to be held at Chicago, Illinois, on February 25 and 26, 1961. Malcolm X further stated that whatever action is decided upon it will embarrass New York City, New York State and the United States governments even more than the NOI has been embarrassed by this publicity.

———————. •———————

DIRECTOR, FBI (25-330971)   SAC, BOSTON (97-145)
NATION OF ISLAM   4/6/61
IS-NOI

On Friday, March 24, 1961, at 8:00 P.M., the Harvard Law School forum presented a program, "The American Negro: Problems and Solution." This program was in the nature of debate with MALCOLM X (LITTLE), identified as a "black Muslim leader," presenting the point of view in favor of complete segregation between the Negro and the white man, as the solution to the Negro problems. WALTER CARRINGTON, a member of the National Association for the Advancement of Colored People and the Massachusetts State Commission Against Discrimination, spoke in favor of integration of the Negro and the white man as a solution to Negro problems.

SA [BUREAU DELETION] attended this affair, which was held in Sanders Theatre, Cambridge, Massachusetts, before an estimated audience of sixteen hundred persons, about twenty percent of whom were Negroes. Most of the Negro audience were judged to belong to the NOI based on the headdress worn by the females and the golden emblem worn in the lapel of the men's suitcoats.

The speakers were introduced by ROGER D. FISHER, Professor of Law, Harvard University, Cambridge, Massachusetts.

The first speaker was MALCOLM X, introduced as one of the leading figures in the "black Moslem" movement and minister of that movement's mosque in New York City. Professor FISHER gave a background sketch of MALCOLM X and stated MALCOLM X was brought up in Michigan, was the only black pupil in his school classes, and his ability and brilliance in school often brought down the resentment of his white classmates upon him. MALCOLM's home burnt to the ground while the local Fire Department refused to fight a fire in a Negro home. MALCOLM

X traveled all about the country committing all types of illegal acts and was confined in Massachusetts State Prison where he became converted to Islam and became a follower of ELIJAH MUHAMMAD.

MALCOLM X commenced his talk by stating that it must be appreciated that the movement he is a part of is not political in nature, but entirely religious. He explained that the followers of ELIJAH MUHAMMAD believe ELIJAH is one of the prophets mentioned in the Bible and is as great as the prophets JESUS or MUHAMMAD. ELIJAH MUHAMMAD's followers believe that he is the last and greatest of the prophets. As a prophet, God, whom Muslims call ALLAH, speaks through ELIJAH MUHAMMAD. When ELIJAH MUHAMMAD sets forth a program of any sort, such as segregation of the Negro from the white man, his followers must accept it as coming directly from ALLAH. They have no choice but to accept it as right and as the will of ALLAH.

MALCOLM X's talk continued in a religious vein. He discussed the three hundred years of slavery of the "so-called American Negro," who are denied the opportunity to be taught or to practice the Muslim religion which MALCOLM X claimed was the religion of their forefathers. MALCOLM X discussed the great Negro civilizations from which the forefathers of the "so-called American Negroes" were brought into slavery. He pointed out that many accusations are made against ELIJAH MUHAMMAD as not being a true Muslim and as not practicing the true Muslim religion. He repudiated these accusations by pointing out that ELIJAH MUHAMMAD recently traveled to the Far [sic] East, even visiting the Holy City of Mecca and was everywhere received by Muslim leaders and welcomed as a true Muslim.

MALCOLM X discussed the program demanded by ELIJAH MUHAMMAD that the United States give land to the Negroes in this country in which the Negroes can set up their own government, be segregated from the white race and build their own economy. MALCOLM X stated that the United States government should assist this new country in any way necessary for a period of forty-five to fifty years until the country can get on its feet and make its own way.

MALCOLM X claimed that God plans to destroy all opposition to ELIJAH MUHAMMAD. This will come about through the War of Armageddon which will end with black supremacy. He mentioned this war as a prophecy in the Bible and made no mention of Muslim participation in it. MALCOLM X referred to his group on several occasions as "the black masters." This reference appeared to describe the position the followers of ELIJAH MUHAMMAD would be in following the War of Armageddon.

WALTER CARRINGTON was introduced as a Negro graduate of Harvard College and Harvard Law School, a member of the Massachusetts Bar and a practicing attorney in Massachusetts. Mr. CARRINGTON attacked MALCOLM X's position of segregation of the Negro as "the greatest boon to the Ku Klux Klan since the invention of the bed sheet." He pointed out that the "black Moslems" claim to number a hundred thousand. He stated that this is a relatively small and insignificant group when the entire twenty million Negroes are considered as a group. Mr. CARRINGTON believes that the remaining nineteen million, nine hundred thousand Negroes are not in sympathy with the "black Moslems" and wanted [sic] integration and want it now. Mr. CARRINGTON pointed out that ELIJAH MUHAMMAD has figured out that the War of Armageddon was to take place in 1914, but God has given seventy years grace to the Negro to afford him an opportunity to join ELIJAH MUHAMMAD. This would place the date of the War of Armageddon at 1984. Mr. CARRINGTON stated that the Negro doesn't want to wait until then, but wants integration and civil rights now. He called the "black Moslems" a segment of the Negro race which has done nothing to advance the Negroes' position. CARRINGTON stated that MALCOLM X has stated his beliefs and explained his religion, but he has not told the audience what he actually teaches inside the temples which the white man is forbidden to enter and what he is teaching on the streets of Harlem in New York City.

It was noted that the NOI members in attendance did not applaud CARRINGTON during his talk except upon the rare occasion when MALCOLM X applauded. At the conclusion they offered no applause for CARRINGTON's address until

MALCOLM X finally started to clap. The entire audience was orderly and no incidents were noted.

————————• •————————

UNITED STATES DEPARTMENT OF JUSTICE
FEDERAL BUREAU OF INVESTIGATION

Report of: [BUREAU DELETION] b7C   Office: New York, New York

Date: 5/17/61

Field Office   Bureau
File No. 105-8999   File No. 100-399321
Title: MALCOLM K. LITTLE
Character: INTERNAL SECURITY - NOI

Synopsis:

Subject continues to reside at 21-11 97th Street, East Elmhurst, Queens, New York, and is a national NOI leader and the full-time minister of NOI Temple No. 7, New York, New York. Subjects's extensive NOI activities at New York and in various parts of the U.S. set forth. Also set forth are the subject's public appearances not sponsored by the NOI, his contact with representatives of the KKK . . . and comments relative to Communism and Russia.

Contact With The KKK

The KKK has been designated by the Attorney General of the United States pursuant to Executive Order 10450.

[BUREAU DELETION] advised on January 30, 1961, that certain Klan officials met with leaders of the NOI on the night of January 28, 1961, in Atlanta, Georgia. One of these NOI leaders identified himself as MALCOLM X of New York, and it was the source's understanding that MALCOLM X claimed to have a hundred seventy-five thousand followers who were complete separationists, were interested in land and were soliciting the aid of the Klan to obtain land. During this meeting subject stated that his people wanted complete segregation from the white race, and that land obtained would be occupied by them and they would maintain their own businesses and government. Subject further stated that the Jew is behind the integration movement, using the Negro as a tool. Subject was further quoted as stating that his people would do anything to defend their beliefs and promote their cause and in his opinion there would be violence some day. Subject was further quoted as saying at this meeting that if one of his people went against their teachings, he would be destroyed. Subject also stated that if his people were faced with the situation that the white people of Georgia now face, that traitors, meaning those who assisted integration leaders, would be eliminated.

Comments and Contacts With Communism and Russia

The Communist Party, USA (CP, USA), has been designated by the Attorney General of the United States pursuant to Executive Order 10450.

[BUREAU DELETION] advised on [BUREAU DELETION] 1960, that during December, 1960, Minister MALCOLM X LITTLE of NOI Temple No. 7, New York City, made the following statements [to the effect that] the white man is the enemy of the black man. The Czarist government suppressed the people and the same kind of revolution as occurred in Russia will take place here in the United States. This revolution will start in Harlem and [the Nation of Islam will be] the leaders of this black man revolution.

MALCOLM X expressed himself as a great admirer of NICOLAI [sic] LENIN and JOSEPH STALIN and stated that they were actually non-white men. He explained that LENIN was of the yellow race descending from the Mongols and STALIN descending from Semitic-Arabs and a Muslim mixture with dark skin. The Americans who are white will fight the Russians because they are non-white; it will be race against race and we American black men will support the Russians. We will kill all the white men in the United States. . . .

MALCOLM X criticized the United States Department of State and stated that the United States Government does not

want free Africans but the Africans will be free with the assistance of the Russian army right in Africa. He stated that the
United States was responsible for encouraging England, France
and Israel to invade the United Arab Republic in 1956.

[BUREAU DELETION] described subject as shrewd, canny
and at times smart but further stated that he actually was a "mad
dog" temporarily on a leash. According to [BUREAU DELE-
TION] subject is violently anti-white and insists that the whites
must be destroyed.

SECTION 7

REPORT: November 17, 1961. New York

This report continues to summarize Malcolm's speeches, reporting his violent anti-white sentiments. It also notes that no comments were made at NOI meetings included in the report "that could be construed as seditious, revolutionary or anarchistic." The Bureau attempts to connect Malcolm and the NOI to other organizations, but with little success; the FBI can make no connection between the NOI and the Workers World Party, nor with labor leader A. Philip Randolph. Links with the Communist Party and several Marxist-Leninist organizations consisted only of the fact that some of these organizations had mentioned Malcolm in a favorable light or had tried to contact him. The report indicates that Malcolm is on the mailing list of the Fair Play for Cuba Committee, and makes a connection between the Communist Party and the Negro American Labor Council (NALC), but the Bureau already had established that there was no known link between the NALC and the NOI. In short, the FBI's quest to establish ties between the NOI and leftist organizations had produced little substantiation.

SUBJECT   MALCOLM X LITTLE
FILE NO.   ___100-399321___
             ___Section 7___
             ___Serials 48-50___

FEDERAL BUREAU OF INVESTIGATION

Reporting Office: New York
Office of Origin: New York
Date: 11/17/61
Investigative Period: 10/2–11/2/61
Report made by: [BUREAU DELETION] b7C
Title: MALCOLM K. LITTLE aka
Character of case: Internal Security - NOI

REFERENCE:
Report of SA [BUREAU DELETION] b7C dated 5/17/61, at
New York.

ADMINISTRATIVE:
Subject is a key figure of the NYO.

It is to be noted that no mention is made of the events occurring at some of the meetings included in this report inasmuch as
no speeches or comments were reported as being made that could
be construed as seditious, revolutionary or anarchistic.

An information copy of this report is being designated for Chicago inasmuch as they are office of origin in the NOI case.

Two information copies of this report are being designated for Los Angeles [BUREAU DELETION]. It should be noted in this regard that Temple No. 27 is considered "subject's temple" [BUREAU DELETION].

It should be further noted that subject was in Los Angeles, California, during September and October, 1961, but there is no information available which indicates that he formulated any relationship between Temple No. 27 and the WWP [Workers World Party], or that he was in contact with representatives of the WWP.

There is not set forth in this report a characterization of the Negro American Labor Council (NALC) or the Emergency Committee for Unity on Social and Economic Problems (EUSEP) since there is no approved characterizations for either organization. It is noted that the NALC is the subject of a Cominfil investigation (NY 100-139834). Both of these organizations are headed by A. PHILIP RANDOLPH, International President of the Brotherhood of Sleeping Car Porters, and a Vice President of the AFL-CIO and of the NAACP [BUREAU DELETION].

[BUREAU DELETION]

Speeches and Comments by Subject
(10/2–11/2/61)

At the NOI meeting held at Temple No. 7, New York City, [BUREAU DELETION] MALCOLM X was the speaker and after playing a tape recording of a debate between himself and a representative of the NAACP, MALCOLM stated that you can now see why it will be necessary for God to destroy the devil (white man) and his sympathizers. He said that a Negro leader (referring to the NAACP representative), though he knows that the work of the Honorable ELIJAH MUHAMMAD is divine, will always stand up to defend the white man. He added that there will come a time when these Negroes will have to stop defending the white man. He further added that the white man should pray that nothing happens to the Honorable ELIJAH MUHAMMAD because then there will be no one to control his followers.

[BUREAU DELETION]

At the NOI meeting held at 541 Henry Street, Oakland, California, [BUREAU DELETION] MALCOLM asked the audience why should we, the Muslims or any so-called Negro, fight for the white man in Germany or Korea? When you come home, he continued, they hang you in your own country, such as Mississippi, and rape your sisters. And then you talk about fighting for the white man.

[BUREAU DELETION]

At the NOI sponsored Street Rally held at Seventh Avenue and 125th Street, New York City, [BUREAU DELETION] MALCOLM stated that there is a law against kidnapping, lynching and raping. He stated that the Federal Bureau of Investigation (FBI) was sent to the South to find the lynchers of MACK PARKER and EMMETT TILL. MALCOLM stated that the FBI found the lynchers, but they went free and were not punished for their crimes. He then stated that Uncle SAM is going to be put on trial for kidnapping, lynching, raping, etc. He further stated Uncle SAM would be judged and sentenced by God and that Uncle SAM now has a chance to repent to God through the Honorable ELIJAH MUHAMMAD and if he (Uncle SAM) sincerely seeks repentance, it will be the only way that he can escape destruction.

[BUREAU DELETION]

At the NOI meeting held at Temple No. 7, New York City, [BUREAU DELETION] MALCOLM was the speaker and asked what is the American way of life? He then stated that no people on earth know the American way of life like the so-called Negro does. He stated that we have helped them fight for freedom but do we have freedom. He continued that the Negroes in America have helped their slavemasters more than any other people but are still second-class citizens.

MALCOLM then described America as a white wolf who sees a black lion coming towards him from the East and asks us, the black men who are like the sheep who have felt the teeth of the wolf, to fight for him. MALCOLM then stated that he has never told anyone that they should or should not fight; however, he added that it seemed to him that the sheep would want to see the wolf destroyed.

MALCOLM continued that the Honorable ELIJAH MUHAMMAD has taught us that we cannot fight the devil with his own weapons and that ELIJAH MUHAMMAD has given the light of truth as a weapon and that this weapon is all that is needed to bring the devil to his knees.

[BUREAU DELETION]

Speeches and Comments by Subject
(4/3–5/7/62)

At the NOI meeting held at Temple No. 7, New York City, [BUREAU DELETION] that subject was the speaker and he said that the Honorable ELIJAH MUHAMMAD said that all of the white men, including their babies, are devils. He also said that you cannot change the nature of the snake nor can you change the nature of the white man. He added that the Muslims of the East do not know that the white man is a devil unless they learn it through the Honorable ELIJAH MUHAMMAD. Subject added that common sense should tell "us" that if the white man is a devil, then the black man has to be God.

[BUREAU DELETION] at the NOI meeting held at Temple No. 1, Detroit, Michigan, [BUREAU DELETION] the subject was the speaker, and he said that the Dred Scott Decision defined the legal rights of the Negro and white man, and that the Negro was the white man's property, and that the white man has regarded the Negro as a chattel. He went on to say that the American Negro does not have civil rights because he does not have human rights. He stated that the Negro is and has been nothing more than the white man's watchdog. All the white man had to say was "sic 'em" and the dumb Negroes went off to war in Germany, Japan and Korea. MALCOLM said that the so-called Negro must learn that there is nothing black in Uncle SAM and that the letters "USA" do not include the Negro. MALCOLM described KHRUSHCHEV and President JOHN F. KENNEDY as maniacs who are about to blow up the world with atomic weapons, and that only Allah and his Messenger offer a solution to the Negro. He further added that the black man in the world today has moved into the era of power and control.

Relationship with Communist, Marxist
and Socialist Organizations
1. Communist Party (CP)

[BUREAU DELETION] at a Board Meeting of the CP of Illinois, held in Chicago, Illinois, on [BUREAU DELETION] a report was given by CLAUDE LIGHTFOOT, from the National Executive Committee of the CP, in preparation for the forthcoming convention of the Negro American Labor Council (NALC).

The Worker, an East Coast Communist newspaper, of May 1, 1960, page MW 2, identified CLAUDE LIGHTFOOT as the National Vice-Chairman of the CP.

In this report, LIGHTFOOT stated that in the Negro liberation movement there has been a growing tendency of nationalism particularly among Negro youth, and that the youth were not convinced that labor can play a role in this liberation since they do not see labor playing a role at the present time. LIGHTFOOT then added that the NALC thus becomes important in the development of the Negro labor alliance and that it will be the policy of the CP at the coming NALC Convention to attempt to change the policy and outlook of the NALC. LIGHTFOOT referred to a recent street corner meeting held in New York City which included speeches by [BUREAU DELETION] and MALCOLM X, head of the New York Muslim Temple, among others. LIGHTFOOT went on to say that [BUREAU DELETION] is still the personality of the NALC, but that he is not an organizer and will allow the Communists to do his organizing.

2. Provisional Organizing Committee
for a Marxist-Leninist Communist Party (POC)

[BUREAU DELETION] that at a meeting of the Chicago Area Chapter of the POC, ARMANDO ROMAN stated that when he was recently in New York City, he learned that the POC there is using its Puerto Rican comrades to try and make contact with the NOI and to set up a meeting with MALCOLM X of New York.

The Worker, October 12, 1958, page 15, contained an article which states, "The New York State Committee of the CP announced last Monday the expulsion of ARMANDO RO-MAN . . . from the CP."

3. Worker World Party (WWP)

[BUREAU DELETION] that at a meeting of the Buffalo Branch of the WWP held at 831 Main Street, Buffalo, New York, [BUREAU DELETION] a member reported on an NOI meeting which she attended and which was held in Buffalo, New York, and at which subject was the speaker. She stated that subject claimed that the black race goes back to ancient history, had formerly ruled the world, and predicted that they would rule again. She said subject also stated that KHRUSHCHEV and President KENNEDY are enemies, but that both of them are the enemies of the Muslims.

[BUREAU DELETION] that at a meeting of the Buffalo Branch of the WWP held at 831 Main Street, Buffalo, New York, [BUREAU DELETION] a member gave a report on a Muslim meeting she had attended and said that MALCOLM X engaged in a panel discussion with several ministers and made "fools" out of them. She stated that she was impressed by the way MAL-COLM handled the discussion and that according to him, Muslims believe in segregation and they should operate businesses independent of the whites. She added that she did not agree with the Muslims' policies regarding segregation.

[BUREAU DELETION] that another member at this same meeting stated that while the Muslims are against white suprem-acists, they are also against segregation and that because of this the Muslims could become fascists rather than socialists, and he advised those present to be cautious in their dealings with the Muslims.

4. Fair Play for Cuba Committee (FPCC)

[BUREAU DELETION] made available the names and addresses of individuals in New York City who currently are on the mailing list of the FPCC, Room 329, 799 Broadway, New York, New York. Among the names furnished was that of:

Malcolm X
c/o Temple No. 7 Restaurant
113 Lenox Avenue
C-62

[BUREAU DELETION] the code letters "C-62" indicates an FPCC member whose membership comes up for renewal in the third quarter of 1962.

SECTION 8

November 16, 1962–May 13, 1963

REPORTS: 1. November 16, 1962. New York
                2. February 4, 1963. SAC, Washington Field
                    Office to Director. Airtel
                3. February 4, 1963. Report of W.C. Sullivan
                4. March 13, 1963. SAC, Charlotte, North
                    Carolina, to Director
                5. May 13, 1963. Washington D.C.

Section 8 outlines the events surrounding the shooting death of NOI member Ronald Stokes by Los Angeles policemen and sketches the growing tension between Malcolm and Elijah Muhammad's family. Malcolm's role in the aftermath of the shooting was highly visible, and Los Angeles Mayor Samuel Yorty increased that visibility on June 6 by playing a tape in which Malcolm publicly referred to a French airline crash as Allah's divine revenge against the white race for the travesty in California. Yorty recommended wide publication of the statement "so the public could understand the threats of this philosophy."

The FBI soon decided that Yorty's methods were impractical because they tended to create interest in the NOI, even though they were designed to create the opposite effect. Assistant Director W.C. Sullivan here divulges an important policy decision, which is the policy of "taking no steps which would give them (NOI) additional publicity." This is one of the few examples of policy analysis which occurs in this edition of the file. An FBI agent offers his analysis of Malcolm's appeal in a memo relating a

Charlotte speech of January 30. The agent discusses in depth how Malcolm "unites the individuals into an emotional entity, how he achieves rapport, reaches common understanding and responsiveness as he fuses individuals into a unit."

SUBJECT   MALCOLM X LITTLE

FILE NO.   100-399321

Section 8

Serials 51-63

UNITED STATES DEPARTMENT OF JUSTICE
FEDERAL BUREAU OF INVESTIGATION

Report of: [BUREAU DELETION] b7C   Office: New York, New York

Date: 11/16/62

Field Office File No.: 105-8999   Bureau file No.: 100-399321

Title: MALCOLM K. LITTLE

Character: INTERNAL SECURITY-NATION OF ISLAM

Synopsis:

Subject continues to reside at 23-11 97th Street, East Elmhurst, Queens, NY, and is Minister of NOI Temple No. 7, NYC and also considered a National NOI official, and the right hand man of ELIJAH MUHAMMAD. Subject's NOI activities and speeches at NYC and around the U.S. set out. Subject attempted to rally other Negroes in Los Angeles, California, to protest against the killing of a NOI member during a shooting incident between NOI members and the Los Angeles Police Department (LAPD). Subject's public appearances set out and he apparently has canceled all future college appearances. Subject invited to integration rally, Englewood, NJ, but did not attend when opposition developed among Negro leaders. Subject's association with Communist movement set out.

Subject's Activities Following the
Los Angeles Shooting Incident

Outlined below are the activities of the subject on behalf of the NOI following a shooting incident on April 27, 1962, between Los Angeles NOI members and the LAPD in Los Angeles, California, at which one NOI member was killed, several wounded and a number arrested. Also set forth are activities by the subject as a result of this incident in concert with various Los Angeles groups who protested alleged police brutality against the Negro population there.

Subject attended and conducted funeral services held at 5606 South Broadway, Los Angeles, California, on May 5, 1962, for NOI member RONALD STOKES who was killed on April 27, 1962, in a shooting incident between Los Angeles NOI members and the LAPD.

[BUREAU DELETION]

The May 10, 1962 edition of the *Los Angeles Herald Dispatch,* a weekly Negro newspaper published in Los Angeles, California, contained an article which reflected that a crowd of over two thousand attended the funeral of RONALD STOKES, a Muslim, who was shot down by local police, which services were held at 5606 South Broadway, Los Angeles, California, on May 5, 1962, and conducted by the subject.

The May 10, 1962 edition of the *Los Angeles Herald Dispatch* also contained an article which reflected that on May 4, 1962, in the Statler-Hilton Hotel, Los Angeles, California, subject had held a press conference relative to the shooting on April 27, 1962, of seven Los Angeles NOI members, one of whom (RONALD STOKES) died.

The article reflected that subject's opening statement was that ". . . Seven innocent unarmed black men were shot down in cold blood by Police Chief WILLIAM J. PARKER's Los Angeles City Police." The article continued that subject referred to the incident as "one of the most ferocious, inhuman atrocities ever inflicted in a so-called 'democratic' and 'civilized' society," and subject referred to the death of STOKES as a "brutal and cold blooded murder by PARKER's well-armed storm troopers."

This article went on to say that according to the subject, the official version of the incident which was related in the "white press" was that the Muslims were engaged in a gun battle with police provoked by the Muslims. Subject ridiculed this article saying that the Muslims obey the law religiously and he further ridiculed the "white press" for helping Chief PARKER "suppress the facts."

Also during this conference, the subject refused to clarify how one of the white policemen was shot, stating that he was acting on the advice of the attorneys of the Muslims who were accused and arrested for assault.

The May 17, 1962 edition of the *Los Angeles Herald Dispatch* contained an article which reflected that a Los Angeles Coroner's Jury inquiring into the death of RONALD STOKES on April 27, 1962, at the hands of the LAPD, ruled that it was "justifiable homicide under lawful performance of duty and in self defense." The article further indicated that only the police officers testified and that the nine Muslims who were arrested at the scene refused to testify and left the hearing after being advised that they were not required to testify if they thought their testimony might incriminate them.

This same article quoted the subject as saying after hearing the above verdict that STOKES's death was "a murder in cold blood" and that the Muslims "despaired of getting justice" and would pray to "God that he gives justice in his own way." The article went on to say that in response to questions the subject stated that Muslims obey the law, do not carry firearms and are never the aggressors but if attacked have their God-given right to defend themselves.

The May 24, 1962 edition of the *Los Angeles Herald Dispatch* contained an article which reflected that a protest rally against police brutality was held in Los Angeles on May 20, 1962, at the Park Manor Auditorium which was sponsored by the "County Civic League," the latter being described in the article as an independent organization dedicated to the protection and preservation of the black community.

The article reflected that the subject spoke at this meeting and is quoted as saying ". . . Not a Muslim but a black man was shot down." The article indicated that the subject reiterated the importance of not letting religious, political, social or economic differences divide the blacks. He further stated, according to the article, "For you're brutalized because you're black and when they lay a club on the side of your head, they do not ask your religion. You're black, that's enough."

At this above mentioned rally held on May 20, 1962, [BUREAU DELETION] during the subject's speech, he said that black people all over the world are uniting. Socialists, Communists and Liberalists [sic] all are coming together to get rid of the common enemy with white skin.

[BUREAU DELETION] that early in June, 1962, [BUREAU DELETION] at the Holman Methodist Church, Los Angeles, California, during which a bulletin was passed out that had on its back "A Manifesto for Clergymen of the Los Angeles Area." [BUREAU DELETION] the bulletin indicated that this manifesto was being issued as a result of the killing of a Muslim by the LAPD. This manifesto indicated that the Negro Ministers did not condone police brutality but that they were in no way related to or in sympathy with the Muslim movement.

The June 6, 1962 edition of the *Los Angeles Herald Examiner* contained an article which reflected that news media of Southern California were asked by Los Angeles Mayor SAMUEL W. YORTY to publicize statements made by the subject at an NOI meeting in Los Angeles, California. The article indicated that Mayor YORTY, during a press conference in his office, played a tape recording of the NOI meeting which included a speech by the subject during which the latter said in regard to the crash of a jet airliner in Paris, France, in which all the passengers were killed:

I would like to announce a very beautiful thing that has happened. As you know, we have been praying to Allah. We have been praying that he would in some way let us know that he has the power to execute justice upon the heads of those who are responsible for the lynching of Ronald Stokes on April 27.

And I got a wire from God today (laughter) wait, all right, well somebody came and told me that he really had answered our prayers over in France. He dropped an airplane out of the sky with over 120 white people on it because the Muslims believe in an eye for an eye and a tooth for a tooth (cheering and applause).

Many people have been saying, "Well, what are you going to do?" And since we know that the man is tracking us down day by day to try and find out what we are going to do so he'll have some excuse to put us behind his bars, we call on our god. He gets rid of 120 of them in one whop. But thanks to God, or Jehovah or Allah, we will continue to pray and we hope that every day another plane falls out of the sky (cheering and applause). I want to just let you understand this.

Whenever you read in the paper or hear on the television about accidents in which these good, blessed, blue-eyed people have lost their lives, you can say amen for that's God's work. God knows you are cowards; God knows you are afraid; God knows that the white man has got you shaking in your boots. So God doesn't leave it up to you to defend yourself.

God is defending you himself. They don't know what makes those airplanes come down; they start looking for mechanical failure. No, that's godly; that's "divinely failure."

Following the playing of the above recording the article indicated that Mayor YORTY stated that he did not believe that MALCOLM X or the black Muslims had the support of the Los Angeles Negro community and urged that wide publicity be given to this statement of MALCOLM X so the public could understand the threats of this philosophy.

Animosity Between Subject and the
Family of ELIJAH MUHAMMAD

On several dates during February, March and April, 1963, [BUREAU DELETION] there was developing a feeling of resentment and animosity against the subject by members of ELIJAH MUHAMMAD's family. This resentment apparently stems from MALCOLM's taking charge and running the NOI Convention in Chicago, Illinois, on February 26, 1963, when illness precluded ELIJAH MUHAMMAD's attendance. The family was especially resentful of subject's attempts to advise and tell the family what to do and of statements he was allegedly making against ELIJAH and his family.

This resentment was further aggravated, [BUREAU DELETION] by subject's remaining in Chicago for several weeks after the convention where he made numerous appearances and speeches in the Chicago area. On the request of members of the family, ELIJAH MUHAMMAD, who was still in Phoenix, Arizona, ordered subject to return to New York City, which he did on March 10, 1963, canceling his future scheduled appearances around Chicago. The excuse utilized for leaving the Chicago area was that subject had to return home and assist his wife who had fallen and broken her leg, which in fact she had done.

A possible incident reflecting the reason for some of this resentment is indicated below:

At the NOI Convention in Chicago, Illinois, on February 26, 1963, subject's speech was interrupted several times by an apparent request to allow ELIJAH's son WALLACE MUHAMMAD, to speak. Subject refused to heed this request and stated that due to the late start it would not be possible for WALLACE to speak. However, subject did introduce those members of ELIJAH's family who were present.

This document contains neither recommendations nor conclusions of any kind. It is the property of the FBI, and is a loan to your agency; it and/or its contents are not to be distributed outside your agency.

───────── • • ─────────

2/4/63

AIRTEL
TO: DIRECTOR, FBI (25-330971)
FROM: SAC, WFO (100-22829)
NATION OF ISLAM
IS-NOI
(OO:CG)

During a simultaneous release of a filmed interview on radio and television stations WMAL, Washington, D. C., on 2/3/63, at 7:00 P.M., MALCOLM X, New York City, described as the official spokesman for the black Muslims and Minister of Muhammad's Mosque, No. 7, New York City's Harlem District, made some comments as follows:

The honorable ELIJAH MUHAMMAD teaches that the black man is closer to God and is actually superior physiologically, psychologically, socially and numerically.

The religion of Islam eliminates drunkenness, dope addiction, vice, immorality, smoking, drinking, stealing, lying, cheating, gambling, and disrespect for womanhood.

Regarding violence, Muslims are taught to obey the law, respect the law and to do unto others as "We would like them to do unto us," but that after having religiously obeyed the law, the Muslims are within their rights to defend themselves when attacked.

Muslims are never involved in riots and are never involved in violence unless attacked.

ELIJAH MUHAMMAD has never advocated the overthrow of the government. If the black man cannot go back to his own people and his own land, ELIJAH MUHAMMAD is asking that a part of the United States be separated and given to the Muslims so they can live separately. ELIJAH MUHAMMAD is the only man the white people can deal with in the solving of problems of the so-called Negro, as ELIJAH MUHAMMAD knows his problems.

Communism does not support the Muslim ideology.

The FBI spends twenty-four hours daily in attempting to infiltrate the Muslims and after Muslim meetings are held, the FBI goes from door to door asking about the meetings. The FBI goes far beyond its duty in the "religious suppression" of the Muslims.

The NAACP has existed for fifty-four years, during which period it has always had a white man as president. MALCOLM believes that the organization is not developing leadership among the black people or it is practicing discrimination.

There is a group of Muslims in every Negro community.

Financial support from the white people is not desired, but would be accepted because it would represent what the white "forefathers" robbed from the black "forefathers" during the 310 years that the Negro spent in bondage while working without pay for the white people.

The above interview was conducted by MATTHEW WARREN and MALCOLM LA PLACE, reporters for WMAL News.

A more complete account of the interview will be furnished to the Bureau, CG and NY when it has been assembled.

———————— • •————————

Mr. W. C. Sullivan   February 4, 1963
[BUREAU DELETION]
NATION OF ISLAM
INTERNAL SECURITY-NOI
MALCOLM X LITTLE
INTERNAL SECURITY-NOI

My memorandum 2/1/63 advised a scheduled program called "Black Muslim" would be presented at 7 P.M., Sunday, 2/3/63 on Channel 7, WMAL Television, Washington, D. C. "Black Muslims" is the term used by the news media in referring to the Nation of Islam (NOI). WMAL, the *Evening Star* (a Washington, D. C., daily newspaper) station, advised that one of the reasons they were presenting the program was because they felt it presented MALCOLM X and the "Black Muslims" in a "bad light."

During the program MALCOLM X did refer to the FBI on one occasion. He said:

The FBI spends twenty-four hours a day infiltrating or trying to infiltrate Muslims and after we hold our religious services they go from door to door and ask questions of persons who come to the meetings to try and harass them and frighten them. The FBI really goes way beyond the call of its duty in the religious suppression of the Muslims in this country. We have many occasions where they have tried to threaten and frighten Negroes from becoming Muslims, but it doesn't work. Today they have a new Negro on the scene and the more harassment and threats the FBI or the police or anyone gives toward Islam or toward the Negro, it only makes us grow that much faster.

OBSERVATIONS:

In carrying out our responsibilities in the security field [BUREAU DELETION]. However, the statements concerning harassment and threats are absolutely false and are additional examples of wild untrue statements made to influence the Negro.

The program did not put MALCOLM X or the "Black Muslims" in a "bad light." The "answers" given by MALCOLM X were not questioned. He was allowed to expound the NOI program in such a way that he created interest in the NOI. This is another example of the effect of publicity concerning the NOI. While it was intended to have an adverse effect, it created interest in the organization which was out of proportion to its importance.

RECOMMENDATION:

It is recommended that we continue to follow the approved policy of taking no steps which would give them additional publicity.

———————• •———————

DIRECTOR, FBI (100-439895)   3/13/63
SAC, CHARLOTTE (100-4273)
NATION OF ISLAM
IS-NOI

[BUREAU DELETION] made available to SA [BUREAU DELETION] a recording of the speech made by MALCOLM X LITTLE at the Hi-Fi Country Club in Charlotte, N. C., on 1/30/63.

[BUREAU DELETION]

Hearing the actual speech of MALCOLM X enables the listener to discover the type of argument and logic employed by a hate peddler. The resulting effect is clearly heard in the background of this particular tape.

[BUREAU DELETION] The listener can hear audience reaction in the background as MALCOLM X stimulates his listeners to the release of their prejudices, grievances and wishes. Some of the content of the tape underlines the inhibitions and repressed attitudes of a segment of Negroes in general and of Charlotte Negroes in particular. These bitternesses are easily identified on the tape through crowd outbursts as MALCOLM X underlines some of the causes of Negro unrest.

This taped speech [BUREAU DELETION] shows clearly how MALCOLM X unites the individuals into an emotional entity, how he achieves rapport, reaches common understanding and responsiveness as he fuses individuals into a unit.

It is interesting to listen to the method of using statements of fact to set a favorable state of mind as he interweaves easy catch phrases of hate into the content of his speech. He continually throws irritants into an atmosphere of growing disapproval of the white race.

MALCOLM X uses his skill as a speaker to direct emotions and hatreds of his audience toward white people whom he sets up as a scapegoat for Negroes, described by him as a people severed from their racial heritage.

UNITED STATES DEPARTMENT OF JUSTICE
FEDERAL BUREAU OF INVESTIGATION

WASHINGTON 25, D. C.
May 13, 1963

NATION OF ISLAM
INTERNAL SECURITY -
NATION OF ISLAM

The *Washington Post,* a Washington, D. C. daily newspaper, in its issue of May 13, 1963, on page B-3, carried an article entitled "400 Hear MALCOLM X Speak Here." This article reflected that MALCOLM X, the Number Two leader of the Black Muslims, spoke on May 12, 1963, to an audience of about four hundred persons in a studio of a Washington, D. C. radio station, WUST. This article stated that the subject had been transferred recently as Minister of the sect's Washington Mosque. MALCOLM X announced that whites had been barred from the meeting "so that we can talk about them like we want to." A squad of young Muslims frisked everyone at the door for weapons. No whites were seen attempting to enter.

The subject warned at this meeting, according to the newspaper article, that Negroes can expect little better treatment from President Kennedy than they get from Alabama Governor George C. Wallace. He characterized the two men as a wolf and a fox. "Neither one loves you," he said. "The only difference is that the fox will eat you with a smile instead of a scowl."

MALCOLM X cited the weekend bombings and fighting in Birmingham, Alabama, as proof of the failure of the turn-the-other-cheek policy advocated by Martin Luther King. He said that Negroes ought to stay away from the white man, "but if he turns his dogs on your babies, your women and your children, then you ought to kill the dogs, whether they've got four legs or two."

SECTION 9

May 23, 1963–January 23, 1964

Rather than policy prescriptions, the Bureau reports in this section limit themselves to reporting Malcolm's public appearances. This section outlines his activities from the time of his May appointment as Minister of Mosque No. 4 in Washington through the end of 1963, including Malcolm's reactions to the August 28 March on Washington, his comments regarding President Kennedy's assassination, and his subsequent suspension from the NOI.

The Bureau reported that any NOI members who participated in the "Farce on Washington," as Malcolm called it, would receive ninety-day suspensions. Yet Malcolm himself attended, as he relates in his autobiography:

Yes, I was there. I observed that circus. Who ever heard of angry revolutionists all harmonizing "We Shall Overcome . . . Suum Day . . ." while tripping and swaying along arm-in-arm with the very people they were supposed to be angrily revolting against? . . . Hollywood couldn't have topped it. (pp. 280–81)

Malcolm clearly disapproved of the march, but instead of acting in the traditional NOI manner by avoiding the event, he actually attended in order to have his militant stance be heard. Thus, he satisfied both Elijah Muhammad and his own increasing desire to become a visible part of mass black nationalism.

The FBI had received information that the schism between Malcolm and Elijah seemed to be healing, but apparently this information was incorrect. After Malcolm's "chickens coming home to roost" comment, Elijah suspended him at first for ninety days, and then indefinitely. Malcolm's submission to the suspension is well-documented in his autobiography, but the FBI also received a report of a conversation in which Malcolm and Elijah try to understand each other's positions. The January 2 conversation is confusing, and many FBI deletions increase the difficulty of understanding the informant's description. However, a close reading reveals that Malcolm appears to be attempting to submit to Elijah in full, but Elijah is intent on perpetuating the widening rift between them.

An interesting letter to Director Hoover and a personal response from him hint at FBI activity against Malcolm X. The September 19, 1963 letter, written by a "concerned citizen," questions "Are we doing anything to curb the activities of Black Muslim leader 'Malcolm X'?" Comparing Malcolm to Hitler, the letter asks why he is not "stopped now before it is too late?" J. Edgar Hoover's personal response to the inquiry states that the FBI is "unable to answer your specific inquiry due to the confidential nature of our files." However, Hoover assures the writer that "the FBI is carrying out its responsibilities in the internal security field with the same dispatch and thoroughness which have characterized our investigations in the past."

UNITED STATES DEPARTMENT OF JUSTICE
FEDERAL BUREAU OF INVESTIGATION

WASHINGTON 25, D.C.
May 23, 1963

MALCOLM K. LITTLE
ALSO KNOWN AS MALCOLM X
INTERNAL SECURITY - NATION OF ISLAM

MALCOLM X was interviewed in the studio of radio station WUST, Washington, D. C. between 1:00 P.M. and 1:30 P.M. on 5/12/63. He appeared on a weekly program of WUST called "Focus," and was introduced as Minister of Muhammad's Mosque No. 4 (MM No. 4), 1519 4th Street, N. W., Washington, D. C.

For the sake of brevity, the interviewer will be identified by the letter "I." The subject will be identified by the letter "M." The interview is as follows:

I.   Would we be correct in assuming here that your being sent here to Washington is not only for the exhilaration of the program locally, but to also create across the country influence here or get national attention to your program.

M. Not so much national attention. I don't think any more attention could be drawn to Mr. MUHAMMAD than has already been drawn, not only nationally but internationally. Our people are confronted today with a very grave problem and many whites who pose as liberals and use Negroes who pose as leaders, to make our people think that integration is going to solve our problem, and as Muslims we look upon this as only a trick designed to blind the black man in this country, to what is really facing the white man. And the Honorable ELIJAH MUHAMMAD teaches us that the only salvation for our people is not integration into a white society, of a society that is on its way out and is on its way down, but separation from that society. And that righteous effort be put forth among our people to solve our own problems; to get on God's side and to integrate with God and imitate God instead of running around here foolishly trying to integrate with the white man or imitate the white man or get on the white man's side.

I. Well, what is the thinking of ELIJAH MUHAMMAD? There are rapid strides being made in the field of integration.

M. I don't see how you could call rapid strides being made in the field of integration when you don't have one city in this country that can honestly say it is an example of sincere integration. The most, the first city to integrate was Washington, D. C. and it has become, because of integration, the only city in the country, according to government statistics, which has a majority population of so-called Negroes. Which shows you that when the black people come in the white men run out and the white liberals run out faster than the white conservatives. The white northerners run out more swiftly than white southerners, so we just don't see where integration has worked in any city, North, South, East or West. It is only a very hypocritical approach to the problem.

I. Now with your being sent here to Washington, what do you propose to do to help this situation?

M. What situation?

I. This matter of having the Negro race, if I understand it correctly, here now, to segregate themselves.

M. Not segregate themselves. MUHAMMAD teaches us there is a difference between separation and segregation. Segregation is that which is forced upon inferiors by superiors. Separation is done voluntarily by two equals. You notice that whenever you have an all-white school, it is not referred to as a segregated school. The Negro school is the segregated school; the Negro community is the segregated community. Chinatown isn't even called a segregated community and only Chinese live there. But because the Chinese voluntarily live among themselves in their own community and control their own economy, their own business and own banks and own schools in their Chinese community, it is never called a segregated community. But the Negro schools in the Negro community are controlled by whites; the businesses in the Negro community are controlled by whites; the economy of the Negro community is controlled by whites; even the mind of the Negro community is controlled by whites; and since the Negro society or community is a controlled or regulated community by outsiders it is a segregated community. But if it was a separate entity, it would be something that we would voluntarily do. Separation, as I said, is that which is voluntarily done by two people, but segregation is that which is forced upon inferiors by superiors, and Muslims who follow the Honorable ELIJAH MUHAMMAD are as much against segregation as we are against integration. We are against segregation because it is unjust and we are against integration because its hypothesis is a false solution to a real problem, and you can talk integration but you can't show me anyplace where it is being practiced.

I. Mr. MALCOLM X, your arrival and stay in Washington has stirred the community, the white and the Negro race. The question is raised by our leading Negro publications: "Why should he come here?" Another question is raised: "Do we need Malcolm here?" If you are a religious sect who submits to the will of God, then why all the concern over the Muslims?

M. Well, I think you will find there was an article in the *New York Herald Tribune* recently, in a series of articles called "Ten Negroes," and one of your leading educators right here in this city, Nabrit, I think that is the way you pronounce his name, the President of Howard University, in this article he pointed out that one of the things that is dangerous about the Muslims is that we don't drink or we don't smoke, we don't, and that the Honorable ELIJAH MUHAMMAD is able to exercise control over his followers that is not matched by any other religious group, and Nabrit went on to point out that we don't drink, we don't smoke, we have no crime, we pay our debts, we take care of our families. . . . Now if Nabrit is in a city that is complaining of crime, not only youth crime but adult crime, and they also confess their own inability to solve this dreadful condition, and they see that MR. MUHAMMAD is able to solve it, yet they don't want MR. MUHAMMAD's doctrine to spread, this shows you the hypocrisy of the Negro leadership; that the Negro isn't the Negro leaders whether they are educators, politicians, or religious leaders, they are not concerned with elevating the condition of the masses of black people or correcting the problem faced by the masses of black people in this country. Most of these Negro leaders are only interested in keeping friendship with the white man, and pleasing the white liberal element with whom they are identified and with whom they are associated. And therefore because these white liberals won't go along with what the Honorable ELIJAH MUHAMMAD is teaching, despite the fact that what he is teaching is able to reform our people, since the white liberals don't endorse MR. MUHAMMAD, these Negro educators and politicians and religious leaders don't endorse the Honorable ELIJAH MUHAMMAD either, and this is why they express fear and concern over my, over the Honorable ELIJAH MUHAMMAD sending me to Washington. They should be happy that a man who has been reformed himself by MR.

MUHAMMAD and who in turn has reformed others, why, they should be happy to see the entry into the city of such a man.

I. Let's take this matter of crime now. How do we account for some of the Muslims being in one institution here, the Lorton Reformatory, where we had a considerable amount of trouble here sometime ago.

M. I am glad you asked that. What the press fails to point out is that no Muslims go to prison. Those men weren't Muslims before they went to prison. These men were Christians before they went to prison. They were Christians, Baptists, Methodists, Catholics, Negroes, and this type of religious concept that they had in the society in which they traveled, circles in which they traveled, led them into a life of crime; and the inability of that religion to reform them of these criminal tendencies is what made them wind up in prison. And after getting in prison they heard about the teachings of the Honorable ELIJAH MUHAMMAD, and then became Muslims, then reformed themselves and were then rehabilitated and changed, and became better men. But despite the fact that the Christian psychologists, the Christian theologists were unable to reform these men and rehabilitate these men . . . It was the Muslims who went in prison and reformed them and are bringing them out of prison and making them better men.

I. . . . Visiting the Mosque or visiting the building here where you are going to hold your meeting later this afternoon: There are some procedures that individuals have to go through before they enter, such as frisking an individual. Why is this necessary?

M. . . . It is not a case of frisking, anyone who enters a Muslim meeting is checked because we don't allow weapons to enter any of our services; we don't allow anyone who comes with alcohol on his breath to enter—everyone who comes is not only checked for weapons but is also checked for alcohol—and this is good because people who attend our meetings over a period of time, it means that these automati-

cally, whenever they did carry weapons, they leave their
weapons at home when they come around us, and after
forming the habit of leaving their weapons at home when
they come around us they realize that they don't need weapons after all. So actually in a psychological sense, this
teaches our people not to carry weapons, it teaches our people that they don't need any type of alcohol; and it reforms
—it puts them on a path toward reformation without them
even realizing it.

I.   About the meeting here this afternoon, why aren't white
      people allowed to attend?

M.   Well, this is another thing, we have had meetings plenty of
      times that white people attended, and it didn't help them.
      We have had meetings where we let white reporters come in.
      They did nothing but distort what was said or took it out of
      context, or blew up what they considered to be negative.
      They don't come to listen objectively and then go out and
      report objectively; they go out to project us as a racist
      group, as a black supremacist group, or as a group that is
      advocating violence. . . . If they want to cover our meet-
      ings, let them get someone black who looks like us to come
      in and cover our meetings. . . . I heard that one television
      network is flying a Negro in all the way from New York
      City just to cover this meeting because we won't let the
      white reporters in, and this means that this particular net-
      work, which is one of the largest in the country, here in this
      city, the Capitol, doesn't even have one Negro in this city
      working for them. So they have to go out of town and bring
      one in. Why, this only further proves what Honorable ELI-
      JAH MUHAMMAD is teaching is true. Any kind of job
      that the white man even gives to a Negro usually is token-
      ism, and is window dressing to try to make the Negro think
      he is sincere in trying to solve this problem when he is
      actually not. . . .

I.   You are advocating that twenty million Muslims will be in
      the sect by 1970; that is about seven years away. And that,
      and also you are advocating that more than ninety percent
      of the Negroes will have turned to the Muslim religion.

That is such a short time. How do you think you can get so many?

M. The Honorable ELIJAH MUHAMMAD has taught us that Islam is the religion of God. There is only one God, the creator of the Universe.

I. Let us take the matter of the religion of Islam now. How do you differentiate, if I may interrupt here, Muslim, M-U-S-L-I-M from Moslem, M-O-S-L-E-M.

M. Well, if you were to go to the Moslem world and ask them what they are, they would say they are Muslims. Muslims is how it is pronounced in the Moslem world. Moslem itself, that word is only to apologize or westernize or white man's way for saying Muslim. So a Moslem is a Muslim, a Muslim and Moslem is just the way the white man says it. And because most Negroes don't understand this and they believe in imitating the white man, they go around saying that we are not Moslems, we are Muslims, because actually they don't understand, they are just parroting what their white master has put inside their mouth.

I. There is a separate language, is there not?

M. Arabic is, well, Arabic is the language that is spoken, that is most commonly spoken in the Muslim world, although the Muslim world stretches from China to the shores of West Africa. . . . The people in the Muslim world don't regard a man according to the color of his skin. When you are a Muslim, you don't look at the color of a man's skin whether he is black, red, white or green or something like that; when you are a Muslim you look at the man and judge him according to his conscious behavior. And many people in this country think we are against the white man because he is white. No, as a Muslim we don't look at the color of a man's skin; we are against the white man because of what he has done to the black man; we are against the white man in America because of his enslavement of our people and his oppression of our people and his exploitation of our people, and today, his continued hypocrisy, his refusal to stop doing this. But his forked tongue that he uses to make the world think that he is getting better now when all he has done is

allowed us to advance from ancient slavery to modern slavery.

I.   You, in this discussion here this afternoon, are talking in
      terms of collective white people, are you not?

M.   The problem is collective, but we are not interested in these
      little individual whites who run around here with a halo
      around their heads. This is not a problem that can be solved
      on an individual basis.

I.   There are many, many people, whom I think you will agree,
      who have done much toward the advancement of the Ne-
      gro. There are many people who are sincere, who are con-
      cerned about Negro problems, and who have tried to do
      something about it. What about the gentlemen who made
      the trip south and was killed in Gaston, Alabama?

M.   We are not interested in these little white individuals. Lin-
      coln was supposed to have been sincere in his efforts to solve
      the problem and today the students of Lincoln agree that he
      was a hypocrite who wasn't interested in freeing the black
      people. He was posing as a liberal. He was interested in
      saving the Union and he said that if he could keep them
      slaves and save the Union he would keep them slaves and if
      he had to let them go to save the Union he would let them
      go. . . . He was interested in perpetuating the power of the
      white man. . . . Also the Emancipation Proclamation
      wasn't designed to free the Negro. If it was, we would be
      free. We wouldn't still be around here begging for civil
      rights. The Thirteenth and Fourteenth Amendments were
      other acts by white liberals that didn't solve our problems
      because if they were enacted in sincerity, we wouldn't have
      the problem today. Then you have nine more hypocrites
      posing as Supreme Court justices who came up with the so-
      called desegregation decision in 1954, which was nothing
      but a doctrine of hypocrisy because those judges, who were
      masters of the English language and legal phraseology, if
      they really wanted the black man to be desegregated in this
      country on an educational basis, they would have come up

and worded that decision in a legal terminology. They would have made it impossible for the crackers in the South to sidestep it. . . . When black people begin to see that, they will get away from that white man and elect leaders themselves, and select leaders themselves, and get together among ourselves and try to solve this problem ourselves instead of waiting around here depending on these hypocrites.

I.   In talking about problems here, how about the Birmingham situation? I understand the Muslim approach would have been different to that particular situation.

M.   We don't force ourselves upon people where we are not wanted, but anybody who sics their dog on us is nothing but a dog who will sic his dog on you, and anybody who sics a dog on children and babies is nothing but a dog himself.

I.   Would Muslims have struck back on this occasion?

M.   I think you will find a Muslim never attacks anyone, but that Muslim is within his God-given right to retaliate against anyone who attacks him. He is never to be the aggressor, but the Holy Koran teaches us to fight against those who fight against us.

I.   History has proven itself down through the years that in a situation like this that when you strike back you tend to start a riot.

M.   No, you can't call a man defending his home a rioter. You can't call a man who is defending his babies and his children and his women, a rioter. You call the rioter the one who is attacking—those white people down there, who are policemen in uniform. The law itself is what is attacking our people and that law in Alabama could never attack black people unless the Federal Government of the United States condones it, and it is not the crackers in the South who are responsible for this . . . it is the President, the Attorney General, the Senators and the Congressmen and the Cabinet and the Supreme Court who are responsible for it.

I.   Dr. King's approach in Birmingham has been one of non-violence.

M. His approach has been one of an Uncle Tom.

I. We have seen as the results of the talks they have had in the past couple days where there have been some results.

M. You can't call it results when someone has bitten your babies and your women and your children and you are to sit down and compromise with them and negotiate with them and then have to pay your way out of prison.

I. We are not talking about the past now. We are talking about what has been provided for the Negro in the Birmingham area for the future.

M. Nothing has been provided for the Negro in the future in the Birmingham area. They have been given promises that they will be able to sit down and drink some coffee with some crackers in a cracker restaurant—desegregated lunch counters. Now, what kind of advancement is that. They still don't have a job.

I. How do you feel about mixing of the races?

M. We are one hundred percent against inter-marriage and the mixing of the races.

I. How do you account for the mixing of the races within your own membership?

M. What do you mean within our own membership?

I. Some of the members that you have are not full-blood Negroes.

M. This did not come through inter-marriage. This came when the white man owned our people during slavery. He was able to take advantage of our women at will. My mother, grandmother, and great-grandmother were the property of the white man.

I. . . . How do you feel about the efforts of the NAACP insofar as improving the relationship is concerned, the advancement of the Negro and so forth?

M. The NAACP has done a job according to its own understanding. I imagine it was effective in its day. But we are living in a new day now and the black people on the scene now aren't willing to wait around here for a white man to make up his mind that we are human beings. The whites don't have to go to the Supreme Court or before the President for freedom. I don't see where black people should have to wait for some presidential proclamation or some senator or congressman to make up his mind that we are free.

I.   One final question, Mr. MALCOLM X, why the use of the "X"?

M.   X stands for the unknown, and if a Chinese were to walk in here with the name of Patrick Murphy you would think he was crazy because Patrick Murphy is an Irish name, a white man's name, and a Chinaman is a yellow man and has no business with a white man's name. And as a yellow man has no business with a white man's name, I don't see how these black people can walk around here calling themselves Murphy, Johnson and Bunche and Powell, which are actually white people's names. So the Honorable ELIJAH MUHAMMAD teaches us that during slavery the white man named us after himself to specify us as his property, and when we wake up and turn back toward the education of Islam and become Muslims, we give him back his name, we give him back his religion, we give him back his flag and everything else that goes with it.

———————— • •————————

TRUE COPY

September 19, 1963

Mr. J. Edgar Hoover
Federal Bureau of Investigation
Washington, D. C.
Dear Mr. Hoover:

Are we doing anything to curb the activities of Black Muslim leader "Malcolm X"?

Aren't his ideas somewhat on a parallel with those of Adolph Hitler?

Isn't "Malcolm X" in the category of traitors to our country in that what he is advocating in black supremacy is the same as plotting to overthrow our government?

Why isn't this hate-full man stopped now before it's too late?

[BUREAU DELETION]

September 23, 1963

[BUREAU DELETION]

Dear [BUREAU DELETION]
Your letter of September 19, 1963, with enclosure, has been received.

I am unable to answer your specific inquiry due to the confidential nature of our files. I would like to assure you, however, that the FBI is carrying out its responsibilities in the internal security field with the same dispatch and thoroughness which have characterized our investigations in the past.

Sincerely yours,
John Edgar Hoover
Director

NOTE: Correspondent is not identifiable in Bureau files.

UNITED STATES DEPARTMENT OF JUSTICE FEDERAL BUREAU OF INVESTIGATION

[BUREAU DELETION]

Report of: [BUREAU DELETION] b7C   Office: New York, New York

Date: 11/15/63

Field Office File No.: 105-8999   Bureau file No.: 100-399321

Title: MALCOLM K. LITTLE

Character: INTERNAL SECURITY - NATION OF ISLAM

Synopsis:

Subject continues to reside 23-11 97th Street, East Elmhurst, Queens, NY, and is Minister of Muhammad's Mosque No. 7,

NYC, and is also a national representative of the NOI. Subject served as an Interim Minister of the NOI in Washington, D. C., from April to 10/63. Since 8/26/63, a new regular minister has been placed in charge of the NOI in Philadelphia, Pa., and subject is no longer in charge of the NOI there. Subject's NOI activity and speeches at NYC and around the U.S. set forth. Sources report animosity between subject and members of ELIJAH MUHAMMAD's family has apparently quieted down. Subject's public appearances, statements and activities around the U.S. including those dealing with the racial situation, set out. Subject reported to be in contact with representative of SIERRA LEONE Mission to the UN.

Animosity Between Subject and the Family of ELIJAH MUHAMMAD

On several dates during March, April and May, 1963, [BUREAU DELETION] advised that there continued to be a feeling of hostility and resentment between subject and members of ELIJAH MUHAMMAD's family.

According to [BUREAU DELETION] this animosity was particularly aggravated by an article which appeared in an April edition of the *New York Times* to the effect that subject overshadowed ELIJAH MUHAMMAD, and was taking over the NOI from ELIJAH who was ill.

In May, 1963, [BUREAU DELETION] advised that this animosity has apparently quieted down during this month since subject had written an apologetic letter to ELIJAH MUHAMMAD and ELIJAH had told subject that they should not be divided but should work together.

Statements and Activities Relative to Racial Matters

The May 15, 1963 edition of the *New York Herald Tribune* contained an article datelined Birmingham, Alabama, which indicated that JEREMIAH X, a black Muslim from Atlanta, was in Birmingham observing the racial trouble there. JEREMIAH X condemned MARTIN LUTHER KING's non-violent movement and he claimed that subject was coming to Birmingham to hold mass rallies there.

[BUREAU DELETION] by a Special Agent (SA) of the Federal Bureau of Investigation (FBI), it was determined that subject did not plan on going to Birmingham as indicated in the above article. It was further determined that subject had not been ordered to Birmingham by ELIJAH MUHAMMAD or specifically invited there by JEREMIAH X, the head of the NOI in that area.

The May 17, 1963 edition of the *New York Times* contained an article datelined Washington, D. C., May 16, 1963, which reflected that subject attacked President KENNEDY for the manner in which he dealt with the Birmingham racial crisis. Subject claimed that President KENNEDY's statement to Alabama editors in a recent meeting with them, that failure of the non-violent movement for Negro rights might spur Negro extremist groups such as the black Muslims, indicated that President KENNEDY did not want Negroes treated right because it was right, but because the world was watching.

The May 25, 1963 edition of the *New York Amsterdam News* contained an article which reflected that in an interview with subject at Washington, D. C., subject had attacked MARTIN LUTHER KING, JACKIE ROBINSON, and FLOYD PATTERSON as unwitting tools of white liberals. Subject claimed that the lesson of Birmingham is that "Negroes have lost their fear of the white man's reprisals and will react today with violence, if provoked."

On June 13, 1963, [BUREAU DELETION] advised that subject had been instructed by ELIJAH MUHAMMAD not to take part or assist the NAACP or any other Negro organization in their demonstrations for civil rights.

On [BUREAU DELETION] 1963, [BUREAU DELETION] advised that in subject's speech at the NOI Bazaar held at the Boston Arena, Boston, Massachusetts, on August 17, 1963, subject had informed the audience that ELIJAH MUHAMMAD and the NOI are in no way supporting or participating in the March on Washington being held by civil rights groups in Washington, D. C., on August 28, 1963. During this speech subject warned that the March would probably end in a bloodbath, and no Negro should be foolish enough to participate.

At an FOI meeting held in MUHAMMAD's Mosque No. 7, New York City, on August 19, 1963, subject informed those in attendance that any members of the NOI who participated in the March on Washington on August 28, 1963, would be given ninety days out of the mosque. Subject further stated that if any member belonged to a union which required them to participate in the March, they had better "get sick."

This document contains neither recommendations nor conclusions of any kind. It is the property of the FBI, and is a loan to your agency; it and/or its contents are not to be distributed outside your agency.

[BUREAU DELETION]

——————— • •———————

(IS) 25-330971

Date: December 6, 1963
To: Chief, U. S. Secret Service
From: John Edgar Hoover, Director
Subject: NATION OF ISLAM
            INTERNAL SECURITY-NOI

[BUREAU DELETION] had confirmed reports that Malcolm X Little, Minister of the Nation of Islam (NOI) Temple in New York City, and leading NOI spokesman, had been suspended from the NOI on December 4, 1963 by Elijah Muhammad for expressing joy over the death of President Kennedy.

Malcolm X Little, who spoke at a rally held by the NOI in New York City on December 1, 1963, stated that the late President Kennedy had been "twiddling his thumbs" at the slaying of South Vietnamese President Ngo Dinh Diem and his brother, Ngo Dinh Nhu. Little added that he "never foresaw that the chickens would come home to roost so soon." He also stated, "Being an old farm boy myself, chickens coming home to roost never did make me sad; they always made me glad." Elijah Muhammad, National Leader of the NOI, was scheduled to speak at this New York rally but canceled his appearance out of respect to the death of President Kennedy and instructed NOI members to make no comments concerning the assassination of the President.

The NOI is an all-Negro, anti-white, semi-religious organization which advocates complete separation of the races and teaches extreme hatred of all white men.

UNITED STATES GOVERNMENT
M E M O R A N D U M

TO: DIRECTOR, FBI (25-330971-38)   DATE: 1/23/64

FROM: SAC, PHOENIX (105-93)
SUBJECT: NATION OF ISLAM
           IS-NOI

[BUREAU DELETION] made available the following information on the dates designated:

1/2/64

ELIJAH MUHAMMAD, MALCOLM LITTLE, [BUREAU DELETION] and another individual [BUREAU DELETION] were in a conversation at which time ELIJAH gave a long religious talk using many parables. ELIJAH told of the great power of Allah and how he has followed everything Allah has told him. He mentioned how Allah has let him know in advance of many things. ELIJAH told them that he is just a man as the rest of them with a message from Allah. He said the people make a great man such as he is now. He stated if he [sic]people understand his mission as well as the devils do everything would be all right. ELIJAH mentioned the President's assassination and MALCOLM's New York speech. He said he feels Allah when everything is right and he knows this is good. He talked about

Moses, Jesus and so forth. He mentioned about after he put
MALCOLM down from public speaking how the devils had
called hinting there was a split between ELIJAH and MAL-
COLM, and ELIJAH told them there was not. ELIJAH told
how he helped MALCOLM in his statements to the press when
MALCOLM first started speaking in Harlem. He said he had
been hearing about MALCOLM this and MALCOLM that and
even MALCOLM being called leader. ELIJAH said now this one
and that one is getting jealous. He told MALCOLM that MAL-
COLM was ELIJAH's property to which MALCOLM agreed.
He told MALCOLM he had made an error. MALCOLM stated
he had asked permission in a letter before he said anything and
he understood it was all right. ELIJAH said he could not understand why MALCOLM took this poison and poured it out and
told them it was poison. He told MALCOLM that one cannot
use fire to fight fire. He said all of the time MALCOLM had been
referring to something else and ELIJAH thought he had a sly
scheme or shrewd plan but not this time. ELIJAH stated we
can't organize the man. He said if anyone had told him that
MALCOLM was going to use things like that he would not have
believed it. He told MALCOLM if he loved Allah then he must
love ELIJAH as the messenger of Allah. MALCOLM stated he
would rather be dead than to say anything against ELIJAH.
MALCOLM said he didn't say anything to anyone about ELI-
JAH and had been using parables to speak. ELIJAH asked
MALCOLM how could [BUREAU DELETION] have gotten
the wrong impression from what MALCOLM had said. ELIJAH
stated they all wrote to him and said the same thing. He told
MALCOLM he could not walk through the woods with fire in
his hands and not start a fire. He said one must carry a bucket of
water and not fire.

ELIJAH stated he had to speak out on KENNEDY's death as
the whole nation would have been against them. MALCOLM
agreed. ELIJAH mentioned even some of the sympathetic devils
were outraged at MALCOLM's statement.

ELIJAH asked MALCOLM why MALCOLM had been
checking into ELIJAH's personal affairs [BUREAU DELE-
TION]. MALCOLM stated that he had not asked anything

about this but had heard it in Chicago. MALCOLM said he talked to [BUREAU DELETION] about it and he already knew it. MALCOLM said he noticed the people in Chicago were very cold to ELIJAH's family in Chicago on Savior's Day (apparently referring to February, 1963). MALCOLM said [BUREAU DELETION]asked him to eat with him that night and brought the matter up. [BUREAU DELETION] told him (MALCOLM) about it and he, MALCOLM, acted as if he knew nothing about it. MALCOLM said [BUREAU DELETION] had stated a lost-found sister in Boston had said the FBI had asked her about it, and told [BUREAU DELETION]. MALCOLM mentioned [BUREAU DELETION] told him, the person she planned on marrying, about this. This brother told [BUREAU DELETION] who called and told [BUREAU DELETION] in New York. MALCOLM stated he called and told [BUREAU DELETION] back (apparently in Boston) and told him he had put pressure on the sister and made her say these things which she did not mean. MALCOLM said he told [BUREAU DELETION] to drop it and that he, MALCOLM, never discussed it with anyone else. ELIJAH told MALCOLM he could not prove any of this. MAL-COLM said he thought ELIJAH had tried to tell MALCOLM of this one time in Phoenix. MALCOLM mentioned ELIJAH asked him what he, MALCOLM, thought of [BUREAU DELETION] and that MALCOLM changed the subject because he was afraid to hear it. MALCOLM said he told [BUREAU DELETION] he thought it would be a good idea to tell some of their trusted people so they would be in a receptive spirit if they heard of it from any of the people and could handle the matter. MAL-COLM told [BUREAU DELETION] he was going to write ELIJAH and tell what [BUREAU DELETION] reaction would be and he hoped ELIJAH would allow MALCOLM to tell others who would understand it too. ELIJAH spoke about how some people have said that he and [BUREAU DELETION] are sepa-rated but that they are not. ELIJAH said he cannot stay in Chicago because of the pressure on him all of the time and because of the weather. He said one of them must stay there all of the time so she stays there in Chicago and ELIJAH lives in Phoenix be-cause of the good weather.

SECTION 10

January 29, 1964–April 15, 1964

Section 10 outlines Malcolm's 1964 activities until his trip to Africa in April. Early in 1964, the division between Malcolm and Elijah continued to widen. In January, Malcolm spent some time in Florida with Cassius Clay, as Clay prepared to meet Sonny Liston for the heavyweight boxing championship. Although he had been silenced, Malcolm still served as spiritual advisor to the victorious Clay, who soon changed his name to Muhammad Ali. Malcolm also valued his friendship during the difficult period of his suspension, as he reflects in his autobiography.

Cassius Clay and I are not together today. But I always must be grateful to him at just this time, when he was in

Miami training to fight Sonny Liston, Cassius invited me,
Betty, and the children to come there as his guests—as a
sixth anniversary present to Betty and me. (p.303)

On March 8, Malcolm declared his break with the NOI and
his desire to form his own "politically oriented black nationalist
party." The FBI had already received information that he was
planning to leave the NOI, predicated on an informant's belief
that Malcolm might oppose the NOI leadership of Elijah
Muhammad with Clay's support.

Ali remained loyal to Elijah Muhammad, who harshly criticized Malcolm's creation of the Muslim Mosque, Inc. (MMI).
Elijah Muhammad predicted that Malcolm "would not be successful and he will come running back and ask to be forgiven."
The report notes that the NOI soon began eviction procedures to
reclaim Malcolm's house in East Elmhurst, Queens, and Elijah
warned Malcolm to stop interfering with NOI affairs. Amidst the
mounting activity, tension, and threats, Malcolm journeyed to
Africa and Asia, where he made his pilgrimage to Mecca. In his
autobiography, Malcolm reported:

I left New York quietly (little realizing that I was going to
return noisily). Few people were told I was leaving at all. I
didn't want some State Department or other roadblocks put
in my way at the last minute. Only my wife, Betty, and my
three girls and a few close associates came with me to Kennedy International Airport. (p.320)

FBI
Date: 1/29/64

Transmit the following in_____
(Type in plain text or code)

Via____AIRTEL____   _____
(Priority or Method of Mailing)

TO: DIRECTOR, FBI (100-399321)
FROM: SAC, NEW YORK (105-8999)
SUBJECT: MALCOLM K. LITTLE AKA
            Malcolm X, Malcolm Shabazz,
            Malik El Shabazz, Malik
            Shabazz
            IS-NOI
            (OO:NEW YORK)
            Re Miami airtel dated 1/21/64.

For the information of Miami, local NYC newspapers have
recently carried stories which indicate that subject has spent a
week in Miami, Florida, vacationing with his wife BETTY, and
their three young daughters. According to the articles, subject

and his family were the guests of heavyweight contender CAS-
SIUS CLAY while in Miami.

CLAY and subject returned together by plane to NYC on 1/
21/64. That same evening, CLAY was the guest of honor and
speaker at a Dinner Social sponsored by the FOI and MGT of
Mosque No. 7, NYC, held in Rockland Palace, 8th Avenue and
155th St., NYC. Subject did not attend the affair, and CLAY
reportedly returned to Miami the following day. In a newspaper
interview CLAY advised that his managers did not know that he
was making this trip to NYC, and they were quite upset about it.

ˋ On 12/4/63, subject was temporarily suspended by NOI leader
ELIJAH MUHAMMAD for remarks subject made in NYC on
12/1/63, relative to the assassination of former President KEN-
NEDY. Since then subject has been forbidden to speak in public
and has not outwardly engaged in any NOI activity, although he
is still considered the Minister of Mosque No. 7. He has spent his
time relaxing in his Queens home and working on a book about
the NOI. [BUREAU DELETION] in New York did not know of
his trip to Miami.

————————• •————————

FEDERAL BUREAU OF INVESTIGATION

Date_____2/5/64_____

ˋMalcolm Little advised he is generally known as Malcolm X
and resides at 23-11 97th Street, Queens, New York City. He
stated that until sometime in December, 1963, he was the Minister in charge of the Nation of Islam (NOI) Mosque in New York
City. In December, 1963, he was suspended by ELIJAH
MUHAMMAD from his duties. He would not say the reason for
his suspension or its duration. He stated that any comment on
this would have to come from ELIJAH MUHAMMAD.

He stated that his suspension from duties caused him to reap-
praise his loyalty to the NOI and ELIJAH MUHAMMAD. He
stated that because of his suspension, he is now more firmly devoted to ELIJAH MUHAMMAD than ever. He pointed out that
his suspension proves that the rules of the NOI apply to everyone
equally. He stated he is in no way bitter towards ELIJAH

MUHAMMAD and that anything that might have caused his suspension was entirely his own fault and he could blame no one else.

He stated that the NOI cooperates with the United States government more than any other Negro organization in that the NOI stops members from smoking, drinking, and committing crimes and many other things which result in a benefit to the United States government but which the government is unable or unwilling to do itself. Because of this, the NOI is the only group that really benefits the Negroes. He pointed out that other Negro groups do not have a program which will benefit the Negro and eventually the Negro will realize this. He stated that when the Negro realizes that the government, white people and so-called Negro leaders are not really helping the Negro or obtaining for the Negro the things which he wants or should have, then the Negro will start helping himself to these things. He did not care to explain this except by stating that at that time there could be a great deal of trouble.

He stated that the so-called Negro leaders are incompetent to lead the Negroes and stated that BAYARD RUSTIN, who was a leader of the one-day school boycott in New York City on February 3, 1964, is nothing but a homosexual. He furnished no other information on either RUSTIN or any other person he considered a Negro leader. He reiterated that he is cooperating with the government in view of the principles of the NOI but to suggest any other means of cooperation was an insult to his intelligence. He stated the teachings of the NOI are public and are well known to the Government. He stated he had no information concerning membership of the NOI, either as to numbers or names and even if he did have such information, he was not disposed to furnish it to the government.

He stated that he would have no objection to being contacted by the Federal Bureau of Investigation regarding demonstrations or other public affairs contemplated by the NOI. He stated he realized that in the past the NOI has been blamed for a number of incidents with which they were, in fact, not involved. He stated he would be most willing to be contacted in order to clear up any such possible misunderstanding.

23-11 97th Street
On___2/4/64___at___Queens, New York City___File #___NY 105-8999___
by___SAS [BUREAU DELETION] and [BUREAU DELE-TION]___
Date dictated ___2/5/64___

———————. •———————

February 10, 1964

The Rift Widens Between Elijah Muhammad
and his Principal Lieutenant Malcolm X Little

The rift between Elijah Muhammad, self-proclaimed Messenger of Allah and the leader of the fanatical Black Muslim hate group, and his erstwhile Lieutenant Malcolm X Little appears to be widening. Little was silenced officially and publicly by Muhammad a short while after President Kennedy's assassination inasmuch as Little had made stupid and ill-timed remarks to the effect that President Kennedy's death gave him pleasure.

Little has not taken this disciplinary action gracefully and he has attempted to develop sympathy and backing for his position among other leaders of the Black Muslims in various sections of the country. He evidently feels that Elijah Muhammad is in his declining years and that he is slipping. It is no secret that Little would not hesitate one moment to take over the leadership of the Nation of Islam (NOI) and incidentally begin living in the regal style which Elijah Muhammad enjoys. While Muhammad may be getting older, he is far from ready to hand over the reins of the NOI and all the affluent service benefits that go with it to Little. Muhammad is reportedly fuming at the temerity Little has exhibited in questioning the "Messenger's" judgment and it would not surprise anyone at all familiar with the works of the NOI to see Little summarily expelled from this organization if he continues to buck the orders and wishes of Elijah Muhammad.

—————. .—————

FBI

Date: 3/3/64

Transmit the following in_____

(Type in plain text or code)

Via____AIRTEL_____   AIR MAIL—

REGISTERED MAIL

(Priority or Method of Mailing)

TO: DIRECTOR, FBI (100-399321)
FROM: SAC, MIAMI (105-8554) (P)
SUBJECT: MALCOLM K. LITTLE, aka
           IS-NOI
           (OO:NEW YORK)

[BUREAU DELETION] of the recent publicity given the NOI in the Miami area in connection with the "LISTON-CLAY fight" [BUREAU DELETION]. He said the Hampton House is the logical gathering place in Miami for any visiting NOI official or other prominent Negroes. [BUREAU DELETION]

[BUREAU DELETION] MALCOLM X stayed at the Hampton House during that period and was to leave on 2/27/64. While there MALCOLM X was in contact with [BUREAU DELETION].

[BUREAU DELETION] MALCOLM X had conferences with CASSIUS CLAY and his brother, RUDOLPH, and he tried to instill confidence in CLAY prior to the fight. He also reported that MALCOLM X said he would return to Miami in March, 1964, and also made the statement, "If you think CASSIUS CLAY was loud, wait until I start talking on the first of March."

[BUREAU DELETION] believed MALCOLM X might oppose the NOI leadership of ELIJAH MUHAMMAD with the assistance of CLAY in the near future.

UNITED STATES DEPARTMENT OF JUSTICE
FEDERAL BUREAU OF INVESTIGATION

New York, New York
March 9, 1964
Malcolm K. Little
Internal Security - Nation of Islam

The March 9, 1964 edition of the *New York Times,* a daily newspaper published in New York, New York, contained an article on page 1 entitled "Malcolm X Splits With Muhammad." It is noted that Little is publicly known as "Malcolm X."

The article reflected that on the night of March 8, 1964, Little announced that he had broken with Elijah Muhammad's Black Muslim movement and he would organize a politically oriented "black nationalist party."

According to the article, Little claimed that he was still a Muslim "but the main emphasis of the new movement will be black nationalism as a political concept and form of social action against the oppressors." Little stated the party would seek to convert the Negro population from non-violence to active self-defense against white supremacists in all parts of the country.

Little stated that he would accept speaking engagements at colleges and universities, and would cooperate in local civil rights actions in the South and elsewhere in order to heighten the political consciousness of the Negroes and intensify their identification against white society. Little claimed that he has already accepted an invitation to help a civil rights committee in Plaquemines Parish, Louisiana.

Little stated, according to the article, that his first task would be to construct an organization based in New York. He claimed support from many Negro intellectuals and professionals who could not accept Islam but accepted the Black Muslim view of race relations in the United States.

Little claimed that he had not been invited to the annual Black Muslim convention in Chicago on February 26, 1964, and he could not get a clarification of his suspension status from Elijah

Muhammad. Consequently, he decided that he could best spread
Mr. Muhammad's message by staying out of the Nation of Islam
(NOI) and working on his own among non-Muslim Negroes. He
further claimed that he was not trying to split the Muslims, and
advised all NOI members to remain in the NOI, stating that he
was not encouraging them to follow him. Little also claimed that
his suspension was due to the jealousy of Elijah Muhammad's
family aroused by his previous popularity.
[BUREAU DELETION]

This document contains neither recommendations nor
conclusions of any kind. It is the property of the FBI, and is
a loan to your agency; it and/or its contents are not to be
distributed outside your agency.

———————— • •————————

3/12/64
AIRTEL   AIR MAIL - REGISTERED MAIL

TO: DIRECTOR, FBI (25-330971-33)
FROM: SAC, PHOENIX (105-93)

NATION OF ISLAM
IS-NOI
On 3/9/64, [BUREAU DELETION] made available the fol-
lowing information:

[BUREAU DELETION] spoke about the other situation and
said that he (believed referring to MALCOLM LITTLE) has
definitely given it to the news media and that MALCOLM was
on the TV "Today" show. ELIJAH stated he could hardly believe it at first, but actually it turned out to be the truth. ELIJAH
stated he had [BUREAU DELETION] to contact him (MAL-
COLM) and [BUREAU DELETION] said that he (MAL-
COLM) told him that he had not given up Islam. ELIJAH said
he wrote MALCOLM the previous week and told him that he

(MALCOLM) is drunk over publicity and leadership. ELIJAH stated he did not intend to give him (MALCOLM) the place (No. 7) back, no matter what he did. ELIJAH stated if he did do so, MALCOLM would set up a crew one hundred percent for him (MALCOLM) and not with them in Chicago. ELIJAH said "he wants to oppose us." ELIJAH stated MALCOLM thinks he is smart, but he (ELIJAH) has too much experience. He said the man is in danger going to an organization he has been criticizing. He said "who is going to back him up?" ELIJAH said no one. [BUREAU DELETION] stated the one who is working with MALCOLM is "MISHHAM" (phonetic). [BUREAU DELETION] stated when they all saw it in the paper, then they divided and they all want to be leaders. ELIJAH said MALCOLM would not be successful and he will come running back and ask to be forgiven. He said they will learn that Allah is with him (ELIJAH) and him alone. It will be a lesson for MALCOLM.

ELIJAH inquired about MALCOLM's house as to who bought it and who was paying the mortgage. [BUREAU DELETION] stated the Nation (NOI) is paying the mortgage and that the house belongs to ELIJAH and the mosque put down $5,000 and paid the note. [BUREAU DELETION] said the house is actually in the name of the mosque and even MALCOLM's car is also. ELIJAH told JOSEPH to send a letter or have the secretary send one to MALCOLM and tell him he must give up the house. ELIJAH suggested the letter be signed by [BUREAU DELETION] as well as several others at the mosque. He said they should demand that MALCOLM vacate the house and give up everything he has that belongs to Islam. [BUREAU DELETION] stated the only records he knew of that MALCOLM has would be the incorporation papers for the mosque. ELIJAH said MALCOLM should be asked to give them up also. ELIJAH stated the letter directed to MALCOLM should be notarized and signed by six or seven of the brothers. Upon speaking about the house that MALCOLM is living in ELIJAH told [BUREAU DELETION]. ELIJAH said [BUREAU DELETION] should not mention this until MALCOLM is out.

FEDERAL BUREAU OF INVESTIGATION

FD-72
(1-10-51)

FORM NO. 1
THIS CASE ORIGINATED AT   DETROIT   FILE NO.

REPORT MADE AT	DATE WHEN MADE	PERIOD FOR WHICH MADE	REPORT MADE BY
BOSTON	MAY 4 1953	3/20;4/1,3,6/53	BA

TITLE

MALCOLM X. LITTLE, was.
Malachi Shabazz; "Rythm Red"; "Detroit Red";
Jack Carlton

CHARACTER OF CASE

SECURITY MATTER-C
SECURITY MATTER-MCI

SYNOPSIS OF FACTS:

Little   *Little*

Subject resides at 4336 Williams Street, Inkster, Michigan. Subject claimed in June, 1950, that he was a Communist and during September, 1952, he indicated membership in the Muslim Cult of Islam.

-RUC-

DETAILS:-

This investigation was predicated upon information received from ████████
Norfolk, Massachusetts ████ to the effect that the Subject ████████ had written two letters ████ that included comments on Communism.

ALL INFORMATION CONTAINED
HEREIN IS UNCLASSIFIED
DATE 11/30/15 BA

I. BACKGROUND

Birth

████████ the Subject was born May 19, 1925, in Omaha, Nebraska, and is a citizen by virtue of his birth.

COPIES DESTROYED
173   JUL 23 1962

Employment

Information received from Boston Informant ████

APPROVED AND FORWARDED	SPECIAL AGENT IN CHARGE	DO NOT WRITE IN THESE SPACES

COPY IN FILE

COPIES OF THIS REPORT

5-Bureau
4-Detroit(100-21719
1-25-17462)
2-Boston (100-27649)

100-1399321 - 2   SE-15

MAY 8 1953

MAY 20 1953

The first page in the FBI file on Malcolm X; it states the Bureau's reason—two letters in which Malcolm refers to Communism—for opening its investigation.

Malcolm Little at fifteen sporting a zoot suit; the photo was taken in Boston. *Schomberg Center for Research in Black Culture*

Harlem's Hotel Theresa, at 125th Street and Seventh Avenue, where Malcolm headquartered his Muslim Mosque Incorporated. *AP/Wide World Photo*

Perhaps the most familiar studio photograph of Malcolm X.
Schomberg Center for Research in Black Culture

Malcolm X on the dais with Elijah Muhammad—the One True Messenger of Allah—and an unidentified sister at a meeting of the Nation of Islam. *Lawrence Henry Collection*

Malcolm (second from left) at an NOI dinner. Seated at his right is Minister James Shabazz, Temple of Islam No. 2, Chicago. Wallace Muhammad, son of Elijah Muhammad, sits at his immediate left, and Herbert Muhammad, another of Elijah Muhammad's sons, is third from Malcolm's left. *New York Amsterdam News Photo*

Malcolm X speaks. This photo was taken in Rev. Milton Galamiason's Shiloh Baptist Church in Harlem during the school desegregation demonstration, March 15, 1964. *Lawrence Henry Collection*

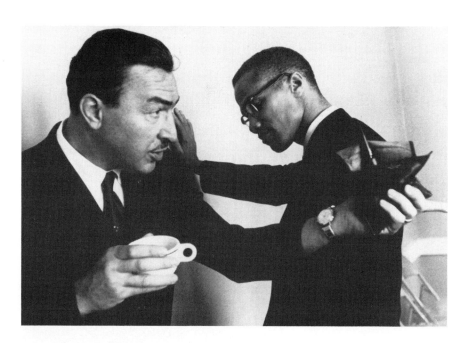

With Adam Clayton Powell during a coffee break at a Harlem rally. *Lawrence Henry Collection*

With Martin Luther King, Jr., on the only occasion the two actually met face to face. King had just completed a news conference in the U.S. Capitol; the date was March 24, 1964. *UPI*

Malcolm on the steps of the State Building in Albany, New York. He is flanked on his right by Charles Rangel and on his left by Percy Sutton, his friend and attorney. *E. M. Somers*

Malcolm in Africa during his last visit there in 1964.
Lawrence Henry Collection

UNITED STATES DEPARTMENT OF JUSTICE
FEDERAL BUREAU OF INVESTIGATION

New York, New York
March 11, 1964
Malcolm K. Little
Internal Security - Nation of Islam

On March 9, 1964, from 10:00 P.M. to 10:30 P.M., Little appeared on the news commentary and interview program "The World at Ten," television station WNDT, Channel 13, New York, New York. He was interviewed by WNDT commentator Joe Durso relative to his announcement on March 8, 1964, that he had split with the NOI.

During the interview Little specifically pointed out that he was not setting up a rival organization to the NOI. He stated that Islam was still his religion, he still believed in Allah, he still considered himself a follower of Elijah Muhammad, and he still considered the separation of races as taught by Muhammad as the solution to the race problem. He advised that he has decided that the best way to serve Muhammad was to stay out of the NOI and work on his own with non-Muslims. This way he will be free of NOI restrictions that previously kept him from reaching all Negroes, and he will urge them to follow Elijah Muhammad. He added that he can now do what "he" thinks is necessary to enlighten the people toward Muhammad and Islam. He stated he intended to teach a political, economic and social philosophy of black nationalism.

In regard to the current civil rights movement, Little predicted that the struggle would "explode" in 1964 and expressed the opinion that young Negroes are now willing to do anything for integration. He feels that if they are not protected in this activity, then they must take up arms. He specifically pointed out that he was not urging or teaching retaliation, only self-protection. As an example he cited the unsolved bombing of a Negro church in Birmingham that resulted in the death of four girls, and it was his opinion that Negroes (not specified) should solve this and other such wrongs and execute those responsible.

Little stated that he was only interested in "freedom, justice and equality" for Negroes. He added that they have not gotten it by being polite, and he feels that they should now get angry.

In regard to his suspension by Muhammad in December, 1963, for his remark concerning the assassination of former President Kennedy, Little advised that the suspension was not for the remark itself. He explained that the suspension was for his disobedience to Muhammad for making the remark, since Muhammad had told him not to comment on the assassination. He further stated that the suspension was originally for a ninety-day period, but he recently learned from Muhammad that it would be for an indefinite period. Consequently, he decided to stay out of the NOI and speak out on his own.

UNITED STATES DEPARTMENT OF JUSTICE
FEDERAL BUREAU OF INVESTIGATION

New York, New York
March 13, 1964
Muslim Mosque, Incorporated
Internal Security - Miscellaneous

On March 12, 1964, Malcolm K. Little, known generally as Malcolm X, held a press conference at 11:00 A.M. in the Tapestry Suite of the Park Sheraton Hotel, 7th Avenue and 55th Street, New York, New York. Approximately sixty persons attended the conference.

Malcolm X opened his press conference by reading a telegram he had sent to Elijah Muhammad on March 11, 1964. In this telegram he indicated that he had not left the NOI of his own free will, but had been pressured out by a conspiracy between Captain Joseph (Gravitt) in New York and national NOI officials at the Chicago Headquarters of the NOI.

Malcolm X continued his press conference by reading a prepared statement.

Editor's note. *Malcolm's prepared statement first of all clarifies his position as a Muslim and as a separatist. No longer a member of the Nation of Islam but a Muslim nonetheless, Malcolm affirms that he still believes Elijah Muhammad's solution to the plight of black people to be the best—i.e. complete separation of the blacks from white America and a return to their African homeland. He also sees it, however, as a long-range plan, and meanwhile twenty-two million American blacks are wanting for adequate food, clothing, housing, education and jobs. These problems demand solutions here and now.*

Because he is no longer a member of the Nation of Islam (and not by his own free will, he points out), Malcolm feels he can take a more independent and flexible approach to the problems of black Americans. He does "not pretend to be a divine man," he says, nor is he an educated man or "an expert in any particular field . . . but I am sincere," he adds, "and my sincerity are my credentials."

Malcolm would use all his personal resources, it would appear, not "to fight other Negro leaders or organizations," but to "find a common approach, a common solution, to a common problem." He continues by emphasizing that "the problem facing our people here in America is bigger than all other personal or organizational differences. Therefore, as leaders, we must stop worrying about the threat that we seem to think we pose to each other's personal prestige, and concentrate our united efforts toward solving the unending hurt that is being done daily to our people here in America."

Malcolm then declares his intent to organize a new mosque in New York. It will be called the Muslim Mosque, Incorporated, and will provide a religious, cultural and moral base for members of the black community. Black Nationalism, he asserts, will be the Mosque's economic, social and political philosophy, which means in essence that blacks themselves "must control the politics and politicians of [their] community." Malcolm also calls for the accent to be upon youth and "new ideas, new methods, new approaches." Because established politicians have failed to solve the problems long facing

American blacks, Malcolm says he wants "to see some new faces . . . more militant faces."

Although at this time Malcolm would not refuse financial aid from whites, he would not as yet allow them into the Mosque membership. "There can be no black-white unity until there is first some black unity," he explains, and "there can be no workers solidarity until there is first some racial solidarity."

Malcolm also speaks briefly to the point of nonviolence. Black people are being forced to be violent; they must fight back, he says, because they are constantly being victimized. As firearms are legal and as he would have his people obey the law, Malcolm advocates forming "rifle clubs" so that blacks can defend themselves and their property when emergencies arise and the government fails to protect them.

Malcolm concludes by challenging that government; if it finds his solution to the problems wrong, then let the government start doing its job, he advises.

Malcolm X then responded to questions from the various news representatives present, furnishing the following information:

Re Muslim Mosque, Incorporated
The mosque would have temporary headquarters at the Hotel Theresa, 2090 Seventh Avenue (at 125th Street), New York, New York, and there are no present plans for any mosque outside of New York City.

He would not have gone out on his own if he had not received evidence of support. He stated that in the last several days he had received numerous calls from all over the country offering him support and asking him to speak. Malcolm X stated he would make absolutely no effort to draw away any of the followers of Elijah Muhammad, but some NOI members have come over to him. He refused to reveal the number of NOI members who have come over to him, nor would he reveal the total number of his followers or identify them by name. He also stated that his mosque would have the same moral standards as the NOI. He stated that he would retain his name "Malcolm X" which he had obtained in the NOI.

Malcolm X also announced that his mosque would hold a "restricted" meeting at 8:30 P.M., Sunday, March 15, 1964, at the George Washington Carver Club, Amsterdam Avenue and 145th Street, New York City.

--------------• •--------------

UNITED STATES DEPARTMENT OF JUSTICE FEDERAL BUREAU OF INVESTIGATION

Chicago, Illinois
March 27, 1964
NATION OF ISLAM
INTERNAL SECURITY -
NATION OF ISLAM

The Nation of Islam (NOI), has not been designated pursuant to Executive Order 10450 and is characterized in later pages.

In late March, 1964, [BUREAU DELETION] advised as follows:

Elijah Muhammad was told by officials of the NOI that Malcolm Little had, on March 23, 1964, sent six of his followers to see one of the leaders of Elijah Muhammad's mosque in New York City with instructions to tell him what to do and what not to do. Muhammad instructed that the police in New York City be notified that Little was interfering and that they should be told of the consequences which might come from acts of this type. Muhammad stated that if the law will not put a stop to this "our own should be told to do it."

Muhammad was also told by NOI leaders that Malcolm Little was using his name, was pretending to be in good with him, and was only feuding with his, Muhammad's, family.

Muhammad stated he had instructed Malcolm Little's brother in Detroit, Michigan, to talk to Malcolm because Malcolm was going to get himself in trouble at the rate he was going.

———————— . ————————

UNITED STATES DEPARTMENT OF JUSTICE
FEDERAL BUREAU OF INVESTIGATION

Boston, Massachusetts
April 3, 1964

MUSLIM MOSQUE, INCORPORATED

On March 19, 1964, [BUREAU DELETION] Harvard University, Cambridge, Massachusetts, advised that Malcolm X spoke at Leverett House, Harvard University, on March 18, 1964. The occasion was one of the periodic seminars held at Leverett House, and Malcolm X's appearance was arranged by a teaching fellow at Harvard University, [BUREAU DELETION].

According [BUREAU DELETION] Malcolm X stated that he was starting a new movement which he believes will change this country's foreign and domestic policies by giving Negroes political, social and economic philosophy.

Malcolm X stated his new movement is not "anti anything." He wants the black man to control the politics in his own residential areas by voting, helping to choose and to support their own candidates. He wishes them to become economically sound by owning and investing in the businesses within the Negro areas, and he feels that they should become socially sound by complete separation from white people and organizing their own separate society: He proceeded that the Negro has become disillusioned with non-violent action and would be ready for any action which will get immediate results in their goal for civil rights. Malcolm X stated that the Negro realizes he is being exploited and lied to and is sick of it.

[BUREAU DELETION] made available the following information on March 25, 1964.

The "Bob Kennedy Show," a program of Radio Station WBZ, Boston, Massachusetts, which is run nightly from 6:30 P.M. to 8 P.M., on March 24, 1964, had as its guest speaker Malcolm X

Shabazz, identified as having been the spokesman for Elijah Muhammad, leader of the Black Muslims, until recently silenced by Elijah Muhammad. The subject of the program on that evening was to be "Negro—Separation and Supremacy."

ꞏMalcolm X was questioned as to whether or not his being silenced by Elijah Muhammad was actually the result of a statement he had made shortly after the death of President John F. Kennedy or whether Elijah Muhammad had "dismissed" him because he was getting too popular with the Muslims and threatened the leadership of Elijah Muhammad, and this leadership being passed on to Elijah Muhammad's son and son-in-law.ꞏ

ꞏMalcolm X stated that his statement, "The chicken had gone home to roost," when mentioning the death of President John F. Kennedy had been taken out of context.ꞏ He stated that at the time the topic of his talk was "God's Judgment on White America"; he had been trying to demonstrate that white America was reaping the harvest of the seed she had sown and had been using incidents all over the world to illustrate this. His remark about "the chicken had gone home to roost" was meant as another illustration of the misfortunes that had come to the United States and was not meant to show any kind of relief over the unfortunate death of the President.ꞏ

He stated that all these incidents that he was using as illustrations were merely prophecies of the Bible coming true and that he had pointed out he was happy to see these prophecies coming true, and he did not mean that he was happy about the death of the president.

———— ꞏ ꞏ ————

FEDERAL BUREAU OF INVESTIGATION
U. S. DEPARTMENT OF JUSTICE

COMMUNICATIONS SECTION

APRIL 14, 1964
TELETYPE

CODED TELETYPE
4-01 PM URGENT 4-14-64
TO DIRECTOR /4/ /100-399321/

FROM NEW YORK /105-8999/
  MALCOLM K. LITTLE, AKA
  IS-NOI
  LITTLE, UNDER ALIAS MALIK SHABAZZ, WITH
PASSPORT NUMBER C TWO NINE FOUR TWO SEVEN
FIVE, DEPARTED JFK INTERNATIONAL AIRPORT,
NYC, AT SEVEN O-CLOCK PM, APRIL THIRTEEN, LAST,
ABOARD LUFTHANSA GERMAN AIRLINE FLIGHT
FOUR ZERO ONE FOR FRANKFURT, GERMANY. TO
DEPART FRANKFURT ON APRIL FOURTEEN IN-
STANT, FOR CAIRO, EGYPT. LITTLE HAS ONE WAY
TICKET WITH ITINERARY: NEW YORK TO FRANK-
FURT, TO CAIRO, TO JEDDA, SAUDI ARABIA, TO
CAIRO. RETURN DATE UNKNOWN. LITTLE AN-
NOUNCED AT MUSLIM MOSQUE, INC., RALLY ON
APRIL TWELVE, LAST THAT HE WOULD MAKE THREE
WEEK AFRICAN TOUR EXPECTING TO LEAVE ON
APRIL SIXTEEN NEXT. LHM FOLLOWS.
END
JS
FBI WASH, DC

UNITED STATES DEPARTMENT OF JUSTICE
FEDERAL BUREAU OF INVESTIGATION

New York, New York
April 15, 1964
Malcolm K. Little
Internal Security - Nation of Islam

On April 14, 1964 [BUREAU DELETION] advised that one
"Shabazz" departed John F. Kennedy International Airport,
New York City, aboard their flight number 401 at 7:00 P.M.,
April 13, 1964.

This flight was to Frankfurt, Germany, where "Shabazz" was
scheduled to make connections for Cairo, Egypt, with Middle
East Airlines. "Shabazz" would depart Frankfurt aboard flight

number 788 of the latter airline at 5:35 P.M., April 14, 1964, due
to arrive in Cairo at 10:55 P.M., April 14, 1964.

[BUREAU DELETION] "Shabazz" had made no advance
reservation with Lufthansa, but appeared at the ticket counter
shortly before flight time. "Shabazz" had purchased a one-way
ticket for $1,300 cash from United Arab Airlines, New York
City. His itinerary is as follows:

New York to Frankfurt, Germany
Frankfurt to Cairo, Egypt
Cairo to Jedda, Saudi Arabia
Jedda to Cairo

On April 14, 1964 [BUREAU DELETION] Immigration and
Naturalization Service, John F. Kennedy International Airport,
New York City, advised that their records reflect that Malik
Shabazz, 23-11 97th Street, East Elmhurst, Queens, New York,
United States Passport number C294275, departed at 7:00 P.M.,
April 13, 1964, for Frankfurt, Germany, aboard Lufthansa flight
number 401.

Malcolm Little is described as follows:

Name	Malcolm K. Little
Aliases	Malcolm X, Malcolm Shabazz
	Malik Shabazz, Malik El Shabazz
Race	Negro
Sex	Male
Age	Thirty-eight

SECTION 11

February 6, 1964–May 22, 1964

REPORTS: 1. May 22, 1964. New York
2. June 9, 1964. New York
3. June 16, 1964. New York to Director. Teletype
4. June 18, 1964. New York

' Section 11 combines information regarding Malcolm's return from Africa on May 21, 1964, with reports of the suit to evict him from his home and repetitious reports from Section 10, added with slight modifications. Upon Malcolm's return, he immediately called a press conference at which he stated that some African nations would support his fight to try the United States in the United Nations for violating the human rights of black Americans. In Africa, he had spoken several times and "he impressed on all of these people the fact that racial discrimination in America is sponsored by the government."'

After the judge had postponed it several times, the NOI's eviction suit against Malcolm finally reached the courts in June, but the judge withheld his sentence until an "unknown future date."

The last portions of the June 18 report can also be found in Section 10, but some reports are elaborated upon here. One of these repetitions, for instance, reports an FBI interview with Malcolm from February, the second of only two such interviews which Malcolm granted. In Section 10, Bayard Rustin's name was in fact deleted from the text, whereas it remains visible in the report included in Section 11. (In this edition the interview has been placed in Section 10, with Rustin's name restored.)

Sketchy details in Section 10 are made concrete. For instance, the full text of Malcolm's speech from Section 10, report 5 is submitted. A brief history of the Muslim Mosque, Inc. appears, and actually refers the reader to Section 10 for details. Relationships with Civil Rights leaders and sports figures are set out, along with a summary of an alleged attempt upon Malcolm's life, which the FBI, the NOI, and Malcolm all seem to agree never happened.

SUBJECT   MALCOLM X LITTLE
FILE NO.   100-399321
           Section 11
           Serials 109–126

UNITED STATES DEPARTMENT OF JUSTICE
FEDERAL BUREAU OF INVESTIGATION

New York, New York
May 22, 1964
Re: Malcolm K. Little
Internal Security - NOI

By means of a pretext by a Special Agent of the Federal Bureau of Investigation (FBI) on May 20, 1964, it was ascertained [BUREAU DELETION] that subject was scheduled to return from his tour of Africa on May 21, 1964, and would arrive at the John F. Kennedy International Airport, New York City, at 4:30 P.M., May 21, 1964. A press conference by subject was scheduled for 7:00 P.M. on that date and a reception for him was scheduled at 8:00 P.M. on May 21, 1964, in the Skyline Room, Hotel Theresa, New York City.

On May 21, 1964, Supervising Inspector John Adams, Immigration and Naturalization Service, New York City, advised that subject, using the name Malik El Shabazz, arrived at 4:25 P.M. that date aboard Pan American flight 115 from Paris, France. He had passport number C294275, and his destination was his residence at 23-11 97th Street, East Elmhurst, Queens, New York City.

Concerning the press conference mentioned above, the following article (in part) appeared in the *New York Times,* a New York City daily newspaper, of May 22, 1964, Late City Edition, page 22, column 5:

MALCOLM SAYS HE IS BACKED ABROAD

Asserts U.N. Will Get Case on U.S. Negro This Year

Malcolm X, the Negro nationalist leader, said yesterday he had received pledges of support from some new African nations for charges of discrimination against the United States in the United Nations.

The case against the United States for its treatment of the Negro people, he said, would be prepared and submitted to the United Nations sometime this year. He did not say which nations intended to lodge the formal charges.

'Malcolm, speaking at a press conference in Harlem following his return from a trip to Africa and Mecca, said the pledges had been received from the heads of all the countries he visited. Among the nations on his itinerary were Ghana, Algeria, Nigeria, Morocco and Saudi Arabia.

The case to be presented to the world organization, he asserted, would compel the United States Government to face the same charges as South Africa and Rhodesia.

The United States, he asserted, has colonized the Negro people just as the people of Africa and Asia were colonized by Europeans. He described the American method as neo-colonialism.

This document contains neither recommendations nor conclusions of any kind. It is the property of the FBI, and is a loan to your agency; it and/or its contents are not to be distributed outside your agency.

UNITED STATES DEPARTMENT OF JUSTICE
FEDERAL BUREAU OF INVESTIGATION

New York, New York
June 9, 1964

Malcolm K. Little
        Internal Security - Muslim Mosque, Incorporated
    From 11:40 P.M., June 8, 1964, to 12:30 A.M., June 9, 1964,
subject was the guest on the "Barry Gray Show" over Radio
Station WMCA, New York, New York. Prior to the interview of
subject by Mr. Gray, the latter telephonically interviewed
Alabama's Governor George Wallace.

In commenting on Governor Wallace, subject stated that he
made no distinction between Governor Wallace and President
Lyndon B. Johnson, except in their methods. Little also characterized the United States government as a racist government
since the majority of all congressional committees are headed and
dominated by congressmen from the South.

꙾ Subject spoke of his recently completed tour of Africa, describing it as the "greatest place on earth." He stated he had toured
Arabia, Egypt, Lebanon, Nigeria, Ghana and Morocco. In Arabia, he made the twelve-day pilgrimage to Mecca, where his outlook was broadened when he saw how belief in Allah by men of
all races eliminates racial distinctions. ꙾

Little claimed that while in Ghana he met with the ambassadors there from Cuba and Communist China, both of whom gave
dinners in his honor. He also addressed members of the Ghana
Parliament and he impressed on all of these people the fact that
racial discrimination in America is sponsored by the government.

FEDERAL BUREAU OF INVESTIGATION
U. S. DEPARTMENT OF JUSTICE

COMMUNICATIONS SECTION

JUNE 16, 1964
TELETYPE

CODED TELETYPE
FBI NEW YORK
.603 PMSSS URGENT 6-16-64
TO DIRECTOR 100-399321
FROM NEW YORK 105-8999
MALCOLM K. LITTLE, IS-MMI.

RE NEW YORK TELETYPE SIX, FIFTEEN, SIXTY FOUR. [BUREAU DELETION]

[BUREAU DELETION] QUEENS COUNTY CIVIL COURT, ADVISED TODAY THAT EVICTION TRIAL BROUGHT BY NATION OF ISLAM /NOI/ AGAINST SUBJECT ENDED AT ONE THIRTY P.M. THIS DATE. JUDGE HAS RESERVED DECISION WHICH WILL BE HANDED DOWN AT UNKNOWN FUTURE DATE.

[BUREAU DELETION] ADVISED THAT APPROXIMATELY TEN MUSLIM MOSQUE INC. /MMI/ MEMBERS AND FIFTY NOI MEMBERS WERE PRESENT IN AND AROUND THE COURTHOUSE BUT THERE WERE NO INCIDENTS. ONE OF SUBJECT/S BODYGUARDS OBSERVED IN CAR OUTSIDE OF COURT WITH A RIFLE AND WAS CHECKED OUT [BUREAU DELETION]. HE HAD TWO UNLOADED RIFLES BUT NO AMMUNITION. NO ARREST MADE SINCE POSSESSION OF RIFLE IS NOT AN OFFENSE. IN SPITE OF ALLEGED THREATS TO SUBJECT HE HAS MADE NO REQUEST TO THE NYCPD FOR PROTECTION.
END
FBI WASHDC

UNITED STATES DEPARTMENT OF JUSTICE
FEDERAL BUREAU OF INVESTIGATION

Report of: [BUREAU DELETION]   Office: New York, New York

Date: 6/18/64

Field Office   Bureau
File No. 105-8999   File No. 100-399321

Title: MALCOLM K. LITTLE

Character: INTERNAL SECURITY - MUSLIM MOSQUE,
          INCORPORATED

Synopsis:

Subject continues to reside at 23-11 97th Street, East Elmhurst, Queens, New York, and is founder and leader of the Muslim Mosque, Incorporated (MMI), with headquarters in the Hotel Theresa, New York City. Subject was a National Representative of the Nation of Islam (NOI) and Minister of NOI Mosque No. 7, New York City, until temporarily suspended by NOI leader ELIJAH MUHAMMAD on 12/4/63, for remarks made by the subject on 12/1/63 concerning the assassination of former President KENNEDY. The suspension was originally for ninety days, but was made indefinite in early March 1964, allegedly because of a power struggle within the NOI between the subject and NOI officials. The subject's NOI activities around the United States and his public appearances as an NOI representative are set forth. Interview with subject at New York City on 2/4/64 [is] set out. Subject broke with the NOI on 3/8/64, and on 3/12/64 publicly announced the formation of the MMI, an organization with Islam as its religious base and a political, economic and social philosophy of black nationalism. the subject outlined the ultimate aim of the MMI as the separation of races and the return of the Negro to Africa. The current aim is to work with civil rights groups to improve conditions of Negroes in the United States, although the subject opposes integration. As MMI spokesman, subject claims Negro struggle should no longer be nonviolent, and he urges Negroes to practice self-defense if and when attacked. He also suggested on 3/12/64 the formation of rifle clubs by Negroes for self-defense in areas where Negroes are not protected by the government. Subsequently, the subject denied he was promoting or organizing Negro rifle clubs, only suggesting that it was legal to own rifles and shotguns and Negroes should do so to protect themselves and their homes, if necessary. He also urged Negroes to vote in order to control their own community politically. Activities and public appearances of subject as MMI leader around the United States [are] set forth. Subject is advisor to civil rights group known as ACT, and his relationship with some Negro civil rights leaders [is] ... out along with comments by other Negro civil rights leaders who apparently reject him. Interests of WWP and SWP in subject and his MMI [are] set out. Also set forth is information on subject's arrest in New York City for speeding, alleged threat against his life and association with sports figures CASSIUS CLAY and JIMMY BROWN. Efforts by NOI in New York City to evict him from his residence are also set forth along with information on his trip to Africa and return in April and May 1964.

BREAK FROM THE NOI
A. Break By Subject

The March 9, 1964 edition of the *New York Times* contained an article on page 1 which reflected that on March 8, 1964, MALCOLM X publicly announced that he had broken with ELIJAH MUHAMMAD and the NOI due to his continued suspension and that he would organize a politically oriented "black nationalist party."

On March 12, 1964, Special Agents of the FBI attended a press conference held by MALCOLM X in the Park Sheraton Hotel, 7th Avenue and 55th Street, New York City. At this press conference MALCOLM X passed out a copy of the public statement he issued on March 8, 1964, concerning his break with the NOI.

Editor's note. *In this public statement Malcolm attempts to make clear his position in regard to the much-publicized split between him and Elijah Muhammad. After praising Muhammad's wisdom and acknowledging Muhammad's wisdom and acknowledging Muhammad as his mentor, Malcolm states his ongoing concern for the twenty-two million blacks in America. "During this ninety days of silence," reads Malcolm's statement, "I have reached the conclusion that I can best spread Mr. Muhammad's message by staying out of the Nation of Islam"; but, he adds, he will nevertheless remain a Muslim and abide by Muhammad's teachings as he understands them. His statement concludes with his assurance that he is not "trying to split the Muslims" and his advice that all Muslims "stay in the Nation of Islam under the spiritual guidance of Elijah Muhammad" and not desert their faith in order to follow Malcolm.*

Also at this press conference MALCOLM X passed out a copy of the telegram he sent to ELIJAH MUHAMMAD on March 11, 1964.

Editor's note. *The telegram emphasized Malcolm's assertion that he has not left the Nation of Islam of his own free will and that he has in fact submitted to pressures both from Captain Joseph in New York and from national officials. His present course of action, Malcolm feels, will help to preserve the unity of the Nation of Islam and the faith of Muhammad's followers. Malcolm then states that he has never criticized Muhammad or his family to the press and continues with an acknowledgment of Muhammad as his "leader and teacher," to whom he gives "full credit for what I know and who I am."*

On March 9, 1964, from 10:00–10:30 P.M., MALCOLM X appeared on the news commentary and interview program "The World At 10," over TV station WNDT, Channel 13, New York

City, where he was interviewed regarding his split with the NOI. MALCOLM X explained that he was suspended (on December 4, 1963) for disobedience to ELIJAH MUHAMMAD as the result of his remark on the assassination of President KENNEDY, since ELIJAH MUHAMMAD had previously told him not to comment on the assassination. He stated the suspension was originally for ninety days, but he recently learned that the suspension would be for an indefinite time.

The March 14, 1964 edition of the *New York Amsterdam News,* a Negro weekly newspaper published in New York, New York, on page 1, contained an exclusive interview by that paper with MALCOLM X concerning his break with the NOI and the formation of the MMI.

In this interview, MALCOLM X charged that NOI headquarters in Chicago had been waging a power struggle against him that led to his suspension in December, 1963. The article quoted MALCOLM X as stating "they forced me to take the stand I am taking because I had to find a way to circumvent the forces in the movement that opposed me and at the same time to expedite Mr. MUHAMMED's program as I understand it."

This article reflected that MALCOLM X's announcement to split with the NOI and form his own group was brought on by a letter he received on March 5, 1964, from ELIJAH MUHAMMAD, informing him that he was to remain on suspension for an indefinite time.

B. Reaction of NOI Officials

The March 10, 1964 edition of the *New York Journal American,* a daily newspaper published in New York, New York, contained an article on page 1 which reflected that NOI leader ELIJAH MUHAMMAD, in Phoenix, Arizona, was on the verge of tears when he heard of subject's break with the NOI and he declared, "I never dreamed this man would deviate from the NOI. My people are adapted to peace. They believe in peaceful solutions."

The March 28, 1964 edition of the *Chicago Defender,* a daily newspaper published in Chicago, Illinois, contained an article on page 1 captioned "Hit MALCOLM X As Judas." This article indicated that PHILBERT X, NOI Minister in Lansing, Grand Rapids and Flint, Michigan, and a brother of subject, denounced subject as a traitor for breaking with the NOI and forming his own group. PHILBERT X stated he had brought his brother into the NOI ten years ago and he claimed subject's actions were caused by "resentment" over the suspension given him by ELIJAH MUHAMMAD. He described subject's new organization as "dangerous," and he denounced subject as a BRUTUS, JUDAS and BENEDICT ARNOLD. He added that subject would do anything to gain mention and news coverage.

Similar articles to that above appeared in the following newspapers:

New York Journal American, March 27, 1964, page 1.

New York Post, a daily newspaper published in New York, New York, of March 27, 1964, page 4.

New York Herald Tribune, a daily newspaper published in New York, New York, March 28, 1964, page 5.

The March 29, 1964 edition of the *Chicago Sunday Tribune,* a newspaper published in Chicago, Illinois, contained an article on page 20, which reflected that subject was not upset by his brother PHILBERT's attack against him, and subject claimed that PHILBERT was using someone else's words and was forced to make the statements he made.

[BUREAU DELETION] of the NOI described subject as a traitor to ELIJAH MUHAMMAD who always wanted to be in the limelight and who left the NOI for personal gain. He further described subject as a disobedient follower who was not satisfied with being the Number Two man in the NOI.

[BUREAU DELETION]

The April 4, 1964 edition of *The New Crusader,* a weekly Negro newspaper published in Chicago, Illinois, contained an article by ELIJAH MUHAMMAD entitled "Mr. MUHAMMAD Speaks."

In this article subject's break with the NOI was discussed. ELIJAH MUHAMMAD stated that subject disobeyed him by failing to keep quiet after his suspension, and when told he would have to remain quiet for a longer time subject went out on his own. ELIJAH stated in the article that he places his trust in ALLAH, while subject is going to trust himself. He then stated, "I am sorry for the poor fools who refuse to trust the god of the Honorable ELIJAH MUHAMMAD, and follow MALCOLM for self-victory."

AFFILIATION WITH THE MUSLIM
MOSQUE, INCORPORATED

On March 12, 1964, Special Agents of the FBI attended a press conference by subject in the Park Sheraton Hotel, New York City, from 11:00 A.M. to 1:00 P.M. which was attended by approximately sixty representatives of the press. At this press conference subject publicly announced the formation and incorporation of his new organization named "Muslim Mosque, Incorporated."

On March 16, 1964, [BUREAU DELETION] New York County, New York, New York, advised that on that date a Certificate of Incorporation was filed for the MMI pursuant to Article IX of the Religious Corporation Law of the State of New York. The certificate was filed under number 2330 for 1964. The certificate was executed on March 9, 1964, notarized on March 10, 1964, and filed on March 16, 1964 by EDWARD W. JACKO, JR., attorney at law, 217 West 125th Street, New York City.

The certificate reflected that on March 9, 1964, in conformity with Section 192 of the Religious Corporation Law, a meeting to decide for incorporation was held at 23-11 97th Street, Queens, New York. Present at this meeting were MALCOLM X LITTLE, who presided, EARL GRANT and JAMES M. K. WARDEN. At this meeting it was decided to incorporate and the name chosen was "Muslim Mosque, Incorporated." It was also decided at this meeting that there would be no less than three nor more than twenty-one trustees, and the meeting then proceeded to elect LITTLE, GRANT and WARDEN as its trustees to serve until the first Sunday of March, 1965. On that date a second election of trustees would be held, and thereafter a new election of trustees would be held on the first Sunday of each calendar year. The certificate further indicated that the principal places of worship were to be in the borough of Manhattan, New York County, New York.

[BUREAU DELETION] that JAMES X (WARDEN) is a former FOI Lieutenant of NOI Mosque No. 7, New York City. In March, 1964, he went over to MALCOLM X's new organization, the MMI, and he is MALCOLM X's Chief Assistant.

The above incorporation record of the MMI set forth its purposes as follows:

(a) To provide a suitable place of worship for its members and others in accordance with the Islamic Faith.

(b) To maintain a house of study for the advancement of the Islamic Faith and Religion.

(c) To stimulate interest among the members in the formation, maintenance and the teachings of the Islamic Faith.

(d) To publish textbooks, pamphlets, brochures, and to solicit, collect and in other manners raise funds for the hereinabove and hereinafter enumerated purposes.

(e) To work for the imparting of the Islamic Faith and Islamic Religion in accordance with the accepted Islamic Religious principles.

(f) To purchase, lease, acquire, sell and mortgage improved or unimproved real property and any interest therein.

(g) The foregoing clauses shall be considered both as objects and purposes, and it is hereby expressly provided that the foregoing enumerated specific objects and purposes shall not be held to limit or restrict in any manner the powers of this corporation, but that this corporation shall be entitled to enjoy all the powers that a religious corporation may have under and by virtue of the Laws of the State of New York.

RELATIONSHIP WITH CIVIL
RIGHTS ORGANIZATIONS AND LEADERS

The March 11, 1962 edition of the *New York Journal American,* on page 2 contained an article which reflected that JAMES

FARMER, National Director of CORE, and WHITNEY YOUNG, Head of the National Urban League, downgraded the influence in the Negro community of MALCOLM X and other black supremacists. They stated that the goals of MALCOLM X did not mesh with the overall civil rights effort since the latter are pledged to integration and not separation, and their modus-operandi is non-violence.

The March 15, 1964 edition of the *New York Herald Tribune,* a daily newspaper published in New York, New York, contained an article which reflected that Dr. MARTIN LUTHER KING of the Southern Christian Leadership Conference denounced the suggestion of MALCOLM X that Negroes form rifle clubs to defend themselves as "a grave error" and an "inefficient and immoral approach."

The March 21, 1964 edition of *The New Crusader,* page 5, quotes New York Congressman ADAM CLAYTON POWELL as saying that MALCOLM's plan to arm Negroes is "totally and completely wrong." He predicted failure for MALCOLM since he is dedicated to separation, while the entire civil rights movement is for desegregation.

The April 26, 1964 edition of the *New York Herald Tribune* contained an article on page 10, relative to the racial situation, by former professional baseball player JACKIE ROBINSON. In a prelude to the article, ROBINSON was described as a "loud and influential voice in the Negro battle for equal rights," who is bitterly opposed to the forces fighting civil rights legislation in Congress, and equally opposed to irresponsible Negro leadership and tactics.

In the article, Mr. ROBINSON wrote that he could not understand why the national "white" press, in reporting on civil rights and racial matters, persisted in "glorifying on their front pages the very persons they condemn in their editorials."

Mr. ROBINSON cited MALCOLM X as an outstanding example of this reporting and he then made the following comments on MALCOLM X:

Mr. X, as he is projected by what we regrettably call the "white press," doesn't even exist. As Dick Gregory has said,

Malcolm was "invented" by the people who edit big newspapers, control big television and radio and publish big newspapers and magazines.

Malcolm has big audiences, but no constructive program. He has big words, but no records on deeds in civil rights. He is terribly militant on soapboxes on street corners of Negro ghettos. Yet, he has not faced Southern police dogs in Birmingham as Martin Luther King has done, nor gone to jail for freedom as Roy Wilkins and James Farmer have done, nor brought about creative dialogue between business and civil rights leaders as Whitney Young does daily.

In fact, here is a man who has been exposed and disowned by the very organization which he had so eloquently espoused—the Black Muslims. In spite of all this, Mr. X receives more publicity in national media than is given to all the responsible Negro leaders we have mentioned above. White colleges flood him with speaking engagement offers. You can count on one hand Negro colleges which have invited him if there are any.

It is the function of media to report, yes. But the Malcolm X image has been distorted rather than reported; distorted so that many whites imagine that Malcolm has a popular following; distorted so that a number of whites and colored people, more concerned with public attention than with civil rights, more hungry for headlines than for jobs and justice, have suddenly reached for mantles of leadership which they are not prepared to wear.

MISCELLANEOUS
B. Alleged Threat Against Subject's Life

The March 21, 1964 edition of the *New York Amsterdam News* contained an article on page 50 which reflected that subject claimed that officials at NOI Mosque No. 7 had tried to persuade NOI members that he was insane after his suspension in December, 1963. After these NOI officials believed they had turned enough NOI members against him, subject alleged that they sent a brother out to kill him in cold blood during February, 1964, but because truth was stronger than falsehood the brother did not believe the charge and instead of killing him told him of the plot and of the actions of NOI officials. Subject claimed that when he demanded an opportunity to refute these charges before NOI Mosque No. 7 his request was refused.

[BUREAU DELETION] had no information to indicate that an attempt was ever made or contemplated against the life of subject by members of the NOI, and that subject had never made such a complaint [BUREAU DELETION].

C. Association With Sports Figures

The January 25, 1964 edition of the *New York Amsterdam News* contained an article on page 1 that subject and his family were in Miami during the past week, vacationing as the guests of Heavyweight Boxing Contender CASSIUS CLAY.

The February 1, 1964 edition of the *New York Amsterdam News* contained a photograph on page 1 of subject, his wife BETTY, and their three daughters sitting together with CASSIUS CLAY in Miami, Florida.

The March 20, 1964 edition of the *New York Herald Tribune* contained an article on page 6 which reflected that subject was in Miami Beach, Florida, presumably to attend the heavyweight boxing championship fight between CASSIUS CLAY and SONNY LISTON.

The March 9, 1964 edition of the *New York Post* contained an article on page 4 which reflected that subject, who had broken with the NOI, had stated that he would not take CASSIUS CLAY with him out of the NOI. The article indicated that subject was generally accredited with CLAY's joining the NOI.

The March 10, 1964 edition of the *New York Journal American* contained an article on page 1 which reflected that CASSIUS CLAY indicated he would not leave the NOI to follow subject.

The May 18, 1964 edition of the *New York Post* contained an article on page 4, datelined "Accra, Ghana." This article indicated that the allegiance of CASSIUS CLAY to Rebel Muslim Leader MALCOLM X seemed to be over. The article indicated that during the separate African tours of subject and CASSIUS

CLAY they met in Morocco on April 17, 1964 and CLAY made the following remarks concerning subject:

"Man, did you get a look at him? Dressed in that funny white robe and wearing a beard and walking with a cane that looked like a prophet's stick? Man, he's gone so far out he's out completely." Then, turning to HERBERT MUHAMMAD, the son of ELIJAH MUHAMMAD, who is accompanying CLAY on his African tour, CLAY stated, "Doesn't that just go to show that Elijah is the most powerful? Nobody listens to that Malcolm anymore."

D. Efforts by NOI to Evict Subject from Residence

As reflected in Section 1, Part A, above, subject resides with his family at 23-11 97th Street, East Elmhurst, Queens, New York.

[BUREAU DELETION] advised that after ELIJAH MUHAMMAD learned subject had broken with the NOI on March 8, 1964, he instructed [BUREAU DELETION] to tell subject that he must give up his residence, which is owned by the NOI.

[BUREAU DELETION] advised that [BUREAU DELETION] sent the following letter under date of March 10, 1964 to subject:

. . . Dear Brother Malcolm,

You have several items such as letters, Mosque film, Negro documents, etc., relative to the Muslims and their affairs . . . [T]he laborers and believers hereby request your cooperation in turning these items over to Muhammad's Mosque No. 7 immediately. Also you are residing in a building which was purchased by Muhammad's Mosque No. 7 for the use by a laborer as designated by the leader and teacher, the honorable Elijah Muhammed, who may serve in ministerial capacity or whatever position he places them. As you no longer hold this position we the laborers and believers request that you vacate premises located at 23-11 97th Street, East Elmhurst 69, New York, upon receiving this letter.

Upon a call to Captain Joseph arrangements can be made to have personal items belonging to the Nation of Islam picked up. This letter will also serve notice your car insurance is in Muhammed's Mosque No. 7. We are requesting that you discontinue using the name of Muhammad's Mosque or the Nation of Islam for your personal effects. We can effect a transferral of title. Also you can bring the necessary papers to make this change. If you continue to use the Nation's name on your car then the Mosque will have to take possession of the car, which we do not want to do because this car is your personal property. The Mosque only desires the withdrawal of its name from your personal effects, etc. This letter also serves notice that Muhammed's Mosque No. 7 will discontinue handling expenses on utilities at said 23-11 97th Street.

At the FOI meeting at NOI Mosque No. 7, New York City, on March 16, 1964, it was publicly announced by [BUREAU DELETION] that efforts will be made to get MALCOLM out of his residence which is owned by Mosque No. 7.

[BUREAU DELETION]

[BUREAU DELETION] Landlord and Tenants Proceedings, Civil Court of the City of New York, Queens County, 126-06 Queens Boulevard, Queens, New York, advised that eviction proceedings were filed by MUHAMMAD's Temple of Islam Incorporated (NOI) on April 8, 1964, and are filed under index number L&T 4845 for 1964. Subject answered on April 13, 1964, and a hearing was set on April 17, 1964. This hearing was postponed until May 26, 1964, and postponed again until June 3, 1964. [BUREAU DELETION] made the papers in the file available.

Subject's answer and counterclaim was filed by the law firm of Sutton and Sutton, 135 West 125th Street, New York City.

On June 3, 1964, [BUREAU DELETION] advised that the trial on the above matter scheduled for that date had been postponed to June 15, 1964.

The April 18, 1964 edition of the *New York Amsterdam News* contained an article on page 1 relative to the above eviction pro-

ceedings and identified the NOI attorney as JOSEPH WIL-
LIAMS, and the attorney for subject as PERCY SUTTON.

This document contains neither recommendations nor
conclusions of any kind. It is the property of the FBI, and is
a loan to your agency; it and/or its contents are not to be
distributed outside your agency.

SECTION 12

July 2, 1964–September 17, 1964

The major events of Malcolm's summer of 1964 were his June 28 founding of the Organization of Afro-American Unity (OAAU) and his July 7 trip to Africa, where he would remain until November, despite race riots in the United States and growing tension within his newly formed group. At a June 30 speech in Omaha, Malcolm related that the OAAU was dedicated to doing "whatever is necessary to bring the Negro struggle from the level of civil rights to the level of human rights." He had altered his philosophy and accepted the possibility that "there were many whites who sincerely wanted to help the Negro cause."

By no means had his change in philosophy reduced his militancy or his commitment to the right to defend oneself when attacked. His new ideology could in fact have made his militancy more effective, because now he could operate within the mainstream of civil rights leaders. Only days after the formation of the OAAU, Malcolm offered to "send some of our brothers . . . on [Dr. Martin Luther] King's word" to Florida to defend Florida blacks from racist attacks.

Soon after the FBI received information that the NOI had released orders to kill him, Malcolm left on his third trip to Africa, his second in less than a year. The FBI kept close watch over him, and reported the audience's warm reception of a speech he delivered at a banquet in Alexandria. Another speech indicated Malcolm's continued interest in pursuing the human rights problem in the international arena.

Malcolm's apparent success abroad must have begun to worry the Justice Department, because J. Walter Yeagley, Assistant Attorney General in the Internal Security Division, indicated to Director Hoover that he had knowledge that Malcolm had urged foreign governments to "take the issue of racialism in America before the United Nations as a threat to world peace." Yeagley requested that the FBI look into Malcolm's dealings and see if there were any "activities abroad indicating a possible violation of the Logan Act," the act forbidding U.S. citizens to influence foreign governments without permission from the state. The FBI seemed to be interested in helping Mr. Yeagley as much as possible; The Logan Act is printed in a September 11 memo from the New York office to Hoover, and investigators were instructed to review Malcolm's foreign travels and report any violations.

SUBJECT MALCOLM X LITTLE

FILE NO.   100-399321

Section 12

Serials 127–174

UNITED STATES DEPARTMENT OF JUSTICE
FEDERAL BUREAU OF INVESTIGATION

Omaha, Nebraska
July 2, 1964

MALCOLM K. LITTLE,
also known as Malcolm X

An article appeared in the *Omaha World-Herald,* Omaha, Nebraska, a daily newspaper, on June 15, 1964, which revealed that Reverend Kelsey Jones, President of the Citizens Coordinating Committee for Civil Liberties, announced that Malcolm X would speak in Omaha, Nebraska, at the Assembly Hall in the City Auditorium at 8:00 P.M. on June 30, 1964. Reverend Jones is quoted as stating, "If you can back Goldwater in Omaha, you ought to be able to listen to Malcolm X."

An article appeared in the *Omaha World-Herald* newspaper on June 30, 1964, which stated that the man who had at one time been the fieriest spokesman for the Black Muslim movement stated his new group hopes to carry the American Negro's plight to the United Nations. The article related that Malcolm X, who was returning to the city where he was born Malcolm Little on May 19, 1925, said his new organization is called Afro-American Unity and dedicated to doing, "whatever is necessary to bring the Negro struggle from the level of civil rights to the level of human rights."

The article continues by stating that Malcolm X's organization had telegraphed the Reverend Martin Luther King that it was ready to send help to St. Augustine if the Federal Government does not provide aid. He stated that the day of "turning the other cheek to those brute beasts is over and that we can send enough help to get results."

The article relates that Malcolm X displayed considerable tolerance toward other Negro rights groups which as a Black Muslim he had berated. In regard to these rights groups he stated, "If they have failed it is because of the terrific opposition they face. If they have not reached their goals, if they have stumbled, it's because they have been tripped by the American people." He warned that if negotiation does not bring more results the United States will face a "new situation in the struggle."

The article quotes him as saying, "I used to believe in Elijah Muhammad (the Black Muslim leader). I believed in him as a person and I believed in his philosophy that the white man is the embodiment of evil." He said he left the organization "because of internal problems" and not because of the punishment given him over the remarks he had made on President Kennedy's death. He said, "If Elijah Muhammad teaches the white race is evil how can he condemn me for remarks made when one of them dies?"

The article relates that he realized there were many whites who sincerely wanted to help the Negro cause. He stated, "But they don't need to join us. They should join each other to change the attitudes of the white community toward the black community."

FEDERAL BUREAU OF INVESTIGATION
U. S. DEPARTMENT OF JUSTICE

COMMUNICATIONS SECTION

JUNE 30, 1964
TELETYPE

CODED TELETYPE
FBI NEW YORK
220 PM URGENT 6-30-64 JAM
TO DIRECTOR /4/ 100-399321 JACKSONVILLE AND NEW ORLEANS
FROM NEW YORK 105-8999 IP
MALCOLM K. LITTLE, AKA IS-MMI.

[BUREAU DELETION] ADVISED INSTANT DATE THAT SUBJECT LEADER OF MUSLIM MOSQUE INCORPORATED /MMI/ AS CHAIRMAN OF NEW ORGANIZATION OF AFRO-AMERICAN UNITY SENT TELEGRAM THIS MORNING TO MARTIN LUTHER KING CONCERNING ATTACKS ON NEGROES IN ST. AUGUSTINE, FLORIDA BY PEOPLE OF WHITE RACE. SUBJECT ADVISED KING THAT IF FEDERAL GOVERNMENT WILL NOT SEND TROOPS TO KING-S ASSISTANCE THAN ON KING-S WORD "WE WILL IMMEDIATELY DISPATCH SOME OF OUR BROTHERS THERE TO ORGANIZE OUR PEOPLE INTO SELF DEFENSE UNITS AMONG OUR PEOPLE AND THE KU KLUX KLAN WILL RECEIVE A TASTE OF ITS OWN MEDICINE. THE DAY OF TURNING THE OTHER CHEEK TO THE HUMAN BRUTE BEASTS IS OVER."

[BUREAU DELETION]

BUREAU AND INTERESTED OFFICES WILL BE ADVISED OF ANY FURTHER DEVELOPMENTS IN THIS MATTER.

LHM FOLLOWS
END

MSL
FBI WASH DC

FBI

Date: 7/7/64

Transmit the following in _____

Via_____AIRTEL_____   _____REGISTERED_____

(Priority)

TO   : DIRECTOR, FBI (100-399321)
FROM   : SAC, NEW YORK (105-8999)
SUBJECT: MALCOLM K. LITTLE AKA
          IS-MMI

On 7/5/64, subject was in contact with [BUREAU DELE-
TION] told him that orders to kill him (MALCOLM) came from
Chicago. [BUREAU DELETION] can furnish witnesses if
MALCOLM wants to take them to court. [BUREAU DELE-
TION] also told MALCOLM he should tell the FBI all about the
threats against him.

On 7/5/64, subject contacted [BUREAU DELETION] MAL-
COLM informed [BUREAU DELETION] had filed suits against
ELIJAH for illegitimacy and non-support, and he urged her to
talk one of the other mothers (not named) into filing suit against
him. He also told her that ELIJAH has been putting money in
Switzerland lately, and CLARA has been putting hers in Beirut
and CAIRO. MALCOLM also told her "that that [BUREAU
DELETION] has been giving ELIJAH money for several years.
    The above is being furnished for information.

FEDERAL BUREAU OF INVESTIGATION
U. S. DEPARTMENT OF JUSTICE

COMMUNICATIONS SECTION

JULY 21, 1964
TELETYPE

CODED TELETYPE
FBI NEW YORK
10-33 PM URGENT 7-21-64 DAE
TO DIRECTOR -19- 100-399321
FROM NEW YORK 105-8999
MALCOLM X LITTLE AKA, IS-MMI.

ARTICLE IN "NEW YORK JOURNAL AMERICAN" DATED JULY TWENTY ONE SIXTY FOUR, REFLECTS THAT MALCOLM X IS OR HAS RETURNED TO THE U. S. FROM HIS AFRICAN TOUR AND WILL BE FORMING RIFLE CLUBS. [BUREAU DELETION] ON JULY TWENTY SIXTY FOUR ADVISED MALCOLM X CONTACTED [BUREAU DELETION] FROM CAIRO, EGYPT, SAME DATE AND INFORMED HER THAT HE WILL NOT RETURN TO THE U. S. THE FIRST TWO WEEKS IN AUGUST SIXTY FOUR, ALTHOUGH HE HAS KNOWLEDGE OF THE RIOTS IN HARLEM, BUT WILL INSTEAD GO TO ARABIA AND OTHER AFRICAN COUNTRIES AND WILL CONTACT [BUREAU DELETION] AGAIN ON JULY TWENTY ONE SIXTY FOUR. [BUREAU DELETION] ADVISED JULY TWENTY ONE SIXTY FOUR THAT THERE IS NO INDICATION THAT MALCOLM X HAS CHANGED HIS PLANS SINCE JULY TWENTY SIXTY FOUR AND IS DEFINITELY NOT IN NYC AT PRESENT TIME. [BUREAU DELETION]
END AND PLS HOLD

FEDERAL BUREAU OF INVESTIGATION
U. S. DEPARTMENT OF JUSTICE

COMMUNICATIONS SECTION

AUGUST 7, 1964
TELETYPE
SENT BY CODED TELETYPE
FBI NEW YORK
10-15 PM URGENT 8-7-64 DAE
TO DIRECTOR -14- 100-399321-ENCODED
FROM NEW YORK 105-8999
MALCOLM K. LITTLE, IS-MMI.

[BUREAU DELETION] ADVISED EIGHT SEVEN SIXTY FOUR, THAT [BUREAU DELETION]ON SAME DATE TOLD [BUREAU DELETION] HE RECEIVED A "WRITE-UP OF A PRESS RELEASE" FROM MALCOLM THAT HE IS GOING TO RELEASE TODAY. RELEASE STATES THAT ON EIGHT, FOUR SIXTY FOUR IN ALEXANDRIA, EGYPT, MALCOLM X ADDRESSED OVER EIGHT HUNDRED MUSLIM STUDENTS REPRESENTING SEVENTY THREE DIFFERENT AFRICAN AND ASIAN COUNTRIES AT A BANQUET GIVEN BY THE SUPREME COUNCIL OF ISLAMIC AFFAIRS IN WHICH HE EXHORTED THEM TO CALL TO THE ATTENTION OF THEIR GOVERNMENTS WHO IN TURN SHOULD BRING TO THE ATTENTION OF THE UN THE PLIGHT OF THE NEGRO IN AMERICA. AT THE CONCLUSION OF THE BANQUET, ACCORDING TO THE RELEASE, ONE [BUREAU DELETION] /LNU/ OFFERED MALCOLM X TWENTY FREE EXPENSE PAID SCHOLARSHIPS TO AL-AZER /PH/ UNIVERSITY IN CAIRO SO THAT MALCOLM X CAN HAVE YOUNG MEN TRAINED IN THE /MUSLIM/ RELIGION, [BUREAU DELETION] STATED THAT ONE [BUREAU DELETION] HAD INVITED MALCOLM-S MUSLIM MOSQUE, INC., /MMI/ TO JOIN THE ISLAMIC FEDERATION IN THE UNITED

STATES AND THAT MALCOLM-S [BUREAU DELETION] SHOULD BE A PERSONAL REPRESENTATIVE OF THE MMI WHICH [BUREAU DELETION] AGREED TO BECOME. THE ABOVE IS DETAIL OF INFO OF THAT SUBMITTED IN SUMMARY TELETYPE THIS DATE.
   LHM FOLLOWS.
END AND PLS HOLD.

------------• •------------

UNITED STATES GOVERNMENT
DEPARTMENT OF JUSTICE

MEMORANDUM

DATE: September 2, 1964

TO   : Director, Federal Bureau of Investigation
FROM   : J. Walter Yeagley
            Assistant Attorney General
            Internal Security Division
SUBJECT: MALCOLM K. LITTLE
            aka 'MALCOLM X'
            INTERNAL SECURITY

   Information has come to our attention reflecting that Malcolm K. Little, aka "Malcolm X," in the course of his recent tour of Middle East and African states has reportedly been in communication and contact with heads of foreign governments urging that they take the issue of racialism in America before the United Nations as a threat to world peace.
   Since such activities could conceivably fall within the provisions of the Logan Act, and are moreover deemed to be inimical to the best interests of our country, prejudicial to our foreign policy, we are requesting the Secretary of State to make appropriate inquiries of our Embassies in the Middle East and Africa for any pertinent information concerning Malcolm X's alleged contacts and communications with heads of foreign governments.
   We would also appreciate having your Bureau furnish us with

any information which you may receive concerning Malcolm X's
activities abroad indicating a possible violation of the Logan Act.

———————— • •————————

SAC, New York (105-8999)   9/11/64
Director, FBI (100-399321)
MALCOLM K. LITTLE
SECURITY MATTER - MMI
Enclosed for your information is a copy of a letter from Assis-
tant Attorney General J. Walter Yeagley, Internal Security Divi-
sion, Department of Justice.
The Logan Act mentioned by the Department's letter is Title
18, Section 953, U. S. Code Annotated and reads as follows:

Any citizen of the United States, wherever he may be,
who, without authority of the United States, directly or indirectly commences or carries on any correspondence or inter-
course with any foreign government or any officer or agent
thereof, with intent to influence the measures or conduct of
any officer or agent thereof, in relation to any disputes or
controversies with the United States, or to defeat the measures of the United States, shall be fined not more than
$5,000 or imprisoned not more than three years, or both.
This section shall not abridge the right of a citizen to
apply, himself or his agent, to any foreign government or the
agents thereof for redress of any injury which he may have
sustained from such government or any of its agents or subjects. June 25, 1948, c. 645, 62 Stat. 744.

While the Logan Act is not a statute over which the Bureau
has primary investigative jurisdiction, your attention is called to
the Assistant Attorney General's request in the last sentence of
his letter. You are to review your file on Little beginning with his
first departure on foreign travel for any information which may
tend to show a violation of the above-mentioned statute. This
request should also be kept in mind during future investigation of
the subject. Any information which appears pertinent to Mr.

Yeagley's request should be promptly submitted in a memorandum suitable for dissemination to the Department.
Note:
Little, former minister of Nation of Islam Temple No. 7, New York City, is now head of the Muslim Mosque, Inc., which he organized as a militant quasi-religious Negro organization deeply involved in the Harlem race demonstrations. His name is included in the Security Index.
Enclosure

UNITED STATES DEPARTMENT OF JUSTICE
FEDERAL BUREAU OF INVESTIGATION

New York, New York
September 17, 1964

Malcolm K. Little
                    Internal Security - Muslim Mosque Incorporated
A confidential source who has furnished reliable information in the past [BUREAU DELETION] made available a press release dated July 17, 1964, under the letterhead "Organization of Afro-American Unity" (OAAU), containing a cover sheet which stated, "During the midst of the racial turmoil here in America, the most militant of the militant Negroes—Malcolm X—was in Cairo, Egypt, where he was the only American allowed into the conference of the Organization of African Unity."

"A resolution was passed at this conference condemning racism in the United States. Sincerely, OAAU."

This press release stated that it is a "Copy of the statement that was prepared by Malcolm X on behalf of the OAAU and the 22 million Afro-Americans, and was delivered by him to the conference which opened in Cairo, Egypt, on July 17, 1964."

The statement alleged to be prepared by Malcolm X was addressed to Their Excellencies, First Ordinary Assembly of Heads of State and Governments, Organization of African Unity, Cairo, U.A.R.

Editor's note. *"Our problems are your problems,"* Malcolm asserts repeatedly throughout this plea to the Independent Af-

rican States for aid in the battle of "twenty-two million African Americans whose human rights are being violated daily
by the racism of American imperialists." Malcolm counts African Americans among the lost—a people taken in chains to
a strange land that has submitted them for three hundred
years to physical abuse and mental torture; a people today left
defenseless by a government that has continually failed to
protect their lives or property simply because they are black
and of African descent. The problem, as Malcolm presents it,
belongs not to a single nation, or even a continent, but the the
world and to humanity; for "it is not a problem of civil rights,
but a problem of human rights."

America, Malcolm argues, is no less guilty of violating the
human rights of her black citizens than is South Africa. In
fact, Malcolm finds the situation in America worse because,
in addition to being racist, "she is also deceitful and hypocritical." South Africa, he points out, "practices what she
preaches"—segregation—whereas in America what is practiced is segregation but what is preached is integration. To
Malcolm's view, "the much publicized, recently passed Civil
Rights bill" amounts to little more than a "propaganda ma-
neuver" designed to blind African nations to the injustices of
American racism and the sufferings of the American black
populace.

According to Malcolm, the struggle of African Americans
for their freedom should not be perceived at all as a domestic
issue, and indeed the intent of the OAAU is "to 'internationalize' it by placing it at the level of human rights." Thus he
beseeches the Independent African States to place this issue
before the United Nations because, firstly, the United States
government is "morally incapable of protecting the lives and
property of twenty-two million African Americans" and, sec-
ondly, their "deteriorating plight is definitely becoming a
threat to world peace."

As Malcolm sees it, "frustration and hopelessness" have
pushed young blacks in America to the breaking point. By
whatever means and whatever the consequences, these blacks,
along with him and the OAAU, will "assert the right of self-

defense . . . and reserve the right of maximum retaliation against [their] racist oppressors." No longer will they be turning the other cheek, Malcolm says, but rather they will meet "violence with violence, eye for eye and tooth for tooth," in a "racial conflict . . . that could easily escalate into a violent, worldwide, bloody race war."

It is "in the interests of world peace and security," then, that Malcolm couches his final plea for an investigation by the United Nations Commission on Human Rights. He does add a final caveat to the Independent African States: "Don't escape from European colonialism only to become even more enslaved by deceitful, 'friendly' American dollarism."

SECTION 13

November 25, 1964–December 3, 1964

REPORTS: 1. November 25, 1964. New York
2. December 15, 1964. Chicago
3. December 22, 1964. New York
4. December 3, 1964. Malcolm X at Oxford

Section 13 is short, containing reports separated by less than a month. It describes the FBI's account of Malcolm's return to the United States on November 24, 1964, after spending eighteen weeks in Africa. He immediately held a press conference, where he answered questions about his trip. Although he was more conciliatory than in the past, he indicted FBI Director Hoover, the Attorney General, and the President for the lack of advances in civil rights and claimed that the United States would soon be on trial for its crimes.

In the month after his return, Malcolm's Pan-African views noticeably solidified, and he spoke frequently about Africa, its resources, and its politics. His view of the world had broadened in scope, and he commented, "I don't care what color you are as long as you want to change this miserable condition that exists on this earth."

During this month, Malcolm also continued to make comments regarding the sexual improprieties of Elijah Muhammad. The NOI clearly would not allow such defamation of its leader, and a December 12 article in the *Crusader* indicated that NOI Fruit of Islam Captain Raymond Sharrieff would "no longer tolerate your (Malcolm) scandalizing the name of our leader and teacher. . . ."

UNITED STATES DEPARTMENT OF JUSTICE
FEDERAL BUREAU OF INVESTIGATION

New York, New York
November 25, 1964

Malcolm K. Little
     Internal Security - Muslim Mosque, Incorporated
[BUREAU DELETION] that passenger list manifest of TWA
Flight 801, from Paris, France, contained the name "Shabazz."
This flight was scheduled to arrive at John F. Kennedy Interna-
tional Airport, New York at 6:00 P.M., November 24, 1964.

     [BUREAU DELETION] that Malcolm X will arrive at John
F. Kennedy (JFK) International Airport at 6:00 P.M. on the
same date. This source also advised that Muslim Mosque, Incorporated (MMI) members are in charge of security for Malcolm X
when he arrives at JFK International Airport, and approximately fifteen to twenty MMI members are expected to guard
Malcolm X upon his arrival. The Organization of Afro-American Unity (OAAU) plans to have about twenty of its members
out at JFK International Airport to greet Malcolm X with "Welcome home" signs.

     [BUREAU DELETION] upon his arrival at the airport, Malcolm X plans to hold a brief press conference and then go directly to his home and family at 23-11 97th Street, East Elmhurst, Queens, New York. The MMI and the OAAU plan on activities to honor Malcolm X on his return home for that evening.

Malcolm X arrived at JFK International Airport on TWA Flight 801, at 6:41 P.M., on November 24, 1964. He was greeted by approximately sixty persons at the airport some of whom carried identical signs stating "Welcome Back Brother Malcolm." After greeting his family and well wishers, he held a press conference.

Malcolm X stated that he had been gone for eighteen weeks, having left the United States on July 9, 1964. He said he traveled to many countries in Africa, traveling as a religious leader through Moslem countries and as Malcolm X in non-Moslem countries. He said he returned by way of Geneva and Paris to New York.

He said the objective of his trip was to get a better understanding of the Africans' problems and to tell them of the problems of the twenty-two million Negroes in the United States. Malcolm X stated all African countries met him with "open minds, open hearts and open doors." According to Malcolm he met with some presidents and ambassadors of African countries and they listened to what he had to say about the Negro problems in the United States. He said the only solution for the Afro-Negro in the United States is to bring our case before the United Nations. He said it will be difficult for African nations to shy away from taking some kind of action against the United States if the United States is brought before the United Nations on charges of violation of the Negroes' human rights, since the African countries themselves have appealed to the United Nations in the past for aid and assistance in gaining their independence.

Malcolm X said "we are advocates of whatever it takes to solve our problems. "I'm for anything that gets results and believe in the right to do anything that gets results."

He said he would be willing to meet with any group, white or black, if they are willing and are honestly sincere in trying to find the problem and present a solution to the racial problem. He said the lack of education for the white as well as the black is one of the causes for the social problem in the United States. He said education will replace deficiency in the Negro and deficiency in the white person. Negro leaders have to accept the fact that there are problems between the white and black people and they must be sincere in trying to obtain a solution to their problems.

When asked about a statement he made in the past calling Elijah Muhammad a "religious faker," Malcolm remarked "no comment," but then said he would "seek a spirit and atmosphere of unity" with him.

Asked to comment on the recent presidential election in the United States, Malcolm X said that the election turned out as he predicted. He said President Johnson now has control of Congress and the Senate and will not have any excuse for not passing good civil rights laws. He said that [because of] the fact that President Johnson got such a large number of votes he may believe that everyone is with him and get a little reckless.

Malcolm X then remarked that it must be remembered that (Senator) Goldwater received twenty-six million votes "which means that twenty-six million people bought what Goldwater had to sell."

Asked to comment on the recent killings in the Congo of Americans, Malcolm X said that it must be remembered that Patrice Lumumba was murdered by Moise Tshombe who is now Premier of the Congo and he is supported by President Johnson. President Johnson is responsible for what happens in the Congo. Malcolm X went on to say that the "Congolese have been killed year after year after year, and whatever the United States gets in the Congo, she is getting what she asked for; the Congo killings is like the chickens coming home to roost."

Malcolm X was asked to comment on Mr. Hoover's recent criticism of Dr. Martin Luther King, Jr. Malcolm X stated that "you can't blame the Federal Bureau of Investigation or Mr. Hoover for the action or lack of action in the South, for Mr. Hoover has a boss, the attorney general, and he in turn has a boss, the president. So, the blame has to be placed upon the president and the United States government."

Asked what is the name of his organization, Malcolm X said it is the "Organization Of Afro-American Unity of which I am the chairman."

This document contains neither recommendations nor conclusions of the Federal Bureau of Investigation. It is the property of the Federal Bureau of Investigation and is loaned to your agency; it and its contents are not to be distributed outside your agency.

UNITED STATES DEPARTMENT OF JUSTICE
FEDERAL BUREAU OF INVESTIGATION

Chicago, Illinois
December 15, 1964
NATION OF ISLAM
INTERNAL SECURITY -
NATION OF ISLAM (NOI)

The *Crusader* in its issue of December 12, 1964, on page 3, carried an article entitled "Nation of Islam Warns Malcolm X." The article reflected as follows:

The following open telegram was dispatched December 7, 1964, by Captain Raymond Sharrieff of the Fruit of Islam of the Nation of Islam in North America to the former Malcolm X, defected from the Muslim movement:

Mr. Malcolm: We hereby officially warn you that the Nation of Islam shall no longer tolerate your scandalizing the name of our leader and teacher the Honorable Elijah Muhammad regardless of where such scandalizing has been.
Signed: Captain Raymond Sharrieff, the Nation of Islam in North America.

The *Crusader* is a weekly newspaper published at 6429 South Park, Chicago, Illinois. It regularly features articles by Elijah

Muhammad, the Messenger of Allah, entitled "Mr. Muhammad Speaks."

UNITED STATES DEPARTMENT OF JUSTICE
FEDERAL BUREAU OF INVESTIGATION

New York, New York
December 22, 1964
Organization of Afro-American Unity
Internal Security - Miscellaneous

[BUREAU DELETION] advised that the OAAU held a public rally in the Audubon Ballroom, Broadway and 166th Street, New York City, from 8:30 P.M.to 10:15 P.M., on December 20, 1964. Approximately 175 persons attended the rally.

Malcolm X spoke on Africa, particularly about the natural resources and industrial potential of that continent. He also stated that the economy of Western Europe and America are dependent on Africa and would collapse if their interests in Africa are lost. This, he claimed, is why the United States and European countries are interested in keeping their foothold in Africa by supporting the Congo regime of Moise Tshombe. He praised the Mau Mau, an anti-white terrorist group that formerly operated in Kenya, and indicated that a Mau Mau was needed in the United States to win freedom and equality for Negroes. He also claimed that black people in America should align themselves with black people of Africa.

Malcolm X also talked about the future of the OAAU indicating that its new philosophy will be one of "alignment with Africa." He stated that the first step in this program will be to teach the Negroes to think along this line after which they can set up a definite program.

Malcolm X also remarked that he had been asked if the newspaper *The Militant* was his paper since it gave him so much publicity. He stated that it was not his paper but that it was a good paper and he urged everyone to buy and read it.

The Militant is a weekly newspaper of the Socialist Workers Party (SWP).
The SWP has been designated pursuant to Executive Order 10450.

Following his speech Malcolm X introduced Milton Henry, an attorney from Detroit, Michigan, who was an unsuccessful candidate there for an unknown office during the 1964 election of the all-Negro Freedom Now Party (FNP). He expressed disappointment over the election and blamed the failure of the FNP on the "established political machine."

MALCOLM X AT OXFORD

Editor's note. *Section 13 of the Bureau file on Malcolm X includes an article printed in* The Daily Telegraph, *a London newspaper, on December 4, 1964. Under the title "Cheers for Malcolm X at Oxford" it reports:*

> *The American Negro leader Malcolm X received a long ovation when he spoke last night in an Oxford Union debate.*
> *He was speaking for a motion "that extremism in the defence of liberty is no vice, moderation in the pursuit of justice is no virtue." . . .*

> *Also included in Section 13 is a transcript from a TV telediphone recording (from transmission 2215 on December 3, 1964) of a substantial portion of Malcolm's address—a defense of extremism—on this occasion.*
> *Extremism, Malcolm asserts, will prove far more effective in the battle for civil rights than all the "little wishy-washy love-thy-enemy approaches" currently being espoused by blacks in the United States. Quoting Patrick Henry's "Give me liberty or give me death"—a statement that, Malcolm notes, is extreme, very extreme"—he observes that far from being a vice, extremism lies at the very heart of the American struggle for human liberty.*

Malcolm then speaks of reading Shakespeare "once, passingly . . . but I remember," he says, "one thing he wrote that kind of moved me. He put it in the mouth of Hamlet, I think it was, who said 'To be or not to be.' He was in doubt about something. Whether it was nobler in the mind of man to suffer the slings and arrows of outrageous fortune in moderation or to take up arms against the sea of troubles [and] by opposing ending [them]. And I go for that. If you take up arms you'll end it, but if you sit around and wait for the one who's in power to make up his mind that he should end it, you'll be waiting a long time."

Viewing his time as "a time of extremism, a time of revolution," Malcolm ends his address with a plea to young people of all races—"I don't care what color you are," he says—to wrest power from those who have misused it and "to change this miserable condition that exists on this earth."

SECTION 14

REPORT: January 20, 1965. New York

Section 14 offers a neatly packaged review of information from 1964, already set out in the FBI file. The only new report is submitted a few weeks after Malcolm apparently checked into a Hilton in New York under the alias M. Khalil, but all the other information contained had been previously documented, at least in outline form. The report elaborates on Malcolm's statements of June 1964 regarding Elijah Muhammad's extramarital affairs, stating that Wallace Muhammad, Elijah's son, had informed him of his father's improprieties. The day after Malcolm stated that "the NOI would even commit murder to keep this secret quiet," he received a recorded telephone message telling him that he was "as good as dead."

Malcolm did not limit his criticism to the Messenger. On June 4, he had appeared on a Philadelphia radio show and stated that John Ali, National Secretary of the NOI, only wanted to "get all the money out of it (the NOI) he possibly [could]." Threats on Malcolm's life continued throughout the month of June and early July until he left for Africa.

The Bureau documents Malcolm's foreign travel extensively, indicating that he traveled in Africa from April 13 through May 21. On this trip the FBI obtained his itinerary, a report of his pilgrimage to Mecca, and the text of some statements he made which incriminated the U.S. government. His last trip of July 9 to November 24 is also documented, during which he met with Mrs. Shirley Graham DuBois, widow of writer W.E.B. DuBois, whose "background is important to show the strange inter-weaving of characters now attempting to infiltrate and agitate the Negro communities of the U.S."

Malcolm details his April and May travels extensively in his autobiography, but his description differs greatly from the FBI's views. For Malcolm, his travels are a learning experience; for the Justice Department, they are an opportunity for him to influence foreign nations to oppose the United States.

The section concludes with a recap of Yeagley's request for an investigation into possible Logan Act violations, and that if the MMI "is receiving funds from any Arab or African government, or is acting at the order, request or direction of the foreign government, it may be obligated to register under the Foreign Agents Registration Act."

SUBJECT   <u>MALCOLM X LITTLE</u>
FILE NO.   <u>100-399321</u>
                 <u>Section 14</u>
               <u>Serials 214–227</u>

FEDERAL BUREAU OF INVESTIGATION

Reporting Office: NEW YORK
Office of Origin: NEW YORK
Date: 1/20/65
Investigative Period: 12/1/64–1/15/65
Report made by: [BUREAU DELETION]
Title of Case: CHANGED
    MALCOLM K. LITTLE aka
    M. Khalil
Character of case: IS-MMI
The title of this case is marked "Changed" to add the alias of
M. KHALIL used by the subject when he registered at the
Hilton Hotel, NYC, on 1/2/65.

AFFILIATION WITH THE MUSLIM
MOSQUE, INCORPORATED (MMI)
A public rally sponsored by the MMI was held on June 7,
1964, at the Audubon Ballroom, New York City. Approximately
450 persons were present at this rally and the featured speaker
was MALCOLM X, the founder and leader of the MMI.
MALCOLM, in his speech, told of his recently completed tour

of Africa. He claimed that Africans were very sympathetic to Negroes in America and that African countries have promised to take the American racial problem to the United Nations for a solution.

He accused the New York City Police Commissioner of being a racist who is attempting to justify a police state by blaming disorder in New York on the Negroes.

During a question and answer period, MALCOLM was asked a question about ELIJAH MUHAMMAD and the Nation of Islam (NOI), which question appeared to be "set up." MALCOLM answered by alleging that ELIJAH MUHAMMAD, the leader of the NOI, was the father of six illegitimate children which the NOI "covers up." MALCOLM X claimed that the NOI would even commit murder to keep this secret quiet. He also claimed that this information concerning ELIJAH MUHAMMAD was told to him by MUHAMMAD's son, WALLACE, who, according to MALCOLM X, has been put out of the NOI by his father.

At an open rally sponsored by the MMI, held on June 21, 1964, at New York City, MALCOLM X was the main speaker. MALCOLM referred to his recent African tour and talked of the Islam religion as the only true faith for the Negroes. He described the civil rights bill passed by the United States Senate in June as a "farce" which will not solve the Negroes' problems.

MALCOLM mentioned that a new group is being formed to deal with the racial problems in the United States. He claimed that this new group will have an educational program to instruct Negroes in the contribution their race has made to history. He indicated that this new group will not sponsor "sit-ins" as current civil rights groups do but their policy will be one of "take-ins," that is, according to MALCOLM X, they will take what is rightfully theirs.

A regular meeting of the MMI was held [BUREAU DELETION]. At this meeting, a letter written by MALCOLM X, who was touring Africa, addressed to an unknown African delegate to the Organization of African Unity Conference in Addis Ababa,

Ethiopia, was read. In the letter, MALCOLM X informed the delegates that if the latter needed recruits to join the rebel military forces in the Congo, to aid in driving the white mercenary forces of Congo President MOISE TSHOMBE out of the Congo, he, MALCOLM X, could obtain ten thousand recruits in the Harlem section of New York City.

There was no answer to the letter to the African delegate and no call for recruits was made at the above meeting. No statement was made that would indicate that any such call for recruitment would be made.

Confidential sources familiar with MMI activity in the New York City and Philadelphia, Pennsylvania areas could furnish no information that would substantiate the allegation that MALCOLM X was sending "vengeance squads" to the South, particularly to Mississippi.

[BUREAU DELETION] advised on several dates during July, 1964, that the [BUREAU DELETION] has no information that would substantiate or indicate that the MMI was involved in sending "vengeance squads" to the South.

A special issue of the magazine *Revolution,* published in Paris, France, for July–August, 1964, contained an exclusive interview with MALCOLM X. During the interview, MALCOLM X stated that he has never employed violence but he felt that if violence is used against "us," we shall defend ourselves. He added that "we" do not believe that one must offer the other cheek.

MALCOLM X appeared on the "Les Crane Television Show" at New York on December 28, 1964. When asked why he preached that Negroes should take up arms to protect themselves, MALCOLM answered that if the government and the Federal Bureau of Investigation cannot protect Negroes in specific areas of the United States, that Negroes should organize and have rifles to protect themselves. He said he did not want them to break any laws but that vigilante groups are being organized at the present time in New York in order to protect their neighborhoods without the police interfering with their organizing. MAL-

COLM X said he cannot see any reason why the Negroes cannot also organize themselves for their own protection. He stated that it is up to the Negro to protect himself if the government fails to give him protection.

Television and/or Radio
Appearances of MALCOLM X

On April 23, 1964, a Special Agent of the Federal Bureau of Investigation observed a debate on "The Negro Revolt" between Negro author LOUIS LOMAX and MALCOLM X, which was held on May 23, 1964, at Chicago, Illinois. During his remarks MALCOLM X stated that since his return from Africa, he has changed his mind to a certain extent regarding the white man. He stated that he found a number of white persons who had been converted to the "Moslem" faith who were good people.

On April 23, 1964, MALCOLM X appeared with other guests on "Kup's Show," a panel television program moderated by IRV KUPCINET, over television Channel 7, Chicago, Illinois. During the program, MALCOLM X stated, while speaking of the racial problems in America, that he did not believe in racism and that there are many white people in America who are also fed up with the racist attitude reflected in American policy. He developed this belief through his pilgrimage to Mecca, and there are many whites who are willing to become involved in a genuine struggle on behalf of the Negro.

On June 9, 1964, SA [BUREAU DELETION] observed the "Mike Wallace News Program" at 11:00 P.M. over NBC-TV (National Broadcasting Company-Television), New York City. During this program, MALCOLM X was interviewed for approximately five minutes during which he stated that many white persons are fed up with the treatment of Negroes in America and he is convinced that there are good white people. When MIKE WALLACE pointed out to MALCOLM that this was contrary to his former teaching, MALCOLM X said that he now speaks for himself and that his previous anti-white statements were made while he was speaking for the NOI.

On June 8, 1964, MALCOLM X was a guest on the "Barry Gray Show" over radio station WMCA, New York City. During the interview, he stated that he made no distinction between Alabama Governor GEORGE WALLACE and President JOHNSON over racial matters except in their methods. He characterized the United States government as a racist government since the majority of all Congressional committees are headed and dominated by southern Congressmen. He further stated that while in Ghana on a recent trip, he had met with many persons, including the ambassadors of Cuba and Communist China, and he told all of these people that racial discrimination in America is sponsored by the government.

On June 25, 1964, MALCOLM X appeared on the BOB KENNEDY show "Contact" over radio station WBZ, Boston, Massachusetts. During the program, he stated that he saw the civil rights struggle as a struggle for human rights. Also, when asked how militant his new group would be, he stated that the black people in this country are justified in obtaining freedom by any means necessary. He then clarified this statement by stating that he would be justified in taking any action which was intelligent, just and legal.

Philosophy Change

The April 18, 1964 edition of the *New York Amsterdam News,* a Negro weekly newspaper published in New York City, contained an article on page 1 which indicated that prior to leaving for his African tour, MALCOLM X stated that the purpose of this trip was "to get spiritual strength" from a visit to the Moslem holy city of Mecca.

The May 8, 1964 edition of the *New York Times* daily newspaper published in New York City contained an article on page 1, captioned "Malcolm X Pleased by White Attitude on Trip to Mecca." This article stated that in a letter dated April 15, 1964, from Mecca, Saudi Arabia, MALCOLM X advised that he had gained new positive insight on race relations through his religious experience in Mecca. He advised that for the first time in his life, he felt no racial antagonism towards whites. He remarked about the hospitality he had received and stated that his experience has forced him to "rearrange" much of his own thought pattern. He indicated that the religion of Islam made everyone equal regardless of race and that if white America would accept the religion of Islam, then they would cease to measure others in terms of "difference in color."

On his appearance on the "Les Crane Television Show" on December 28, 1964, at New York City, MALCOLM X stated that his trip to Mecca in April, 1964, caused him to change his attitude towards the white people. He stated that he became a member of the true Islam faith in which it teaches brotherhood for all man and that he has met many true Moslems of the white race.

Efforts to Discredit NOI
Leader ELIJAH MUHAMMED

On June 8, 1964, MALCOLM X, in attempting to make arrangements with [BUREAU DELETION] Columbia Broadcasting System (CBS) Television, New York City, to provide the full story of the illegitimate children of ELIJAH MUHAMMAD on a film interview, told [BUREAU DELETION] that there are six women involved. MALCOLM said all are former members of MUHAMMAD's secretarial staff who have had illegitimate children by him since 1956 or 1957. According to MALCOLM two of these women have had two children and one of the two women at that time was pregnant with a third child of MUHAMMAD's. MALCOLM claimed that the real reason for his split with the NOI was that when he heard of these indiscretions, he told NOI officials who had in turn told ELIJAH MUHAMMAD in a manner that made it look like he was "stirring up things" instead of trying to resolve them. MALCOLM X told [BUREAU DELETION] that his life is at stake because he poses a threat to the NOI since public revelation of this information would cause NOI members to desert ELIJAH MUHAMMAD. On the same date, [BUREAU DELETION] received a telephone message for MALCOLM X from an anonymous caller who said "Just tell him he is as good as dead."

On [BUREAU DELETION] 1964, [BUREAU DELETION] advised that at an MMI public rally held in the Audubon Ballroom, New York City, on June 7, 1964, MALCOLM X, in answer to a question from the audience, stated that ELIJAH MUHAMMAD was the father of six illegitimate children. He claimed the NOI covers this up and would even murder to keep it quiet. MALCOLM indicated that he had learned this from ELIJAH's son, WALLACE MUHAMMAD.

On June 12, 1964, MALCOLM X was the guest on the program "Conversation for Peace" over radio station WEEI, Boston, Massachusetts. During the program, he stated that the real reason for his break with the NOI was due to a moral problem. He then told the story of several teenage NOI members who went to work for the NOI since 1957, and became pregnant. It was always assumed that a non-Muslim male was involved since no one ever stood with the girls when they were brought before the temple to stand charges for their actions. In February, 1963, according to MALCOLM X, he learned that ELIJAH MUHAMMAD was the father of these children and that he talked to MUHAMMAD about it and the latter admitted it. In October, 1963, MALCOLM said he was informed by ELIJAH's son, WALLACE, that it was still going on and he then realized that he could no longer represent ELIJAH MUHAMMAD. MALCOLM indicated that ELIJAH MUHAMMAD had children by six of his secretaries.

[BUREAU DELETION]

It is to be noted that since June, 1964, MALCOLM X and the MMI have attempted to publicize the illegitimate children of ELIJAH MUHAMMAD through various news media. MALCOLM X has been successful in getting the story on several radio programs during interviews, but a fear of a libel suit has apparently kept such publicity at a minimum. However, representatives of various news agencies have advised MALCOLM that they could publicize it if the women involved instituted legal action against ELIJAH MUHAMMAD.

AFFILIATION WITH THE ORGANIZATION
OF AFRO-AMERICAN UNITY (OAAU)

On June 30, 1964, [BUREAU DELETION] advised that
MALCOLM X sent [a] telegram on that date to Dr. MARTIN
LUTHER KING, Southern Christian Leadership Conference at
Saint Augustine, Florida, and also to [BUREAU DELETION]
the Student Non-Violent Coordinating Committee at Philadelphia, Mississippi, where both of the above were engaged in activities and demonstrations on behalf of the civil rights movement.

> Editor's note. *In this telegram Malcolm as Chairman of
> the OAAU offers to dispatch OAAU members to St. Augustine,
> Florida, to help blacks there organize themselves "into self-
> defensive units" so that they can effectively protect themselves
> against "the vicious attack of the white race" in the event that
> the federal government fails to send troops to their aid. He
> suggests that this would give the Ku Klux Klan "a taste of
> their own medicine" and demonstrate that "the day of turn-
> ing the other cheek to the inhuman brute beasts is long over."*

An OAAU-sponsored public meeting was held on December
13, 1964, at New York City, attended by about five hundred
people.

The featured speaker was OAAU Chairman and MMI leader
MALCOLM X. He devoted most of his speech to the Congo
situation, claiming that the United States is responsible for the
situation there because of its support for the Congo Premier MO-
ISE TSHOMBE. MALCOLM X charged that it was the United
States who was hiring white mercenaries for TSHOMBE and
these white mercenaries described by MALCOLM X as "hired
killers" are the ones who are killing innocent Africans.

MALCOLM X also spoke on Mississippi and indicated that
the struggle for independence by Africans was synonymous with
the struggle for freedom by Afro-Americans in the United States.
MALCOLM X also stated that the Federal Bureau of Investigation cannot stop the murders in Mississippi so "they" would have
to take care of it. He did not elaborate further on what "they"

would do other than to remark in jest that he would pay a reward of $1,000 to anyone who would "get" the sheriff and his deputy who were recently released after being arrested for killing three civil rights workers.

After giving his speech MALCOLM X introduced Negro comedian DICK GREGORY who joked for forty minutes, chiefly concerning law enforcement and the racial situation in the South.

BREAK FROM THE NATION OF ISLAM (NOI)

On June 4, 1964, MALCOLM X appeared on Radio Station WDAS, Philadelphia, Pennsylvania, and was asked why he left the Nation of Islam. MALCOLM stated that WALLACE MUHAMMAD, son of ELIJAH MUHAMMAD, is the one who really told him what was going on and told him to wake up and leave the organization. He said he learned from WALLACE MUHAMMAD that ELIJAH MUHAMMAD, NOI leader, fathered six illegitimate children by women who were secretaries at the NOI in Chicago. He said two of the women went to Phoenix and were put up in a motel in that city. Two other women were from Detroit. MALCOLM stated that JOHN ALI, National Secretary of the NOI, is currently running the NOI. He said ELIJAH MUHAMMAD's sons had him go to Phoenix so that JOHN ALI could run the organization. All members of the NOI were told to have absolutely nothing to do with MALCOLM. MALCOLM said JOHN ALI is running the organization (NOI) for one purpose and that is to get all the money out of it that he possibly can.

[BUREAU DELETION]

On June 12, 1964, MALCOLM X appeared on the PAUL VINCAQUIN program "Conversation for Peace," on Radio Station WEEI, Boston, Massachusetts. The program commenced at 2:10 P.M. and continued until 5:00 P.M. During the interview, MALCOLM stated that he was forced from the NOI because of a moral issue which he could no longer put up with and consequently severed relations with ELIJAH MUHAMMAD. . . .

MALCOLM stated that he realized that he could never again represent ELIJAH MUHAMMAD, knowing that one of the most high officials in the Muslim movement was the father of the children of six secretaries.

An article in the June 26, 1964 issue of the *New York Post,* a local New York newspaper, captioned "MALCOLM X to ELI-JAH; Let's End the Fighting." This article states:

Malcolm X today called for an end to the three month dispute which has split the black Muslim movement in Harlem.

In an open letter to ELIJAH MUHAMMAD, he urged an end to hostilities which threaten to flare into open warfare between the two groups, his dissidents and the parent body headed by ELIJAH. He called for unity in solving the problems of Negroes in Mississippi, Alabama, Georgia and other parts of the South.

"Instead of wasting all this energy fighting each other," he wrote, "we should be working in unity with other leaders and organizations in an effort to solve the very serious problems facing all Afro-Americans."

He asked ELIJAH MUHAMMAD how, since the Muslims did not resort to violence when they were attacked by "white racists" in Los Angeles and Rochester, N. Y., they could justify declaring war on each other.

MALCOLM X's statement came on the heels of an announcement by MUHAMMAD's followers that they had received a "tip" from one of MALCOLM's followers that plans were being made to assassinate ELIJAH MUHAMMAD when he arrives at Kennedy International Airport Sunday morning.

MALCOLM X, reached at his Boston hotel, denied that he or his followers were plotting to kill the Muslim leader. "I'm surprised at the accusation," he said. "No Muslim would think of assassinating MUHAMMAD. He has never been in any danger in his life.

"We don't have to kill him. What he has done will bring him to his grave."

MUHAMMAD's followers said that they would take every precaution to protect their leader. "We have our own security guards," they said. "We just want the police to know about the threat. MALCOLM wants to regain his position by killing the Messenger."

MALCOLM X scoffed at the accusation and said that the assassination threat was an excuse by MUHAMMAD to bypass the June 28th speaking engagement [in New York]. "I just don't think he'll come," he said.

ALLEGED THREATS AGAINST MALCOLM X
At New York

The *New York Herald Tribune,* a local New York daily newspaper, dated June 16, 1964, contained an article captioned "Eight Guards, Thirty-two Police for MALCOLM X." In this article it is stated that the police and guards were guarding MALCOLM X because of anonymous telephone tips to the wire service and a newspaper that MALCOLM would be shot if he appeared in court for an eviction trial. MALCOLM is quoted as saying, "There is no people in the United States more able to carry out this threat than the Black Muslims. I know; I taught them myself."

"MUHAMMAD was nobody until I came to New York as his emissary," MALCOLM stated. "If they had left me alone I would not have revealed any of this."

The *New York World Telegram and Sun,* dated June 18, 1964, contained an article captioned "MALCOLM X Man Marked for Death." This article states in part that "police fear that MALCOLM X is a marked man. The former East Coast leader of the Black Muslims goes nowhere without police shadows and his own core of rifle-bearing bodyguards. His own adherents insist he is targeted for assassination by June 29.

MALCOLM X contacted the New York City Police Department on July 7, 1964 and advised them that an attempt was made on his life that day.

[BUREAU DELETION]

MALCOLM X contacted the New York City Police Department on July 3, 1964, and advised them that he was returning home alone in his car at 11:30 P.M.the same date and stopped in front of his home at 33-11 [sic] 97th Street, East Elmhurst, New York, when two unknown Negro males approached his car and touched the door, at which time he sped away, drove around the block and returned to his residence and the two unknown Negro males were nowhere in sight.

A police guard was placed in front of MALCOLM's home until 4:00 P.M., July 4, 1964. It is believed that the complaint of MALCOLM X was a publicity stunt since he apparently notified the wire and news service as well as the police department about the incident.

[BUREAU DELETION]

MALCOLM X was contacted on July 5, 1964 [BUREAU DELETION], who advised MALCOLM that orders to kill him, MALCOLM, have come from Chicago and that witnesses can be furnished if MALCOLM wants to take the NOI to court.

[BUREAU DELETION]

At Boston, Massachusetts

On June 12, 1964, [BUREAU DELETION] Boston, Massachusetts, advised that at approximately 1:40 P.M. on the same date [BUREAU DELETION] had received an anonymous phone call concerning MALCOLM X. The caller stated that "MALCOLM X is going to be bumped off."

[BUREAU DELETION] advised that police were sent to guard MALCOLM X who was appearing on a radio program, Station WEEI at 182 Tremont Street, Boston, Massachusetts from 2:10 P.M. until 5:00 P.M. and at 10:00 P.M. the same date MALCOLM X was to appear on Radio Station WMEX, Boston.

MALCOLM X appeared on the JERRY WILLIAMS Radio Program on WMEX, Boston, from 10:00 P.M., June 12, 1964, to 1:00 A.M., June 13, 1964. WILLIAMS introduced MALCOLM X as the former spokesman for ELIJAH MUHAMMAD and the Muslims. He stated he understood several threats had been made on MALCOLM's life that day and MALCOLM stated that several threats had been made on his life during the last five months.

MALCOLM then remarked that recently on a radio program in Chicago known as "Hot Line," JOHN ALI, National Secretary of the Muslims, had been asked by a telephone caller if it was true that the Muslim Movement was trying to kill MALCOLM X. According to MALCOLM, JOHN ALI replied that they were trying to kill MALCOLM X and that he should be killed.

FOREIGN TRAVEL OF MALCOLM X
To Africa, April 13, 1964
through May 21, 1964

On May 21, 1964, Supervisor JOHN ADAMS, Immigration and Naturalization Service (INS), John F. Kennedy (JFK) International Airport, New York, advised that MALCOLM X LITTLE, Passport Number C294275, using the name MALIK EL SHABAZZ arrived in the United States at 4:25 P.M., aboard Pan American flight 115 from Paris, France.

On July 13, 1964, [BUREAU DELETION] furnished an itinerary of MALCOLM X during his trip to Africa which indicated the following schedule:

April 13, 1964	He departed the United States for Cairo, Egypt.
April 14 to May 5, 1964	In Cairo, United Arab Republic, Beirut, Lebanon and Saudi Arabia, where he completed pilgrimage to Mecca.
May 6, 1964	In Lagos, Nigeria.
May 8, 1964	In Ibadan, Nigeria.
May 10, 1964	In Accra, Ghana.
May 18, 1964	Morocco.
May 19, 1964	In Algiers.
May 21, 1964	Returned to the United States.

At Ibadan, Nigeria

[BUREAU DELETION] made available on May 27, 1964 a copy of the newspaper *Pilot,* datelined Ibadan, Nigeria, dated May 8, 1964, [which] contained an article of an interview with MALCOLM X. According to this article MALCOLM X stated

"United States Peace Corps are spies. They are missionaries of neo-colonialism and although white American Peace Corps were dangerous, enough to invoke protest from any country they were operating, Negro American Peace Corps were more dangerous and objectional." This article also stated that MALCOLM X remarked that the "Negroes in Peace Corps were being used by the American Government to place a wedge between American Negroes and Africans with views toward ending concept of Africanization of Negroes."

MALCOLM X added, "Peace Corps has been instructed to present such a repugnant image of American Negroes to the extent that Africans would be compelled to be unsympathetic to Negro causes in America."

MALCOLM X arrived in Ibadan, Nigeria on May 8, 1964. He visited the university of Ibadan where he spoke before an audience of from four hundred to five hundred persons sponsored by the National Union of Nigerian Students.

At Accra, Ghana

[BUREAU DELETION] advised on June 11, 1964 that MALCOLM X arrived in Accra, Ghana on May 11, 1964. He was not officially invited to Ghana by the Ghanaian Government but came at the invitation of the "Marxist Forum," a new student organization in the University of Ghana. He did not have an interview with President NKRUMAH nor did the government hold any official reception for him.

During his visit, MALCOLM spoke to the Association of Ghanaian Journalists and gave a lecture at the University of Ghana entitled "Will Africa Ignite America's Racial Powder Keg?" He also spoke before the students of Kwame Nkrumah Ideological Institute and to an informal group of Parliament members.

MALCOLM emphasized the following basic themes during his tour to Ghana.

1. The Negroes were stolen from Africa and forced to forget their culture and traditions, yet they never have been accepted into American society.

2. The Christian religion has been used to oppress Negroes and encourage them to accept an inferior position.

3. Force is the only possible way to achieve equality.

4. The United States is the "master of imperialism" without whose support other imperialistic nations could not exist.

5. White America is guilty of dehumanizing the American Negro and putting him to death as a human being.

6. If America is not interested in human rights in America, how can she be interested in human rights in Africa? The American Government should not send the Peace Corps to Africa, they should send them to Mississippi and Alabama.

7. The only difference between apartheid in South Africa and racism in the United States is that "while South Africa preaches and practices segregation, the United States preaches integration and practices segregation."

The *New York Amsterdam News,* local New York Negro newspaper, dated May 23, 1964, contained an article captioned "Is Mecca Trip Changing Malcolm X?" This article in part states:

Has the visit of Malcolm X, now El Hajj Malik El Shabbazz, to Mecca and with Muslim leaders in Africa changed him to become more soft in his anti-white feelings and to become more religious?

This is the feeling of this reporter following receipt of a newsletter this week from Nigeria in which Malcolm, who is due to return to New York next week, said that he was being received with warm hospitality throughout Africa where he said "they love us as their long-lost brothers."

Asserting that his trip to Mecca had officially established his new religious Muslim Mosque, Inc., at the Hotel Theresa, Malcolm said his trip had also established that Africans are interested in the plight of the nation's 22 million African-Americans.

A possible clue to Malcolm's suspected change in his militant racial attitudes was seen in a newsletter received this week by the Amsterdam News.

"As far as the Muslims of Asia, Arabia, and even Europe,

are concerned, in regards to the plight of the 22 million
African-Americans, the Koran compels all people who accept the Islam religion to take a firm stand on the side of
anyone whose human rights are being violated, no matter
what the religious persuasion of the victims may be."

Fresh from a visit to the Muslim holy city of Mecca and a
tour of several African nations, Malcolm X is scheduled to
return to New York Thursday afternoon, May 21, to launch
a drive urging closer ties between American Negroes and
Africans.

Malcolm hinted his new philosophy in a letter to the Amsterdam News in which he said that "we can learn much
from the strategy used by the American Jews. They have
never migrated physically to Israel, yet their cultural, philo-
sophical and psychological ties to Israel have enhanced their
political, economic and social position right there in America.

"Pan Africanism will do for people of African descent all
over the world the same that Zionism has done for Jews all
over the world," Malcolm wrote.

Malcolm's letters to this newspaper during his almost two
months in Africa indicate something of a change in his position to work for closer ties with civil rights leaders and a
lessening of his anti-white attitudes. During his visit to
Mecca he was the guest of the government for 12 days and
was treated as a dignitary in most of the places he traveled,
his letters asserted.

On May 23, 1964, MALCOLM X appeared on "Kup's Show,"
Channel 7-TV, Chicago, Illinois. On the panel show he was asked
if he was able to get into Mecca, a closed city, by his own identification or did he have to pass some kind of test to prove that he
was a Muslim.

MALCOLM said he arrived in Cairo about three in the morning and his inability to speak Arabic plus his American passport
made him automatically suspect. So he was taken from the group
that he originally started out from Cairo with and placed in a
compound which has been built there in Jedda which houses all

of the incoming pilgrims, and he thought about ninety thousand came in this year by plane alone. He was put in this place and he had to admit he was worried because he couldn't communicate. And he stayed there about twenty hours and he was in a haram (phonetic) which is a two-piece towel outfit. Your waist from the belt downward is wrapped in one towel and from the waist upward in another. And after being in this particular plight for about twenty hours, he recalled that Dr. SCHWARBE (phonetic) from New York had given him a book that had been sent to him by ABDARAKMAN AZAM (phonetic). The name of the book is "The Eternal Message of Muhammad." "So [MALCOLM] called his son and after reaching his son, his son came to the place where he was and used his authority to get him released, get [his] passport. He took him to his home where he met AZAM PARSHA (phonetic), and he gave him his suite at the Jedda Palace Hotel and the next morning he was visited by the son of Prince FAISAL (phonetic), MUHAMMAD FAISAL (phonetic). He informed him that he was to be a state guest so that the remaining twelve days that he was in Arabia, he was a guest of the state. They gave him a car—they placed a car at his disposal, gave him a guide—a mualam (phonetic), and a chauffeur and made it possible, after going before the highest committee of the court, for him to travel back and forth between Mecca and Jedda and Medina almost at will. He was given the highest honor and respect and hospitality that a visitor could receive anywhere.

On [BUREAU DELETION] 1964, [BUREAU DELETION] furnished a copy of a letter written by MALCOLM X from Jedda, Saudi Arabia, dated April 20, 1964, which stated that during his pilgrimage to Mecca, he observed many white persons who displayed the spirit of unity and brotherhood that he did not believe could ever have existed based on his previous American experience. He stated that America needs to understand Islam because it is the one religion that erases the race problem from society. He also stated that if whites and non-whites would accept Islam they would become changed people since it removes racism, and all members thus automatically accept each other as brothers and sisters. He went on in the letter to state "you may be shocked at these words coming from me" and he added that his pilgrimage has taught him that if Islam can replace the spirit of true brotherhood in the hearts of whites he has met there, it can also remove the "cancer of racism" from the heart of white America.

Travel to Africa from July 9, 1964 to November 14, 1964

On July 6, 1964, MALCOLM X, using the name HAJJ MALIK EL SHABAZZ with passport number C294275, purchased a one-way ticket to Cairo, Egypt via London, England. He was scheduled to depart from JFK International Airport, New York, on July 9, 1964, aboard Trans World Airlines (TWA) flight 700, due to arrive in London, England, 7:30 A.M., July 10, 1964. He was scheduled to depart London, England, 3:30 P.M., July 11, 1964, aboard United Arab Airlines, flight 790 to Cairo, Egypt. MALCOLM failed to make return reservations or airline bookings when he arrived in Cairo for his return trip to the United States.

At Cairo, Egypt

The *New York Times,* dated July 14, 1964, captioned "Malcolm X in Cairo Says He'll See African Leaders." This article, datelined Cairo, July 13, states:

Malcolm X the black nationalist leader said today that he had come to attend a meeting of the council of ministers of the Organization of African Unity as an observer. He arrived yesterday.

He said he intended to acquaint African heads of state "with the true plight of America's Negroes and thus show them how our situation is as much a violation of the United Nations human rights charter as the situation in Africa and Mongolia.

The *New York Journal American,* dated August 5, 1964, contained an article captioned "Malcolm X and the Red Chinese" written by VICTOR RIESEL. This article, datelined Cairo, stated that:

Malcolm X, whom the Chinese Communists call the "chairman of the Afro-American unity organization," spent a considerable amount of his time in the presence of international Communist propagandists here.

Not only did he endorse the rioting back home, but he publicly called for retaliation against the white community. He said the time had come to meet "violence with violence; an eye for an eye and a tooth for a tooth."

He prepared a series of inflammatory anti-U.S. documents here on the pretext of presenting them to the recent meeting of the Organization of African Unity, and it was reported across the world that he attended the conference. This is nonsense. He did not get near the parley. He was not accredited to it.

Malcolm X was not at any of the conference sessions. I was informed that it "is ridiculous" and "undignified" to think for a moment that anyone such as Malcolm X would be heard by the African counterpart of the Organization of American States.

Malcolm X's activity here was strictly a propaganda operation which he set up at the Hotel Semiramis, where some newsmen gathered. He made certain that his violent anti-U.S. diatribes were put in the hands of the Chinese Communist correspondents planted here by the New China News Agency.

But when Malcolm X wanted to be with his pro-Communist friends he came over to the Hotel Omar Khayam, a former palace. I vouch for this personally, I was there when he met Mrs. Shirley Graham DuBois, widow of the late Dr. W. E. DuBois, in the lobby. When the aged Dr. DuBois died recently, he was a member of the Communist Party, U.S.A. and had switched his citizenship to Ghana.

Hotel Omar Khayam was also the headquarters of the violently anti-U.S., pro-Communist Ghanaian delegation to the African States' conference. On Thursday, July 16, Malcolm X and his frequent companion, Mrs. DuBois, met for hours in the garden restaurant of the hotel.

Mrs. DuBois and her late husband spent much time in Peking. They were frequent guests of Mao-Tse-tung. Dr. DuBois delivered many anti-U.S. speeches which were broadcast across the world by the powerful Chinese mainland radio.

Mrs. DuBois has long been active in world Communist circles. Her background is important here to show the strange inter-weaving of characters now attempting to infiltrate and agitate the Negro communities of the U.S.

Mrs. DuBois knew the Castro brothers, Fidel and Raoul, in Mexico as far back as the late '40s. She is now associated with the pro-Communist *Freedomways,* a publication allegedly devoted to the Negroes.

In the past few years she has been a prolific writer in defense of the pro-Communist dictatorial state of Ghana.

Intelligence agents of several countries now are eager to learn just how Black Nationalist leader Malcolm X made contact with such Communist activists as Mrs. DuBois. Of considerable interest is the source of Malcolm X's funds now that the Muslims under Elijah Muhammad have declared war on him.

Malcolm X has been making expensive and extensive trips across Africa. I ran into his trail in several cities—especially in Ibadan, Nigeria, where he delivered speeches so anti-U.S., so incendiary, that they could be printed only on asbestos.

It is also being noticed that the Chinese Communist broadcasts have been featuring him and his splinter sect.

Why?

At Ibadan, Nigeria

The *New York Journal American,* dated July 25, 1964, contained an article written by VICTOR REISEL, captioned "Malcolm X Gives Africa Twisted Look." This article, datelined Ibadan, Nigeria, states:

I'm a long way from Harlem but not very far from Malcolm X and his Moslem Mosque, Inc. The effect of what he told university students in this city still reverberates in this land of 40 million people—good people, friendly people—eager to reach across the sea to us. But many of the young men and women in this town now shudder when they think of us—for Malcolm X was here, brutalizing us, charging us with being a vast national torture chamber.

He so aroused students at the Ibadan University during a lecture here that they threw a university staff member off the platform when the latter attempted to defend the U.S.

The least of what Malcolm shouted here was an ultimatum to the whites in America that they soon must face violence from his forces back home.

He literally screamed that the whites had made the American Negroes "drunkards and trained (them) to be hardened criminals, as the result of which American Negroes think of themselves as no more than above wild animals."

Knowing full well the hatred of the African for the African government of the Union of South Africa, Malcolm X then screamed: "Racial discrimination in the U.S. is worse than apartheid in South Africa."

Then he endangered the lives of many American youngsters of all races who are now teaching Africans in the veld, in the bush and in the Kraals and villages how to string electric lights, build schools, put in windows, and read their native language. Malcolm X did this by charging:

The U.S. Peace Corps members are all espionage agents and have a special assignment to perform. They are spies of the American government, missionaries of colonialism and neo-colonialism.

From here he went to Winneba, Ghana, where he addressed the students at the Kwame Nkrumah Ideological Institute, which is pro-Communist and where they hate us, anyway. There he said to hundreds of students that "the only language the whites understand is force and nothing else." He was cheered.

In other cities he got tougher. A cause is a cause, but trying to start an international racial war gets to be mighty dangerous.

The *New York Times,* dated August 13, 1964, contained an article captioned, "Malcolm X Seeks UN Negro Debate—He Asks African States to Cite United States Over Rights." This article, datelined Washington, August 12, states:

> The State Department and the Justice Department have begun to take an interest in Malcolm X's campaign to convince African states to raise the question of persecution of American Negroes at the United Nations.
>
> The Black Nationalist leader started his campaign July 17 in Cairo, where the 33 heads of independent African states held their second meeting since the Organization of African Unity was founded in Addis Ababa 14 months ago. . . .
>
> Malcolm also warned the heads of the African states that their countries would have no future unless the American Negro problem was solved. He said:

> Your problems will never be fully solved until and unless ours are solved. You will never be fully respected until and unless we are also respected. You will never be recognized as free human beings until and unless we are also recognized and treated as human beings.

Asserting that the Negro problem is not one of civil rights but of human rights, Malcolm said:

> If United States Supreme Court Justice Arthur Goldberg a few weeks ago, could find legal grounds to threaten to bring Russia before the United Nations and charge her with violating the human rights of less than three million Russian Jews—what makes our African brothers hesitate to bring the United States Government before the United Nations and charge her with violating the human rights of 22 million African-Americans?

We pray that our African brothers have not freed themselves of European colonialism only to be overcome and
held in check by American dollarism. Don't let American
racism be "legalized" by American dollarism.

Malcolm argued that "if South African racism is not a
domestic issue, then American racism also is not a domestic
issue."

The Black Nationalist, who quit the Chicago-based Black
Muslim movement led by Elijah Muhammad to form his
non-sectarian Organization of Afro-American Unity, said it
was the intention of his group in coalition with other Negro
groups "to elevate our freedom struggle above the domestic
level of civil rights."

                    At Addis Ababa, Ethiopia
[BUREAU DELETION] advised on 10/6/64 that on 10/3/64
MALCOLM X, during a three day visit to Addis Ababa, addressed the open student assembly of the university college at the
invitation of the University College Student Union. There was an
estimated audience of five hundred to six hundred persons consisting primarily of Ethiopian students and others consisting of
faculty members and outside visitors.

After a flattering and enthusiastic introduction by a student
leader ("known throughout Africa as a man standing for princi-
ple, truth and justice") Malcolm X presented a rather surpris-
ingly low-keyed lecture which stressed two major purposes of his
safari in Africa: 1) to remain away from the U.S. until after the
election in order to avoid making the decision as to whether he
(and presumably American Negroes in general) would be de-
voured by "a fox or a wolf"; and 2) to attempt to persuade the
independent African nations to haul the U.S. before the UN on
charges of being "unable or unwilling" to give the American
Negro his civil rights.

Malcolm X's speech employed clever distortions of truth to
lead to distorted conclusions—e.g., when World War II started,
the U.S. was not taking Negroes into the army or navy for fear

they would learn to use weapons against whites. The tone of the speech reflected Malcolm's assertion at the beginning that he had just concluded two months of "quiet rearrangement" of his "thinking" in Cairo. He was not nearly so emotional as he sometimes has been in the past, nor did he lay himself open to traps as often as he is sometimes prone to do.

The audience response was good, with several interruptions for applause, particularly during his attacks on the United States' effort in Africa.

Following Malcolm's speech the student moderator felt compelled to note that of course African students don't believe that United States aid comes "out of human kindness." The four questions from the audience were rather bland, but did permit Malcolm to develop the theme that while Goldwater was a rather open racist, Johnson ("the fox") was more subtle, but that the latter's record during thirty years in Congress was also that of a racist. In discussing the coming election, he stated that the American people don't govern, that southern-dominated congressional committees control under the seniority system and it is they "who send military equipment to Tshombe."

In answering the final question, he emphasized the relative unity between himself and such leaders as Martin Luther King, saying that their differences were primarily differences of method rather than goals. "The main difference is that he doesn't mind being beat up and I do."

[BUREAU DELETION] advised on 10/19/64 that the local press in Nairobi (not further identified) reported that MALCOLM X flew from Dar-es-Salaam to Kenya with African leaders KENYATTA and OBOTE on October 18, 1964. MALCOLM is quoted as saying that Americans will never voluntarily give American Negroes freedom until forced to and that as ministers they (Negroes) do not have the forces. According to MALCOLM, Africa has the key to the Negro problem solution and will determine the degrees of freedom because the African leaders hold the strategic power balance in world affairs. He said that part of his mission to Africa was to make (African) leaders aware of their position of power. He stated that American aid was not a favor to Africa because Africa contributed human flesh to the

American economy. MALCOLM further stated that he was surprised at the support which African leaders have for the American Negro cause. According to MALCOLM they had all showed
him unlimited concern and sympathy.

MALCOLM X left Addis Ababa on October 19, 1964.

At Lagos, Nigeria

[BUREAU DELETION] advised on 11/6/64 that MAL-
COLM X visited Lagos for the second time on October 29, 1964.
He previously visited Lagos in May, 1964.

On his arrival on October 29, 1964, he held a press conference.
MALCOLM X was quoted as saying that he was "touring Africa
to better acquaint himself with the problems facing the continent
so that he could tell his people at home about these problems,
factually and in detail." MALCOLM X said that "one of the
greatest problems facing Africa was internal squabbling" and
continued, "in East Africa it is the Africans against the Asians,
and in West Africa, it is the Moslem against Christians and all
these are fed by outside force."

At Conakry, French West Africa

[BUREAU DELETION] advised on 11/14/64 that MAL-
COLM X left Conakry by plane on November 13, 1964. He was
"GOG Guest" and carried a visitor's visa. He visited the hospital
ship "SS Hope" twice accompanied by a GOG interpreter and
took pictures. He was enthusiastic about "Project Hope," saying
"it was the best United States project he had seen in Africa and
especially commended integration aboard ship."

Return to United States from African Tour on 11/24/64:

[BUREAU DELETION] New York City, advised on November 24, 1964, that passenger manifest list of TWA flight 801,
Paris, France, contained the name "SHABAZZ." This flight was
scheduled to arrive at JFK International Airport, 6:00 P.M., November 24, 1964.

Special Agents of the Federal Bureau of Investigation (FBI)
observed MALCOLM X arriving JFK International Airport via

TWA flight 801 from Paris, France, at 6:41 P.M., November 24, 1964.

At London, England, November 30
1964 to December 6, 1964

On November 27, 1964, [BUREAU DELETION] British Overseas Airways Corporation (BOAC), New York City, advised that MALCOLM LITTLE was scheduled to leave New York City via BOAC from JFK International Airport and to arrive in London, England, December 1, 1964. He further stated that MALCOLM LITTLE planned to return to the United States on December 6, 1964 [BUREAU DELETION].

At a reception for MALCOLM X held on November 29, 1964, sponsored by the OAAU, he remarked that he was traveling to London, England, on November 30, 1964, and would debate at Oxford University on December 1, 1964.

[BUREAU DELETION]

MISCELLANEOUS

On September 4, 1964, [BUREAU DELETION] Rome, New York, furnished the following information to SA [BUREAU DELETION].

[BUREAU DELETION] stated that on September 1, 1964, he visited the office of ALEXANDER PALMER HALEY, a Negro writer and newspaper correspondent at 414 West Dominick Street, Rome, New York, on an official matter. According to [BUREAU DELETION] HALEY advised he had just completed a book he had written concerning MALCOLM X LITTLE. [BUREAU DELETION] HALEY indicated he had been in contact with MALCOLM X on more than one occasion in regard to this writing, and that he, HALEY, and MALCOLM are to share in the royalties expected from this book.

OPINION OF THE DEPARTMENT OF STATE
A. Re MALCOLM X

By letter dated September 2, 1964, J. WALTER YEAGLEY, Assistant Attorney General, Internal Security Division, Department of Justice, advised that MALCOLM K. LITTLE aka

MALCOLM X, in the course of his recent tour of the Middle East and African countries, has reportedly been in communication and contact with heads of foreign governments urging that they take the issue of "racialism" in America before the United Nations as a threat to world peace.

Mr. YEAGLEY indicated that since such activities could conceivably fall within the provisions of the Logan Act, and are moreover deemed to be inimical to the best interests of our country and prejudicial to our foreign policy, the Department of Justice requested the Secretary of State to make appropriate inquiries of our embassies in the Middle East and Africa for any pertinent information concerning MALCOLM X's alleged contacts and communications with heads of foreign governments.

Mr. YEAGLEY expressed concern over the fact that MALCOLM X's activities abroad indicate a possible violation of the Logan Act.

B. Re MMI

By letter dated September 28, 1964, Mr. YEAGLEY advised that if evidence is available which will establish the MMI has been or is receiving funds from any Arab or African government, or is acting at the order, request or under the direction of the foreign government, it may be obligated to register under the Foreign Agents Registration Act.

SECTION 15

February 4, 1965–February 25, 1965

REPORTS: 1. February 4, 1965. SAC, Chicago to Director. Airtel
2. February 8, 1965. New York
3. February 9, 1965. New York
4. February 10, 1965. Paris, Jack Monet article, *New York Herald Tribune*
5. February 16, 1965. New York
6. February 17, 1965. SAC, Detroit to Director. Airtel
7. February 17, 1965. Detroit
8. February 16, 1965. New York
9. February 19, 1965. SAC, Chicago to Director. Airtel
10. February 18, 1965. New York to Director. Teletype
11. February 22, 1965. New York to Director. Teletype
12. February 22, 1965. New York to Director. Teletype
13. February 23, 1965. Washington D.C. to Director. Teletype
14. February 24, 1965. Memo. Philadelphia
15. February 22, 1965. Memo. Baumgardner to Sullivan
16. February 22, 1965. Memo. Bland to Sullivan
17. February 22, 1965. Chicago to Director. Teletype
18. February 22, 1965. Memo. Bland to Sullivan

19. February 22, 1965. Memo. Bland to Sullivan
20. February 24, 1965. New York to Director. Teletype
21. February 25, 1965. Memo. SAC, New York to Director

This section, one of the most confusing, covers the period leading up to the assassination and the assassination itself. The furious pace of his schedule increased even more in the month of February as Malcolm inwardly conceded that his life was nearing its end. He actively rethought his philosophy and was, as he said in his autobiography, "man enough to tell you that I can't put my finger on exactly what my philosophy is now, but I'm flexible" (p.428).

He apparently covered his finances for this final period with a $20,000 advance on his autobiography from the publishers, Doubleday and Co., but even these funds would be spent by the time of his death.

His final weeks were clearly frustrating for him. Authorities denied him entrance into France on February 9, causing him to exclaim, "I thought I was in South Africa. They let . . . Tshombe in. He's the worst person on earth."

This episode also caused him to reconsider his indictment of the NOI as his killers, as he noted in his autobiography:

But you know . . . the more I keep thinking about this thing, the things that have been happening lately, I'm not at all sure it's the Muslims. I know what they can do, and what they can't, and they can't do some of the stuff recently going on . . . the more I keep thinking about what happened to me in France, I think I'm going to quit saying it's the Muslims. (pp. 430–431)

His home in East Elmhurst, Queens was firebombed in the early morning of February 14, and he was soon after evicted by a court order. The FBI clearly believes that he attempted to burn the house himself. He was killed one week later, on Sunday, February 21 at the Audubon Ballroom.

The extent of the FBI's knowledge about Malcolm's assassination is difficult to surmise from the correspondence provided in this edition of the file, but it seems that lower-level agents were taken by surprise. It also seems that from the moment of Malcolm's death, the FBI suspected groups other than just the NOI. One informant told FBI agents that it looked like an inside job of the MMI. One source, with confirmation from another, indicated that investigators should "check out Washington and [the] CIA because they wanted Malcolm out of the way because he 'snafued' African relations for the U.S."

The reports of the shooting and evidence continue into the next section, but enough reports from this section indicate that the FBI might have thought that Malcolm's own people were responsible, due to the fact that Malcolm's guards appeared negligent that afternoon, and, according to a witness, there was "a definite lack of security at this rally." It is interesting to note that the FBI was aware that a pack of Camel cigarettes was found in a green suit coat with the sawed-off shotgun. Muslims are not supposed to smoke.

The FBI had to deal with the most prominent suspects, which at the time were Hayer and the NOI. Talmadge Hayer had been apprehended, and an OAAU member had turned in the .45 caliber pistol he had used in the shooting. This member would apparently figure heavily in the trial of Hayer in 1966. The FBI questioned this witness extensively along with witnesses who stated that MMI members would attempt to retaliate against the NOI and Elijah Muhammad.

FBI

Date: 2/4/65

Transmit the following in _____
                                                    (Type in plain text or code)

Via_____AIRTEL_____ _____
                                                    (Priority or method of Mailing)

TO   : DIRECTOR, FBI (100-399321)
FROM   : SAC, CHICAGO (100-33593) (P)
SUBJECT:
MALCOLM K. LITTLE, aka
          IS-MMI
          (OO: New York)

Re Chicago teletype to Director dated 1/29/65.

Referenced teletype stated that MALCOLM X was to appear on "Kup's Show," a TV panel-type discussion, on 1/30/65 in Chicago.

"Kup's Show" is a local TV show televised over WBKB-TV, Chicago, from approximately 12:15 A.M. to 3:00 A.M. on Sunday mornings. This show was televised on 1/31/65 but was taped on

1/30/65 P.M. at studios of WBKB-TV, Chicago. IRVING
KUPCINET, Chicago newspaper columnist and TV moderator,
conducts the show.

The following is the transcript:

KUPCINET: MALCOLM, you know you've changed a lot
since your first appearance on this show some
years ago. At that time you were sort of a stormy
individual and you hated all whites you said.

MALCOLM: I've gotten older.

KUPCINET: Now you have a different attitude completely
and you told me that your religious experience in
Cairo has changed your attitude and your outlook.

MALCOLM: Well, as a Muslim, since I left ELIJAH
MUHAMMAD's Black Muslim movement, I
should say since they put me out 'cause that is
what they did, I have had a chance to do some
traveling and travel does broaden your scope,
and as a Muslim whose religion is Islam, as it is
practiced and taught in the Muslim world, I realize that it is impossible to call oneself a Muslim,
to call one's religion Islam and at the same time
judge a man by the color of his skin. . . .

KUPCINET: This poses two very interesting things. In other
words, you no longer believe as ELIJAH
MUHAMMAD has been quoted as saying that
all white men are devils. You have changed everything.

MALCOLM: If ELIJAH MUHAMMAD says that all white
men are devils, then you have the King of Arabia, King Faisal, who is white. He is the keeper
of the Holy City of Mecca and many other
Arabs, in Egypt, in Algeria, and in other places.
They are from all appearances white.

KUPCINET: Now this poses a second problem I would like to
get your opinion on. Of course, you may be bi-

ased because you no longer are a member of the
so-called Black Muslims, but is the Black Muslim a religion or not, because this is coming up in
a case in Chicago where a prisoner in Stateville
converted from Roman Catholicism to Black
Muslim and demanded to be allowed to practice
his religion in jail. The warden denied this because he said the Black Muslims were not a bona
fide religion. How do you feel?

MALCOLM: I want to answer that with this explanation first.
Number one: no one can use me against ELIJAH
MUHAMMAD or against the Black Muslim
movement. On the other hand, anything that
ELIJAH MUHAMMAD says or does, or the
Black Muslim movement says or does, which I
feel is against the best interest of the Black community, then I will attack it myself, but I won't
attack it because someone sics me on it. . . . Islam teaches that belief in all of the prophets, especially MUHAMMAD ibn ABD ALLAH,
who was born and died in Arabia fourteen hundred years ago and the Muslim believes that
MUHAMMAD of Arabia was the last prophet,
the last messenger, whereas ELIJAH MUHAM-
MAD teaches that MUHAMMAD of Arabia
was not a prophet, but an enthusiast, and that he,
himself, ELIJAH, is the prophet, so that . . .
what ELIJAH MUHAMMAD is teaching is dia-
metrically opposed to the principles of Islam and
the Muslim world itself, the religious officials at
Mecca and other religious officials and those at
the top authority on Islam theology, totally reject what ELIJAH MUHAMMAD teaches as
being any phase, even of Islam. On the other
hand, what he is teaching can be easily defined as
a religion, but it cannot be labeled Islam . . .
and I think that if the penal authorities were far-
sighted enough to permit the religion of Islam,

real Islam, true Islam, to be taught in prison by qualified Islamic religious leaders as they let Judaism, Catholicism and the Protestant religions be taught there, then many of the people that are in prison would not be misled like I, myself, was because there is a vacuum in this country where Islam is concerned . . . and in that vacuum, it is easy for any phony or faker to come along with a concocted, distorted product of his own making, and say that this is Islam.

KUPCINET: Are you by inference saying that ELIJAH MUHAMMAD is a faker and a phony?

MALCOLM: If ELIJAH MUHAMMAD really believed in the same God that I believed in—I believe in ELIJAH MUHAMMAD stronger than he believed in himself. I believed in his God more than he did and I was not aware of this until I found he was confronted with a crisis in his own personal moral life and he did not stand up as a man. Anybody could make a moral mistake, but when they have to lie about it and will be willing to see that murder is committed to cover up their mistake not only are they not divine, they are not even a man. . . .

KUPCINET: Are you trying to tell us that there has been an attack on your life because of your withdrawal from the Muslim religion?

MALCOLM: I have had several.

KUPCINET: You have?

MALCOLM: And just thanks to ALLAH, so far I have been successful. I believe that when you are a black man born in this particular society, you are faced with certain dangers already. You get used to it and plus the stand that I took when I was in the Black Muslim movement was uncompromising. I defended an indefensible position. Anyone that defends an indefensible position as I did—they must have believed in it.

UNITED STATES DEPARTMENT OF JUSTICE
FEDERAL BUREAU OF INVESTIGATION

New York, New York
February 8, 1965

Malcolm K. Little

Internal Security—Muslim Mosque, Incorporated

On February 5, 1965 [BUREAU DELETION] advised that they recently received the following information concerning the source of finances of MMI and OAAU leader Malcolm K. Little, better known as Malcolm X. This information [BUREAU DELETION]

Malcolm X has recently received the sum of $20,000 which represents an advance on his forthcoming book, to be published by Doubleday and Company, Incorporated; and, as payment for the autobiography on him which appeared in the September 12, 1964, edition of the magazine, "The Saturday Evening Post."

[BUREAU DELETION] also advised that Malcolm X has also undoubtedly received some compensation for appearances and speeches he has recently made on radio and television and at several colleges.

This document contains neither recommendations nor conclusions of the Federal Bureau of Investigation; it is the property of the Federal Bureau of Investigation and is loaned to your agency; it and its contents are not to be distributed outside your agency.

UNITED STATES DEPARTMENT OF JUSTICE
FEDERAL BUREAU OF INVESTIGATION

New York, New York
February 9, 1965

Malcolm K. Little

Internal Security—Muslim Mosque, Incorporated

On February 5, 1965, Malcolm K. Little was observed by agents of the Federal Bureau of Investigation boarding Trans World Airlines, (TWA), Flight 700, at John F. Kennedy (JFK) International Airport for London, England. TWA Flight 700 departed JFK International Airport at 8:11 P.M., and was scheduled to arrive at London, England at 11:15 P.M., London time.

[BUREAU DELETION] TWA, JFK International Airport, advised, on February 5, 1965, that Malcolm Little purchased an economy class ticket under the name M. Shabazz for London, Paris, Geneva, and return to New York. [BUREAU DELETION] stated that Little departed for London, England on TWA Flight 700, on February 5, 1965, with "open dates" to continue his trip to Paris, Geneva, and return trip to New York.

[BUREAU DELETION] that Little paid $478.80 cash for his plane tickets.

FBI

Date: 2/10/65

Transmit the following in_____
(Type in plain text or code)

Via____AIRTEL____ _____
(Priority or method of mailing)

TO   :   DIRECTOR, FBI (100-399321)
FROM   :   LEGAT, PARIS (100-2171) (P)
SUBJECT: MALCOLM K. LITTLE, also
            known as Malcom X, M.
            Shabazz
            IS-MMI

[BUREAU DELETION]

Clipping from the *New York Herald Tribune* . . . enclosed herewith for the Bureau.

If we receive any additional information from [BUREAU DELETION] relative to subject we will promptly furnish it to the Bureau and interested offices.

New York Herald Tribune, European Edition
February 10, 1965, page 3

France Bars Malcolm X To Avoid "Trouble" at Meeting

By Jack Monet

Paris, Feb. 9.—French authorities today barred Malcolm X from entering the country to deliver a talk.

The American black nationalist leader arrived from London at Orly International Airport this morning, learned from French security officials that his presence was "undesirable" and was put on a flight back to London two hours later.

An Interior Ministry spokesman said it was decided that a meeting Malcolm X was to address tonight could "provoke demonstrations that would trouble public order."

Malcolm X, the most outspoken exponent of violent activities to further Negro-as-such strength in the United States, was to speak at the Salle de la Mutualité on "The Afro-American Struggle for Freedom."

The meeting tonight was sponsored by the Federation of African Students in France, the principal African student organization here, and the Committee of Members of the Afro-American Community in Paris.

Despite the proscription of Malcolm X, the Prefecture of Police maintained its authorization for the meeting, so the sponsors decided to go ahead later tonight with a quickly organized "protest" session.

About 300 persons, a third of them white, attended the meeting. The speakers denounced the ban on Malcolm X, white mercenary intervention in the Congo and American raids on North Vietnam, all interpreted as attacks on non-white peoples.

In London, Malcolm X expressed shock at his treatment in France. "The authorities would not even let me contact the American embassy," he said."

"I thought I was in South Africa. They let (Congolese Premier) Tshombe in. He's the worst person on earth."

————— • • —————

UNITED STATES DEPARTMENT OF JUSTICE FEDERAL BUREAU OF INVESTIGATION

New York, New York
February 16, 1965

Malcolm K. Little

        Internal Security—Muslim Mosque, Incorporated
[BUREAU DELETION] New York City Police Department (NYCPD), advised the New York Office of the Federal Bureau of Investigation (FBI) on February 14, 1965, that early that morning Malcolm X's home was destroyed by a fire.

On February 14, 1965, a conference was held at the 114th Precinct, NYCPD, at 23-16 30th Avenue, Queens, New York, with Special Agents (SAs) of the FBI, [BUREAU DELETION] Detective District, New York City, [BUREAU DELETION] New York City, concerning the burning of the residence of Malcolm X, 23-11 97th Street, East Elmhurst, Queens, New York, leader of the MMI and the OAAU.

[BUREAU DELETION] stated that the first alarm was received by telephone at 2:46 A.M. February 14, 1965, from [BUREAU DELETION] East Elmhurst, Queens, New York. [BUREAU DELETION] later interviewed by the fire department, stated she was awakened by the noise of glass breaking. She looked out the window and saw a round hole in Malcolm X's living room window, and the room was in flames. [BUREAU DELETION] stated she saw no one near Malcolm X's residence at that time.

[BUREAU DELETION] advised that the second alarm was sounded by [BUREAU DELETION] Queens, New York, a cab

driver who, with an unidentified passenger, noticed a bush burning in front of Malcolm X's residence. [BUREAU DELETION]
said he put the bush fire out and while doing so, he heard glass
breaking twice. He stated he then looked along the side of the
house, and saw a fire in the rear of the home. He then stated he
knocked at the front door of Malcolm X's home and at the same
time, heard voices inside. He then knew that they were awake so
he ran to set off the fire alarm.

[BUREAU DELETION] said that from the time he first saw
the bush fire in front of the home to the time the fire department
arrived, he neither saw nor heard any person or vehicle leaving
the area.

[BUREAU DELETION] stated the fire engines arrived at
Malcolm X's home at 2:50 A.M. on 2/14/65. He stated the fire
was confined to the living room area, with smoke and water dam-
aging areas of the home. He stated Malcolm X, his wife and four
children, ages six months to six years, escaped through the back
door and were in the back yard when the fire apparatus arrived.

[BUREAU DELETION] stated that an investigation conducted by the New York City Police and Fire Departments disclosed the following:

Investigation of Fire

1. The bushes and front of the home on the right side of the
   front steps were scorched.
2. The fire was confined to the living room only.
3. The rear bedroom window was broken, the ground and
   fence in the vicinity of the broken rear window were
   scorched.
   The venetian blind on the broken rear window was closed
   and down, and was scorched at the bottom, although there
   was no evidence of fire in the rear bedroom.

Evidence Obtained At Scene of Fire

1. The bottom 1/8 part of a whiskey bottle containing gasoline
   was found in the enclosed front porch. The glass of the bottle was
   scorched, although there was no evidence of a fire in the front
   porch area.

2. A quart whiskey bottle filled with gasoline was located standing upright on the dresser in the rear bedroom where Malcolm X's other daughters slept. This bottle had a screw cap which was intact and did not have rags attached to it.

It is noted that all firemen who entered Malcolm X's home during the fire were interviewed and all stated they did not place the bottle on the dresser.

3. A broken neck of a whiskey bottle with a scorched cloth wick attached to the neck of the bottle was located in the rear of the said home at approximately 15 feet from the house and near the bedroom with the broken window and scorched ground and fence.

4. A broken neck of a whiskey bottle and shoulder of a whiskey bottle which matched the neck section was found in the center of Malcolm X's bedroom. A piece of cloth soaked with gasoline but unscorched, was on the bedroom floor a few feet from the broken whiskey bottle. No evidence of a fire could be located in this bedroom.

The youngest daughter, age six months, slept in a third bedroom opposite Malcolm X's room.

No evidence of bottles could be located in the living room where the fire was confined, but according to [BUREAU DELETION] there was evidence that gasoline was used in the living room fire.

[BUREAU DELETION]

The investigation by [BUREAU DELETION] and [BUREAU DELETION] determined that Malcolm X stated he awoke himself and discovered the fire and that his wife, Betty, stated that she awoke him and then grabbed their children and left their home through the rear door.

Malcolm X, after the fire, and during the interview, showed no emotion or anger and actually laughed when he was asked who he thought may have burned his home.

Malcolm X left his family with friends, returned to his home after the fire was put out, secured some clothing and recording tapes and left about 9:00 A.M. for a meeting in Detroit.

[BUREAU DELETION] NYCPD, advised on February 14, 1965, that Malcolm X and his family are staying at the home of

Thomas Wallace, 34-50 110th Street, East Elmhurst, Queens, New York, who is a known member of the MMI.

[BUREAU DELETION] advised on February 14, 1965, that Malcolm X departed from New York City by plane at 9:30 A.M. February 14, 1965, for Detroit, Michigan.

———————— • •————————

2/17/65

AIRTEL
TO: DIRECTOR, FBI
FROM: SAC, DETROIT (157-838)(P)
AFRO-AMERICAN BROADCASTING
AND RECORDING COMPANY
DETROIT, MICH.
RACIAL MATTERS

[BUREAU DELETION]
On 2/14/65, at approximately 11:30 A.M., [BUREAU DELETION] MALCOLM LITTLE from the city limits of Detroit to the Statler Hilton Hotel where he registered in room 638. [BUREAU DELETION]

Upon arriving at the Statler Hilton Hotel, [BUREAU DELETION] immediately began to question MALCOLM LITTLE regarding the bombing of his home in New York. LITTLE related that he did not see any of the perpetrators but he believed that the bombing was a result of a feud between himself and ELIJAH MOHAMMAD; however, it is the opinion of [BUREAU DELETION] that LITTLE did see at least one of the men responsible for the bombing because he later stated that he had attempted to fire a .25 caliber automatic to frighten off the men, but the gun misfired.

About this time, [BUREAU DELETION] became concerned about LITTLE's health and he called for the services of a [BUREAU DELETION] who arrived [BUREAU DELETION] and administered a sedative to MALCOLM LITTLE. After the drug was administered MALCOLM became very drowsy and incoherent for the remainder of the day.

At approximately 4:00 P.M. on 2/14/65, MALCOLM LIT-
TLE was awakened to be interviewed by a news crew from
WXYZ-TV. During the remainder of the day and up to approxi-
mately one-half hour before his speech, he slept.

────────── • •──────────

UNITED STATES DEPARTMENT OF JUSTICE
FEDERAL BUREAU OF INVESTIGATION

Detroit, Michigan
February 17, 1965
Re:Afro-American Broadcasting
and Recording Company
Detroit, Michigan

[BUREAU DELETION] that Malcolm Little was the featured
speaker at the First Annual Dignity Projection and Scholarship
Award ceremony sponsored by the Afro-American Broadcasting
and Recording Company on February 14, 1965, at the Ford Auditorium, 20 East Jefferson Avenue, Detroit, Michigan.

Editor's note. *Excerpted in the file are Malcolm's comments
on the hyprocrisy of a society that preaches brotherhood on
Sunday but fails to practice it any day, a society that in the
name of brotherhood every day practices violence against people of color everywhere. Emphatically stating that he "would
not call upon anybody to be violent without a cause," Malcolm then makes it clear that black Americans have long had
cause and that the time has come for them to protect themselves against their oppressors "no matter how many necks
[they have] to break and heads [they have] to crack."*

*Malcolm later points up the need of his people to "start
learning a new language"—a language that the Ku Klux
Klan, "a cowardly outfit," can understand. It is the duty of
blacks themselves to stop the crimes being committed against
them and assert the human rights the federal government, for
all its talk, has continually failed to grant them.*

*After commenting on the role of the Organization of Afro-
American Unity in the struggle for human rights at an inter-*

national level, Malcolm speaks of the organization's need na-
tionally for involvement in voter registration—but not without
voter education. He would not, however, send any civil rights
workers to states like Mississippi and Alabama "without some
kind of protection" and without training in the arts of self-
defense.

Malcolm concludes by stating "again that I am not a rac-
ist; I do not believe in any form of segregation or anything
like that; I am for the brotherhood of everybody, but I do not
believe in forcing brotherhood upon people who do not want
it."

UNITED STATES DEPARTMENT OF JUSTICE
FEDERAL BUREAU OF INVESTIGATION

New York, New York
February 16, 1965
Organization of Afro-American Unity
Internal Security—Miscellaneous

[BUREAU DELETION] OAAU held a public rally from 8:15
P.M. to 10:15 P.M., February 15, 1965, at the Audubon Ballroom,
Broadway and 166th Street, New York City. Approximately six
hundred persons were in attendance. There was extensive press
coverage of the rally.

The meeting was opened by MMI Assistant Minister Benjamin
X Goodman who made a few introductory remarks and then
introduced the featured speaker, OAAU and MMI leader, Malcolm X Little.

Malcolm X talked at length on the firebombs which were
thrown into his house in the early morning of February 14, 1965,
destroying the house. He was quite angry and upset that the
incident had placed his wife and daughters in danger and he
angrily accused the NOI of doing it on the direct orders of NOI
leader, Elijah Muhammad. He ridiculed the suggestion by the
NOI that he set the fire himself and claimed that he knew absolutely nothing about his being evicted from the house on Febru-

ary 15, 1965, based on a court action by the NOI, until he heard it on the radio on February 15, 1965.

Malcolm X then claimed that a conspiracy exists between the NOI and the Ku Klux Klan that is not in the best interest of the black people. He alleged that both the NOI and the Klan have agreed to leave each other alone and that the Klan has offered land in North Carolina to the NOI for the latter's "separate state" for Negroes plan. Malcolm X also implied that Elijah Muhammad and his NOI are sympathetically linked with George Lincoln Rockwell and his American Nazi Party.

[An article in the February 16, 1965, edition of the *New York Times*] explained that the house of Malcolm X at 23-11 97th Street, East Elmhurst, Queens, New York, was set aflame by firebombs thrown into it on February 14, 1965, and a NOI official had previously indicated that he believed that Malcolm X had set off the firebombs himself to get publicity. This article further indicated that the NOI held title to the house and had obtained a court order in June, 1964, calling for Malcolm X to vacate the house, an order he had appealed to the New York Appellate Division. However, Malcolm X was evicted from the ruined house on February 15, 1965, when the (Queens County) Civil Court refused Malcolm X a further stay of the eviction.

This article went on to state that at the OAAU Rally on February 15, 1965, Malcolm X stated that in the racial situation he has switched his attack to the (Ku Klux) Klan and (George Lincoln) Rockwell, leader of the American Nazi Party. Malcolm X indicated that he was doing this because he had seen NOI leader Elijah Muhammad make agreements with Rockwell and the Klan that were not in the interests of Negroes.

———— • • ————

FBI

Date: 2/19/65

Transmit the following in_____
                    (Type in plain text or code)

Via_____AIRTEL_____ _____
                    (Priority or method of Mailing)

TO   : DIRECTOR, FBI
FROM   : SAC, CHICAGO (100-35635)
SUBJECT: NATION OF ISLAM
          IS—NOI

Re Philadelphia teletype to Director, Chicago and New York
dated 2/16/65, entitled "Organization of Afro-American Unity,
IS—MISCELLANEOUS."

Referenced teletype reflected a meeting of the OAAU was held
on 2/15/65, at Audubon Ballroom, in New York City; that
MALCOLM LITTLE was the main speaker and alleged that
while he was active in the NOI in 12/60, he attended a meeting
with [BUREAU DELETION] of ELIJAH MUHAMMAD's
Mosque [BUREAU DELETION] and KKK officials at [BU-
REAU DELETION] home in Atlanta for the purpose of negoti-
ating for land for ELIJAH MUHAMMAD to set up a separate
state in Georgia or in South Carolina. LITTLE further alleged
that GEORGE LINCOLN ROCKWELL and his American
Nazi Party and KKK and ELIJAH MUHAMMAD were connected.

Regarding MALCOLM's allegations concerning the meeting
with officials of the KKK in Atlanta in 1960, attention is directed
to report of SA [BUREAU DELETION] dated 4/14/61. Pages
44 and 45 carry information reflecting ELIJAH MUHAMMAD
spoke at Magnolia Ballroom in Atlanta, Georgia, on 9/11/60.
Pages 96 and 97 set forth information regarding a meeting between MALCOLM LITTLE and [BUREAU DELETION] with

KKK leaders at Atlanta in late [BUREAU DELETION] This is apparently the meeting LITTLE was referring to.

Regarding LITTLE's allegations that MUHAMMAD is connected with the American Nazi Party, attention is directed to report of SA [BUREAU DELETION] dated 4/24/62. Pages 122 through 125 set forth information regarding an appearance by GEORGE LINCOLN ROCKWELL at the Annual Muslim Convention held at Chicago, Illinois, on 2/25/62, and also sets forth information regarding MUHAMMAD's comments regarding ROCKWELL and his associates. Attention is also directed to report of SA [BUREAU DELETION] dated 10/24/62. Page 132 sets forth information regarding alleged cooperation between the American Nazi Party and the NOI.

FEDERAL BUREAU OF INVESTIGATION
U. S. DEPARTMENT OF JUSTICE

COMMUNICATIONS SECTION

FEBRUARY 18, 1965
TELETYPE
SENT BY CODED TELETYPE
FBI NEW YORK
7-16 PM URGENT 2-18-65 DAE
TO DIRECTOR -10- 100-399321
FROM NEW YORK 105-8999
MALCOLM K. LITTLE, AKA IS-MMI.

RENYAIRTELS AND LHM-S DATED FEB. SIXTEEN, SIXTY FIVE CAPTIONED AS ABOVE AND OTHER CAPTIONED OAAU, IS-MISC.

AT NINE AM FEB. EIGHTEEN, SIXTY FIVE MALCOLM X OFFICIALLY EVICTED FROM HIS RESIDENCE TWENTY THREE-ELEVEN NINETY SEVENTH ST., EAST ELMHURST, QUEENS, NY, AT WHICH TIME REGINALD THORPE, MARSHAL OF CITY OF NEW YORK TURNED RESIDENCE OVER TO [BUREAU DELETION] NOI MOSQUE NUMBER SEVEN, NYC. MALCOLM X MOVED BELONGINGS FROM RESIDENCE AT ONE AM FEB.

EIGHTEEN, SIXTY FIVE. [BUREAU DELETION] AD-
VISED FEB. EIGHTEEN, SIXTY FIVE MALCOLM X NOW
RESIDING AT THIRTY FOUR-FIFTY ONE HUNDRED
TENTH ST., EAST ELMHURST, QUEENS, NY WITH MMI
MEMBER.
SND AND PLS HOLD............

———————. •———————

FEDERAL BUREAU OF INVESTIGATION
U. S. DEPARTMENT OF JUSTICE

COMMUNICATIONS SECTION

FEBRUARY 22, 1965
TELETYPE

FBI PHILA
1-58 PM URGENT 2-22-65 RM
TO DIRECTOR /100-399321/ AND NEW YORK /105-8999/
   NEW YORK VIA WASH
FROM PHILADELPHIA /100-39918/
   MALCOLM K. LITTLE, AKA IS-MMI.
   RE NEW YORK TELETYPE 2-21-65.
   [BUREAU DELETION] THEY POSSESSED NO INFO ON
KILLING OF SUBJECT OR ATTEMPT TO RETALIATE
BY HIS FOLLOWERS. THEY WILL IMMEDIATELY AD-
VISE THIS OFFICE SHOULD THEY OBTAIN INFO CON-
CERNING ABOVE.
   [BUREAU DELETION] WAS AT RALLY NEW YORK
CITY WHEN MALCOLM X WAS KILLED. [BUREAU DE-
LETION] BALLROOM BENJAMIN X WAS SPEAKING.
MALCOLM WAS NOT IN SIGHT. ABOUT THREE PM
MALCOLM APPEARED ON STAGE RIGHT AND
WALKED TO LECTERN. BENJAMIN THEN LEFT STAGE.
MALCOLM GAVE MUSLIM GREETING AND THEN
SAID QUOTE BROTHERS AND SISTERS UNQUOTE. AT
THIS POINT A NEGRO MALE, WEARING THREE QUAR-
TER LENGTH BLACK LEATHER JACKET, PUSHED HIS
CHAIR BACK STOOD UP AND ACCUSED NEGRO MALE
SITTING ON HIS LEFT OF HAVING HIS HAND IN HIS

POCKET. THE NEGRO MALE WHO STOOD UP WAS VERY DARK COMPLEXED [sic], SLENDER BUILD, ABOUT FIVE FEET TEN INCHES TALL, WEIGHT ONE HUNDRED SIXTY POUNDS, AGE IN LATE TWENTIES, LEAN FACE MEDIUM LENGTH STRAIGHT HAIR.

THIS MAN PUSHED HIS COAT BACK AND PRODUCED AN OBJECT WHICH LOOKED TO BE METALLIC AND RAISED HIS ARM. PEOPLE FROM THE AUDIENCE OF ABOUT FOUR HUNDRED PERSONS BEGAN JUMPING TO THEIR FEET. MALCOLM TOLD EVERYONE TO QUOTE TAKE IT EASY UNQUOTE. THE NEXT THING [BUREAU DELETION] RECALLS WAS THAT THEY HEARD ABOUT FOUR GUNSHOTS WHICH WERE RAPID, SOUNDING LIKE THEY CAME FROM A SEMI-AUTOMATIC PISTOL. [BUREAU DELETION] THEN FELL TO THE FLOOR AND BELIEVED HE SAW BLOOD ON MALCOLMS FACE.

WHILE LYING ON THE FLOOR ABOUT FOUR MINUTES LATER [BUREAU DELETION] AT LEAST TEN OR ELEVEN MORE SHOTS WHICH SOUNDED LIKE THEY CAME FROM THE SAME TYPE GUN MENTIONED ABOVE AND FROM SAME LOCATION. WHILE STILL LYING ON THE FLOOR AND IMMEDIATELY AFTER LAST BURST OF GUNFIRE, [BUREAU DELETION] OBSERVED A MAN FROM THE WAIST DOWN PAST HIM, LOADING A GUN CLIP. [BUREAU DELETION] BELIEVED THIS CLIP TO BE SMALLER THAN A FORTY-FIVE CALIBER CLIP BUT COULD NOT BE MORE SPECIFIC. [BUREAU DELETION] DID NOT BELIEVE THIS MAN TO BE THE ONE WEARING THE BLACK LEATHER JACKET AS HIS HANDS APPEARED TO BE THAT OF A LIGHT NEGRO. THIS MAN WORE BROWN OR CORDOVAN COLORED SHOES WITH MEDIUM SIZE FEET. SOURCE COULD FURNISH NO FURTHER INFO AS SCENE WAS NOW IN UTTER CONFUSION.

[BUREAU DELETION] COULD FURNISH NO INFO CONCERNING ANY PLANS OF RETALIATION BY MALCOLM X FOLLOWERS. [BUREAU DELETION]

[BUREAU DELETION]

[BUREAU DELETION] WAS AT BALLROOM WHEN MALCOLM KILLED AND MAY POSSIBLY COME TO PHILA. [BUREAU DELETION]

[BUREAU DELETION] AND BUREAU AND NEW YORK WILL BE KEPT IMMEDIATELY ADVISED OF ANY PERTINENT DEVELOPMENTS.

SECRET LHM FOLLOWS.
WA FOR RELAY HOLD CORR
E
WA FOR RELAY LRA
FBI WASH DC AND RELAY
TU AND SI DISC 5

—————. •—————

FEDERAL BUREAU OF INVESTIGATION
U. S. DEPARTMENT OF JUSTICE

COMMUNICATIONS SECTION

FEBRUARY 23, 1965
TELETYPE
SENT BY CODED TELETYPE
FBI NEW YORK
5-58 AM URGENT 2-22-65 RDB
TO DIRECTOR /100-399321/ -01- AND SACS, CHICAGO AND PHILADELPHIA
FROM NEW YORK /105-8999/ 12 PAGES
MALCOLM K. LITTLE, AKA IS-MMI.

RE NEW YORK TELEPHONE CALLS TO AND FROM THE BUREAU AND TO CHICAGO, FEBRUARY TWENTY ONE AND TWENTY TWO, NINETEEN SIXTY FIVE.

[BUREAU DELETION] MALCOLM X WAS JUST SHOT AT THE AUDUBON BALLROOM, NEW YORK CITY, WHILE ADDRESSING AN ORGANIZATION OF AFRO DASH AMERICAN UNITY RALLY. AT THE TIME MALCOLM WAS SHOT AN EXCHANGE OF GUNFIRE FROM THE SPEAKING PLATFORM WAS OBSERVED. REUBEN X FIRED SEVERAL SHOTS AT THE ASSASSINS. NYCPD

CAPTURED ONE PERSON OUTSIDE OF AUDUBON BALLROOM WHO WAS LATER IDENTIFIED AS THOMAS HAGAN NEGRO MALE AGE TWENTY TWO. HAGAN HAD IN HIS POSSESSION AT THIS TIME A FORTY FIVE AUTOMATIC CLIP CONTAINING FOUR ROUNDS OF AMMUNITION. HAGAN WAS SHOT IN THE LEFT THIGH AND WAS ADMITTED TO JEWISH MEMORIAL HOSPITAL FOR TREATMENT, AND AT FIVE THIRTY PM, FEBRUARY TWENTY ONE, NINETEEN SIXTY FIVE, WAS TRANSFERRED TO BELLEVUE HOSPITAL, NYC [BUREAU DELETION] WAS ADVISED THAT A SAWED OFF, DOUBLE BARREL SHOTGUN WAS FOUND ON THE STAGE OF THE BALLROOM WRAPPED IN A GREEN SUIT COAT, CONTAINING A KEY FOR YALE LOCK, PACK OF CAMEL CIGARETTES, EMPTY GLASS CASE BEARING OPTOMETRIST-S NAME, M.M. PINE, MAIN STREET, FLUSHING NY. SHOTGUN CONTAINED TWO DISCHARGED REMINGTON EXPRESS SHELLS, SINGLE O BUCKSHOT SHELLS AND INDICATIONS THAT GUN WAS RECENTLY USED. ALSO LOCATED IN THE HALL WERE THREE FORTY FIVE CALIBER SHELLS AND SLUGS, SIX NINE MILLIMETER SHELLS AND TWO SLUGS AND THREE THIRTY TWO CALIBER SLUGS AND TEN PIECES OF LEAD, PRESUMABLY FIRED FROM A SHOTGUN.

[BUREAU DELETION] MALCOLM WAS PRESENTED TO THE AUDIENCE AT APPROXIMATELY THREE TWO PM AND HAD MOVED TO A POSITION BEHIND THE PODIUM. AS HE ROSE FROM BEHIND THE PODIUM AND WALKED TO THE SPEAKER-S POSITION TO GREET THE AUDIENCE SOMEONE FROM THE LEFT SIDE OF THE HALL, APPROXIMATELY FOUR ROWS FROM THE FRONT, DESCRIBED AS A NEGRO MALE, YELLED QUOTE GET YOUR HANDS OUT OF MY POCKET UNQUOTE. AS THIS WAS DONE, MALCOLM-S BODY GUARDS MOVED IN THE DIRECTION OF THIS INDIVIDUAL AND ATTEMPTED TO SUBDUE HIM, WHEREUPON MALCOLM X SAID QUOTE HOLD IT UN-

QUOTE. [BUREAU DELETION] WALKING TOWARD THIS MAN IN FRONT OF THE AUDIENCE [BUREAU DELETION] AS A RESULT OF MALCOLM-S COMMAND TO QUOTE HOLD IT UNQUOTE. WITHOUT HESITATION, TWO MEN, OCCUPYING FRONT SEATS, LEFT SIDE OF MIDDLE AISLE, APPROXIMATELY EIGHTEEN FEET FROM MALCOLM X GOT INTO A CROUCHED POSITION AND FIRED SEVERAL SHOTS IN THE DIRECTION OF MALCOLM X. THESE MEN WERE DRESSED IN DARK CLOTHES. STILL IN A CROUCHED POSITION THE GUNMEN HASTILY MOVED TOWARD THE EXIT AND SEEMED TO BE STILL FIRING. [BUREAU DELETION] REUBEN FRANCIS, MEMBER OF MALCOLM-S GROUP, HAD SHOT ONE OF THE QUOTE DECOYS UNQUOTE AND THAT ONE OF THE GUNMEN WAS CAUGHT BY SEVERAL OF THE MMI MEMBERS.

[BUREAU DELETION]

[BUREAU DELETION] IN ADDITION TO MALCOLM AND HAGAN, THE SUSPECT, BEING SHOT, TWO PEOPLE IN THE AUDIENCE WERE STRUCK BY FLYING BULLETS. ONE [BUREAU DELETION] A MEMBER OF MALCOLM-S ORGANIZATION, WAS SHOT IN THE RIGHT SIDE AND [BUREAU DELETION] WAS WOUNDED IN THE LEFT FOOT. BOTH WERE TAKEN TO COLUMBIA PRESBYTERIAN HOSPITAL AND THEIR CONDITIONS ARE CONSIDERED GOOD. POLICE CONSIDER BOTH [BUREAU DELETION] AND [BUREAU DELETION] TO BE MERELY ONLOOKERS AND NOT TO HAVE BEEN INVOLVED IN THE SHOOTING. AUTOPSY ON MALCOLM X REFLECTED THAT HE HAD TEN BULLET WOUNDS IN HIS CHEST, THIGH AND ANKLE, PLUS FOUR BULLET CREASES IN THE CHEST AND THIGH. THIS AUTOPSY LOCATED ONE NINE MILLIMETER SLUG, ONE FORTY FIVE CALIBER SLUG AND SEVERAL SHOTGUN PELLETS IN HIS BODY. THE POLICE HAVE CHARGED HAGAN WITH HOMICIDE ON MALCOLM X AND HAVE CHARGED REUBEN X FRANCIS WITH FELONIOUS ASSAULT AND POSSESSION OF

A DEADLY WEAPON. THE POLICE SAY THAT IN VIEW OF THE NATURE OF HAGAN-S INJURY HE BE HOSPITALIZED FOR UP TO SIX WEEKS. [BUREAU DELETION] HAVE A WITNESS WHO HAS IDENTIFIED FRANCIS AS FIRING BACK AT ASSAILANTS OF MALCOLM X. FRANCIS IS PRESUMED TO HAVE FIRED SHOT WHICH STRUCK HAGAN. POLICE ALSO SUSPECT FRANCIS SHOT THE THIRTY TWO CALIBER REVOLVER USED IN THESE SHOOTINGS, THOUGH THE GUN HAS NOT BEEN LOCATED. [BUREAU DELETION] NOW ESTIMATE THAT THE NUMBER OF MALCOLM-S ASSAILANTS NUMBER FROM TWO TO FOUR INCLUDING THE CAPTURED HAGAN. FBI IDENTIFICATION DIVISION IDENTIFIED FINGERPRINTS OF HAGAN AS IDENTICAL TO TALMADGE HAYER, ALSO KNOWN AS THOMAS HAYER, FBI NUMBER ONE FOUR TWO FOUR NINE SIX F, NEGRO MALE, BORN MARCH SIXTEEN, NINETEEN FORTY TWO AT HACKENSACK, NEW JERSEY, RESIDES THREE FOUR SEVEN MARSHALL STREET, PATTERSON, NEW JERSEY, [BUREAU DELETION].

[BUREAU DELETION] NYO AND NEWARK INDICIES NEGATIVE ON HAYER. DESCRIPTION OF ONLY ONE OTHER ASSAILANT HAS BEEN DETERMINED. HE IS A NEGRO MALE, AGE TWENTY EIGHT, SIX FEET TWO INCHES, TWO HUNDRED POUNDS, HEAVY BUILD, DARK COMPLEXION, WEARING GRAY COAT AND BELIEVED TO BE ASSAILANT WHO USED SHOTGUN. HAGAN HAS REFUSED TO FURNISH ANY INFORMATION OTHER THAN HIS NAME AND AGE, WHICH IS TWENTY TWO YEARS. NYO INDICIES ON HAGAN NEGATIVE.

[BUREAU DELETION] SELF-ADMITTED OAAU MEMBER, [BUREAU DELETION]TELEPHONICALLY CONTACTED NYO AND ADVISED HE HAS ONE OF THE GUNS USED TO KILL MALCOLM X. CONTACTED BY BUREAU AGENTS, [BUREAU DELETION] TURNED OVER TO THEM A UNITED STATES ARMY COLT

FORTY FIVE, MODEL ONE NINE ONE ONE, SERIAL NUMBER THREE THREE FIVE ZERO FIVE FIVE, WITH CLIP CONTAINING THREE ROUNDS OF AMMUNITION. DURING INTERVIEW, [BUREAU DELETION] HE WITNESSED THE SHOOTING FROM THE REAR OF THE AUDUBON BALLROOM AND BELIEVED FOUR TO FIVE NEGRO MALES PARTICIPATED IN THE SHOOTING. [BUREAU DELETION] STATED THAT TWO MEN PASSED HIM WHEN LEAVING THE BALLROOM. TWO OTHERS WERE RUNNING OUT OF THE BALLROOM, ONE TURNED TO RETURN THE FIRE AT MALCOLM-S MEN. AS THIS MAN TURNED TO RUN OUT THE DOOR, HE, [BUREAU DELETION] THREW A BODY BLOCK AT HIM, AND THIS PERSON FELL ON THE STEPS DROPPING THE GUN. THE LAST MAN RUNNING OUT OF THE BUILDING JUMPED OVER THE PERSON HE STRUCK AND WAS APPARENTLY ARRESTED WHEN HE LEFT THE BUILDING. THE PERSON WHO WAS STRUCK DOWN FELL DOWN THE STAIRS, SCRAMBLED TO HIS FEET, AND BEGAN RUNNING OUT OF THE BUILDING. [BUREAU DELETION] STATED HE PICKED UP THE GUN AND TRIED TO SHOOT HIM BUT THE GUN JAMMED. ABOUT THIS TIME, SOME OF MALCOLM-S MEN PUSHED HIM BACK INSIDE THE BUILDING WHERE HE THEN PUT THE GUN IN HIS POCKET AND WAITED UNTIL MALCOLM WAS TAKEN AWAY, AND LEFT THE BALLROOM. [BUREAU DELETION] THE MAN WITH THE GUN AS BEING MALE NEGRO, AGE TWENTY, FIVE FEET SEVEN INCHES, MEDIUM BUILD, SHORT BLACK HAIR, BROWN SKIN, WEARING A DARK BROWN, DIRTY SUEDE JACKET. THE LAST MAN LEAVING THE BUILDING WAS DESCRIBED AS MALE, NEGRO, THIRTY YEARS OF AGE, SIX FEET TALL, ONE HUNDRED AND SIXTY POUNDS, SHORT BLACK HAIR, MAY HAVE HAD A SMALL MUSTACHE, WORE DARK TROUSERS, MEDIUM GRAY TOP COAT AND NO HAT.

[BUREAU DELETION] CAME TO THE NYO AND

PICKED UP THE FORTY FIVE CALIBER GUN MADE AVAILABLE BY [BUREAU DELETION] AND WERE ADVISED THAT THE INDIVIDUAL WHO GAVE AGENTS THIS GUN DESIRED HIS IDENTITY BE KEPT CONFIDENTIAL AT THIS TIME, AND THAT THE FBI WOULD ATTEMPT TO PREVAIL UPON THIS SOURCE TO COOPERATE AND IDENTIFY HIMSELF TO THE POLICE. [BUREAU DELETION] ADVISED THAT HE DID NOT DESIRE THAT WE ATTEMPT TO APPROACH [BUREAU DELETION] AT THIS TIME AND PREFERRED THAT WE WAIT UNTIL THE FBI IS CONTACTED BY HIM AT A LATER DATE AS AN APPROACH AT THIS TIME MAY FRIGHTEN THIS POTENTIAL WITNESS, CAUSING HIM TO LEAVE THE NY AREA. NY WILL NOT RECONTACT [BUREAU DELETION] AT THIS TIME PURSUANT TO [BUREAU DELETION] REQUEST.

POLICE INDICATE THEY HAVE THE FOLLOWING WITNESSES TO THIS SHOOTING. [BUREAU DELETION] MALE, AGE SIXTY NINE.

[BUREAU DELETION] CITY DESK, ASSOCIATED PRESS, FIFTY ROCKEFELLER PLAZA, NYC, ADVISED FEBRUARY TWENTY ONE, SIXTY FIVE, THAT ONE OF THEIR SOURCES WHOSE RELIABILITY IS UNKNOWN BY THIS OFFICE, HAD STATED THAT SOME MEN, INCLUDING [BUREAU DELETION] /KNOWN OAAU MEMBERS IN NYC/, WERE GOING TO CHICAGO EITHER BY PLANE OR CAR FOR THE PURPOSE OF KILLING ELIJAH MUHAMMAD, NOI NATIONAL LEADER. AP SOURCE ALSO ADVISED THAT PLANS HAVE BEEN MADE TO KILL [BUREAU DELETION] AND MARTIN LUTHER KING. AP SOURCE INDICATED THAT KING WAS TO HAVE BEEN KILLED WHEN THE STATUE OF LIBERTY WAS SUPPOSED TO HAVE BEEN DESTROYED. HE ALSO STATED THAT MALCOLM X WAS NOT DUE TO BE ASSASSINATED UNTIL TWO WEEKS FROM TODAY /FEBRUARY TWENTY ONE SIXTY FIVE/ BUT THAT THE SCHEDULE HAD BEEN MOVED AHEAD.

IT IS TO BE NOTED IN REFERENCE TO [BUREAU DE-

LETION] THAT [BUREAU DELETION] IS DESCRIBED AS NEGRO, MALE, AMERICAN, LATE TWENTIES, FIVE FOOT NINE INCHES, ONE SEVENTY FIVE POUNDS, MEDIUM BUILD, BROWN EYES, BLACK HAIR, SMALL MUSTACHE, SMALL BEARD, VERY PRONOUNCED HOOK NOSE, COFFEE BEAN COMPLEXION, VERY NERVOUS, EXCITABLE MANNER. WEARS PAKISTANIAN TYPE GINNAHA CAP. [BUREAU DELETION] WAS DESCRIBED BY [BUREAU DELETION] AS FOLLOWS . . . NEGRO, MALE, AMERICAN, THIRTY ONE YEARS OF AGE, SIX FEET TWO OR THREE INCHES TALL ONE SEVENTY FIVE TO ONE EIGHTY POUNDS, WELL KNIT BUILD, SHAVED HEAD, THIN MUSTACHE, VERY DARK COMPLEXION, DARK EYES, FALSE TEETH IN FRONT OF MOUTH, WEARS GINNAHA TYPE CAP AND A BLACK COAT.

[BUREAU DELETION] OVERHEARD [BUREAU DELETION] REPORTER "LIFE" MAGAZINE, IN CONVERSATION WITH A [BUREAU DELETION] WASHINGTON, D.C., APPROXIMATELY ELEVEN THIRTY PM FEBRUARY TWENTY ONE SIXTY FIVE DURING WHICH CONVERSATION [BUREAU DELETION] STATED THAT THE KILLERS OF MALCOLM X WERE POSSIBLY IMPORTED TO NYC. [BUREAU DELETION] BELIEVED THE FOLLOWING STATEMENTS BY [BUREAU DELETION] TO BE ACCURATE, THAT [BUREAU DELETION] ADVISED [BUREAU DELETION] TO CHECK OUT WASHINGTON AND CIA BECAUSE THEY WANTED MALCOLM OUT OF THE WAY BECAUSE HE "SNAFUED" AFRICAN RELATIONS FOR THE U.S. [BUREAU DELETION] ALSO OVERHEARD [BUREAU DELETION] CALL [BUREAU DELETION] IN CHICAGO AT TELEPHONE AB FOUR EIGHT SIX TWO THREE DURING WHICH CONVERSATION [BUREAU DELETION] ADVISED [BUREAU DELETION] THAT TWO OF MALCOLM-S MEN WERE THEN IN CHICAGO HAVING FLOWN THERE TO HIT EITHER ELIJAH OR THE UNIVERSITY /PRESUMABLY UNIVERSITY OF

ISLAM./ [BUREAU DELETION] TO STAY OUT OF THE WAY WHEN BULLETS START FLYING.

[BUREAU DELETION] FEBRUARY TWENTY ONE SIXTY FIVE AT ELEVEN PM THAT THE [BUREAU DELETION] HAD CONTACTED THEM TO ADVISE THAT THEY HAD PICKED UP ONE [BUREAU DELETION] / BELIEVED TO BE A MMI MEMBER IN PHILADELPHIA/ WHO CAME TO ST. LUKE-S HOSPITAL IN PHILADELPHIA WITH A BROKEN ARM AND ADMITTED BEING AT THE AUDUBON BALLROOM WHEN THE SHOOTING TOOK PLACE INVOLVING MALCOLM LITTLE. NO FURTHER DETAILS WERE FURNISHED AT THIS TIME IN THIS REGARD [BUREAU DELETION] THIS BEING SUBMITTED FOR PHILADELPHIA-S INFORMATION.

BUREAU WILL BE KEPT ADVISED.

AM COPIES BEING FORWARDED TO BOSTON, CLEVELAND, LOS ANGELES, SAN FRANCISCO, NEWARK AND WASHINGTON FIELD OFFICE.

ALL INFORMATION CONTAINED HEREIN PERTAINING TO CHICAGO HAS BEEN PREVIOUSLY FURNISHED TO THEM BY TELEPHONE.

END
OMS FBI WASH DC

FEDERAL BUREAU OF INVESTIGATION
U. S. DEPARTMENT OF JUSTICE

COMMUNICATIONS SECTION

FEBRUARY 23, 1965
TELETYPE

FBI WASH DC 0724
2-40 AM DEFERRED 2-23-65 RM
TO DIRECTOR /100-399321/ AND NEW YORK /105-8999/
FROM PHILADELPHIA /100-39918/

MALCOLM K. LITTLE, IS-MMI.

REPHTEL 2-22-65.

[BUREAU DELETION] AT RALLY NYC WHEN MAL-

COLM X WAS KILLED. [BUREAU DELETION] ARRIVED AT BALLROOM ABOUT TWO FORTY FIVE PM, 2-21-65 WITH [BUREAU DELETION]. BENJAMIN X WAS SPEAKING AND WAS ALONE ON STAGE. ABOUT THREE PM, MALCOLM APPEARED ON STAGE RIGHT AND WALKED TO PODIUM. BENJAMIN X LEFT STAGE TO RIGHT WING THROUGH DOOR MALCOLM HAD JUST ENTERED.

MALCOLM AT PODIUM SAID SOMETHING LIKE QUOTE GOOD AFTERNOON BROTHERS AND SISTERS UNQUOTE. AT THIS TIME A NEGRO MALE, WEARING SUIT COAT LENGTH BLACK LEATHER COAT STOOD UP AND LOUDLY TOLD NEGRO MALE ON HIS LEFT QUOTE GET YOUR HAND OUT OF MY POCKET UNQUOTE, MAN STANDING UP WORE KHAKI PANTS, WHITE SHIRT OPEN AT COLLAR. HE WAS ABOUT FIVE FEET ELEVEN INCHES TALL, WEIGHT ONE SIX FIVE LBS., SLENDER BUILD, AGE ABOUT TWENTY NINE, SLIGHT BEARD AND MUSTACHE TRIMMED IN CIRCLE AROUND MOUTH, LOOKED LIKE AFRICAN WITH SHORT CUT WOOLLY HAIR, MEDIUM DARK COMPLEXION.

MALCOLM THEN STEPPED TO RIGHT OF PODIUM PAREN MALCOLM/S LEFT END PAREN AND SAID QUOTE WE WILL HAVE NONE OF THAT UNQUOTE. THE MAN STANDING PUT HIS LEFT HAND IN LEFT POCKET OF JACKET AND REMOVED SOMETHING. HE EXTENDED HIS ARM TOWARD MALCOLM. MALCOLM SAID EXCITEDLY DON/T DO IT UNQUOTE AND STEPPED FARTHER TO HIS LEFT. [BUREAU DELETION] HEARD FOUR OR FIVE RAPID SHOTS AND SAW WHAT APPEARED TO BE GUN FLASHES FROM STANDING MAN/S EXTENDED LEFT ARM. RED STAINS APPEARED ON MALCOLM/S SHIRT FRONT. MALCOLM SLUMPED AND FELL TO FLOOR.

[BUREAU DELETION]

STANDING MAN THEN RAN TO LEFT AISLE AND WAS LAST SEEN TURNING INTO MIDDLE EXIT. [BU-

REAU DELETION] WAS THEN PULLED TO FLOOR [BU-
REAU DELETION] AND SAW NO MORE.

[BUREAU DELETION] WHEN SHOOTING STARTED
PEOPLE IN AUDIENCE BEGAN FALLING TO FLOOR
YELLING AND SCREAMING.

SECONDS AFTER [BUREAU DELETION] PULLED TO
FLOOR A QUOTE LOT MORE UNQUOTE SHOTS WERE
HEARD. THEY SOUNDED LIKE PEOPLE WERE SHOOT-
ING AT EACH OTHER FROM OPPOSITE SIDES OF
ROOM.

[BUREAU DELETION] DID NOT GET GOOD LOOK AT
MAN ON LEFT WHO WAS ACCUSED OF PUTTING
HAND IN STANDING MAN/S POCKET BUT BELIEVES
HE MAY BE IDENTICAL WITH THOMAS HAGAN
WHOSE PICTURE [BUREAU DELETION] IN AP WIRE-
PHOTO 2-22-65. [BUREAU DELETION] BELIEVED HE
WORE A DARK SUIT AND WHITE SHIRT.

[BUREAU DELETION] BEFORE MALCOLM CAME ON
STAGE A MAN WHO [BUREAU DELETION] SHOT MAL-
COLM APPEARED TO BE ACQUAINTED WITH MAN ON
HIS LEFT AND MAN ON HIS RIGHT AS THE THREE
WERE ENGAGED IN CONVERSATION. THE MAN ON
RIGHT WAS A LIGHT COLORED NEGRO, HAD CLOSE
CUT HAIR, AND WORE BEIGE OR LIGHT BROWN SILK
LOOKING SUIT. [BUREAU DELETION] NO FURTHER
DESCRIPTION OF THESE MEN, AND NO ADDITIONAL
INFO CONCERNING THEM.

[BUREAU DELETION] ADVISED THERE WERE
AISLES ON EACH SIDE OF BALLROOM, BUT NO CEN-
TER AISLE. [BUREAU DELETION] SAT ABOUT MIDDLE
OF THE SIXTH ROW. THE THREE ABOVE MENTIONED
MEN SAT RIGHT OF CENTER IN THE THIRD ROW.

[BUREAU DELETION] NO INFO CONCERNING ANY
PLANS OF RETALIATION BY MALCOLM/S FOLLOW-
ERS.

[BUREAU DELETION]

ANY ADDITIONAL INFO DEVELOPED [BUREAU DE-

LETION] WILL IMMEDIATELY BE FURNISHED THE
BUREAU AND NEW YORK.
   SECRET LHM FOLLOWS.
WA F OR RELAY LRA
FBI WASH DC 0724
TU DISC

————————. . ————————

FEDERAL BUREAU OF INVESTIGATION

Date   February 24, 1965
[BUREAU DELETION]
[BUREAU DELETION] was at the rally in New York City on
February 21, 1965 at the Audubon Ballroom, where MALCOLM
X was killed. This meeting was sponsored by the Organization of
Afro-American Unity (OAAU).
   [BUREAU DELETION] arrived at the ballroom BENJAMIN
X was speaking. MALCOLM X was not in sight. About 3 P.M.
MALCOLM X appeared on stage right and walked to the po-
dium. BENJAMIN X then left the stage.
   MALCOLM X gave the Muslim greeting, "As Salaam
Alaikem," and then said "Brothers and Sisters." At this time a
Negro male, wearing a three-quarter length black leather coat,
pushed his chair back, stood up, and said to the Negro male
sitting on his left "Get your hand out of my pocket."
   The Negro male who stood up was very dark complected, slender build, about 5'10" tall, weighing 160 pounds, age in the late
twenties, lean face, with medium length straight hair.
   This man then pushed his coat back and produced an object
which looked to be metallic and raised his arm. At this point,
people from the audience, which consisted of about four hundred
individuals, began jumping to their feet. MALCOLM X told everyone to "take it easy."
   The next thing [BUREAU DELETION] was that [BUREAU
DELETION] heard about four gunshots, which were fired in
rapid order, and which sounded like they came from a semiauto-
matic pistol.
   [BUREAU DELETION] then fell to the floor and [BUREAU

DELETION] believed [BUREAU DELETION] blood on MAL-COLM X's face. While lying on the floor about five minutes later [BUREAU DELETION] heard at least ten or eleven more gunshots, which sounded like they came from the same type gun mentioned above and from the same location.

While still lying on the floor and immediately after the last burst of gunfire, [BUREAU DELETION] a man from the waist down walk [BUREAU DELETION] loading a gun clip [BUREAU DELETION] believed this clip to be smaller than a .45 caliber clip but could not be more specific. [BUREAU DELETION] did not believe this man to be the one wearing the black leather jacket, as his hands appeared to be those of a light-skinned Negro.

This man wore brown or Cordovan-colored shoes and had medium-sized feet. [BUREAU DELETION] he could furnish no further information regarding the murder of MALCOLM X, as the scene was, by this time, "utter confusion."

[BUREAU DELETION] possessed no information concerning any plans of retaliation by the followers of MALCOLM X or any other individuals.

[BUREAU DELETION] did not know who shot MALCOLM nor did he see any firearms. [BUREAU DELETION] it appeared to him there was a definite lack of security at this rally. In addition, [BUREAU DELETION] there did not appear to be enough guards in the front of the hall nor any guards near the exits.

[BUREAU DELETION] the Audubon Ballroom is rectangular shaped, with exits at the left center side and left rear side. He said that chairs were set up in rows for the audience to sit in, with aisles on either side and an aisle down the middle. [BUREAU DELETION] the podium behind which MALCOLM X stood was directly in front of the center aisle.

[BUREAU DELETION] The man who stood up, mentioned above, sat about in the middle of the left row of chairs, about three rows [BUREAU DELETION] and about four rows from the front row of chairs.

[BUREAU DELETION] that MALCOLM X was the leader of the OAAU and Muslim Mosque, Inc., (MMI).

On　2/21/65　at Philadelphia, Pa.
　　　　　　　　　　　File #Philadelphia 100-39918
　SA [BUREAU DELETION] and
by　SA [BUREAU DELETION]
　　　　　　　　　　Date dictated　2/24/65

UNITED STATES GOVERNMENT

MEMORANDUM

　　　　　　　　　　　　　　　　　Date:　February
TO　　:　Mr. W. C. Sullivan　　　　　22, 1965
FROM　:　Mr. F. J. Baumgardner
SUBJECT:　MALCOLM K. LITTLE, also
　　　　　known as Malcolm X
　　　　　INTERNAL SECURITY—
　　　　　MMI

Malcolm K. Little, leader of the Muslim Mosque, Incorporated (MMI), and the Organization of Afro-American Unity (OAAU), was shot and killed on the afternoon of February 21, 1965, at approximately 3:10 P.M. while speaking at a meeting of the OAAU being held in the Audubon Ballroom, 166th Street and Broadway, New York City. The New York Office was immediately advised of the incident [BUREAU DELETION] who was present at the meeting.

[BUREAU DELETION] was [BUREAU DELETION] at the back of the hall when someone in the audience called out indicating that his pocket had been picked. [BUREAU DELETION] observed two men standing near the front of the hall in about the third or fourth row, apparently firing some sort of weapons. He also recalls seeing two other men standing at the time, one several feet behind the first two, and the other several feet to the side. He presumed that they were also involved in the shooting. [BUREAU DELETION] two shots and saw Malcolm X fall backward to the floor. He then heard a volley of shots, probably twenty. [BUREAU DELETION] believes the assailants were also shooting at Malcolm's guards. At this point, [BUREAU DELETION] ran to the foyer of the hall and [BUREAU DELETION] which commanded a view of the entrance to the hall. He observed a man, later identified as John Hagen, running down the aisle crouching and weaving with a .45 caliber pistol in his hand. [BUREAU DELETION] one of Malcolm's followers who was behind the man, fired three shots, one of which evidently hit Hagen. [BUREAU DELETION] learned that Hagen was caught outside by Malcolm's followers.

[BUREAU DELETION] that one John Hagen, Negro male, age 22, was arrested when leaving the Audubon Ballroom by an officer stationed outside. During the arrest, a warning shot was fired in the air. A .45 caliber clip with four bullets was found in Hagen's pocket and it was discovered he was wounded in the left thigh. He is presently in Jewish Memorial Hospital under police detention. Hagen subsequently identified by Identification Division through fingerprints, submitted by New York Police Department, as Talmadge Hayer, also known as Thomas Hayer, FBI Number 142496F, a Negro, born March 16, 1942, Hackensack, New Jersey. [BUREAU DELETION] Bureau files contain no other information identifiable with this individual.

An anonymous call was received by the New York Office. The caller indicated he had found a gun used in the shooting and would furnish the gun to Bureau Agents, but would not give it to the police. Upon arriving at the meeting place designated by the caller, the Agents [BUREAU DELETION] as the caller. [BUREAU DELETION] turned over a .45 caliber automatic, Model 1911, U. S. Army Serial Number 335055. [BUREAU DELETION] said he was at the meeting in back of the hall when he observed four or five men, all Negroes, standing approximately nine rows back from the stage firing weapons toward the stage. After firing, the men ran past him and as the third man passed, [BUREAU DELETION] knocking the .45 caliber automatic to the ground. [BUREAU DELETION] picked the gun up, attempting to fire the weapon at the man; however, the gun jammed. [BUREAU DELETION] said there were three rounds left in the chamber. He stated he could possibly identify the fourth man, but not the man that dropped the gun. The weapon was turned over to the New York Police Department. [BUREAU DELETION] would not indicate whether he intended to make his identity known to the New York police.

[BUREAU DELETION] has recovered a 12 gauge sawed-off shotgun, Model 1017, J. C. Higgins, from the hall where the shooting occurred. The police believe the shotgun, which was recently fired and contained #0 buckshot shells, was used in the shooting. In addition to the shotgun, the [BUREAU DELETION] believe two other guns were used, a .45 caliber automatic and a .9 millimeter automatic.

[BUREAU DELETION] Negro male, [BUREAU DELETION] was shot in the left foot and is presently confined in the Columbia Presbyterian Hospital. Other witnesses being questioned by the police are [BUREAU DELETION].

ACTION BEING TAKEN:

The New York Office was instructed to alert [BUREAU DELETION] the Nation of Islam (NOI) and MMI as well as [BUREAU DELETION] to report any information indicating there might be retaliatory riots and information indicating the involvement of any organization. New York Office was instructed to not furnish the New York Police Department with any information developed without prior Bureau clearance. New York Office has alerted pertinent offices where MMI and NOI are active, to alert their sources for any information bearing on the situation. Information concerning the assassination of Little was telephonically furnished to the Duty Officer, [BUREAU DELETION] Secret Service. Pertinent information was also furnished to Acting Assistant Attorney General John Doar of the Civil Rights Division, and Assistant Attorney General J. Walter Yeagley of the Internal Security Division, and to Mr. DeLoach's office.

You will be kept advised of pertinent developments.

Up to now, this appears to be a murder case, basically a problem of the New York Police Department, and the FBI should not become involved. We are maintaining contact with the New York Police Department for any information of Bureau interest. As indicated above, [BUREAU DELETION].

———— • •————

UNITED STATES GOVERNMENT

MEMORANDUM

TO   : Mr. W. C. Sullivan   DATE: February
                                                              22, 1965
FROM   : Mr. J. F. Bland
SUBJECT: MALCOLM K. LITTLE
                INTERNAL SECURITY—
                MMI

At 1:45 A.M., February 22, 1965, [BUREAU DELETION] New York Office, telephonically furnished the following additional information which had been received from the [BUREAU DELETION]:

The autopsy of subject's body was concluded and there was found: one .45 caliber slug, one nine millimeter slug from an automatic, and several pellets from a shotgun. There were ten holes in the body; seven of which were in the left chest (probably from shotgun blast), two in left thigh and one in left ankle. There were also four creases, three of which were across the chest and one on right knee of Little.

In addition to the above, [BUREAU DELETION] stated that the police found the following items from a search of the Audubon Ballroom where Little was killed:

1. One "sawed-off" two-barrel shotgun with two "expended" shells in the chambers. The shells (which had been discharged) were 12 gauge Remington Express, Single 0 buckshot. The shotgun was found wrapped in a jacket. A search of the jacket by the New York City Police Department revealed one Yale key, some cigarettes, and an empty case for eyeglasses. On top of the case was the following: M. M. Pine, Optometrist, 3901 Main Street, Flushing, New York.

2. Ten pieces of lead, presumably from shotgun.

3. Two, nine millimeter slugs from the nine millimeter automatic weapon.

4. Three .45 caliber slugs from .45 automatic.

5. Three .32 caliber slugs from revolver.

6. Six, nine millimeter shell casings.

7. Three .45 caliber Western shell casings.

SA [BUREAU DELETION] stated he had learned from the police that Thomas Hagan (later identified as Talmadge Hayer) would be charged with homicide in the death of Malcolm Little.

ACTION:

For information. This is being followed closely, and you will be kept advised.

DECODED COPY

____AIRGRAM   ____CABLEGRAM   ____RADIO
__xx__ TELETYPE
12:12 PM CST URGENT 2-22-65 PAK
TO DIRECTOR AND NEW YORK
  NEW YORK VIA WASHINGTON-ENCODED
FROM CHICAGO 221641
MALCOLM LITTLE, IS-MMI

[BUREAU DELETION] ADVISED FEBRUARY 21 LAST ELIJAH MUHAMMAD'S REPRESENTATIVES ALERTED THAT FOLLOWERS OF LITTLE MAY COME CHICAGO TO ATTACK HIM AND HIS TEMPLE. MUHAMMAD DENIED KNOWLEDGE OF ASSASSINATION, COMMENTING HE WAS AWARE LITTLE FOLLOWERS MAY COME TO CHICAGO. MUHAMMAD SAID HE WAS NOT AFRAID, ADDING "THEY KILLED THEIR OWN MAN, RIGHT IN HIS OWN PLACE. HE WASN'T EVEN THERE."

[BUREAU DELETION] REPORTS CASSIUS CLAY'S APARTMENT IN CHICAGO GUTTED BY FIRE-POSSIBLY ARSON. LATER PD REPORT REFLECTS [BUREAU DELETION] RESIDING IN APARTMENT BELOW CLAY'S, IN CUSTODY AND HAD SET FIRE UNINTENTIONALLY WHILE DRUNK. CLAY NOT HOME AT TIME

OF FIRE. NEWS MEDIA, CHICAGO, GAVE EXTENSIVE COVERAGE THIS FIRE.

[BUREAU DELETION] AND G-2 FURNISHED INFO RE POSSIBILITY SIX FOLLOWERS OF LITTLE COMING CHICAGO AND PD FURNISHED NAMES AND DESCRIPTION [BUREAU DELETION] AND [BUREAU DELETION] SECRET SERVICE BEING ADVISED.
RECEIVED: 1:22 PM JLD

UNITED STATES GOVERNMENT

MEMORANDUM

DATE: February 22, 1965

TO   : Mr. W. C. Sullivan
FROM   : Mr. J. F. Bland
SUBJECT: MALCOLM K. LITTLE, also known as Malcolm X
          INTERNAL SECURITY—
          MMI

[BUREAU DELETION] who witnessed the killing of Malcolm X on 2/21/65, advised the New York Office on the night of 2/21/65 that he had been given an [BUREAU DELETION] eyewitness account of the incident.

Upon discussing this assignment with [BUREAU DELETION] on the night of [BUREAU DELETION] also told him he expected something to happen to Nation of Islam (NOI) Temple No. 7, 102 W. 116th Street, New York City, and the nearby NOI Shabazz Restaurant before 3 A.M., 2/22/65, and requested [BUREAU DELETION] to cover the situation. [BUREAU DELETION] did not disclose the basis for his belief and possibly it was only conjecture on his part, based on his knowledge of the violent feud existing between the NOI and Malcolm's group, the Muslim Mosque, Incorporated (MMI).

[BUREAU DELETION] also advised that [BUREAU DELETION] called one [BUREAU DELETION] in Chicago, Illinois, at about 11:30 P.M., 2/21/65, and told him that two of Malcolm's men flew out of New York for Chicago and should then be in Chicago. He said they will "hit" either Elijah Muhammad (NOI leader) or the University of Islam (NOI school in Chicago). Again [BUREAU DELETION] did not indicate the source of his information.

This is one of numerous reports received that Malcolm's followers may attempt to kill Elijah Muhammad to avenge the death of Malcolm X. The Chicago office reported on 2/21/65 that [BUREAU DELETION] had advised that the [BUREAU DELETION] a Chicago NOI member, had received a long-distance telephone call from one [BUREAU DELETION] informing her that six of Malcolm's followers were proceeding to Chicago to take the life of the Messenger (Elijah Muhammad). [BUREAU DELETION] also advised that one [BUREAU DELETION] (not further identified) had informed one [BUREAU DELETION] that cars were loading up with unknown individuals who were going to the "Temple" (presumably the Chicago NOI Temple) to blow it up. [BUREAU DELETION] was appropriately advised of these reports.

The New York Office advised that [BUREAU DELETION] City Desk, Associated Press, stated one of their sources, whose reliability is unknown, had stated two Negroes, [BUREAU DELETION] were going to Chicago to "get" Elijah Muhammad. The Chicago Office has furnished this information to the [BUREAU DELETION] said someone was to kill James 67 X Warden, Executive Secretary of the MMI, and Martin Luther King. The threatened action against King was not further explained. Shanahan had furnished the same information to the [BUREAU DELETION] Department.

Threat against King has been furnished to the Atlanta Office with instructions to furnish to [BUREAU DELETION]. Bureau files are being checked on [BUREAU DELETION].

ACTION:
You will be kept advised of pertinent developments.

———————. •———————

UNITED STATES GOVERNMENT

MEMORANDUM

DATE: February
TO   : Mr. W. C. Sullivan   22, 1965
FROM   : Mr. J. F. Bland
SUBJECT: MALCOLM K. LITTLE,
          AKA, MALCOLM X
          IS-MMI

At 12:10 A.M. the Chicago Office advised that the information received by the [BUREAU DELETION] that two Negroes, [BUREAU DELETION] are on their way to Chicago to do harm to Elijah Muhammad, leader of the Nation of Islam (NOI), a black nationalist group, has been furnished to the [BUREAU DELETION]. The NOI has been at violent odds with Malcolm Little's group, The Muslim Mosque, Inc. (MMI).

The [BUREAU DELETION] is on the lookout for the arrival of these two individuals and any other suspicious persons who may seek to avenge the murder of Malcolm K. Little by injuring or killing Elijah Muhammad. The Chicago residence of Elijah, the Chicago NOI temple and the University of Islam, the NOI school in Chicago, are being covered by the [BUREAU DELETION].

Information has been received by the Chicago Office from [BUREAU DELETION] that Elijah is aware of the danger to his life and he so indicated this during a call he received from [BUREAU DELETION] Phoenix, Arizona. [BUREAU DELETION] told Elijah that he had been contacted by the Phoenix Police Department and informed that it had been requested by the New York City Police Department to afford Elijah protection in the event he returns to Phoenix where he also maintains a residence. Elijah's only comment was to tell [BUREAU DELE-TION] to express his appreciation to the Phoenix Police Department. He did not indicate when he plans to go to Phoenix. Elijah also stated that the press has been after him for a statement on Malcolm Little's death but he intends to make no comment until he learns the truth of what went on.

The Chicago Office is closely following this matter and has instructed [BUREAU DELETION] to immediately furnish any information they receive concerning the killing of Little and possible reprisals by his followers against Elijah or other NOI members.

ACTION:
You will be kept advised of pertinent developments.

-----------. •-----------

FEDERAL BUREAU OF INVESTIGATION
U. S. DEPARTMENT OF JUSTICE

COMMUNICATIONS SECTION

FEBRUARY 24, 1965
TELETYPE
SENT BY CODED TELETYPE
FBI NEW YORK
006//// 1006 AM URGENT 2-24-65 IRR
TO DIRECTOR /4/
FROM NEW YORK /105-8999/
MALCOLM K. LITTLE, AKA, MALCOLM X, IS DASH MMI.

NEWS MEDIA THIS MORNING CARRYING COMMENTS REPORTEDLY MADE YESTERDAY BY JAMES FARMER, NATIONAL DIRECTOR OF THE CONGRESS OF RACIAL EQUALITY /CORE/, THAT FARMER BELIEVES "KILLING OF MALCOLM X WAS A POLITICAL ACT, WITH INTERNATIONAL IMPLICATIONS." FOR INFORMATION OF BUREAU, NEW YORK OFFICE NOT IN POSSESSION OF ANY INFORMATION WHICH WOULD CORROBORATE OR SUBSTANTIATE THIS THE-

ORY OF JAMES FARMER. [BUREAU DELETION] BEING PARTICULARLY ALERTED TO IMMEDIATELY REPORT TO THIS OFFICE ANY INFORMATION WHICH WOULD TEND TO SUPPORT THIS THEORY. RECOMMEND BUREAU CONSIDER INTERVIEWING FARMER, THROUGH ESTABLISHED BUREAU LIAISON WITH HIM, TO DETERMINE WHETHER HE HAS ANY SPECIFICS IN SUPPORT OF HIS BELIEF.
END
HOLD FOR SECOND MSG

———————. •——————

SAC, New York (105-8999)   2/25/65
Director, FBI (100-399321)
MALCOLM K. LITTLE
INTERNAL SECURITY—MMI

In view of the subject's death, his name is being removed from the Security Index at the Bureau and you should handle accordingly in your office.

Submit an appropriate memorandum noting his death, for dissemination at the Bureau.

ATTENTION [BUREAU DELETION]

Cancel SI cards.

SECTION 16

February 25, 1965–March 12, 1965

REPORTS: 1. February 25, 1965, 9:30 P.M. Philadelphia to
Director, Chicago, Newark, New York Office.
Teletype
2. February 25, 1965. New York Office to
Director. Coded Teletype
3. February 26, 1965. New York Office to
Director. Coded Teletype
4. February 27, 1965. New York Office to
Director. Coded Teletype
5. February 25, 1965. Memo. DeLoach to Mohr
6. February 27, 1965. Chicago
7. February 28, 1965. New York
8. March 8, 1965. Boston
9. March 12, 1965. New York

The reports from Section 16 both repeat information and elaborate on certain elements of the assassination. On February 26, Norman 3X Butler was arrested for the shooting after three witnesses placed him at the scene. One witness could not identify the third suspect, Thomas 15X Johnson, but identified Butler as the man who said "Get your hands out of my pocket." It should be noted that Hayer was earlier reported to have made this comment. On March 8, a witness placed all three suspects at the scene and stated that Johnson had run out of the side exit after the shooting.

More reports implicate the MMI in the shooting. The FBI noted that all the witnesses to the shooting "seem to have the same 'clear cut' story that they were in the ballroom when Malcolm X was shot and when the shots rang out they fell to the floor and never got a look at the assassins." Also, an informant indicated that one of Malcolm's bodyguards had been seen in Harlem with expensive clothing and $100 bills soon after the shooting, although the man had "no visible means of support at this time."

Also included in the section is a report of Elijah Muhammad's denial of taking any part in the assassination, and reports of Malcolm's funeral, attended by several black celebrities and political figures, including Ossie Davis, Ruby Dee, James Farmer, and Bayard Rustin.

DECODED COPY

____AIRGRAM   ____CABLEGRAM   ____RADIO
__x__TELETYPE
9:30 PM URGENT 2-25-65 NWL
TO DIRECTOR CHICAGO NEWARK AND NEW YORK
  NEW YORK VIA WASHINGTON—ENCODED
FROM PHILADELPHIA 252025
MALCOLM K. LITTLE, AKA, IS-MMI.
  RE PHILADELPHIA CALL TO NEW YORK TODAY.
  [BUREAU DELETION] HE RECOGNIZED NEWSPAPER
PHOTO OF TALMADGE HAYER, AKA THOMAS HA-
GAN, AS PERSON HE KNEW AS NOI AND FOI MEMBER
IN 1963 AND 1964. CANNOT RECALL X NUMBER, BUT
BELIEVES FIRST NAME WAS TALMADGE OR THOMAS.
ATTENDED NOI MEETINGS WITH HAYER [BUREAU
DELETION] ALWAYS ASSUMED HAYER MEMBER OF
MM NUMBER 25, NEWARK; HOWEVER, NOW FEELS
MAY HAVE BEEN MEMBER OF TEMPLE IN PATERSON.
AT MEETINGS, BOTH NEWARK AND PATERSON,
HAYER WAS SECURITY GUARD AND SEARCHED [BU-
REAU DELETION] MOST THOROUGHLY ON SEVERAL
OCCASIONS. [BUREAU DELETION] ALSO OBSERVED

HAYER AT MEETING AT ARENA, 4537 MARKET STREET, PHILADELPHIA, ON SEPTEMBER 29, 1963 AT WHICH ELIJAH MUHAMMAD WAS PRINCIPAL SPEAKER. HAYER WAS ON SEARCH DETAIL INSIDE ARENA ON NORTH CORRIDOR.

LAST SAW HAYER IN CHICAGO FEBRUARY 1964 AT SAVIOR'S DAY CONVENTION. HAYER SAT ON EITHER FIRST OR SECOND ROW WHEN ELIJAH MUHAMMAD SPOKE AS A GUARD FOR MUHAMMAD IN EVENT OF TROUBLE.

————— • —————

FEDERAL BUREAU OF INVESTIGATION
U. S. DEPARTMENT OF JUSTICE

COMMUNICATIONS SECTION

FEBRUARY 25, 1965
TELETYPE
SENT BY CODED TELETYPE
FBI NEW YORK
8-37 AM URGENT 2-25-65 DAE
TO DIRECTOR -2-
FROM NEW YORK 105-8999
MALCOLM K. LITTLE, AKA IS-MMI.

[BUREAU DELETION] ADVISED FEB. TWENTY FOUR, SIXTY FIVE, THAT THE POLICE DEPARTMENT HAS ONE SUSPECT OTHER THAN TALMADGE HAYER, WHICH HE DECLINED TO IDENTIFY AT THIS TIME IN THE KILLING OF MALCOLM X. [BUREAU DELETION] INDICATED THAT BECAUSE OF THE NUMBER OF CRANK CALLS BEING MADE AT THE PRESENT TIME, THEY ARE WAITING UNTIL AFTER THE FUNERAL OF MALCOLM X BEFORE QUESTIONING THIS SUSPECT. [BUREAU DELETION] ALSO STATED THAT A NUMBER OF WITNESSES TO THE SHOOTING OF MALCOLM X CANNOT BE LOCATED AND ARE BELIEVED TO BE STAYING WITH FRIENDS UNTIL THE SITUATION "COOLS OFF."

IN RESPECT TO THE HEADLINES IN THE "NEW
YORK POST," A DAILY NEWSPAPER, DATED FEB.
TWENTY FOUR, CAPTIONED "POLICE HINT MAL-
COLM-S KILLERS KNOWN" [BUREAU DELETION] SAID
[BUREAU DELETION] WISHED IT WAS TRUE AND RE-
MARKED THAT IT IS JUST ANOTHER WAY FOR THE
"NEW YORK POST" TO SELL NEWSPAPERS. CLOSE LI-
AISON WITH [BUREAU DELETION] CONTINUING.
END
WA
JH
FBI WASH DC

FEDERAL BUREAU OF INVESTIGATION
U. S. DEPARTMENT OF JUSTICE

COMMUNICATIONS SECTION

FEBRUARY 26, 1965
TELETYPE
SENT BY CODED TELETYPE
6-03 PM URGENT 2-26-65 NHH
TO NEW YORK /18/
FROM DIRECTOR /25-330971/ 1P
NATION OF ISLAM INTERNAL SECURITY DASH NOI.

REURTEL FIVE TWENTY A.M. INSTANT DATE, CAP-
TIONED QUOTE MALCOLM K. LITTLE, ALSO KNOWN
AS, END QUOTE, AND YOUR AIRTEL JANUARY THIR-
TEEN LAST, CAPTIONED QUOTE NATION OF ISLAM,
INTERNAL SECURITY DASH NOI, END QUOTE, WITH
ENCLOSED LETTERHEAD MEMORANDUM.

RETEL ADVISED OF ARREST OF TWO INDIVIDUALS
FOR MURDER OF MALCOLM X. ONE IDENTIFIED AS
NORMAN THREE X BUTLER. IMMEDIATELY SUTEL
IDENTITY OF SECOND INDIVIDUAL ARRESTED.
REAIRTEL ADVISED OF ARRESTS OF NORMAN THREE
X BUTLER, THOMAS FIFTEEN X JOHNSON, AND [BU-
REAU DELETION] IN CONNECTION WITH SHOOTING

OF BENJAMIN BROWN ON JANUARY SIX LAST. [BUREAU DELETION] POSSIBLE INVOLVEMENT IN THE MURDER OF MALCOLM X LITTLE AND ANY FUTURE REPRISALS.
END
DAE
FBI NEW YORK

FEDERAL BUREAU OF INVESTIGATION
U. S. DEPARTMENT OF JUSTICE

COMMUNICATIONS SECTION

FEBRUARY 27, 1965
TELETYPE
SENT BY CODED TELETYPE
FBI NEW YORK
5-15 PM URGENT 2-27-65 RGF
TO DIRECTOR -7- /100-399321/
FROM NEW YORK /105-8999/ 2P
MALCOLM K. LITTLE, AKA IS-MMI
RE NEW YORK TELETYPE TO BUREAU FEBRUARY TWENTY SIX LAST CAPTIONED AS ABOVE, WHICH REPORTED THAT [BUREAU DELETION] HAD ADVISED THAT WITNESS [BUREAU DELETION] HAS NOW IDENTIFIED BOTH TALMADGE HAYER AND NORMAN BUTLER AS ASSAILANTS OF MALCOLM X AT THE TIME OF HIS KILLING. AS BUREAU HAS BEEN PREVIOUSLY ADVISED, [BUREAU DELETION] WAS FIRST CONTACTED BY NEW YORK OFFICE AGENTS, [BUREAU DELETION] WHEN HE TURNED OVER FORTY FIVE AUTOMATIC [BUREAU DELETION] RECOVERED AT SCENE OF KILLING. [BUREAU DELETION] WAS AT FIRST RELUCTANT TO SERVE AS WITNESS BUT IS NOW COOPERATING FULLY WITH POLICE.
ON FEBRUARY TWENTY SIX [BUREAU DELETION] ALL EXPRESSED THEIR DEEP APPRECIATION TO NEW YORK OFFICE AGENTS FOR THE EXCELLENT

COOPERATION IN TURNING OVER WITNESS [BUREAU DELETION] AND THE GUN. [BUREAU DELETION] ONE POLICE OFFICER SAID THAT AS OF FEBRUARY TWENTY SIX [BUREAU DELETION] WAS THE MOST IMPORTANT WITNESS THEY HAD.

FOR BUREAU/S INFORMATION
END
UU
SXC
FBI WASH DC

UNITED STATES GOVERNMENT

MEMORANDUM

Date: February 25, 1965

TO   : Mr. Mohr
FROM   : C. D. DeLoach
SUBJECT: MALCOLM X
         INFORMATION CONCERNING

The *New York Journal American* issue of 2/24/65 carries a story concerning the murder of Malcolm X under the headline, "G-Men in Harlem—The Plot Deepens." The story states that, "Negro FBI Agents were working under cover in Harlem today in an investigation reportedly aimed at ferreting out possible international political motives behind the assassination of Malcolm X." Further on in the story it is stated, "The Federal Bureau of Investigation confirmed that there are Negro FBI agents in Harlem, but dodged saying anything specific about their assignments." The Director inquired, "What about this?"

Assistant Director Malone of the New York Office advises that neither he nor any of his men in the New York Office confirmed the FBI has Special Agents working in Harlem. Mr. Malone said all inquiries from whatever source had been answered with a "no comment" in connection with this matter.

No one in my office, in answer to inquiries, confirmed to anyone that Negro Agents are working in Harlem.

OBSERVATION:

It is a well-known fact among news media people that the FBI
has Negro Agents working in large Negro communities. In fact,
we publicize this repeatedly. An example of such highlighting the
work of our Negro Agents is the attached reprint from the September, 1962, issue of *Ebony,* wherein on page 3 this point is
specifically made. Reporters Flynn and Pearl, who work under
Guy Richards at the *Journal-American* are known for their flam-
boyancy and speculative stories.

Enclosure
REW: bsp

UNITED STATES DEPARTMENT OF JUSTICE
FEDERAL BUREAU OF INVESTIGATION

Chicago, Illinois
February 27, 1965

NATION OF ISLAM

On February 22 and 23, 1965, Wesley South, moderator of the
question-answer program "Hot Line" over Chicago radio station
WVON, interviewed Elijah Muhammad. This program, which is
on the air 11:00 P.M. to midnight, was monitored by a Special
Agent of the Federal Bureau of Investigation.

In response to questions regarding the assassination of Malcolm K. Little and the NOI, Muhammad stated as follows:

The murder of Malcolm X was a shock and surprise to us.
We are investigating the charge all over the country to see if
the NOI is responsible and to see if we can come up with the
man's name in our records, but as of now we have no record.
I have preached for thirty-four years we are against this type
of thing. Malcolm left and began teaching hate and the arm-
ing of his members. We in the NOI are against this position

as it would be suicide to take up arms against this country. Allah teaches us not to carry guns and we do not carry any. We have no guns, bombs or artillery pieces to field. The Koran teaches that if one opposes the Messenger and repents he is forgiving, but if he does not repent he is subject to divine chastisement such as death or hell fire.

Muhammad stated he did not know the reason why Malcolm was killed nor who killed him. Muhammed has not asked police protection but appreciates it, adding he was a taxpayer.

Muhammad stated he has heard assassins are coming for him but that he was not frightened, as he was on Allah's mission and was not running.

Muhammad stated he had two hundred thousand to three hundred thousand members all over the world. He said some people in order to keep their racial pride teach hate. Muhammad doesn't teach violence except to fight back if attacked. The NOI is never the aggressor. Muhammad does not teach hate, only the truth and the white men are a wicked, devil race. A Muslim is one who has submitted himself to Islam.

Muhammad stated he would not back any man who used violence and in the event it subsequently might be discovered a member of the NOI killed Malcolm, added he would not back any man who used violence as the Koran only teaches us to kill on the order of Allah. This would be handled in the same way that God advised Moses to lead and help his people as set forth in the Bible.

On February 23, 1965, Elijah Muhammad in response to questions submitted by individuals who called in to radio station WVON advised as follows:

That when Malcolm X remarked that the "Chickens had come home to roost" in regards to the assassination of President Kennedy he meant that this individual had come to his end. The son who had denounced him had now returned and confessed and did not have knowledge of the truth when this occurred. Now he has true knowledge.

[BUREAU DELETION] that Wallace Muhammad, son of Elijah Muhammad, was a former minister in the NOI, but deviated from the NOI in late May, 1964, and was dismissed there from by Muhammad.

The February 25, 1965, issue of *Chicago's American,* a Chicago, Illinois daily newspaper, contained an item on page 1, that Wallace Muhammad would be permitted by his father to rejoin the NOI.

UNITED STATES DEPARTMENT OF JUSTICE FEDERAL BUREAU OF INVESTIGATION

New York, New York
February 28, 1965

Malcolm K. Little

Internal Security—Muslim Mosque Incorporated

[BUREAU DELETION] the body of Malcolm K. Little commonly known as Malcolm X, formerly the founder and leader of the Muslim Mosque, Incorporated (MMI), leader and chairman of the Organization of Afro-American Unity (OAAU), who was shot and killed on February 21, 1965 in New York City, was removed from the Unity Funeral Home, 2352 Eighth Avenue, New York City on February 27, 1965 at approximately 9:20 A.M. to the Faith Temple Church of God, Amsterdam Avenue and West 147th Street, New York City.

[BUREAU DELETION] further advised that the funeral services, which ran approximately fifteen minutes behind schedule, formally began at 9:50 A.M.

[BUREAU DELETION] advised that there were no incidents during the removal of the body from the funeral home to the church; that approximately one thousand persons were in the church itself and that at 9:30 A.M. there were approximately five hundred persons outside the church. [BUREAU DELETION] further advised that a detail of the NYCPD was in evidence in the area of the church during the entire funeral.

At 9:30 A.M., the National Broadcasting Company (NBC) Television Station, WNBC, New York City, broadcasted a one-hour television program covering the services. The television coverage began with scenic scanning photographs of the area surrounding the Faith Temple Church of God at Amsterdam Avenue and West 147th Street, New York City. Included were various views of the funeral procession as it entered the church. At 9:50 A.M. the television cameras were focused on the podium within the church.

Ossie Davis, Negro Playwright and Actor, acted as Master of Ceremonies. Davis made mention of the cooperation rendered the family of the late Malcolm X and those responsible for planning his funeral by the various news media, civic leaders, New York City officials and the NYCPD. He then read excerpts from various telegrams, letters and messages of condolence received by the widow of Malcolm X. Among such messages of condolence as mentioned by Ossie Davis were messages from the Los Angeles Youth Chapter of the National Association for the Advancement of Colored People (NAACP) and Whitney M. Young, Jr., Executive Director of the National Urban League.

Among those present at the Faith Temple Church of God were James Farmer, National Director of the Congress of Racial Equality (CORE), Bayard Rustin, leader of the 1963 March on Washington, Dick Gregory, Negro comedian and John Lewis, Director of the National Urban League.

Ossie Davis was assisted in reading the messages of condolence by his wife, the actress Ruby Dee.

The church services also included eulogies by a male individual who was only identified as a representative of the Islamic Center of Geneva and the United States. This male Negro mentioned that Malcolm X made a trip to the Middle East and Africa in 1964 and that thereafter his views changed and that he no longer advocated racism or violence but believed in integration. This individual characterized Malcolm X as a martyr and stated that it is "better to die on the battlefield than in bed" and that "those who die in battle are not dead."

The concluding speaker was an individual only identified as a leader of the Muslim Students in the United States and Canada. This individual characterized Malcolm X as a Negro leader, who had given his life for the advancement of the Negro cause throughout the world.

[BUREAU DELETION] advised that between 10:45 A.M. and

11:10 A.M. on 2/27/65, the funeral services at the Faith Temple
Church of God, New York City, were concluded without incident and that the funeral procession proceeded through Harlem
in an orderly fashion to the Major Deegan Expressway and traveled north from New York City under NYCPD escort to the City
line at the beginning of the Thomas E. Dewey Expressway, Westchester County, New York, where the procession was taken over
by the New York State Police Department en route to Ferncliff
Cemetery, Hartsdale, New York. [BUREAU DELETION] advised that the funeral procession started with approximately fifteen cars and that the procession itself became entwined with
New York City traffic in Harlem and on the expressway.

[BUREAU DELETION] advised on February 27, 1965 that
the funeral procession under convoy of the New York State Police entered the grounds of the Ferncliff Cemetery, Hartsdale,
New York, Town of Greenburgh, Westchester County, New
York, at 11:35 A.M. on February 27, 1965 with approximately
fifty-two automobiles parked behind the hearse, that approximately two hundred passengers from these automobiles joined
another two hundred persons who had been waiting at the scene
for the funeral procession to arrive.

[BUREAU DELETION] advised that the funeral service at
the grave was concluded at approximately 12:45 P.M., by which
time the group which appeared to be members of the immediate
funeral procession itself had left the cemetery. [BUREAU DE-
LETION] advised that there were no disturbances or incidents in
the cemetery or at the gravesite itself; that the funeral was carried
on in an orderly fashion but that shortly before the end of the
ceremony itself a woman believed to be [BUREAU DELETION]
Boston, Massachusetts, [BUREAU DELETION] in a slight
emotional outburst was heard to say that she would be "willing
to die for the cause."

[BUREAU DELETION] that two individuals known to him
only as former members of a personal bodyguard or close associates of Malcolm X, also in an emotional outburst indicated that
the death of Malcolm X would eventually be avenged.

[BUREAU DELETION] advised on February 27, 1965 that
Harlem Rent Strike Leader Jesse Gray advocated that retail mer-

chants on 125th Street in Harlem close their stores during the Malcolm X funeral hours on February 27, 1965 under the threat of a picket line and boycott. [BUREAU DELETION] further advised that [BUREAU DELETION] noted that the Jesse Gray picket line included no more than thirty persons; that the picket line which appeared at 125th Street, New York City, was completely ineffective and that reports indicate that the retail merchants in the area paid no attention to it and that business was conducted without incident.

[BUREAU DELETION]

UNITED STATES DEPARTMENT OF JUSTICE
FEDERAL BUREAU OF INVESTIGATION

Boston, Massachusetts
March 8, 1965
MALCOLM K. LITTLE, aka
INTERNAL SECURITY—MMI

[BUREAU DELETION] Malcolm Little never considered who might succeed him as leader if anything happened to him. Even though Little believed that his life was in danger, he seemed to be convinced that nothing would happen. Malcolm had stated to his friends that when he left the NOI he was penniless. He made enough money on magazine articles and television appearances to keep himself going, but he said that he had to leave the country to try to establish some permanent source of income for himself. He contacted the heads of the legitimate Moslem religion and, at their request, made the required pilgrimage to Mecca. They arranged to have a religious leader sent to New York City to teach and perform the religious rights of the Moslem religion. This leader was to reside with Malcolm Little, for which Little would be reimbursed the sum of $500 a month.

UNITED STATES DEPARTMENT OF JUSTICE
FEDERAL BUREAU OF INVESTIGATION

New York, New York
March 12, 1965
Malcolm K. Little
Internal Security—MMI

On February 21, 1965, at 3:10 P.M. [BUREAU DELETION] advised that Malcolm X had just been shot in the Audubon Ballroom, New York City, while addressing an OAAU public rally. [BUREAU DELETION] that Reuben X Francis, one of Malcolm's officers, fired back at those shooting at Malcolm X. [BUREAU DELETION] a Negro male (later identified as Talmadge Hayer) was captured outside the Audubon Ballroom immediately after the shooting.

[BUREAU DELETION] advised on February 21, 1965, that at approximately 3:10 P.M., this date, he received a call at the station that a homicide was committed at the Audubon Ballroom, 564 West 166th Street, New York City.

He stated that Patrolman [BUREAU DELETION] New York City Police Department, advised the same date that Malcolm X, Negro, male, age 39, of Suite 128, Hotel Theresa, 7th Avenue and 125th Street, New York City, while on the stage of the Audubon Ballroom, was shot and killed by unknown persons. Patrolman [BUREAU DELETION] stated that Malcolm X was pronounced dead on arrival by [BUREAU DELETION] at Vanderbilt Clinic, Presbyterian Hospital at 168th Street and Broadway, New York City, on February 21, 1965. [BUREAU DELETION] stated that the Police Department determined that the shooting of Malcolm X occurred at about 3:10 P.M., February 21, 1965.

On February 21, 1965, [BUREAU DELETION] and [BUREAU DELETION] both of the [BUREAU DELETION] advised that Malcolm X was shot that afternoon during a rally of the OAAU at the Audubon Ballroom. They stated that [BUREAU DELETION] was on patrol on Broadway when he heard shots coming from the Audubon Ballroom. He immediately proceeded in that direction where he saw people coming out of the said ballroom shouting that Malcolm X had been shot. Others were shouting "Don't let him get away." [BUREAU DELETION] at that time arrested person identified as Thomas Hagan as he was running out of the ballroom. When arrested, Hagan (true name Hayer) had in his pocket a .45 caliber automatic clip containing four rounds. Hayer had been shot in the left leg.

[BUREAU DELETION] further stated on February 21, 1965, that the Police Department obtained two witnesses immediately after the shooting, namely [BUREAU DELETION] both free-lance reporters and photographers of [BUREAU DELETION].

[BUREAU DELETION] stated that [BUREAU DELETION] and [BUREAU DELETION] gave statements in which they say they saw Hayer with a gun in his hand while Malcolm X was on the stage speaking. They said Malcolm X suddenly called out "Hold it" and after this, [BUREAU DELETION] dropped to the floor and did not actually see Malcolm X shot, but stated before they dropped to the floor, they saw Hayer with a gun in his hand pointing it towards Malcolm X. The next thing they saw was Hayer trying to run out of the ballroom with a gun in his hand. According to [BUREAU DELETION] as Hayer ran out, one of Malcolm's group shot three times at Hayer with an automatic pistol. Hayer did not have the pistol on him when he was arrested outside the ballroom.

[BUREAU DELETION] also stated that [BUREAU DELETION] who was sitting in the front row in the Audubon Ballroom was shot in the foot during the shooting spree in which Malcolm X was shot. He also stated that [BUREAU DELETION] was also hit during the shooting spree in the ballroom and both [BUREAU DELETION] and [BUREAU DELETION] were treated at Columbia Presbyterian Hospital, New York City.

[BUREAU DELETION] later advised that the police found a 12 gauge sawed-off double-barrel shotgun manufactured by J. C. Higgins, model 1017, also bearing the number 5100. The police advised, upon examination, that the shotgun had been fired and left at the scene.

At approximately 7:45 P.M., on February 21, 1965, [BUREAU

DELETION] advised that Hayer was being detained in the prison ward at Bellevue Hospital, under guard. He stated that Hayer had one bullet in him which entered his left thigh and shattered the thigh bone. He stated the hospital plans to put Hayer's left leg in traction and that the bullet would stay in the leg for about two weeks until such time as the bone would be healed enough to permit an operation.

On February 21, 1965, [BUREAU DELETION] New York, contacted the office of the Federal Bureau of Investigation (FBI) at New York City and stated that he had one of the pistols used to kill Malcolm X. [BUREAU DELETION] was at that time in [BUREAU DELETION] and asked that Bureau Agents meet him at the [BUREAU DELETION] address as soon as possible. [BUREAU DELETION] when contacted the same date by Agents of the FBI, [BUREAU DELETION] was in the back of the Audubon Ballroom, the same date, to hear Malcolm X speak. He stated that he is a member of the OAAU. He said Malcolm X was just introduced and began to speak when some people began to scream somewhere about eight rows from the front of the auditorium. He said people in that area began to move away and Malcolm X put up his hands as though to quiet the people down and was heard to say "Keep your seats." Just then, [BUREAU DELETION] shots rang out, but [BUREAU DELETION] could not see who was doing the shooting. After the shots were fired [BUREAU DELETION] the persons shooting headed for the exit. Some of the people in the audience tried to stop them by throwing chairs at them or in their way. At this time, two of Malcolm X's men were shooting at the assailants as they were trying to leave the ballroom. [BUREAU DELETION] said the two men involved in the shooting passed him, but as the other two men involved were running towards the exit, one turned to fire back at Malcolm X's men. As this man then turned to run through the exit, [BUREAU DELETION] threw a "body block" into him knocking him down the stairs, at which time, this person dropped a .45 caliber pistol. [BUREAU DELETION] picked up the gun and attempted to shoot the man he knocked down as he was running down the stairs, but the gun jammed and he ran out of the building. [BUREAU DELETION] said he checked the

gun and noticed that three rounds were still in the clip. [BU-
REAU DELETION] then turned over to Special Agents of the
FBI a .45 caliber automatic pistol, serial number 335055, con-
taining a clip with three rounds of ammunition.

At 10:15 P.M., February 21, 1965, [BUREAU DELETION]
came to the office of the FBI, at which time, they were furnished
a .45 caliber automatic pistol, which was obtained by Agents of
the FBI from [BUREAU DELETION].

[BUREAU DELETION] stated that Hayer, who was arrested
immediately after shooting Malcolm X, has been charged with
homicide and that Reuben X Francis, a member of Malcolm X's
group, was charged with felonious assault and possession of a
deadly weapon.

[BUREAU DELETION] also stated that the Police Department has a witness who identified Francis as the person firing
back at assailants of Malcolm X. He said Francis was believed to
have fired a shot which struck Hayer in the leg. He said Francis
is suspected of being the person who fired a .32 caliber pistol,
which has never been recovered by the Police Department. [BU-
REAU DELETION] stated that it is estimated that up to four
persons may be involved in the killing of Malcolm X.

[BUREAU DELETION] further advised that an autopsy performed on Malcolm X reflected that he had ten bullet wounds in
his chest, thigh and ankle plus four bullet creases in the chest and
thigh. The autopsy located one nine millimeter slug and one .45
caliber slug, and several shotgun pellets in the body of Malcolm
X.

[BUREAU DELETION] said that when the Police Department examined the Audubon Ballroom after the shooting they
found a sawed-off double-barrel shotgun wrapped in a green suit
coat. In the suit coat pocket was found a key for a Yale lock, a
package of camel cigarettes and an empty eyeglass case bearing
the optometrist name "M. M. Fine, Main Street, Flushing." The
shotgun contained two discharged Remington express shells, single 0 buckshot shells, and there were indications that the gun was
recently fired.

[BUREAU DELETION] also stated that in the ballroom were
found three .45 caliber shells and slugs, six nine millimeter shells

and two slugs, and three .32 caliber slugs and 10 pieces of lead, presumably fired from the shotgun.

The FBI Identification Division, on February 22, 1965, identified prints of the person arrested in the shooting of Malcolm X as Talmadge Hayer, who up until then, was known to the Police Department only as Thomas Hagen. Identification records reflect that Hayer, FBI #142496F, is a male, Negro, born March 16, 1942, at Hackensack, New Jersey, last known residing at 347 Marshall Street, Paterson, New Jersey. [BUREAU DELETION]

[BUREAU DELETION] that Malcolm X arrived at the Audubon Ballroom, February 21, 1965, in a white 1965 Cadillac. Malcolm X was surrounded by his bodyguards and was then escorted into the front corridor of the Audubon Ballroom and then to the stage. When Malcolm X began to speak, a disturbance occurred between two men. Up in the front near the stage, Malcolm X's bodyguards started to move towards the two men causing a disturbance, when Malcolm X said "Hold it." Without hesitation, two men occupying the front seats, left side, middle aisle, looking towards the stage, got into a crouched position and fired several shots in the direction of Malcolm X. The fire "spitting" from the guns "crashed" into the chest of Malcolm X and he fell backwards as if knocked down by a sudden powerful force. Still in the crouched position, the gunmen hastily moved toward the exit in the back of the hall, stepping over persons who were laying on the floor. It is believed that approximately twenty shots in all were fired during the shooting.

[BUREAU DELETION] reviewed a photograph of Talmadge Hayer and identified him as one of the persons who shot and killed Malcolm X on February 21, 1965, at the Audubon Ballroom.

[BUREAU DELETION] advised on that date Hayer's fingerprints were found on the clip of the .45 caliber pistol that was picked up by [BUREAU DELETION]at the Audubon Ballroom the day Malcolm X was killed and turned over to the FBI.

On February 26, 1965 [BUREAU DELETION] Norman 3X Butler, 661 Rosedale Avenue, Bronx, New York, was arrested at 3:00 A.M., same date, by the New York City Police Department, as one of the assassins in the killing of Malcolm X on February

21, 1965. [BUREAU DELETION] said that three witnesses including [BUREAU DELETION] placed Butler in the Audubon Ballroom at the time that Malcolm X was shot and he was identified as one of the persons who actually shot at Malcolm X.

[BUREAU DELETION] a photograph of Norman 3X Butler, who was arrested by the Police Department for the killing of Malcolm X as one of the persons who participated in the shooting of Malcolm X at the Audubon Ballroom.

On February 27, 1965, [BUREAU DELETION] advised that [BUREAU DELETION] identified Talmadge Hayer and Norman 3X Butler, both now in the custody of the New York City Police Department, as assassins in the killing of Malcolm X. Butler was arrested in January 1965, for shooting a Correctional Officer who broke away from the NOI and, at the time he was arrested for killing Malcolm X, he was on $10,000 bail.

[BUREAU DELETION]
[BUREAU DELETION]
[BUREAU DELETION]

[BUREAU DELETION] identified Norman 3X Butler from photographs as the man who was sitting [BUREAU DELETION] and said "Get your hands out of my pocket" in the Audubon Ballroom, just before Malcolm X was killed. [BUREAU DELETION] cannot recognize Thomas 15X Johnson from photographs as being in the Audubon Ballroom on February 21, 1965.

On March 4, 1965, [BUREAU DELETION] stated that as of this date, Hayer, Butler and Johnson, all arrested for the killing of Malcolm X, have refused to furnish any information other than their name and age.

On March 8, 1965, [BUREAU DELETION] advised that [BUREAU DELETION] was interviewed by the New York City Police Department on the same date. According to [BUREAU DELETION] stated that he saw Hayer shoot Malcolm X and also observed Butler and Johnson in the Audubon Ballroom the day Malcolm X was killed. [BUREAU DELETION] saw Johnson run out the side exit after the shooting.

[BUREAU DELETION] stated that Johnson, when arrested, denied being in the Audubon Ballroom on February 21, 1965.

[BUREAU DELETION] stated that [BUREAU DELETION] after the shooting, he picked up the shotgun used to kill Malcolm X and gave it to Rueben X Francis. He said he also picked up a German Luger pistol and gave it to another person to hold until the police arrived.

[BUREAU DELETION] stated that the German Luger was never turned over to the Police Department and this gun could probably account for the nine millimeter slug in Malcolm's body. [BUREAU DELETION]

On March 10, 1965, [BUREAU DELETION] advised that the [BUREAU DELETION] in conducting interviews of persons, particularly MMI members who were present in the Audubon Ballroom when Malcolm X was shot, seem to have the same "clear cut" story that they were in the ballroom when Malcolm X was shot and when the shots rang out they fell to the floor and never got a look at the assassins. [BUREAU DELETION] stated that the Police Department learned that [BUREAU DELETION] of the MMI in New York City, has instructed members of the MMI and the OAAU to cooperate with the Police Department but only say that they fell on the floor when the shooting started and cannot identify the person who shot Malcolm X.

[BUREAU DELETION] said the [BUREAU DELETION] is now shifting their investigation towards officials of the MMI [BUREAU DELETION]. In reference to [BUREAU DELETION] stated that information has been received that [BUREAU DELETION] also was one of Malcolm X's bodyguards the day he was shot, and has been seen in the Harlem area "dressed to kill," "wearing one hundred dollar suits" and a "pocket full of hundred dollar bills" since the death of Malcolm X. [BUREAU DELETION] said that [BUREAU DELETION] has no visible means of support at this time.

[BUREAU DELETION] also stated that on March 10, 1965, the New York County Grand Jury handed down first-degree murder indictments in the killing of Malcolm X on February 21, 1965, against Talmadge Hayer, Norman 3X Butler and Thomas 15X Johnson.

The *New York Times,* a local daily newspaper dated March 11,

1965, contained an article captioned "4 Are Indicted Here In Malcolm X Case." This article states:

A grand jury indicted three Negroes yesterday in the slaying of Malcolm X, Black Nationalist leader, and indicted Malcolm's bodyguard for shooting and wounding one of the trio.

Charges of willfully killing Malcolm "with a shotgun and pistols" were made against Thomas Hagen, also known as Talmadge Hayer and Thomas Hayer, 22 years old, of 347 Marshall Street, Paterson, N.J.; Norman 3X Butler, 26, of 661 Rosedale Avenue, the Bronx; and Thomas 15X Johnson, 29, of 932 Bronx Park South, the Bronx.

A separate indictment accused Rueben [sic] Francis, under that spelling and also as Rueben [sic] X, on one count of first-degree felonious assault for "aiming and discharging a pistol" at Hagan, two counts of second-degree assault and a fourth count of possessing a pistol. Francis, 33, has given his address as 871 East 179th Street, the Bronx.

Hagan is in Bellevue Hospital's prison ward. Butler and Johnson, [who] are being held without bail, and Francis, whose bail has been set at $10,000, are to be arraigned in Supreme Court, tomorrow.

This document contains neither recommendations nor conclusions of the FBI. It is the property of the FBI and is loaned to your agency; it and its contents are not to be distributed outside your agency.

SECTION 17

March 25, 1965–May 25, 1965

REPORTS: 1. March 25, 1965. Boston
2. March 30, 1965. SAC, Philadelphia to Director. Airtel
3. April 1, 1965. SAC, New York to Director. Teletype
4. April 6, 1965. SAC, New York to Director
5. April 28, 1965. SAC, New York to Director
6. May 25, 1965. SAC, New York to Director

Section 17 continues with reports speculating about the shooting. The FBI receives more information indicating that a conspiracy within the MMI was responsible for the murder. An informant at the funeral felt that the two guards on duty at the Audubon participated. Another indicated that "before the killing someone asked a high official about extra guards for the meeting on 2/21/65. A person in authority said no extra guards would be needed."

Further information surrounding the case is included. A witness contradicts the previous informant by stating that Hayer was the individual who shouted, "Get your hand out of my pocket." Soon it becomes evident that the case against Butler and Johnson is thin at best. On April 28, the Bureau indicates that the NYCPD might be concluding their investigation in order to prepare for trial.

SUBJECT   MALCOLM X LITTLE

FILE NO.   100-399321

Section 17

Serials 366-408

UNITED STATES DEPARTMENT OF JUSTICE
FEDERAL BUREAU OF INVESTIGATION

Boston, Massachusetts
March 25, 1965
[BUREAU DELETION]

On [BUREAU DELETION] who is registered at the Sherry Biltmore Hotel, Boston, Massachusetts, [BUREAU DELETION] was interviewed at the Sherry Biltmore Hotel by an FBI Agent.

[BUREAU DELETION] stated that he had attended the funeral of Malcolm X Little in New York City. He claims that on his arrival in New York City, he was taken into protective custody by the [BUREAU DELETION] and was allowed to attend the funeral. Subsequent to the funeral, he went to a friend's home for the evening and then returned to Boston, Massachusetts.

While at the funeral, he chatted with former members of the Newark Nation of Islam (NOI) Temple whom he recognized from having had contact with them while visiting that temple [BUREAU DELETION] stated, however, that he does not know them by name.

One of these, to the best of [BUREAU DELETION] was present when Malcolm X was shot. This man described the person who handled the shotgun as a tall, dark-skinned Negro whom he recognized as a member of the Newark Temple, but whom he did not know by name. [BUREAU DELETION] believes that this former Muslim, who told him this, identified the Negro who handled the shotgun as a lieutenant in the Newark Temple. The man handling the shotgun shot from the hip and appeared to be an expert in the handling of this type of gun.

On guard at the rostrum at which Malcolm X was speaking were Robert 35X, formerly of the New York Temple, and Charles 26X, formerly of the Newark Temple.

When the distraction was created just before Malcolm X was shot, both of these guards left the immediate area of the rostrum which [BUREAU DELETION] is in violation of all the rules of "standing post" both in the Muslim Temples and in Malcolm Little's organization.

This fact made the persons participating in the discussion [BUREAU DELETION] convinced that the shooting was a conspiracy in which the two guards participated. [BUREAU DELETION] has no factual knowledge about such a conspiracy, how the shooting occurred or who participated in it. The man who started the distraction by claiming someone's hand was in his pocket was described [BUREAU DELETION] as a short, dark-skinned Negro with bushy hair and a mustache, who was believed to be a member of the Newark Temple.

[BUREAU DELETION] that one night during the current week, [BUREAU DELETION] on the telephone. [BUREAU DELETION] is not known to him and he does not know why [BUREAU DELETION] selected him to call. [BUREAU DELETION] identified himself as a representative of the Progressive Labor Movement in the greater Boston area and claimed he had the responsibility of the distribution of the Progressive Labor Movement publication "Challenge" in this area.

[BUREAU DELETION] that he would like him to join the Progressive Labor Movement and help organize it in the greater Boston area. [BUREAU DELETION] stated that from his conversation with [BUREAU DELETION] understood that [BUREAU DELETION] had been associated with or was familiar with [BUREAU DELETION] would be attending a testimonial to Malcolm Little on Saturday evening, March 13, 1965, at 295 Huntington Avenue, Boston, Massachusetts. [BUREAU DELETION] intended to go to the same testimonial and would probably see [BUREAU DELETION] there.

[BUREAU DELETION] the Organization of Afro-American Unity is presently dormant, waiting for someone to assume its leadership.

[BUREAU DELETION] is currently unable to find anybody with the ability or willingness to assume leadership of the group. [BUREAU DELETION] that in conversation with [BUREAU DELETION] in New York, she had decided that [BUREAU DELETION] would assume some of the responsibilities of leadership and would have to depend on Malcolm X's lieutenants in the Organization of Afro-American Unity (OAAU) to assume the rest of the responsibility.

In Boston, Massachusetts, [BUREAU DELETION] does not believe the organization exists except in the desire of [BUREAU DELETION] to develop it.

[BUREAU DELETION] does not belong to any Negro organizations at the present time. He stated that although he had a close friendship with Malcolm Little and that although Little thought very highly of [BUREAU DELETION] was not actually a member of the Organization of Afro-American Unity or a follower of Little.

[BUREAU DELETION]

On March 13, 1965, [BUREAU DELETION] advised that at about 2:30 P.M. on that date, a hotel employee, [BUREAU DELETION] was in his hotel room tried to contact [BUREAU DELETION] but not being able to arouse him gained entrance to the room with a passkey and found [BUREAU DELETION].

[BUREAU DELETION]

Because of the circumstances surrounding the death, namely, that no one was present at the time of death, and the cause of death was unknown, and the victim had been subject to violence in the recent past the body was removed to the Southern Mortuary, Boston, Massachusetts for an autopsy.

[BUREAU DELETION] stated that a medical examination of the body at the time of death, led to a primary diagnosis [BUREAU DELETION] had died of natural causes after falling into a coma.

On March 18, 1965 [BUREAU DELETION] advised that the final report on the autopsy of [BUREAU DELETION] was not yet complete. However, the autopsy had definitely established [BUREAU DELETION] died of natural causes, namely, [BUREAU DELETION] seizure. This occurred apparently [BUREAU DELETION] asleep. [BUREAU DELETION] also suffering at the time of death from an overdose of a medical drug called Domadeen which induces sleep. This is a pill which had apparently been prescribed for him and which he apparently took regularly.

[BUREAU DELETION] stated that the autopsy was performed with great care since he was aware that the death could possibly be of interest to the local police department and the Federal Bureau od Investigation. He stated that it was interesting to him to note that although [BUREAU DELETION] reported to have been severely beaten on [BUREAU DELETION] in the [BUREAU DELETION] and, in fact, [BUREAU DELETION] claimed to have been severely beaten, there is no medical evidence that he received any severe or lasting damage from whatever beating he did receive.

On March 15, 1965, [BUREAU DELETION] types, stated that on Wednesday, March 10, 1965, he had received a phone call [BUREAU DELETION] claimed that he had two suitcases full of NOI documents which he kept in New Haven. He suggested to [BUREAU DELETION] that if [BUREAU DELETION] would drive him to New Haven to pick up the suitcases, he would arrange for [BUREAU DELETION] to examine them and suggested that they could be of great value to [BUREAU DELETION] to New Haven on Monday, [BUREAU DELETION] advised he did not know whether or not to believe but felt that the trip would be well worth it if he actually had such material. From the tone of the telephone conversation, [BUREAU DELE-

TION] felt [BUREAU DELETION] had he intended to try to sell it to [BUREAU DELETION] rather than give it to him.

This document contains neither recommendations nor conclusions of the FBI. It is the property of the FBI and is loaned to your agency; it and its contents are not to be distributed outside your agency.

———— • •————

FBI

Date: 3/30/65

Transmit the following in_____Confidential_____

Via____AIRTEL____   _____REGISTERED MAIL_____

(Priority)

TO   : DIRECTOR, FBI (100-399321)
FROM   : SAC, PHILADELPHIA (100-39918)
SUBJECT: MALCOLM K. LITTLE, AKA
                IS-MMI

[BUREAU DELETION] was interviewed by SA [BUREAU DELETION] and he advised [BUREAU DELETION] was interviewed the previous night by [BUREAU DELETION] and [BUREAU DELETION] of the [BUREAU DELETION] He admitted membership in the MMI and OAAU and told [BUREAU DELETION] where he was sitting when MALCOLM LITTLE was killed. [BUREAU DELETION] showed [BUREAU DELETION] a photo of an individual they identified as a member from NYC and asked [BUREAU DELETION] if this person was on the door when he entered the Audubon Ballroom. [BUREAU DELETION] told the police he thought he observed this person on the door on 2/21/65 either when he was entering or leaving.

[BUREAU DELETION] was then shown a photo of TALMADGE HAYER. He identified HAYER as a person who stood up and told an individual to his left to "get your hand out of my pocket." HAYER, according to [BUREAU DELETION], then took something from his clothes, either from a pocket or from his belt, and pointed it toward MALCOLM LITTLE.

[BUREAU DELETION] was shown a photo (full length) of NORMAN BUTLER. After seeing the full length photo of BUTLER he identified BUTLER as being present at [BUREAU DELETION] had previously been shown a mug shot of BUTLER which he said looked familiar but he could not make a positive identification from the mug shot.

[BUREAU DELETION] was also shown a full length photo of THOMAS JOHNSON and identified JOHNSON as an individual who was present at the last OAAU meeting. At the time he could not state whether he was definitely present at the meeting [BUREAU DELETION] was previously shown a mug shot of JOHNSON. He stated JOHNSON looked familiar but could not make a positive identification.

[BUREAU DELETION]

[BUREAU DELETION] also told police that as soon as the first shot was fired he fell to the floor. While on the floor he observed a man running out of the ballroom loading a clip for an automatic gun. He only saw this man as high as his hands. He could not identify this individual.

[BUREAU DELETION] was also present in New York City when MALCOLM LITTLE was killed. While the [BUREAU DELETION] were interviewing her one of them left the interview room to talk with [BUREAU DELETION] told [BUREAU DELETION] that he felt the killing was an "inside job" because on [BUREAU DELETION] night before the killing someone asked a high official about extra guards for the meeting on 2/21/65. A person in authority said no extra guards would be needed. [BUREAU DELETION] that the [BUREAU DELETION] had offered [BUREAU DELETION] if he would admit shooting HAYER; however, [BUREAU DELETION] would only tell the [BUREAU DELETION] that he was not present at the meeting.

[BUREAU DELETION]

On 3/23/65 SAs [BUREAU DELETION] and [BUREAU DELETION] interviewed [BUREAU DELETION] concerning information he could furnish [BUREAU DELETION] in the event he was called on to testify. [BUREAU DELETION] furnished the same information as previously set forth in this communication. [BUREAU DELETION] was also advised to contact [BUREAU DELETION] in NYC prior to contacting the Philadelphia [BUREAU DELETION] told [BUREAU DELETION] to cooperate with the police as he wanted whoever killed LITTLE brought to justice.

In regard to MMI security, [BUREAU DELETION] tried to start an FOI in the MMI but that MALCOLM LITTLE would not allow it. [BUREAU DELETION] told [BUREAU DELETION] felt the MMI security was inadequate but that MALCOLM LITTLE gave the final orders on security. [BUREAU DELETION] told [BUREAU DELETION] knew nothing about the shooting as he was in the back room when the shooting occurred.

[BUREAU DELETION] stated he felt the police were indirectly responsible for the murder of MALCOLM LITTLE as they did not furnish LITTLE sufficient protection when he appeared in public.

With regard to [BUREAU DELETION] statement that he was in the back room when the shooting occurred, it is to be noted that the [BUREAU DELETION] after the shooting on 2/21/65 stated she observed [BUREAU DELETION] on top of the Muslim who came to the United States from Africa with MALCOLM LITTLE. She stated that [BUREAU DELETION] was attempting to protect this individual.

[BUREAU DELETION]

They asked him who was speaking when he entered and he stated BENJAMIN.

BENJAMIN then introduced MALCOLM LITTLE and MALCOLM LITTLE began his speech. LITTLE gave the MUHAMMAD greeting and then stated "Brothers and Sisters."

After LITTLE stated "Brothers and Sisters" a commotion started a few rows in front of him. LITTLE stopped speaking, came from behind the rostrum and a few people started to stand. LITTLE then told the people to take it easy and sit down. While this was going on the individual [BUREAU DELETION] TAL-

MADGE HAYER, stood up and told a person to his left "Get your hand out of my pocket." The person beside HAYER stated, "I wasn't in your damn pockets." This was occurring at the same time as LITTLE was speaking. After standing up HAYER pushed his coat back and pulled an object from his left side, either from a pocket or from his belt. The object looked metallic [BUREAU DELETION]. HAYER then pointed the object he took from his clothing toward LITTLE. [BUREAU DELETION] then heard what sounded like a gunshot and fell to the floor. He told [BUREAU DELETION] to get down but she was still sitting. He later pulled her down.

[BUREAU DELETION]

[BUREAU DELETION] again stated that the first shots he heard were from directly in front of him, While lying on the floor he felt other shots came directly in front of him and from the right of the ballroom.

[BUREAU DELETION] was then asked if the individual on HAYER's left could be identified. [BUREAU DELETION] he was not sure.

[BUREAU DELETION]

[BUREAU DELETION] observed JOHNSON sitting to his right.

[BUREAU DELETION]

FBI

Date: 4/1/65

TO   : DIRECTOR, FBI (100-399321)
FROM   : SAC, NEW YORK (105-8999)
SUBJECT: MALCOLM K. LITTLE, aka
         IS-MMI

ReNKteletype, 3/5/65, captioned "NORMAN HOWARD MORTIMORE, aka; SM-NOI."
[BUREAU DELETION] viewed numerous photographs, including the photographs of TALMADGE HAYER, THOMAS

JOHNSON,[BUREAU DELETION]. HAYER and JOHNSON have been indicted for the homicide of Malcolm X on 2/21/65, at New York City. [BUREAU DELETION] is a suspect of the [BUREAU DELETION] in the homicide of MALCOLM X. [BUREAU DELETION] is considered one of the Nation of Islam (NOI) "strong armed men" from Newark.

[BUREAU DELETION] upon reviewing a photograph of HAYER, stated that he observed an individual resembling HAYER in the front section of the Audubon Ballroom on 2/21/65, when MALCOLM X was shot and killed. He said this individual was one of two men who were standing to the right of the rostrum, one of whom was observed shooting a pistol in the direction of MALCOLM X. [BUREAU DELETION] however, that he could not make a positive identification of the photograph.

Upon reviewing photographs of [BUREAU DELETION] JOHNSON, [BUREAU DELETION] that these photographs resembled two individuals who sat in about the middle of the audience at the Audubon Ballroom on 2/21/65 and who jumped up at about the time MALCOLM X appeared at the rostrum. One of the two individuals [BUREAU DELETION] shouted that someone "got into his pocket." This caused a disturbance and drew the attention of the audience and MALCOLM X's bodyguards to themselves. The guards approached them and left MALCOLM X unguarded, at which time some shooting occurred down in front near the rostrum. [BUREAU DELETION] could not make a positive identification of the photographs.

[BUREAU DELETION] upon reviewing a photograph of [BUREAU DELETION] remarked that he saw a person resembling [BUREAU DELETION] at the Audubon Ballroom when MALCOLM X was shot, but did not believe that this person took an active part in the killing of MALCOLM X. [BUREAU DELETION] he could not make a positive identification of the photograph.

[BUREAU DELETION] advised on 3/31/65, that at the present time HAYER, JOHNSON and NORMAN 3X BUTLER are the only persons known to them to have had anything to do with the death of MALCOLM X.

Bureau authority is requested to furnish information made available [BUREAU DELETION] to the NYCPD on a confidential basis. If Bureau approves, this information will be furnished to NYCPD through [BUREAU DELETION] NYCPD.

———— • • ————

FBI

Date: 4/6/65

TO : DIRECTOR, FBI (100-399321)
FROM : SAC, NEW YORK (105-8999)
SUBJECT: MALCOLM K. LITTLE, aka
IS-MMI

Extreme caution should be exercised in utilizing information furnished below in order that the identity of [BUREAU DELETION] is not disclosed.

On 3/12/65, [BUREAU DELETION] made available a photograph of a letter dated 3/2/65, written by [BUREAU DELETION].

This letter sets forth that the SWP was making a concerted effort to speed the publication of a book under the tentative title "Malcolm X Speaks." [BUREAU DELETION] sets forth that it appeared that the movement led by MALCOLM X was very interested in getting out such a book in view of the problems facing them following the assassination of MALCOLM X. [BUREAU DELETION] further wrote that the SWP expected to get full collaboration from MALCOLM X's group in gathering possible material for this project.

[BUREAU DELETION] letter was directed to [BUREAU DELETION] and asked if [BUREAU DELETION] could obtain material available from the visit of MALCOLM X to France and England. This could possibly include dates or interviews, excerpts from the press and so forth.

[BUREAU DELETION]

In view of the sensitivity of this information, no letterhead memorandum is being submitted.

UNITED STATES GOVERNMENT

MEMORANDUM

TO   :   DIRECTOR, FBI   DATE: 4/28/65
                  (100-399321)
FROM :   SAC, NEW
                  YORK (105-8999)
SUBJECT:
MALCOLM K. LITTLE, aka
                  IS-MMI
                  (00: NEW
                  YORK)

[BUREAU DELETION] NYC, advised on 4/27/65, that the [BUREAU DELETION] at this time has no important suspects at large arising out of their investigation of the murder of MALCOLM X. [BUREAU DELETION] stated that he is trying to determine from police officials and the NY District Attorney's Office if the NYCPD is to continue with the investigation of the shooting of MALCOLM X or to prepare for trial against TALMADGE HAYER, THOMAS JOHNSON and NORMAN BUTLER for the murder of MALCOLM X.

[BUREAU DELETION] stated the PD is still trying to locate and interview [BUREAU DELETION] both of whom, according to [BUREAU DELETION], were in front of the stage acting as bodyguards for MALCOLM X when he was shot and killed on 2/21/65 at NYC.

DIRECTOR, FBI (100-   5/25/65
SAC, NEW YORK [BUREAU DELETION] (C)
EUGENE 2X
SM-NOI
(00: NEW YORK)

ReNYtel 3/29/65, to Director, FBI, captioned "MALCOLM K. LITTLE aka IS-MMI."

Retel contained information to the effect that [BUREAU DELETION] advised on 3/29/65 that the [BUREAU DELETION] has learned from interviewing NOI members concerning the killing of MALCOLM X, that one [BUREAU DELETION] had been connected with a few homicides in the NY area.

On 4/22/65, [BUREAU DELETION] advised SA [BUREAU DELETION] that the identity of [BUREAU DELETION] has never been obtained by the [BUREAU DELETION] through its investigations. He commented that [BUREAU DELETION] is not a suspect in the killing of MALCOLM X at this time. According to [BUREAU DELETION] has been running into the problem of obtaining information on persons with the identical X numbers, and without the persons' true last name, they are unable to make a true identification of possible suspects.

SECTION 18

August 25, 1965–February 23, 1967

Section 18 continues the story of the investigation and the subsequent trial of Hayer, Butler and Johnson. Reuben Francis had jumped bail, so he could not be tried for his alleged shooting of Hayer. Evidence against the NOI appears in the file, including an interview with Los Angeles attorney Gladys Towles Root, who indicated that Malcolm was to be a witness in the paternity suits of her clients against Elijah Muhammad. She stated that Malcolm had said, "If these cases are not hurried, I'll never be alive." Information regarding who used which weapons in the shooting is clarified, and a final consensus seems to be reached that Hayer stood up first and used the .45, not Butler, as a previous informant had hypothesized.

As the trial begins, the prosecution's key witnesses in the FBI's eyes seem to be the Special Agent who received the .45 caliber pistol and the OAAU member who turned it in. This informant would only testify "after the courtroom was cleared of reporters and spectators, claiming his life was in danger if his identity was known." The agent's testimony was apparently a great success, as Assistant DA Vincent Dermody called the Bureau to thank them "for making available SA [BUREAU DELETION]."

The February trial reports include only information regarding testimony and the basic facts of the case, with little indication of any opinions with respect to the guilt or innocence of the suspects. The file reflects that Hayer at first denied any involvement, but later "admitted he was hired to kill MALCOLM X for money, and had three other confederates whom he refused to identify." Little concrete evidence is presented against Butler and Johnson, although it is noted that "Butler's actions on the witness stand [were] very detrimental to his case" (referring to his disrespectful behavior). No analysis is offered on the March 11 guilty verdict rendered by the jury or the April 14 life sentences by Justice Marks.

On February 23, 1967, a Memorial March took place at the Audubon. Speakers were: Akiyele Awolowo, Baba Oseijeman Adefumi, Stokely Carmichael, Charles 37X Morris, Ella Collins (President of the OAAU).

UNITED STATES GOVERNMENT

MEMORANDUM

DATE: August 25, 1965

TO   : Mr. W. C. Sullivan
FROM   : F. J. Baumgardner
SUBJECT: MALCOLM X LITTLE
          INTERNAL SECURITY—
          MMI

The New York Office has advised that Rueben [sic] X Francis, who is being sought by the New York City Police Department after failure to appear in court, is possibly residing in [BUREAU DELETION] Mexico. New York requests authority to advise the New York City Police Department of the address at which Francis could possibly be located.

Malcolm X Little, leader of the Muslim Mosque, Incorporated, Black Nationalist organization, was murdered on February 21, 1965. The New York City Police Department has arrested three individuals suspected of being the assassins. In addition, the police arrested Rueben [sic] X Francis who was with Little at the time of his murder and shot and wounded one of the assassins. Francis was charged with felonious assault and was released on $10,000 bond. Francis was scheduled to appear in court on May 20, 1965 in connection with this charge. He did not appear and the New York City Police Department has been attempting to determine his whereabouts ever since.

[BUREAU DELETION]

The charge for which Francis is being sought comes within the scope of the Unlawful Flight Statute and the New York Office previously has discussed with police officers handling this matter the possibility of seeking Bureau assistance under the Unlawful Flight Statute. While the New York Office is receiving a continuing flow of unlawful flight cases from the New York Police Department there has been a hesitation in asking our assistance in this particular case. The New York Office advises that officers responsible for the Francis case have been convinced that Francis has been hiding out in the New York City area. We have received similar reports; however, the current information clearly indicates Francis has fled to Mexico. The New York Office on August 24, 1965, advised that with the current information indicating the subject is out of the country, the New York City Police Department in all likelihood would request Bureau assistance under the Unlawful Flight Statute.

If a Federal unlawful flight warrant is obtained, our [BUREAU DELETION] would very likely be able to have Francis deported to the United States where he could be taken into custody by Bureau Agents.

With this in mind the New York Office is being instructed to contact the New York City Police Department and, utilizing the current information indicating subject has fled the country, fully explore the possibility of obtaining a Federal unlawful flight warrant. [BUREAU DELETION]

ACTION:

There is attached for approval an airtel instructing the New York Office, based on information that subject has fled to Mexico, to fully explore the possibility of obtaining a Federal unlawful flight warrant concerning subject Francis.

UNITED STATES DEPARTMENT OF JUSTICE
FEDERAL BUREAU OF INVESTIGATION

Los Angeles, California
September 2, 1965

MALCOLM K. LITTLE

Reference the letterhead memorandum dated June 15, 1965, at Philadelphia, Pennsylvania, wherein Malcolm Little was identified as the former leader of the Muslim Mosque, Incorporated . . . and Elijah Muhammad as the leader of the Nation of Islam.

The *Chicago Tribune,* which is a daily newspaper published in Chicago, Illinois, on February 25, 1965 reported an interview with Los Angeles Attorney Mrs. Gladys Towles Root, who represented clients who filed the paternity suits in Los Angeles against Elijah Muhammad. Root disclosed on February 24, 1965, that Malcolm X, the Negro Nationalist Leader slain Sunday in New York, planned to be a witness against Elijah Muhammad, the Black Muslim leader in the two paternity suits. Malcolm X was reported to be the intermediary for Elijah Muhammad in trying to settle out of court the claims of the two women plaintiffs before he split with Muhammad. Mrs. Root reiterated that after the paternity suits were filed on July 2, 1964, Muhammad had tried to induce an assistant to assume responsibility for the paternity so that Muhammad could keep his spiritual image on a high plane in the eyes of his followers. She stated that Malcolm X had stated he had intended to tell all of this in court when the cases came to trial and he also said, "If these cases are not hurried, I'll never be alive." The two women who filed paternity suits were reportedly residing together and they moved twice since the suits were filed, according to the lawyer. She said that there had recently been an explosion at the dwelling next to the one occupied by the two plaintiffs. Mrs. Root explained she had not attempted to get an early trial set for the two cases because the women had been receiving $100 a month support for each child. The money was described as having come "from the church" by the attorney, and she said that she could not define the source of the money more specifically. It was developed during the interview that the paternity actions may have to be transferred to Chicago because that is where Muhammad has property in his own name.

UNITED STATES DEPARTMENT OF JUSTICE
FEDERAL BUREAU OF INVESTIGATION

Copy to:

Office: New York,
New York

Report of: SA JOHN C. SULLIVAN
Date: 9/8/65

Bureau File No.: 100-399321

Field Office File No.: 105-8999
Title: MALCOLM K. LITTLE
Character: INTERNAL SECURITY—
            MUSLIM MOSQUE, INCOR-
            PORATED

Synopsis:

LITTLE, formerly known as MALCOLM X, leader of the MMI, was shot and killed while addressing an OAAU public rally in the Audubon Ballroom on 2/21/65, at New York City. Three members of the NOI were arrested by the NYCPD in connection with the death of MALCOLM X. MALCOLM X was buried in Ferncliff Cemetery, Hartsdale, New York, on 2/27/65. . . .

ASSASSINATION OF MALCOLM X

On February 21, 1965, at 3:10 P.M., [BUREAU DELETION] advised that MALCOLM X had just been shot in the Audubon Ballroom, New York City, while addressing an OAAU public rally. [BUREAU DELETION] that REUBEN X FRANCIS,

one of MALCOLM's officers, fired back at those shooting at
MALCOLM X. He stated that a Negro male was captured outside the Audubon Ballroom immediately after the shooting.

[BUREAU DELETION] advised Special Agent (SA) [BU-
REAU DELETION] on February 21, 1965, that at approximately 3:10 P.M., this date, he received a call at the station that a
homicide was committed at the Audubon Ballroom, 654 West
166th Street, New York City.

He stated that [BUREAU DELETION] advised the same date
that MALCOLM X, Negro, male, age 39, of Suite 128, Hotel
Theresa, Seventh Avenue and 125th Street, New York City, while
on the stage of the Audubon Ballroom, was shot and killed by
unknown persons. [BUREAU DELETION] stated that MAL-
COLM X was pronounced dead on arrival by Dr. J. A. COL-
LINS at Vanderbilt Clinic, Presbyterian Hospital, 168th Street
and Broadway, New York City, on February 21, 1965. [BU-
REAU DELETION] stated that the NYCPD determined that
the shooting of MALCOLM X occurred at about 3:10 P.M., February 21, 1965.

On February 21, 1965, [BUREAU DELETION] both of the
[BUREAU DELETION] advised SA [BUREAU DELETION]
that MALCOLM X was shot that afternoon during a rally of the
OAAU at the Audubon Ballroom. [BUREAU DELETION] was
on patrol on Broadway when he heard shots coming from the
Audubon Ballroom. He immediately proceeded in that direction
where he saw people coming out of the said ballroom shouting
MALCOLM X had been shot. Others were shouting, "Don't let
him get away." [BUREAU DELETION] at that time, arrested a
person identified as "THOMAS HAGAN" as he was running
out of the ballroom. When arrested, HAGAN had on him a .45
caliber automatic clip with four rounds. He had been shot in the
left leg.

[BUREAU DELETION] further advised SA [BUREAU DE-
LETION] on February 21, 1965, that the [BUREAU DELE-
TION] obtained two witnesses immediately after the shooting,
namely [BUREAU DELETION].

[BUREAU DELETION] gave statements in which [BU-
REAU DELETION] saw HAGAN with a gun in his hand while

MALCOLM X was on the stage speaking. They said MAL-
COLM X suddenly called out "Hold it" and after this, [BU-
REAU DELETION] dropped to the floor and did not actually
see MALCOLM X shot. They stated before they dropped to the
floor, they saw HAGAN with a gun in his hand pointing it toward MALCOLM X. The next thing they saw was HAGAN
trying to run out of the ballroom with a gun in his hand. According to [BUREAU DELETION] as Hagan ran out, one of
MALCOLM's group shot three times at HAGAN with an automatic pistol. HAGAN did not have the pistol on him when he
was arrested outside the ballroom.

[BUREAU DELETION] who was sitting in the front row in
the Audubon Ballroom, was shot in the foot during the shooting
spree in which MALCOLM X was shot. He also stated that
[BUREAU DELETION] was also hit during the shooting spree
in the ballroom and both [BUREAU DELETION] were treated
at Columbia Presbyterian Hospital, New York City.

[BUREAU DELETION] 12 gauge sawed-off double-barrel
shotgun manufactured by J. C. Higgins, Model 1017, also bearing the number 5100. [BUREAU DELETION] upon examination, that the shotgun had been fired and left at the scene.

At approximately 7:45 P.M., on February 21, 1965, [BUREAU
DELETION] advised SA [BUREAU DELETION] that HA-
GAN was being detained in the prison ward at Bellevue Hospital, under guard. He stated that Hagan had one bullet in him
which entered his left thigh and shattered the thigh bone. He
stated the hospital plans to put HAGAN's left leg in traction and
that the bullet would stay in the leg for about two weeks until
such time as the bone would be healed enough to permit an
operation.

On February 21, 1965, [BUREAU DELETION] contacted the
New York Office of the Federal Bureau of Investigation (FBI)
and stated that he had one of the pistols used to kill MALCOLM
X. He stated he was, at that time, [BUREAU DELETION] and
asked that Bureau Agents meet him at the [BUREAU DELE-
TION] address as soon as possible. [BUREAU DELETION]
when contacted the same date by SAs [BUREAU DELETION]
was in the back of the Audubon Ballroom, the same date, to hear

MALCOLM X speak. He stated he is a member of the OAAU. He said MALCOLM X was just introduced and began to speak when some people began to scream somewhere about eight rows from the front of the auditorium. He said people in that area began to move away and MALCOLM X put up his hands as though to quiet the people down and was heard to say "Keep your seats." Just then, according to [BUREAU DELETION] shots rang out, [BUREAU DELETION] could not see who was doing the shooting. After the shots were fired, [BUREAU DELETION] the persons shooting headed for the exit. Some of the people in the audience tried to stop them by throwing chairs at them or in their way. At this time, two of MALCOLM X's men were shooting at the assailants as they were trying to leave the ballroom. [BUREAU DELETION] said the two men involved in the shooting passed him, but as the other two men involved were running toward the exit, one turned to fire back at MALCOLM X's men. As this man turned to run through the exit, [BUREAU DELETION] threw a "body block" into him, knocking him down the stairs, at which time, this person dropped a .45 caliber pistol. [BUREAU DELETION] picked up the gun and attempted to shoot the man he knocked down as he was running down the stairs, but the gun jammed and he ran out of the building. [BUREAU DELETION] checked the gun and noticed that three rounds were still in the clip. [BUREAU DELETION] then turned over to Special Agents of the FBI a .45 caliber automatic pistol, serial number 335055, containing a clip with three rounds of ammunition.

At 10:15 P.M., February 21, 1965, [BUREAU DELETION] came to the Office of the FBI, at which time they were furnished a .45 caliber automatic pistol which was obtained by Agents of the FBI [BUREAU DELETION]

[BUREAU DELETION] HAGAN, who was arrested immediately after the shooting of MALCOLM X, has been charged with homicide and that REUBEN X FRANCIS, a member of MALCOLM X's group, was charged with felonious assault and possession of a deadly weapon.

[BUREAU DELETION] has a witness who identified FRANCIS as the person firing back at assailants of MALCOLM X. He said FRANCIS was believed to have fired a shot which struck HAGAN in the leg. He said FRANCIS is suspected of being the person who fired a .32 caliber pistol, which has never been recovered [BUREAU DELETION] it is estimated that up to four persons may be involved in the killing of MALCOLM X.

[BUREAU DELETION] an autopsy performed on MALCOLM X reflected that he had ten bullet wounds in his chest, thigh and ankle plus four bullet creases in the chest and thigh. The autopsy located one nine millimeter slug and one .45 caliber slug and several shotgun pellets in the body of MALCOLM X.

[BUREAU DELETION] examined the Audubon Ballroom after the shooting, they found a sawed-off double-barrel shotgun wrapped in a green suit coat. In the suit coat pocket was found a key for a Yale lock, a package of Camel cigarettes and an empty eyeglass case bearing the name of an optometrist, "M. M. FINE, Main Street, Flushing." The shotgun contained two discharged Remington express single 0 buckshot shells and there were indications that the gun was recently fired.

[BUREAU DELETION] in the ballroom was found three .45 caliber shells and slugs, six nine millimeter shells and two slugs, and three .32 caliber slugs and ten pieces of lead, presumably fired from the shotgun.

The FBI Identification Division, on February 22, 1965, identified prints of the person arrested in the shooting of MALCOLM X as TALMADGE HAYER who, up until then, was known to the [BUREAU DELETION] only as THOMAS HAGAN. [BUREAU DELETION]

On March 10, 1965, [BUREAU DELETION] advised that persons interviewed by the [BUREAU DELETION], particularly OAAU and MMI members, who were present in the Audubon Ballroom when MALCOLM X was shot, seem to have the same "clear cut" story that they were in the ballroom when MALCOLM X was shot and when the shots rang out, they fell to the floor and never got a look at the assassins. [BUREAU DELETION] stated that the [BUREAU DELETION] learned that [BUREAU DELETION] also known as [BUREAU DELETION] the [BUREAU DELETION] has instructed members of the MMI and the OAAU to cooperate with the Police Department but only say that they fell on the floor when the shooting started and cannot identify the person who shot MALCOLM X.

[BUREAU DELETION] is now shifting their investigation toward officials of the MMI, particularly toward [BUREAU DELETION]. He said witnesses have stated that, at the time of MALCOLM X's death, [BUREAU DELETION], supposedly MALCOLM X's trusted friend and associate, showed very little concern for MALCOLM X and did not even come over to look or assist MALCOLM X who was lying on the stage of the Audubon Ballroom dying. In reference to [BUREAU DELETION] that information has been received that [BUREAU DELETION] the day he was shot and has been seen in the Harlem area [BUREAU DELETION].

[BUREAU DELETION] also stated that on March 10, 1965, the New York County Grand Jury handed down first degree murder indictments in the killing of MALCOLM X on February 21, 1965, against TALMADGE HAYER, NORMAN 3X BUTLER and THOMAS 15X JOHNSON.

The *New York Times,* a local daily newspaper, dated March 11, 1965, contained an article on these indictments.

AFFILIATION WITH THE REVOLUTIONARY ACTION MOVEMENT (RAM)

[BUREAU DELETION] a copy of a four-page memorandum [BUREAU DELETION] from a RAM official in New York City. This memorandum was entitled "Malcolm Lives," and bore the subtitle "Analysis of the Assassination." The last page of this memorandum indicates that it is published by "RAM-Revolutionary Action Movement."

This memorandum states that MALCOLM X had become a threat to "Charlie" (the white man) when he broke with the NOI and made his African trips. This threat was based on his growing influence in Africa and Asia, all of which was reason for the Central Intelligence Agency (CIA) to want MALCOLM X to be assassinated.

The memorandum describes the burning of MALCOLM X's house as the "set up" which would make it look like MAL-

COLM X and the NOI were fighting each other, thus creating a motive for the assassination.

The memorandum discussed the assassination of MALCOLM X and described it as "well planned" and indicated that "Negro CIA Agents-hired killers" were in the audience.

This memorandum stated that the meaning of the assassination of MALCOLM X is that whenever a black man attacks the "white" power structure, he will be assassinated, jailed, or forced into exile. The memorandum further stated that the assassination of MALCOLM X shows that either black people or the white American government will be destroyed.

The memorandum ended with the following phrase: "Black Soul Brothers and Soul Sisters: Unite or Perish! Keep on Pushin'!"

UNITED STATES GOVERNMENT

MEMORANDUM

TO   : Mr. Sullivan   DATE: 2/8/66
FROM   : F. J. Baumgardner
SUBJECT: MALCOLM K. LITTLE
          SECURITY MATTER—
          MUSLIM MOSQUE

The trial of Thomas Hagan, Norman 3X Butler and Thomas 15X Johnson, accused of the murder of Malcolm K. Little, better known as Malcolm X, head of the Muslim Mosque, Inc. (MMI), a politically oriented black nationalist movement for Negroes, began in New York State Supreme Court on 1/12/66. Malcolm X had formerly been a leading spokesman for the Nation of Islam, an all-Negro, semi-religious, anti-white organization.

By letter dated 12/23/65, the Bureau authorized SA [BUREAU DELETION] of the New York Office to appear as a witness in this trial in order to identify one of the murder weapons used in the killing of Malcolm X, and to show the chain of evidence up until the time it was turned over to the New York City Police Department.

By way of background, [BUREAU DELETION], who was present at the scene of the murder, on 2/21/65 telephonically contacted the New York Office advising he had one of the weapons used to kill Malcolm X, which he desired to turn over to the FBI. On that same date, SAs [BUREAU DELETION] and obtained the weapon and also a statement from [BUREAU DELETION] as to how the weapon came into his possession. Later that same date, SA [BUREAU DELETION] turned the weapon over to the New York City Police Department.

On 2/8/66, SAC Donald E. Roney, New York Office, advised that SA [BUREAU DELETION] would testify in the Malcolm X murder trial on Wednesday, 2/9/66. Roney advised that the New York County District Attorney had stated that it would probably be necessary for SA [BUREAU DELETION] to produce the interview report form (FD 302) indicating receipt of the gun. Roney further stated that the New York Office had discussed production of the above-mentioned FD 302 with the United States Attorney's Office and had been advised by the United States Attorney that under the "Jencks Decision" and in conformity with New York State Supreme Court procedures, it will be necessary for SA [BUREAU DELETION] to produce the FD 302 if so requested by the Defense Counsel. Therefore, SAC Roney stated that SA [BUREAU DELETION] will have the FD 302 ready for production in court in the event the Defense Counsel requests it.

———————— • •————————

UNITED STATES GOVERNMENT

MEMORANDUM

TO   :   DIRECTOR, FBI (100-399321)   DATE: 2/9/66
FROM   :   SAC, NEW YORK (105-8999)
SUBJECT: MALCOLM K. LITTLE, aka
            SM-MMI

MALCOLM X

ReBulet dated 12/23/65, granting authority for SA [BU-REAU DELETION] to appear as a witness in the New York State trial concerning the death of captioned subject.

SA [BUREAU DELETION] testified on 2/9/66. During the cross examination, SA [BUREAU DELETION] was asked by the Defense Attorney to produce any notes taken in reference to his contact [BUREAU DELETION]. SA [BUREAU DELE-TION] produced an FD 302 which the Defense Attorney returned after his questioning. Defense Attorney's line of questioning centered upon whether or not SA [BUREAU DELETION] checked FBI reports to see if FBI Agents were in the audience at the Audubon Ballroom when MALCOLM X was killed. SA [BUREAU DELETION] was also questioned as to whether the FBI Lab examined the .45 caliber pistol used in the murder of MALCOLM X before it was turned over to the NYCPD. SA [BUREAU DELETION] advised the court that the FBI Lab did not examine the .45 caliber revolver before it was turned over to the NYCPD and that he did not check FBI files to determine if FBI Agents were present in the ballroom when MALCOLM X was killed.

The courtroom was cleared of the news media and spectators when SA [BUREAU DELETION] testified in view of the fact that his testimony, in effect, centered around [BUREAU DELE-TION] who gave SA [BUREAU DELETION] the above mentioned .45 caliber automatic pistol.

[BUREAU DELETION] testified in court on 2/3 and 4/66, after the courtroom was cleared of reporters and spectators, claiming his life was in danger if his identity was known.

New York County Assistant District Attorney VINCENT DERMODY advised on 2/9/66 that he did not believe it would be necessary to recall SA [BUREAU DELETION] as a witness at a later date.

Mr. DERMODY expressed his appreciation to SA [BUREAU DELETION] for testifying and the NYO for its assistance during the State's investigation of the case.

Addendum

(SAC D. E. RONEY):

On the late afternoon of 2/9/66, Mr. VINCENT DERMODY, Assistant District Attorney, New York County, telephoned me to convey his great appreciation to the Bureau for making available SA [BUREAU DELETION] to testify in the MALCOLM K. LITTLE trial. Mr. DERMODY said SA [BUREAU DELETION] was a wonderful witness, and used the word "terrific" to describe his testimony and demeanor on the witness stand. He said SA [BUREAU DELETION] certainly reflected great credit on the FBI. Mr. DERMODY also said he wanted to express his appreciation for the wonderful cooperation on the part of the NYO with the New York City Police Department and the District Attorney's office in this case. Mr. DERMODY said that the cooperation from the beginning of this case had been "terrific," and said this was a perfect example of real effective cooperation.

—————. .—————

FBI

Date: 2/25/66

Transmit the following in_____
                         (Type in plain text or code)
Via____AIRTEL_____ _____
                              (Priority)

TO   : DIRECTOR, FBI (100-399321)
FROM   : SAC, NEW YORK (105-8999)
SUBJECT: MALCOLM K. LITTLE aka
          SM-MMI

Re Bulet dated 2/21/66, requesting the NYO to closely follow the trial in progress concerning the assassination of captioned subject and to keep the Bureau advised of all pertinent developments.

On 2/21/66, Detective JOSEPH REISCH, a ballistics expert, testified at the MALCOLM X murder trial at NY County Supreme Court, NYC, that cartridges taken from TALMADGE HAYER, one of 3 men charged with MALCOLM X's assassination, were linked with a .45 caliber weapon used to kill MALCOLM X. Detective REISCH said extraction marks found on .45 caliber cartridges taken from TALMADGE HAYER matched markings made by the weapon used to shoot MALCOLM X.

Detective REISCH continued by stating that a microscopic examination of the shell casings of the cartridges taken from HAYER matched three shells found in the Audubon Ballroom when MALCOLM X was slain. REISCH said the extraction marks on a gun are significant and peculiar to that particular weapon. He said the markings are similar to an individual's fingerprints.

It is noted that the .45 caliber pistol mentioned above was made available to the NYPD by SA [BUREAU DELETION] on 2/21/65, the day MALCOLM X was slain.

On 2/16/66, SA [BUREAU DELETION] made available to NY County Assistant District Attorney VINCENT J. DERMODY three photographs. Two of the photographs consisted of a group of male Negroes including HAYER in karate uniforms, the third photograph consisted of three persons, one being TALMADGE HAYER with the photographer who took the group photographs.

These photographs were made available to SA [BUREAU DELETION] by SA [BUREAU DELETION] of the NK Office. SA [BUREAU DELETION]

Assistant District Attorney DERMODY stated that the photographs would be "excellent evidence" that HAYER is or was associated with the Black Muslims since HAYER has denied being a Muslim or even being "associated with them." Mr. DERMODY said he could only use the photographs if HAYER is even called to the stand by his attorney.

Mr. DERMODY and SA [BUREAU DELETION] then arranged that if HAYER was ever called to the stand during the trial, Mr. DERMODY would call SA [BUREAU DELETION] who would then contact SA [BUREAU DELETION] in NK to have him present copies of photographs mentioned above to [BUREAU DELETION] to determine if he took the pictures, where and when and if he could identify HAYER. It was pointed out by Assistant District Attorney DERMODY [BUREAU DELETION] would have to be contacted only when HAYER is testifying [BUREAU DELETION].

On 2/23/66, Assistant District Attorney DERMODY contacted SA [BUREAU DELETION] and advised that HAYER was called by his attorney to testify on his own behalf and that he planned to show the above mentioned photographs to HAYER when he cross examined him [BUREAU DELETION].

While on the stand, HAYER denied charges that he had killed MALCOLM X a year ago, that he was ever a member of the Black Muslims, that he had ever learned or practiced karate or that he had a gun in his hand at the Audubon Ballroom the day MALCOLM X was killed.

While HAYER was being cross examined by Assistant District Attorney DERMODY, he was shown photographs of himself with a karate group and was "quite surprised," remained silent for a moment and said it looks like him but it wasn't him.

In the meantime while HAYER was testifying, SA [BUREAU DELETION] of the NK Office contacted [BUREAU DELETION] and exhibited copies of the above mentioned photographs. [BUREAU DELETION] stated that he took the pictures at Muhammad's Mosque No. 25 at a Black Muslim bazaar in March, 1963. He identified the group photographs as that of a karate group which put on an exhibition and identified HAYER as TALMADGE only.

The results of the contact with [BUREAU DELETION] was made available to Mr. DERMODY on 2/23/66, who was very pleased.

Arrangements were made between Mr. DERMODY, SA [BUREAU DELETION] of the NYO and SA [BUREAU DELETION] NK, to have three members of the District Attorney's Office meet with SA [BUREAU DELETION] at 8:30 A.M., 2/24/66, who in turn would show the officials of the District Attorney's Office [BUREAU DELETION] in order that they could interview [BUREAU DELETION] to return to NYC to testify.

On the afternoon of 2/24/66, Assistant District Attorney DERMODY advised SA [BUREAU DELETION] that DURANT testified on behalf of the State and identified the photographs as those taken by him in March, 1963, at Muhammad's Mosque No. 25, Newark, NJ, of a karate team that put on a karate exhibition. He then identified HAYER as TALMADGE who actually introduced himself to him during the affair.

Assistant District Attorney DERMODY again expressed his appreciation for the cooperation given to him by SA [BUREAU DELETION] and SA [BUREAU DELETION]. He stated that the state has just about completed its case and described the photograph and DURANT's testimony "as frosting on the cake" as far as the presenting of his case to the court is concerned.

——————— • •———————

FBI

Date: 3/7/66

Transmit the following in_____
　　　　　　　　　　　　　　(Type in plain text or code)
Via___AIRTEL___　_____
　　　　　　　　　　　　　　(Priority or Method of Mailing)

TO　　　: DIRECTOR, FBI (100-399321)
FROM　: SAC, NEW YORK (105-8999)
SUBJECT: MALCOLM K. LITTLE aka
　　　　　SM-MMI

ReNYairtel dated 3/3/66.

For the information of the Bureau and Newark Office. [BUREAU DELETION] NYC, advised SA [BUREAU DELETION] on 3/4/66, that THOMAS 15X JOHNSON and his wife testified at the MALCOLM X murder trial on 3/3 and 4/66.

Mrs. JOHNSON testified on 3/3/66, and stated that her husband was home all day on 2/21/65, when MALCOLM X was killed. When questioned by the prosecutor as to whether her husband ever had a gun at home, she refused to answer the question. Later during the trial, Defense Attorney WEAVER asked Mrs. JOHNSON if her husband ever had a gun, and she answered yes. The prosecutor then told Mrs. JOHNSON that he asked her the same question only a few moments ago and she refused to answer the question. Mrs. JOHNSON then remarked "I don't have to answer to the police."

THOMAS JOHNSON took the witness stand on 3/3/66 and the morning of 3/4/66. He denied ever leaving his home on 2/21/65, let alone killing MALCOLM X at the Audubon Ballroom on that date. He also stated he never handled a gun at any time in his life. Under cross-examination, JOHNSON admitted that he once bought a gun while he was unemployed and obtaining funds from the NYC Welfare Department.

[BUREAU DELETION] believed the case will go to the jury on or about 3/10/66.

———————— • •————————

AIRTEL   3/3/66
TO   :   DIRECTOR, FBI (100-399321)
FROM   :   SAC, NEW YORK (105-8999)
SUBJECT: MALCOLM K. LITTLE aka
              SM-MMI

ReNY teletype dated 2/28/66.

For the information of the Bureau and Newark Offices. [BUREAU DELETION] New York City, advised SA [BUREAU DELETION] on 3/2/66 that TALMADGE HAYER, while testifying on the stand in the MALCOLM X murder trial on 2/28/66 and 3/1/66, admitted he was hired to kill MALCOLM X for money, and had three other confederates whom he refused to identify. He did state that NORMAN 3X BUTLER and THOMAS 15X JOHNSON, also charged with the killing of MALCOLM X, are innocent.

[BUREAU DELETION] stated that the defense called a Dr.

KENNETH SESSLOWE, Lincoln Hospital, Bronx, to the witness stand on behalf of NORMAN BUTLER, who claimed the doctor treated him for an injured leg when MALCOLM X was killed. During the cross examination by Assistant District Attorney VINCENT J. DERMODY, the doctor admitted that he treated BUTLER, but four days after the killing of MALCOLM X and that the injury could have been caused by a person falling down a flight of stairs. It is noted that when [BUREAU DELETION] testified at the trial, he stated that one of the assassins jumped over TALMADGE HAYER while running down the stairs to get out of the Audubon Ballroom after MALCOLM X was killed. The defense attorneys, according to [BUREAU DELETION], were disturbed by the doctor's testimony and said they would impeach the doctor. Judge CHARLES MARKS reminded the defense attorneys that the doctor was their witness.

[BUREAU DELETION] stated that District Attorney DERMODY requestioned BUTLER about meeting with JOHN ALI, NOI National Secretary, at the Americana Hotel, NYC, the night before MALCOLM X was killed. BUTLER stated he knew JOHN ALI but never met him. [BUREAU DELETION] said information was received that JOHN ALI met with HAYER the night before MALCOLM X was killed, but that the witness to this meeting was later arrested for theft and was now considered undesirable as a state witness.

[BUREAU DELETION] stated that CHARLES 37X MORRIS, was this date again called to the witness stand, this time on behalf of the defense. During cross examination MORRIS admitted that he was once a member of the NOI in NY and at that time knew BUTLER and JOHNSON as members of the NOI "Enforcement Squad" whose duty it was to talk to and sometimes "shake up people."

According to [BUREAU DELETION], while BUTLER was on the witness stand Judge MARKS stated that if BUTLER's manners on the stand did not change, he would charge the jury to take into consideration BUTLER's mannerism and demeanor in determining if he was telling the truth on the witness stand. [BUREAU DELETION] stated that BUTLER's action on the witness stand was very detrimental to his case.

[BUREAU DELETION] stated THOMAS 15X JOHNSON is scheduled to be called to the witness stand on his own behalf on the afternoon of 3/2/66.

--------- • •---------

TELETYPE UNIT

MARCH 11 1966

ENCODED MESSAGE

FBI NEW YORK
1/43 P URGENT 3-11-66 JAM
TO DIRECTOR /4/ 100-399321
FROM NEW YORK 105-8999 1P
MALCOLM K. LITTLE, SM-MMI

NEW YORK STATE SUPREME COURT JURY FOUND TALMADGE HAYER OF PATERSON, NEW JERSEY, NORMAN THREE X BUTLER AND THOMAS FIFTEEN X JOHNSON OF NEW YORK, GUILTY OF FIRST DEGREE ON MARCH ELEVEN NINETEEN SIXTY SIX FOR THE MURDER OF MALCOLM K. LITTLE COMMONLY KNOWN AS MALCOLM X.
SENTENCE SCHEDULED FOR APRIL FOURTEEN NEXT.
LETTER FOLLOWS.
COPY OF INSTANT TELETYPE BEING SENT TO NEWARK BY MAIL.
CORR TIME SHD BE 143 PM
END
2- HL
FBI WASH DC

--------- • •---------

UNITED STATES GOVERNMENT

MEMORANDUM

TO   :   DIRECTOR, FBI   DATE: 3/16/66
              (100-399321)

FROM   :   SAC, NEW YORK
            (105-8999) (P)
SUBJECT: MALCOLM K. LIT-
            TLE, aka
            SM-MMI

ReNYtel, 3/11/66.

[BUREAU DELETION] advised SA [BUREAU DELE-
TION] on 3/11/66, that on that date NORMAN 3X BUTLER,
THOMAS 15X JOHNSON and TALMADGE HAYER were
found guilty of murder in the first degree for the killing of MAL-
COLM X on 2/21/65, at NYC.

On 3/14/66, Assistant District Attorney VINCENT J.
DERMODY, NYC, advised SA [BUREAU DELETION] that
the NY State Supreme Court jury deliberated over 20 hours and
at 12:20 A.M. on 3/11/66, returned a verdict of murder in the
first degree on the defendants BUTLER, JOHNSON and
HAYER for the assassination of MALCOLM X. Mr.
DERMODY stated that Justice CHARLES MARKS set 4/14/
66 for sentencing. He further stated that if BUTLER, JOHN-
SON and HAYER are sentence to life imprisonment, as is man-
datory for murder in the first degree, the trio would have to serve
a minimum of 26 years 8 months before they will be eligible for
parole.

The NYO will continue to follow this case and report results of
sentencing on 4/14/66.

————————. .————————

FBI

Date: 4/14/66

Transmit the following in_____
                           (Type in plain text or code)
Via____AIRTEL____ _____
                                (Priority)

TO   : DIRECTOR, FBI
          (100-399321)
FROM   : SAC, NEW YORK
          (105-8999) (RUC)
SUBJECT: MALCOLM K. LITTLE aka
          SM-MMI

On 4/14/66, [BUREAU DELETION] NY County, NYC, advised that on this date, NY County Supreme Court Judge CHARLES MARKS sentenced NORMAN BUTLER, THOMAS JOHNSON and TALMADGE HAYER to life imprisonment for the murder of MALCOLM LITTLE, commonly known as MALCOLM X.

It is noted that a person sentenced to life imprisonment for murder in the first degree in NY County must serve a minimum of 26 years, 8 months before they can be eligible for parole.

[BUREAU DELETION] also advised that as of this date, it has not been determined where the trio will be incarcerated to serve their sentences.

UNITED STATES DEPARTMENT OF JUSTICE
FEDERAL BUREAU OF INVESTIGATION

New York, New York
February 23, 1967
Memorial March and Service
Commemorating the Death of Malcolm X
Information Concerning

On February 23, 1967, [BUREAU DELETION] advised that a Memorial March and Service Commemorating the Death of Malcolm X took place at approximately 12 noon on February 22, 1967, at the Audubon Ballroom, West 166 Street and Broadway, New York City.

Approximately one hundred people marched in a parade down Broadway to 145 Street, and then crossed over to Seventh Avenue. At this point, they marched down to 125 Street, where they were joined by about another one hundred people. Here a Memo-

rial Service of Malcolm X was conducted and a small bust of
Malcolm X was unveiled.

Speakers were as follows:

Akiyele Awolowo, Chief of Information of the Harlem People's Parliament.

Baba Oseijeman Adefumi, the Prime Minister of the Harlem
People's Parliament, and High Priest of the Yoruba Temple, who
stated that the Negro people should buy goods from black people.

Stokely Carmichael, Executive Director of the Student Non-
Violent Coordination Committee, who stated that from now on
they will no longer celebrate the death of Malcolm X, but instead
will celebrate his birthday.

Charles 37X Morris, a Militant black nationalist who spoke in
general laudatory terms about Malcolm X.

Ella Collins, President of the Organization of Afro-American
Unity, who also spoke in general terms about the good that Malcolm X did while he was living.

The affair terminated at 2:30 P.M. with about two hundred
people in attendance.

There were no arrests or incidents.

SECTION 19

April 29, 1969–June 20, 1980 plus Recordings
and Appendix

REPORTS: 1. April 25, 1969. Memo to W.C. Sullivan.
            Book Review
            2. June 6, 1970. Memo to W.C. Sullivan. Book
            Review
            3. August 20, 1970. Memo to C.D. Brennan.
            Book Review
            4. August 1, 1970. Memo to E.S. Miller. Book
            Review
            5. April 19, 1972. SAC, Albany to Director
            6. May 16, 1972. San Diego to Bureau
            7. May 17, 1972. Memo. SAC, Seattle to Acting
            Director
            8. May 19, 1972. New York to Acting Director.
            Teletype
            9. May 20, 1972. Washington Field to Acting
            Director
            10. May 20, 1972. Cincinnati to Acting Director.
            Teletype
            11. May 31, 1972. Jackson, Mississippi
            12. June 6, 1972. Memo. SAC, New Haven to
            Acting Director
            13. June 9, 1972. Memo. SAC, Miami to Acting
            Director
            14. June 21, 1972. Baltimore
            15. May 29, 1980. Congressman W. Hughes to
            Director Webster
            16. June 20, 1980. Asst. Director Revell to W.
            Hughes

17. Technical Surveillance Recordings. June 3–
    Oct 3, 1964
18. APPENDIX

This final section offers book reviews, information regarding celebrations of Malcolm's birthday in 1972, a request from New Jersey Congressman Hughes to reopen the case against Butler and Johnson, and telephone surveillance recordings from 1964. An appendix then offers reference assistance for the entire FBI file.

The book reviews are submitted in the form of memos written by b7C informants to agents with a summary of the publication followed by a reference as to whether or not the FBI is mentioned in the book. During 1972, FBI Director J. Edgar Hoover died, so some memos from that year are addressed to "Acting Director."

The telephone recordings from 1964 were useful to the FBI because they could supply immediate information regarding Malcolm's activities and could confirm informant reports as well. No reason is listed as to why they were discontinued after exactly four months.

UNITED STATES GOVERNMENT

MEMORANDUM

TO   : Mr. W. C. Sullivan   DATE: 4/25/69
FROM   : [BUREAU DELETION]
SUBJECT: BOOK REVIEW
          "MALCOLM X, THE MAN
          AND HIS IDEAS"
          BY GEORGE BREITMAN
          RACIAL MATTERS

This memorandum presents a review of captioned book published in 1965 by Merit Publishers, which is being placed in the
Bureau Library.

REVIEW OF BUREAU FILES
The author is [BUREAU DELETION] former editor of *The
Militant* a publication of that organization [BUREAU DELE-
TION].

BOOK REVIEW

The author describes the life of Malcolm X from his childhood to his assassination in February of 1965. After the death of his parents, he lived at state institutions and boarding homes until the age of fifteen when he went to live with his sister in Boston, Massachusetts, and drifted into a life of crime including gambling, drugs, hustling, and burglary. In 1946 at the age of twenty, he was convicted of burglary and sentenced to ten years in prison.

During his incarceration, which continued for six years, he was introduced to the Nation of Islam headed by Elijah Muhammad. During this period he educated himself and learned to speak and debate. The author described him as the most respected debater in the country. After parole, he traveled to Chicago, Illinois; met Elijah Muhammad; was accepted into the Nation of Islam; and in a few short years his work, through his plain direct speaking style, helped transform the Black Muslims from a virtually unnoticed to a well-known organization.

While in the Black Muslims, Malcolm X traveled throughout the country as Muhammad's troubleshooter and came to know the ghetto areas nationally. According to the author, Malcolm X became attuned to the needs and wants of a growing multitude of black people looking for a new road. In 1964 he decided his place was with the Negro masses rather than with Muhammad's organization.

He split with Muhammed's organization and undertook the difficult task of building a new movement based on the black unity of all Negroes regardless of their religion and philosophies as long as they were ready to fight for freedom. His new organization was known as Muslim Mosque, Incorporated. He traveled to Africa and the Middle East to mobilize African support behind a project to put the United States government on trial in the United Nations for continued oppression of the American Negroes. He favored Negroes organizing politically, electing their own candidates, and driving "black stooges" from office in the major political parties. Malcolm X was revolutionary and became increasingly more anticapitalist and prosocialist. He read the Socialist Workers Party publication, "The Militant," and urged other Negroes to do likewise.

No mention is made of the FBI in the book.

———————. •———————

UNITED STATES GOVERNMENT

MEMORANDUM

TO   : Mr. W. C. Sullivan   DATE: 6/5/70
FROM   : [BUREAU DELETION]
SUBJECT: BOOK REVIEW
          "THE SPEECHES OF
          MALCOLM X AT HAR-
          VARD"
          BY ARCHIE EPPS
          RACIAL MATTERS

This is a review of captioned book published in 1969 by Apollo Editions. The book is being placed in the Bureau Library.

[BUREAU DELETION] Epps is Assistant Dean of Harvard College. He is described as founder and advisor of "The Harvard Journal of Negro Affairs."

Book, 191 pages, divided into two parts, latter part being verbatim texts of speeches by Malcolm X on 3/24/61, 3/18/64 and 12/16/64. First 112 pages are analysis by Epps of the speeches in effort to determine personal motivations and goals of Malcolm X (true name Malcolm Little). Epps noted first speech given at time when Malcolm X was deeply involved in Nation of Islam (NOI) and was dedicated follower of NOI head Elijah Muhammad. His remarks showed Black Muslim view of the white man as a lowly animal but freedom of the black man from yoke of white man was placed in terms of redemption by God. Shortly before second speech, Malcolm X resigned from the NOI because of disillusionment. In the second speech, he appeared no longer to believe to rely upon God to save the black man from the white man but presented the Negro people as both judge and executioner of the whites. The final speech was made shortly after he had returned from an extensive trip to Africa and just two months before his assassination. The author concludes that Malcolm X saw himself and the Negroes as exiles in a society which was a jungle for them, threatened by daily violence. He was a mixture of prophet, escapist and revolutionary.

No mention of the FBI is made in the book.

ACTION:

For information.

—————. •—————

UNITED STATES GOVERNMENT

MEMORANDUM

TO   : Mr. C. D. Brennan   DATE: 8/20/70
FROM   : [BUREAU DELETION]
SUBJECT: BOOK REVIEW
           "THE ASSASSINATION OF
           MALCOLM X:
           UNANSWERED QUESTIONS
           AND THE TRIAL"
           BY GEORGE BREITMAN
           AND HERMAN PORTER
           RACIAL MATTERS

This is a review of captioned booklet published in 1969 by Merit Publishers, which is being placed in the Bureau Library.

REVIEW OF BUREAU FILES:

Breitman is [BUREAU DELETION] a former editor of *The Militant,* a publication of the SWP. Porter is [BUREAU DELETION] a writer for *The Militant.* [BUREAU DELETION]

BOOK REVIEW:

This booklet consists of twelve articles which appeared in *The Militant* between July, 1965, and March, 1966. Of the three subjects arrested, convicted and sentenced to life imprisonment for the murder of Malcolm X the authors claim that one was undoubtedly guilty but he was not proved to be a member of the Black Muslims. The other two subjects who were Black Muslims were not a part of the assassination and were framed by the police in order to show Malcolm's death was caused by the rival organization. Breitman writes in an introductory note, "Readers should also understand that if the New York police were involved in the assassination (and nothing said or done at the trial, or in the four years since the crime, has absolved them of this charge), that involvement could not have been on their own initiative, but must have resulted from the decision and direction of the Government in Washington, that is, the CIA."

MENTION OF THE FBI:

The FBI is mentioned on pages 5, 6, 9, 11, 22, and 29. On the first three listed pages, mention is made of the Bureau in connection with its investigations and development of informants in extremist groups. On the last three mentioned pages the FBI is referred to as to testimony given during the trial and evidence obtained.

ACTION:

For information.

--------. .--------

UNITED STATES GOVERNMENT

MEMORANDUM

TO   : Mr. E. S. Miller   DATE: 8/1/72
FROM : [BUREAU DELETION]
SUBJECT: BOOK REVIEW
           "THE END OF WHITE
           WORLD SUPREMACY"
           (FOUR SPEECHES BY
           MALCOLM X)

EDITED BY
BENJAMIN GOODMAN
EXTREMIST MATTERS

This is a review of captioned book, published in 1971 by Merlin House, Inc. The book is being placed in the Bureau Library.

REVIEW OF BUREAU FILES:
Malcolm X (true name Malcolm Little) was Harlem hoodlum and ex-convict who became Muslim while imprisoned. He rapidly rose to become Nation of Islam (NOI) minister and major spokesman until split with NOI in March, 1964, and formed Muslim Mosque, Inc. (a quasi-religious, politically oriented black nationalist group), and Organization of Afro-American Unity (OAAU), (a militant civil rights action group aligned with all African descendants). He was assassinated, at age 39, by three Muslims 2/21/65 while addressing four hundred OAAU followers in New York City (NYC). He has since been considered hero and martyr by many revolutionaries.

Editor Benjamin Goodman (true name Augustus Benjamin Goodman) is Negro, aged 40, former NOI Assistant Minister, who defected from NOI with Malcolm X and was his primary assistant.

BOOK REVIEW:
This book is collection of four speeches by Malcolm X introduced by Goodman, who relates background of this "impassioned and inspired" black nationalist and describes setting for each speech.

These speeches were delivered during period 12/62–12/63, the final year of Malcolm X's NOI affiliation, and all except one were presented in NYC.

The first and longest speech entitled "Black Man's History" was presented at Malcolm X's NOI Mosque No. 7 in Harlem 12/23/62. It includes rambling, grossly distorted anti-white view of history emphasizing blacks' oppression by "white devils."

"The Black Revolution," the second speech, was delivered at Adam Clayton Powell's Abyssinian Baptist Church, NYC. Text relates view only lasting solution to race problem is complete racial separation. Malcolm X proposed that U. S. should give blacks land in proportion to population ratio or send blacks back to Africa and provide their subsistence there for twenty-five years.

"The Old Negro and the New Negro," the third speech, is actually Malcolm X's comments during appearance on Philadelphia radio station, Fall 1963, following address at University of Pennsylvania. Comments include his views on decline of European colonialism, awakening of "dark" world, and development of black pride and self-reliance.

The last speech, "God's Judgement [*sic*] of White America," (subtitled "The Chickens are Coming Home to Roost"), was delivered at Manhattan Center, NYC, on 12/3/63. He declares that decline of U. S. as world power is God's punishment for enslavement of 22 million blacks and, unless whites "repent," further retribution will occur.

MENTION OF FBI:
FBI is not mentioned in book.

ACTION:
For information.

——————— • •———————

SAC, Albany   4/19/72
Director, FBI
BIRTHDAY ANNIVERSARY—MALCOLM X
MAY 19, 1972
EXTREMIST MATTERS

Malcolm K. Little, better known as Malcolm X, a black militant leader, was born 5/19/25. He was killed in New York City (NYC) 2/21/65.

Because many of today's black revolutionaries regard Malcolm X as a hero and a martyr, the possibility exists that the anniversary of his birthday may be marked by them with acts of violence. As an example, last year two NYC police officers were

seriously wounded in a machine gun attack by black assailants
the night of 5/19. Anonymous letters claiming credit for the
attack linked the shooting to "Malcolm's Birthday."

Bring this to the attention of all Agents handling black extremist matters so that they may be alert for any information concerning possible violence in connection with Malcolm X's birthday.
Instruct black extremist informants to be particularly alert to
obtain and report such information.

If any such information developed, promptly advise Bureau
under appropriate caption and handle in accordance with existing instructions.

2—All Offices

HEH:aso (124)

NOTE: See memorandum [BUREAU DELETION] to Mr. E. S.
Miller, dated 4/18/72, captioned as above, prepared by
HEH:aso.

─────────── • •───────────

FEDERAL BUREAU OF INVESTIGATION

COMMUNICATIONS SECTION

MAY 16, 1972
TELETYPE

NR 10 SD CODE
1100PM N1TEL 5-15-72 LLC
TO BUREAU (ATTENTION D I D)
FROM SAN DIEGO (157-3191) (P) 4P
BIRTHDAY ANNIVERSARY—MALCOLM X, MAY NINE-
TEEN NEXT, EXTREMIST MATTERS.

TWO SAN DIEGO SOURCES ADVISED SUBSTAN-
TIALLY AS FOLLOWS ON MAY TWELVE LAST:

THE BIRTHDAY ANNIVERSARY OF THE LATE MAL-
COLM X, EARLY LEADER IN THE BLACK NATIONIST
MOVEMENT, WILL BE OBSERVED WITH FESTIVITIES
MAY NINETEEN AND TWENTY NEXT AT SOUTH-
CREST PARK, FORTIETH AND KEELER STREETS, AND
AT RUSS AUDITORIUM AT SAN DIEGO HIGH SCHOOL,
SAN DIEGO, CALIFORNIA.

FESTIVITIES AT SOUTHCREST PARK WILL START ELEVEN THIRTY AM MAY NINETEEN AND WILL FEATURE SONGS, DANCES AND POETRY READING, AS WELL AS TALKS BY COMMUNITY LEADERS. LAST YEAR'S MALCOLM X CELEBRATION AT THE PARK WAS ATTENDED BY AN ESTIMATED FIVE THOUSAND PERSONS.

AMONG THOSE SCHEDULE TO ATTEND AND ENTERTAIN THE GUESTS WILL BE LE ROI JONES, REFERRED TO AS IMAMU BARAKA, POET AND BLACK POLITICAL ACTIVIST; CAIPHUS SEMANYAN, LEADER OF A MUSICAL GROUP CALLED THE UNION OF SOUTH AFRICA; LETTA MBULU, AN ENTERTAINER FROM AFRICA; DAVID NELSON OF THE LAST POETS, A POETRY READING GROUP, AND RUPERT CROSSE AND TATANISHA, STARS OF THE TELEVISION PROGRAM "ROOM TWO TWENTY TWO."

HIGHLIGHT OF THE CELEBRATION WILL BE THE FIFTH ANNUAL MISS AFROAMERICA SAN DIEGO PAGEANT AT EIGHT PM MAY TWENTY NEXT AT RUSS AUDITORIUM. THE THEME OF THE PAGEANT IS "BLACK WOMEN DASH AFRICAN ESSENCE REBORN." MASTER OF CEREMONIES DURING THE PAGEANT WILL BE BLACK ACTOR RICHARD ROUNDTREE CURRENTLY STARRING IN A MOTION PICTURE TITLED "SHAFT."

THE TWO DAY CELEBRATION IS BEING SPONSORED BY THE CONGRESS OF AFRICAN PEOPLE (CAP), THE NATIONAL INVOLVEMENT ASSOCIATION (NIA), THE BLACK STUDENT UNIONS (BSU) IN VARIOUS LOCAL SAN DIEGO COLLEGES AND HIGH SCHOOL CAMPUSES, AND OTHER COMMUNITY ORGANIZATIONS.

CAP'S BASIC GOAL IS THE GLOBAL EXPRESSION OF BLACK NATIONALISM.

NIA IS A LOCAL SAN DIEGO BLACK ORGANIZATION SELF DESCRIBED AS A MOVEMENT FOR REVOLUTIONARY BLACK NATIONALISM AND IS DIRECTLY AFFILIATED WITH CAP.

THE BSU IS A STUDENT DASH BASED BLACK MILITANT ORGANIZATION.

VERNON JOHN FONTENETTE, JR., REFERRED TO AS IMAMU SUKUMU, WESTERN REGIONAL COORDINATOR FOR CAP, WILL BE THE OFFICIAL HOST OF THE EVENT.

_____. ._____

UNITED STATES GOVERNMENT

MEMORANDUM

TO   : ACTING DIRECTOR, FBI   DATE: 5/17/72
FROM   : SAC, SEATTLE
             (157-1882)(RUC)
SUBJECT: BIRTHDAY ANNIVERSARY
             —MALCOLM X
             5/19/72
             EXTREMIST MATTERS

Re Bureau letter to Albany, 4/19/72.

During May, 1972, Seattle sources and informants familiar with black extremist activity were contacted and advised they did not have any information relating to any possible violence in connection with MALCOLM X's birthday.

_____. ._____

FEDERAL BUREAU OF INVESTIGATION
COMMUNICATIONS SECTION

MAY 19, 1972
TELETYPE

NR 054 NY CODE
1219 AM 5-19-72
URGENT 5-18-72 PAC
TO ACTING DIRECTOR
  ATT DID
FROM NEW YORK 157-7584 3P

BIRTHDAY ANNIVERSARY—MALCOLM X
MAY NINETEEN, NEXT
EXTREMIST MATTERS

RE NEW YORK LETTER TO BUREAU, MAY NINE, IN-
STANT.

ON MAY EIGHTEEN, INSTANT, A CONFIDENTIAL
SOURCE, WHO HAS FURNISHED RELIABLE INFORMA-
TION IN PAST, ADVISED FOLLOWING DEMONSTRA-
TIONS AND ASSEMBLIES ARE TO TAKE PLACE ON
MAY NINETEEN, NEXT IN CONJUNCTION WITH THE
BIRTHDAY ANNIVERSARY OF MALCOLM X:

ELEVEN O'CLOCK AM—PILGRIMAGE TO FERN-
CLIFF CEMETERY HARTSDALE, WESTCHESTER, NEW
YORK, BURIAL SITE OF MALCOLM X, AND SPON-
SORED BY ORGANIZATION OF AFRO-AMERICAN
UNITY (OAAU), TWO TWO FOUR WEST ONE THIRTY
NINTH STREET, NYC.

TWELVE TO SEVEN O'CLOCK PM—MALCOLM X ME-
MORIAL ASSEMBLY AT FULTON STREET BETWEEN
LEWIS AND SCHENECTADY AVENUE, BROOKLYN. UN-
SPONSORED.

TWO O'CLOCK PM—BIRTHDAY CELEBRATION AT
SEVENTH AVENUE AND ONE HUNDRED TWENTY
FIFTH STREET, KNOWN IN BLACK COMMUNITY AS
MALCOLM X SQUARE, WITH NO SPECIFIC SPONSOR
INDICATED.

THREE O'CLOCK PM—DEMONSTRATION AT
UNITED NATIONS BUILDING, FORTY SECOND
STREET AND FIRST AVENUE, NYC, SPONSORED BY
SEVERAL BLACK ORGANIZATIONS FOR PURPOSE OF
DISCUSSING PLIGHT OF UNITED STATES POLITICAL
PRISONERS ALSO TRIBUTES MAY BE GIVEN TO MAL-
COLM X.

ABOVE CONFIDENTIAL SOURCE ADVISED NO ACTS
OF VIOLENCE TO HIS KNOWLEDGE ARE BEING
PLANNED, AND ABOVE ASSEMBLIES ARE TO BE ME-
MORIAL TRIBUTES. NEW YORK CONFIDENTIAL
SOURCES WERE RECONTACTED REGARDING ABOVE

AND NONE WERE ABLE TO FURNISH ANY ADDITIONAL INFORMATION.

————————• •————————

FEDERAL BUREAU OF INVESTIGATION
COMMUNICATIONS SECTION

MAY 20, 1972
TELETYPE

NR 008 WF PLAIN
455 PM NITEL 5-28-72 MWM
TO   ACTING DIRECTOR
        (ATTENTION DOMESTIC INTELLIGENCE)
FROM WASHINGTON FIELD (157-4953) (FIVE PAGES)
        BIRTHDAY ANNIVERSARY, MALCOLM X
        MAY NINETEEN, SEVENTY TWO
        EXTREMIST MATTERS

ALL SOURCES MENTIONED HEREIN HAVE FURNISHED RELIABLE INFORMATION IN THE PAST.

MALCOLM X (LITTLE) WAS A MILITANT CIVIL RIGHTS ACTIVIST WHO WAS ASSASSINATED IN FEBRUARY NINETEEN SIXTY FIVE IN NEW YORK CITY.

THE UNITED STATES PARK POLICE, WASHINGTON, D.C., ADVISED ON MAY TWELVE, SEVENTY TWO THAT A DEMONSTRATION WAS SCHEDULED TO BE HELD IN MERIDIAN HILL PARK, SIXTEENTH AND EUCLID STREETS, N.W., WASHINGTON, D.C., ON MAY NINETEEN SEVENTY TWO TO COMMEMORATE MALCOLM X (MX). AN ESTIMATED THREE HUNDRED PARTICIPANTS WERE ANTICIPATED.

ON MAY SIXTEEN, SEVENTY TWO SOURCE ONE ADVISED A FLIER HAD BEEN PREPARED FOR PUBLIC DISTRIBUTION ANNOUNCING A BLACK ARTS FESTIVAL TO BE HELD IN HONOR OF MX ON MAY NINETEEN, SEVENTY TWO AT MX PARK, SIXTEENTH AND EUCLID STREETS, N.W., WASHINGTON, D.C., FROM SIX O'CLOCK A.M. TO NINE O'CLOCK P.M. INCLUDING A SUNRISE SERVICE, AFRICAN DANCING AND DRUM-

MING, AND ARTS AND CRAFTS EXHIBITS. ATTACHED
TO THE FLIER WAS A POSITION PAPER OF THE MX
MEMORIAL COMMITTEE WHICH EXTOLS THE VIR-
TUES OF MX, STRESSES THE UNITY OF BLACK PEO-
PLE EVERYWHERE AND URGING BLACK PEOPLE TO
BECOME TOTALLY INVOLVED IN THE STRUGGLE FOR
BLACK SURVIVAL.

SOURCE TWO ADVISED THAT ON FRIDAY MORN-
ING, MAY NINETEEN, SEVENTY TWO, AT APPROXI-
MATELY SIX THIRTY A.M., NINE MALE NEGRO INDI-
VIDUALS DRESSED IN DASHIKIS AND AFRICAN-TYPE
GARB WERE OBSERVED AT THE SPEAKER'S STAND IN
MERIDIAN HILL PARK (MX PARK). THEY STOOD
ABOUT FOR A BRIEF PERIOD OF TIME, SOME WITH
HEADS BOWED, AND DEPARTED FROM THE PARK.
BETWEEN SIX THIRTY A.M. AND SEVEN FORTY A.M.
ON THAT DATE, NO OTHER ACTIVITY IN THE PARK
WAS NOTED. BETWEEN THE HOURS OF FOUR
O'CLOCK P.M. AND SIX O'CLOCK P.M. ON MAY NINE-
TEEN, SEVENTY TWO, MUSIC AND BONGO DRUM-
MING ENTERTAINMENT WAS FURNISHED AND
ABOUT SEVEN TABLES HAD BEEN SET UP IN THE
PARK DISPLAYING AFRICAN TRINKETS, SOUVENIRS,
AFRICAN ART AND CRAFTWORK. APPROXIMATELY
TWO HUNDRED PERSONS, ADULTS AND CHILDREN,
WERE MOVING ABOUT IN THE PARK. THERE WERE
NO SPEECHES DURING THIS PERIOD OF TIME AND
NO INCIDENTS WERE OBSERVED. A HEAVY RAIN BE-
GAN FALLING SHORTLY AFTER FIVE THIRTY P.M.
THE EXHIBITS WERE TAKEN UP AND THE CROWD BE-
GAN TO DISPERSE.

SOURCE THREE ADVISED THAT A LOCAL RADIO
STATION HAD ANNOUNCED ON LATE FRIDAY AF-
TERNOON, MAY NINETEEN, SEVENTY TWO, THAT
THE EVENING ACTIVITY AT MX PARK HAD BEEN
CANCELED BECAUSE OF RAIN.

[BUREAU DELETION]
IN VIEW OF ABSENCE OF EXTREMIST ACTIVITY, NO
DISSEMINATION BEING MADE LOCALLY. CASE
CLOSED, NO LHM BEING SUBMITTED. C.
END

——————— • •———————

FEDERAL BUREAU OF INVESTIGATION
COMMUNICATIONS SECTION

MAY 20, 1972
TELETYPE

NR 003 CI CODE
157AM NITEL 5/20/72 DAH
TO ACTING DIRECTOR
FROM CINCINNATI (157-403) C 2P
RALLY AND MARCH IN HONOR OF MALCOLM X,
FRANKLIN PARK, COLUMBUS, OHIO
MAY NINETEEN, NINETEEN SEVENTY TWO
ON MAY NINETEEN LAST, A RELIABLE CONFIDEN-
TIAL SOURCE ADVISED THAT A RALLY CONSISTING
OF APPROXIMATELY ONE THOUSAND NEGROES WAS
HELD IN FRANKLIN PARK, COLUMBUS, ON MAY
NINETEEN LAST IN HONOR OF MALCOLM X. SOURCE
ADVISED HOWARD FULLER, PRESIDENT OF MAL-
COLM X UNIVERSITY, GREENBOROUGH, N.C. TOLD
THE RALLY HE RECENTLY SPENT EIGHT WEEKS
WITH RHODESIAN FREEDOM FIGHTERS AND THAT
THEY MUST UNITE BEHIND THEIR AFRICAN BROTH-
ERS. FULLER CLAIMED POLICE IN THE U.S. ARE IN
COLLUSION WITH BLACK DRUG PUSHERS TO PRE-
VENT BLACKS FROM BEING INVOLVED IN REVOLU-
TIONARY ACTIVITIES. FULLER URGED CROWD TO
TRAVEL TO W DC FOR AFRICAN LIBERATION DAY,
MAY TWENTY SEVEN NEXT.
SOURCE ADVISED CROWD MARCHED FROM PARK
THROUGH EAST SIDE OF COLUMBUS RETURNING TO

PARK AND DISPERSING AT TEN PM MAY NINETEEN
LAST ALL WITHOUT INCIDENT.

———————. •———————

UNITED STATES DEPARTMENT OF JUSTICE
FEDERAL BUREAU OF INVESTIGATION

Jackson, Mississippi
May 31, 1972

BIRTHDAY ANNIVERSARY-MALCOLM X
MAY 19, 1972

On May 23, 1972, a confidential source, who has furnished
reliable information in the past, advised that The Black Unity
Coordinating Committee and the Social Science Division of Tougaloo College, Tougaloo, Mississippi, furnished a program in
connection with Malcolm X's birthday of May 19, 1972.

Source stated this meeting was held on May 17, 1972, and that
the principal speaker, Norman Hodges, was invited to speak by
Roy Walker, senior student at Tougaloo College and president of
The Black Unity Coordinating Committee, Tougaloo College.

Source stated that during the afternoon and evening sessions
actual attendance was only sixty to seventy persons, primarily
students.

———————. •———————

UNITED STATES GOVERNMENT

MEMORANDUM

TO   : ACTING DIRECTOR, FBI   DATE: 6/5/72
FROM   : SAC, NEW HAVEN
           (157-3115) (ROC)
SUBJECT: BIRTHDAY ANNIVERSARY
          —MALCOLM X
          MAY 19, 1972
          EXTREMIST MATTERS

RE: Bureau Letter to Albany, 4/19/72.

No information concerning above captioned matter has come to the attention of agents of the New Haven Office handling extremist matters.

UACB, no further investigation being conducted by New Haven in this matter.

————. •————

UNITED STATES GOVERNMENT

MEMORANDUM

TO   : ACTING DIRECTOR, FBI   DATE: 6/9/72
FROM   : SAC, MIAMI (157-3337) (C)
SUBJECT: BIRTHDAY ANNIVERSARY
—MALCOLM X
MAY 19, 1972
EXTREMIST MATTERS

ReBulet dated 4/19/72.

All appropriate sources of the Miami Office were alerted for any information concerning possible violence in connection with MALCOLM X's birthday.

The date of his birthday has passed and no information was received that any individual or organization planned violence in connection with his birthday.

Also, no violence took place in the Miami area concerning MALCOLM X's birthday.

————. •————

UNITED STATES DEPARTMENT OF JUSTICE
FEDERAL BUREAU OF INVESTIGATION

Baltimore, Maryland
June 21, 1972
RE: BIRTHDAY ANNIVERSARY
MALCOLM X

MAY 19, 1972
EXTREMIST MATTERS

On May 21, 1972, [BUREAU DELETION] advised that the members of the Ujamma Shop, Soul School, Black United Front, and Black Student Union, all from Baltimore, Maryland presented a Malcolm X festival at old Polytech, located at North Avenue and Calvert Streets on May 19, 1972. The admission fee was $1.50 for students, $2.00 for adults. About five hundred people attended in spite of the rain. The affair was given to help raise money for the expenses of the African Liberation Demonstration Day march in Washington, D.C.

[BUREAU DELETION] advised that members of the Ujamma Shop, Soul School, and other brothers presented a play showing how the black man was exploited by the white slavemaster throughout civilization. The white man came to Africa, killed, raped, and robbed the black man of his land and possessions. He then brought them into bondage to America. These same problems went on until the black man was so called "freed" after the Civil War. This so-called freedom turned into a political and economical stage where the white man still controlled the life of the black brother. Next the black man is forced to go to war to fight a man who has done him no harm. When the black brother reaches the war zone he finds that the man who he has been told to fight calls him brother. Then the black brother returns home to find out that the white man has enslaved his brothers and sisters by filling the community with dope. The black brothers should form a force and kill the white dope peddler and clean up [their] community.

There was a group of singers call the "Vandals" who the audience liked very much. The Super Simba Boot dancers of New Jersey performed African military marches directed by a leader, who spoke Swahili.

The main speaker was OWUSU SADAUKAI (master teacher) from Malcolm X University. He informed the audience it was "nation" time and all black brothers must march in the African Liberation Demonstration in Washington, D.C. The purpose of the march is to protest the exploitation of the blacks by white nations. SADAUKAI stated that he fought . . . with black brothers and sisters and saw that most of the military equipment came from America. America has raised corporations and has billions of dollars invested in the lands of Africa and do[es] not wish to see the black man free to own his own land because it would bankrupt [its] holdings. All of the persons attending the festival were invited to attend the celebration of Malcolm X's birthday to be held at Druid Hill Park, Sunday, May 21, 1972.

On May 22, 1972, [BUREAU DELETION] advised that no information came to the attention of [BUREAU DELETION] concerning any incidents which arose out of the Malcolm X festival which was held in Baltimore on May 19–21, 1972.

CONGRESS OF THE UNITED STATES
HOUSE OF REPRESENTATIVES

WASHINGTON, D.C. 20515

May 29, 1980

Mr. William H. Webster
Director
Federal Bureau of Investigation
J. Edgar Hoover Building
10th and Pennsylvania Avenue, N.W.
Washington, D. C. 20535
Dear Mr. Webster:

I have recently received a petition signed by many of my constituents who are urging a new investigation into the assassination of Al-Hajji [sic] Malik Shabazz (Malcolm X). A copy of the petition is enclosed.

According to the petition, new evidence has come to light which identifies all of the persons involved in the assassination and exonerates two of the three men convicted of the crime. In consequence, my constituents urge a new investigation of the assassination.

I would respectfully request that the FBI look into the statements made in the petition and inform me of its findings. I also would like to know if the FBI is currently conducting, or planning to conduct, a new investigation in the assassination of Al-Hajji [sic] Malik Shabazz (Malcolm X).

In advance, I appreciate your attention to this matter.

With kind personal regards.

Sincerely,

(signed)

William J. Hughes

Member of Congress

WJH:emr

Enclosure

———————. .———————

The undersigned citizens of the United States respectfully request that you use your best efforts to have the Congress investigate the assassination of Al-Hajji [sic] Malik Shabazz (Malcolm X) on February 21, 1965. We understand that there is new evidence identifying all of the persons involved in the assassination and exonerating two of the three men convicted of the crime, namely Muhammad Abdel Aziz (Norman 3X Butler), and Khalil Islam (Thomas 15X Johnson), and that this material has already been furnished to you. The House Committee on Assassinations investigated only the deaths of John F. Kennedy, and Martin Luther King, Jr. In view of the new evidence relating to the killing of Al-Hajji [sic] Malik Shabazz (Malcolm X), it is high time that a thorough investigation of his death took place so that two innocent men, who have already spent more than fourteen (14) years in jail, can win their freedom.

Name and Address

[BUREAU DELETION]

———————. .———————

June 20, 1980

Honorable William J. Hughes

House of Representatives

Washington, D. C. 20515

Dear Congressman Hughes:

This is to acknowledge receipt of your communication dated May 29, 1980, with its enclosure on behalf of your constituents.

For your information, the complaint regarding Al-Hajji [sic] Malik Shabazz (Malcolm X) is being furnished to the Civil Rights Division (CRD), U. S. Department of Justice (USDJ).

A review of records of the FBI and CRD, USDJ, fails to reveal any information that the FBI has investigated, or been requested to investigate, the assassination of Al-Hajji [sic] Malik Shabazz (Malcolm X).

A copy of your communication and its enclosure have been furnished to the CRD, USDJ, for its review as to whether any Federal investigation is warranted.

If you have any further questions regarding this matter, you may wish to write directly to the Assistant Attorney General, CRD, USDJ, Washington, D. C. 20530.

Sincerely yours,
(signed)
Oliver B. Revell
Assistant Director
Criminal Investigative Division

SUBJECT   MALCOLM X LITTLE
FILE NO.   <u>105-8999-Sub 1</u>
              <u>(Elsur Logs)</u>
              <u>6/3/64–10/3/64</u>

Editor's note *Technical surveillance was installed in the residence of Malcolm X at 23-11 97th Street, East Elmhurst, Queens, New York, at 4:00 P.M. on June 3, 1964, for a period of four months. The following selections from the electronic surveillance logs in the month of June highlight in particular the causes, and the ramifications, of the rift between Elijah Muhammad and Malcolm X.*

Day: Thursday
Date: 6-4-64

Employee's Name: [BUREAU DELETION] b7C
Activity Recorded:

Time: A.M.
IC/OG: OG

. . . tells MALCOLM that "by the way" [BUREAU DELETION] contacted a paper [BUREAU DELETION] "and he told them about it—" and that "they" told him "we don't print no scandals." MALCOLM interrupts to ask if this is "a white newspaper." [BUREAU DELETION] replies affirmatively and asks if there are any Negro newspapers "there." MALCOLM mutters something (not completely intelligible) about "a Negro newspaper," but he tells [BUREAU DELETION] "Everybody's afraid of it." [BUREAU DELETION] then indicates that [BUREAU DELETION] they don't print scandals "like that" because "these type of things" sometime involve long lawsuits. MALCOLM confirms that "that's what it involves" and tells [BUREAU DELETION] "Nobody can bring this out but those sisters themselves." [BUREAU DELETION] "Isn't that horrible" and MALCOLM agrees it is. . . .

[BUREAU DELETION]

[BUREAU DELETION] that he gave "the whole story" to the *Amsterdam News* and that none of it came out. [BUREAU DELETION] incredulous at first but then says that maybe it's just as well "at this point—until we can plan the right attack." MALCOLM agrees but comments that "it makes you wonder what you're up against." . . . tells MALCOLM that [BUREAU DELETION] suggested that she contact "that hush-hush magazine . . . and those kind of magazines" and let "them" bring "it" out. MALCOLM says he wishes [BUREAU DELETION] had not even let [BUREAU DELETION] know that he (MALCOLM) was involved. [BUREAU DELETION] didn't mention MALCOLM by name; [BUREAU DELETION] "a Muslim Minister." MALCOLM indicates he thinks [BUREAU DELETION] could tell it was him from that. . . .

[BUREAU DELETION] inquiring about how MALCOLM is, etc. MALCOLM says he has a combination of problems that he has to get solved and that he has to get them solved immediately; and that it looks as though he is going to have to solve them himself. MALCOLM indicates they are not financial problems.

[BUREAU DELETION] asks MALCOLM to let her tell him something else "this person" [BUREAU DELETION] told her that "from every angle it seems that they—they have a higher protection than just themselves . . . Now, he told me this." [BUREAU DELETION] what he meant and that "he" said, "Well, you know no one could get that much protection on—and

being black in America, and—all—all around the country."
MALCOLM says that is true but that he is going to break
through it—"I know how to do it. . . . With Allah's help I'll do
it. . . ."

Time: A.M.
IC/OG: OG

. . . M said he spoke to [BUREAU DELETION] and he told
her "he" had [BUREAU DELETION] and others on the East
Coast trying to kill him (Malcolm) because "he" wants me out of
the way before "this comes out." M stated that "he" was being
pressured by his children and that they were afraid that if this
comes out the Muslims will leave "him" and follow me (M). M
said that they feel with him out of the way the Muslims will have
no place to go if this breaks and so they will stay with "him." M
said that they were misusing "brothers" in New York and that
the brothers don't know what it's all about. He said "they" were
pumping these brothers with poison and they were trying to get a
shot at him (M). M [BUREAU DELETION] now that he has let
them know how he is in danger they have disappointed him with
their reaction. M said the only way to end this was to expose
him. [BUREAU DELETION] M said he agreed and that he
would not be surprised if "he" had already left the country. [BU-
REAU DELETION] M said that "this man" has so many followers whom he has misled, followers that M has gotten for him
and that he can turn them against anyone. M said that as long as
he has the public on his side no lawyer will take the case. [BU-
REAU DELETION] M said he told the whole story to the *Amsterdam News* but that they would not print it until one of the
sisters will talk. M said the "Messenger" had [BUREAU DELE-
TION] telling this to "The Fruit" in such a way that they think
Malcolm is bad and is trying to say false things about the Messenger and that M should be killed for this. [BUREAU DELE-
TION] M said that if he thought he could get out there he would
but that he would be recognized as soon as he got on the plane.
[BUREAU DELETION]

Day: Sunday
Date: 6-7-64

Employee's Name: [BUREAU DELETION] b7C
Activity Recorded:

Time: 3:25 P.M.
IC/OG: OG

MALCOLM X to Unwoman asking her to tell [BUREAU DELETION] about the MESSENGER's escapades with his secretaries and how the MESSENGER made them all pregnant. MALCOLM says that [BUREAU DELETION] must be told that the NOI is factionalized and that both factions will commit murders on each other unless the truth is publicized about the MESSENGER's bad deeds. MALCOLM says he is not fooling or speaking for effect when he says that bloodshed will take place as "it almost happened yesterday in New York when those who were in the Mosque came up to the corner where he had a meeting going on and absolutely tried to start some trouble." MALCOLM continued "The only thing that saved us and stopped trouble from starting was that one of my brothers went to the trunk of his car and got a shotgun out and chased away the black Muslims." MALCOLM says that if any violence takes place it will mean [BUREAU DELETION] and [BUREAU DELETION] are trying to "create a situation of bloodshed so that I (MALCOLM X) will get caught up in it." Unwoman asks "You mean the MESSENGER is that ruthless?" MALCOLM answers "that any man who will go to bed with his brother's daughter and then turn and make five other women pregnant and then accuse all these women of committing adultery is a ruthless man." MALCOLM says that the only reason the MESSENGER wants him dead is that he, MALCOLM, is the only one who can make the girls the MESSENGER has violated tell the truth about the MESSENGER. MALCOLM tells Unwoman to tell all [BUREAU DELETION] will be interested in knowing that the MESSENGER is now living in Phoenix, Ariz. with two teenage girls, [BUREAU DELETION]. MALCOLM says that both these teenage girls are natives of California, and have lived at Los Angeles [BUREAU DELETION]. MALCOLM says that if the two sisters [BUREAU DELETION] are now in Los Angeles [BUREAU DELETION] and that if these two sisters do not tell their story to the public within the next twenty-four hours, there will be bloodshed all over this country. MALCOLM continues "what I just said I really mean, [BUREAU DELETION] there will be bloodshed and murder all over this country." MAL-COLM says that the true story on the evil ways of the MESSEN-GER are known by many newspapers but that they will not print the story realizing that they (the newspapers) can hold it like a whip over the heads of the Black Muslim movement and keep it from being effective in any way. MALCOLM says that every day he stays alive causes worry to the MESSENGER and that the MESSENGER has given orders to sincere, but ignorant, Mus-lims to get MALCOLM X. MALCOLM says he is not afraid. MALCOLM tells [BUREAU DELETION] to also call [BU-REAU DELETION] and tell [BUREAU DELETION] (MAL-COLM spells name) was the second one the MESSENGER made pregnant and [BUREAU DELETION] and that the MES-SENGER made her pregnant and then accused her of adultery and put her out of the Mosque. MALCOLM says that [BU-REAU DELETION] should also know that [BUREAU DELE-TION] (name spelled out by MALCOLM X) [BUREAU DELE-TION] will make the calls that MALCOLM has asked her to make.

Time: 4:02 P.M.
IC/OG: IC

Unwoman to MALCOLM X. MALCOLM says the split in the NOI has brought about nothing but negative results. He says "every time I think of how those niggers threw me out of the NOI, I get mad." He continues "that it is dangerous to have the Muslims controlled by criminals of the ilk of [BUREAU DELE-TION] and the like." He says there must be some way we can salvage the Black Muslim movement before it is too late. Un-woman says she is sure MALCOLM can save the Muslims from the clutches of the MESSENGER. He says he feels he can save the Muslims if he can lift the cloud of the MESSENGER's misdeeds from them by exposing the MESSENGER to the public. MALCOLM says that the FBI and the local police department do not want public exposure of the MESSENGER's sexual escapades as the (FBI and PD) would lose the whip they use to control the Black Muslims. MALCOLM says that the MESSENGER's fear of exposure by law enforcement agencies keeps the MESSENGER from leading the Black Muslims to their full potential. Unwoman says that if MALCOLM has faith in Allah all will go well with his cause.

Time: 5:46 P.M.
IC/OG: OG

MALCOLM X to [BUREAU DELETION] at Los Angeles, Calif., [BUREAU DELETION] MALCOLM asks "When did you get there and did you drive?" [BUREAU DELETION] MALCOLM says that she should be careful who she talks to as the MESSENGER might have a tap on her telephone. He says he believes that MESSENGER has a tap on [BUREAU DELETION] telephones. [BUREAU DELETION] tells the MESSENGER everything so she does not see why he should tap her telephone. MALCOLM asks if [BUREAU DELETION] accomplished anything in Phoenix? [BUREAU DELETION] would feel better if they had some legal backing to the allegations they were making. MALCOLM says that the truth of the statements is all the legal backing that they need and that they should not worry about the MESSENGER suing them. MALCOLM says that the best thing [BUREAU DELETION] could do would be to tell their story [BUREAU DELETION] then gets on the telephone and MALCOLM tells him that he had better get on the ball [BUREAU DELETION]. MALCOLM says that he has never tolerated failure in the past and will certainly not accept anything [BUREAU DELETION] less than [BUREAU DELE-

TION] complete disclosure of the sins of the MESSENGER. [BUREAU DELETION] MALCOLM says "if you know what's good for you, you will succeed." MALCOLM tells [BUREAU DELETION] MALCOLM tells [BUREAU DELETION] to keep working [BUREAU DELETION] and to do whatever else is necessary. [BUREAU DELETION]

Day: Monday
Date: 6-8-64

Employee's Name: [BUREAU DELETION] b7C
Activity Recorded:

Time: 9:08 A.M.
IC/OG: IC

Unman to Unwoman. Caller asks to speak to "Brother MAL-COLM." Woman answering asks who is calling. Man replies that he just wants to speak to Brother MALCOLM. Then when woman again asks who is calling the man says she can just give MALCOLM the message: "Just tell him he's as good as dead." He then hangs up.

Time: 10:37 A.M.
IC/OG: OG

. . . I told MR. MUHAMMAD—about what was being said —and at that time he explained—he knew it all the time and explained to me—in the religious way. You know how in a religious cult there's always a religious explanation for these things —so I accepted it, and I didn't say anything more about it, but in October [BUREAU DELETION] told me that this thing was as bad as it ever was; that the person who was responsible for making these sisters pregnant had not stopped. Two of them had two children by him, six of them had become pregnant, two of the six had two children by him, one of the two who had two children by him was pregnant again—and having his third child—and he

told me that the person who was responsible had not stopped in
any way and what he was using to make these sisters stay under
his control was the fact that they were supposed to be fulfilling
the prophecy and all that kind of stuff. So I came back to New
York and told [BUREAU DELETION] sent a report back in to
MR. MUHAMMAD, and to the official staff in Chicago, giving
them the impression that instead of me pouring water on the fire,
that I was pouring gas on the fire. This is what caused the split—
and then they thought that I was going to talk about it and so
they put in motion machinery to try and silence me forever—and
my only reason for never telling it was my fear that the, that the
psychological effect that it would have upon the Muslims—the
only thing that kept them with such moral discipline was the fact
that MR. MUHAMMAD and the others had an image of high
morals. But MR. MUHAMMAD, himself, is the one who is the
father of these children—MR. MUHAMMAD, himself. Two of
them showed up in Phoenix last week demanding to get into his
house. They had three children with them. The one who is pregnant and going to have a baby right now was there—and he had
a fit—because he was frightened. These are the only two that
seem to have nerve enough to try and make him do, do something for them—and they didn't succeed. He sent them, with his
chauffeur, off to a motel—and he thought that they had left and
gone back to the city from whence they had come. But they
stayed right in that city for three or four days trying to reach
him, which they couldn't. Now the two of them—two of them
are back in Los Angeles, and what is happening, the officials here
in New York and in some of the other Mosques, they know about
it—but the Muslims in the Mosques overall don't know about it.
So MR. MUHAMMED is using his ministers and other officials
to make the Muslims think that, that I have turned insane—in an
effort to try and get them—some innocent, ignorant, well meaning Muslim to do something that I, myself, would have done, had
I not found out what I now know."

Day: Monday
Date: 6-15-64

Employee's Name: [BUREAU DELETION] b7C
Activity Recorded:

Time: 1:26 A.M.
IC/OG: IC

   Unknown person called. [BUREAU DELETION] received no response, gave phone to MALCOLM X. MALCOLM X gave Unknown person a six minute sermon on the affairs of MUHAMMAD, naming the six women that he (MUHAM-MAD) had relations with in the past. MALCOLM X at end of his sermon told Unknown person—now you get your rifle, come around to my house and talk some stuff.

Time: 8:10 A.M.
IC/OG: IC?

   Unman (possibly radio or television reporter?; long distance? —from ??) to (MALCOLM X). Man interviews MALCOLM about his rift with ELIJAH MUHAMMAD, asking questions, which MALCOLM replies to. (Note: Intermittent "beep" signals indicate that interviewer was having the interview recorded.) In the interview MALCOLM claims that his statement about President KENNEDY's assassination gave ELIJAH MUHAMMAD the opportunity to suspend him but that the real reason for his suspension was the fact that ELIJAH knew MALCOLM had knowledge of ELIJAH's violation of seven Muslim sisters by whom he had eight children, with another child expected to be born shortly. MALCOLM confirms that he thinks that ELIJAH MUHAMMAD would like to see him killed and mentions that "the National Secretary" of the Muslims stated on the radio that MALCOLM should be killed. In answer to query MALCOLM claims that he has some rifles and that other brothers associated with him have either rifles or shotguns and have no compunction about using them.

Time: 8:53 A.M.
IC/OG: IC

[BUREAU DELETION] had heard that MALCOLM X was supposed to be killed today on the Courthouse steps because he had not moved out of the house which they bought.

Day: Thursday
Date: 6-18-64

Employee's Name: [BUREAU DELETION] b7C
Activity Recorded:

Time: 9:36 A.M.
IC/OG: IC

Unwoman, [BUREAU DELETION] to MALCOLM X. Unwoman says "we plan to do a story today and have information that you are a 'marked man.' " MALCOLM says that it is common knowledge that Mr. MUHAMMAD has been after me since I broke with him. MALCOLM says that the Black Muslims tried to attack him in Boston, Mass., last Sunday night but failed because he did not go to Boston that night. Unwoman asks if MALCOLM has taken any security precautions or if he has asked for police protection? MALCOLM says "I'm more watchful now but I have never asked for police protection as I have my own rifle." Unwoman asks "ELIJAH MUHAMMAD is coming to New York on 6/28/64, do you (MALCOLM X) intend to see him?" MALCOLM says "No. We have nothing to say to each other." MALCOLM says "You newspaper people won't print the truth about ELIJAH MUHAMMAD but you don't let the libel laws bother you when it comes to printing something unfavorable about me." MALCOLM says "If you newspaper people would check with the FBI you wouldn't be afraid to print the truth about ELIJAH MUHAMMAD as the FBI knows all about the things I've told you before about Mr. MUHAMMAD making the girls pregnant." Unwoman ask "Why would the FBI know about this?" MALCOLM answers "Oh, they have it, the FBI was one of the first in Boston to know. The FBI mentioned it to a non-Muslim woman. An FBI man in Boston mentioned it to a non-Muslim woman that ELIJAH MUHAMMAD was the father of [BUREAU DELETION] one of his former secretary's babies. One of the Muslim women mentioned this to [BUREAU DELETION] of the Boston Mosque, and I discussed this with [BUREAU DELETION]. Unwoman says "That is very interesting. I'll pass that along. I think we will publish all the charges made against ELIJAH MUHAMMAD today." Unwoman says she will call MALCOLM again if she needs any more information.

Day: Sunday
Date: 6-21-64

Employee's Name: [BUREAU DELETION] b7C
Activity Recorded:

Time: 9:53 A.M.
IC/OG: IC

[BUREAU DELETION] and all "I" asked was "one little hearing in front of the Muslims." She relates an argument she had with her husband during which she asked him why "they" wouldn't give MALCOLM a hearing, and he answered that "the Messenger has his reasons." She says "he" didn't know himself, because he is "too spooked up to ask a question." MALCOLM says if "he" could be made to think about a couple of things, he would wake up overnight, and says that "if this doesn't happen, then what they're going to do, especially between now and Sunday, they're going to try and provoke an incident." She says that "they" will, and somebody will get hurt. He agrees, "because the brothers that are out will absolutely retaliate against anybody, and the only reason that I have been avoiding public situations is to try and avert any unnecessary bloodshed between innocent brothers. . . ."

Day: Friday
Date: 6-26-64

Employee's Name: [BUREAU DELETION] b7C
Activity Recorded:

Time: 2:30 A.M.
IC/OG: IC

(Malcolm, who appeared upset at being called at 2:30 A.M. made several remarks concerning the time of the call. [BUREAU DELETION] explained time of call was necessitated by newspaper deadline.) [BUREAU DELETION] (spelled) [BUREAU DELETION] inquired if Malcolm X had heard of the remarks of [BUREAU DELETION] and what did Malcolm think of these remarks? MALCOLM X said the charges were absurd and he thought they were made up by Mr. Muhammad himself in order to have an excuse not to come here. Discussion between Malcolm X and [BUREAU DELETION] followed concerning: Whether or not Muhammad would come to NY; division in Muhammad's followers; Muhammad's involvement sexually with nine teenage secretaries; Muhammad's feelings (acc to Mal X) that if he came to NY he would never be able to answer questions of the press. Mal X said Muhammad is not anxious to come here (NY) at this time because too many people are beginning to ask themselves— are the charges that Mal X leveled at Muhammad true? Acc to Mal X Muslim officials when questioned answer that Mal X is crazy or trying to seek publicity, etc. Mal X said you would never get a yes or no answer from them regarding the adultery charges. [BUREAU DELETION] was sure Mal X was aware of the libel laws, and added that as far as he knew none of the press had printed any of this. Mal X pointed out that it had been printed last week on the front page of the Phil. Tribune. Mal X also said that the NY Post printed it the day that he made the statement from the witness stand in Queens in a court trial. [BUREAU DELETION] if only there were some way that this could be proved so that it could be printed. Mal X said that it would be proved that it was only a matter of time. Mal X said that in the Chicago Mosque it was being taught that they were divine babies. He continued that in Boston they were also teaching in the temple that these were divine babies, giving the explanation that Mr.

Muhammad was told by God that the nations would be blessed through his seed, therefore he should plant his seed everywhere. . . . Mal X said that Muhammad as well as his whole family have been living off the fat of the land. Mal continued that there's no program ever been put before his followers (Muhammad) designed to correct conditions that our people live under. Mal X said he would challenge MUHAMMAD to unite his followers and use some of the energy they are now wasting on each other and use it in Miss., Ala., and Georgia to help solve some of our peoples problems. Mal X said that Muhammad was not interested in the problems of Negroes. He then discussed Muhammad's weaknesses and the fact that his (Mal X) concept of Muhammad's divinity had been shattered. . . . He said they were going to unfold a new organization based in NYC designed to involve the masses of our people in an action program to eliminate some of those evils that the other organizations have failed to eliminate. It's not going to be a Muslim movement but probably the first mass organized movement non-religious that has existed in this country since MARCUS GARVEY (ph). . . . [BUREAU DELETION] Mal if he felt himself in danger? Mal said I think a Negro in America is born in danger. [BUREAU DELETION] from a specific source. Mal X said they are coming into town and they have been whipping up hatred inside the Muslims on a national scale for the past two or three months, they have something in mind. [BUREAU DELETION] asked if Mal had a bodyguard? Mal answered I have my rifle in my home and anyone who puts their feet on my doorstep without good reason will have to suffer the consequences. [BUREAU DELETION] he wished to God he could print the bit about the divine babies and so forth. Mal X told [BUREAU DELETION] to check the Queens Civil Court records for Tuesday a week ago (Eviction Case). Mal said he testified revealing to the Muslims in NY that Muhammad had taken nine teenage sisters and made six of them pregnant. Mal said that the NY Post had printed it and other newspapers had printed it and had never been sued. Mal X said that he had spoken it on the following Radio Programs: CBS Radio Station WEEI—Paul Benziquin (ph) program; Jerry Williams (ph) show; WDAS in PH.; Long John Nebel show last Fri night. Mal said there were no lawsuits as a result of any of the above. Mal said that Muhammad is not going to sue anybody over these babies because its too true. Its something that will destroy him. The only thing that holds the Muslim movement together is its image of morality, unity and militancy. Mal continued that most of the defectors from the movement were in Phila., NY, Boston and Chicago, the hdqtrs. but he could not say how many there were.

Day: Saturday
Date: 6-27-64

Employee's Name: [BUREAU DELETION] b7C
Activity Recorded:

Time: P.M.
IC/OG: OG

MALCOLM X to [BUREAU DELETION] asks if CLARENCE JONES has called him, and he says JONES tried but has not reached him. She says that JONES told her to ask MALCOLM to call him. She says that what it is is that Rev. KING would like to meet as soon as possible on the idea of getting a human rights declaration. She says "he" is quite interested and so is [BUREAU DELETION] and they would like to meet as soon as possible. MALCOLM tells her that since he has been back from Africa "we" have been working on an organization, and "we are launching it tomorrow night, the Organization of Afro-American Unity, and the basic aim of it is to lift the whole freedom struggle from civil rights to the level of human rights, and also to work with any other organization and any other leader toward that end. . . ."

The recommendations submitted on July 2, 1964, to the Director of the FBI in File No. 100-399321 on the efficacy of the electronic surveillance read as follows. [E.N.]

Little is a former national official of the Nation of Islam (NOI) who broke with that organization on 3/8/64 and formed Muslim

Mosque, Incorporated (MMI), which he announced would be a broadly based black nationalist movement for Negroes only. Little has urged Negroes to abandon the doctrine of non-violence and advocated that Negroes should form rifle clubs to protect their lives and property. At MMI rallies, Little has surrounded himself by guards armed with rifles and there have been numerous incidents recently involving gun-wielding MMI members where violence has been averted only by timely police action. At an MMI rally on 6/28/64, Little announced the formation of a new non-white civil rights action group called the "Organization of Afro-American Unity" with headquarters at MMI headquarters in New York City, the aim of which would be to bring the United States racial problem before the United Nations and which would engage in civil rights demonstrations using the theme "by any means necessary."

In the past thirty days this technical surveillance has furnished valuable information on Little's travel plans, on the new Organization of Afro-American Unity, facts concerning the arrest of MMI members in Boston on a weapons charge following an altercation with Boston NOI members and information on a threat to Little's life by a person unknown. It also furnished information that Little was sending an assistant to Phoenix and Los Angeles to contact two women who had illegitimate children by Elijah Muhammad, NOI leader. Public announcement of these children by Little has caused the virtual state of war now existent between the NOI and MMI. On 6/30/64 information was received that Little sent telegrams to civil rights leaders Dr. Martin Luther King and James Forman, offering to send his followers to teach self-defense to Negroes if the government did not provide Federal troops for protection.

All of the above information was furnished immediately to the Bureau and was disseminated to the Department and interested agencies. The Domestic Intelligence Division concurs with the recommendations of the SAC, New York, that this installation be continued for an additional three months.

Editor's note. *The report dated October 2, 1964, to the Director of the FBI on the technical surveillance from July through September follows. Surveillance was discontinued on October 4, 1964, at 12:00 noon.*

7/3/64   Information that MALCOLM notified New York City Police Department that an attempt was made on his life.

7/4/64   Information that MALCOLM and his followers were attempting to make a big issue out of the reported attempt on MALCOLM's life in order to get the Negro people to support him. (Police believed complaint on an attempt on MALCOLM's life was a publicity stunt by MALCOLM.) (Teletype to Bureau 7/4/64)

7/6/64   Information that [BUREAU DELETION] attempted to contact MALCOLM.

7/6/64   Information that MALCOLM was leaving JFK International Airport, New York, on 7/9/64, for Cairo, Egypt, with a one day stopover in London where he was to meet with a representative of the Islamic Center of London. While in Cairo, Egypt he was to be met by one [BUREAU DELETION] (Airtel and LHM to Bureau 7/7/64)

7/7/64   Information that one of two women who had illegitimate children by ELIJAH MUHAMMAD contacted MALCOLM by phone from Los Angeles, collect, to advise him that another illegitimate child was born on 7/7/64 and ELIJAH MUHAMMAD was named as the father. (Airtel to Bureau, Chicago, Phoenix and Los Angeles, 7/7/64)

7/21/64   Article in *New York Journal American* newspaper dated 7/20/64, stated MALCOLM is or has returned to the U.S. from Africa and will form a rifle club. Information from source refuted newspaper article and advised MALCOLM was not returning to the U.S. until August, 1964. (Teletype to Bureau 7/21/64)

7/23/64   Information that [BUREAU DELETION] (Letter to Chicago dated 8/12/64)

7/30/64   Article in *New York Daily News* dated 7/30/64, which stated MALCOLM was returning to the United States to hold a mass rally and to urge the Negro to fight against the police with no holds barred. Source advised 7/30/64, that [BUREAU DELETION] no information that MALCOLM planned to return before the middle of August, 1964, thus refuting the above newspaper article. (Teletype to Bureau 7/30/64)

8/7/64   Information about MALCOLM traveling to Alexandria, Egypt and attending a banquet given by the Supreme Council of Islamic Affairs. He gave a speech against the U.S. government's treatment of the Negro people in the U.S. and urged Muslim students to persuade their governments to bring the U.S. before the United Nations for mistreating the American Negroes. (Teletype to Bureau 8/7/64 and airtel and LHM 8/10/64)

9/2/64   Information that MALCOLM was being evicted from his residence and was given until January, 1965, to leave the residence owned by the NOI. (Airtel to Bureau 9/3/64) Information received that MALCOLM was staying at the Hotel Shepherd, Cairo, Egypt and he is having a book about himself published. (Airtel to Bureau and Philadelphia 9/8/64)

9/10/64   Information that MALCOLM sent a letter from Egypt that was to be read at a Muslim Mosque Inc. meeting at New York on 9/9/64. According to the letter MALCOLM informed an unknown delegate to the Organization of African Unity conference in Addis Ababa, Ethiopia, that he, MALCOLM, could supply ten thousand recruits from Harlem if needed to fight in the Congo against Moise Tshombe. (Airtel and LHM to Bureau dated 9/10/64)

9/26/64   Information that MALCOLM will return to the U.S. on 11/15/64 having toured Africa since July, 1964, with the Egypt Government paying his hotel bills and Supreme Council governing Islamic Affairs paying for his plane expenses.

9/26/64   Information that MALCOLM and his wife are now "Orthodox Muslims" and MALCOLM was appointed to the board of the Supreme Council governing Islamic Affairs, and, therefore qualified himself to "spread Islam in America among the Afro-Americans." (Airtel to Bureau 9/29/64 and LHM 10/2/64)

The information received from this source has been used to supplement and corroborate information from live informants and has been channelized to appropriate files.

Appendix

A. American Nazi Party of the World Union of Free Enterprise National Socialists, also known as The George Lincoln Rockwell Party

B. Fair Play for Cuba Committee (FPCC)

C. Freedomways Associates, Incorporated

D. Fruit of Islam (FOI)

E. Independent Socialist Youth (ISY) and Independent Socialist Club (ISC)

F. May 2 Movement (M2M), formerly known as May 2 Committee

G. Muhammad's Temple of Islam No. 11, Boston, Massachusetts, also referred to as Nation of Islam (NOI)

H. Muhammad's Temple of Islam No. 13, Springfield, Massachusetts, also referred to as Nation of Islam (NOI)

I. Muhammad's Temple of Islam No. 14, Hartford, Connecticut, also referred to as Nation of Islam (NOI)

J. Muslim Girls Training (MGT)

K. Muslim Mosque, Incorporated (MMI)

L. Nation of Islam (NOI), formerly referred to as the Muslim Cult of Islam, also known as Muhammad's Temples of Islam

M. Nation of Islam, Mosque No. 7

N. Organization of Afro-American Unity, Incorporated (OAAU)

O. Progressive Labor Party, Progressive Labor Movement, "Progressive Labor"

P. Provisional Organizing Committee for a Marxist-Leninist Communist Party (POC); also known as Provisional Organizing Committee For the Reconstitution of a Marxist-Leninist Party; Provisional Committee For the Reconstitution of the Marxist-Leninist Communist Party; Provisional Committee to Reconstitute the Communist Party, USA

Q. Revolutionary Action Movement (RAM)

R. Socialist Workers Party-Los Angeles Local (SWP-LAL)

S. Socialist Workers Party-Philadelphia Branch

T.   Socialist Workers Party-New York Local
U.   Socialist Workers Party-San Francisco Division
V.   Socialist Workers Party-Seattle Branch
W.   Workers World Party
X.   Young Socialist Alliance (YSA)
Y.   Young Socialist Club of Wayne County (YSC); also known as Wayne University Young Socialist Club; Wayne Young Socialist Club; Young Socialist Club

---

A. American Nazi Party of the World Union of Free Enterprise National Socialists, also known as the George Lincoln Rockwell Party

In his book *This Time The World,* copyrighted in 1961, GEORGE LINCOLN ROCKWELL identified himself as Commander, American Nazi Party of the World Union of Free Enterprise National Socialists (ANP–WUFENS), Arlington, Virginia.

The April 4, 1963 issue of *The Richmond News Leader,* a Richmond, Virginia daily newspaper, reported that GEORGE LINCOLN ROCKWELL had, on the previous day, again applied for the American Nazi Party to be chartered in the State of Virginia, but this request was turned down by the Virginia State Corporation Commission. This action was taken pursuant to an act of the 1962 Virginia Assembly which prohibits the use of "Nazi" or "National Socialism" in a Virginia charter. This article further pointed out that ROCKWELL's party is presently chartered in the State of Virginia as the George Lincoln Rockwell Party.

On August 19, 1963, a source advised that the ANP-WUFENS was organized by GEORGE LINCOLN ROCKWELL at his residence in Arlington, Virginia, on February 26, 1959, as an international "National Socialist" movement based on the German Nazi Party headed by ADOLF HITLER. He added that ROCKWELL is the dominant force and personality in this party; that he is espousing a "line" of hatred against the Jews and Negroes; and that he is seeking, through speeches, distribution of literature and picketing, to establish a cohesive and dominant political party in the United States and in foreign countries.

On December 13, 1963, this source advised that in about September, 1960, the ANP initiated the Fighting American Nationalists (FAN) as a front group for the ANP, although it has never been a separate organization. He said the FAN name is merely used on occasion instead of the ANP name and there are no separate officials for FAN, the FAN officials being identical with the ANP officials. He stated that GEORGE LINCOLN ROCKWELL has informed him the FAN name was originally used as a device to attract supporters to his organization who might rebel at the use of the Swastika and at being labeled a Nazi.

He added that the ANP has operated under the FAN name throughout the country with the exception of a group operating under the FAN name in Baltimore, Maryland. He said the FAN group in Baltimore is now, and always has been, a separate organization and not a part of the ANP.

On October 3, 1963, RICHARD BERRY NORTON, the admitted former director of the FAN group in Baltimore, Maryland, advised that the Baltimore FAN, which was organized in the Spring of 1961, has no official connection with the ANP, although until December, 1962, it received its literature from GEORGE LINCOLN ROCKWELL's ANP.

According to the "Stormtrooper's Manual," an official publication of the ANP, the phases of ANP struggle for power are fourfold, namely, first "to make ourselves known to the masses"; second, "the dissemination of our program and the truth about the party"; third, "organizing the people who have been converted to our propaganda"; and fourth, "the attainment of power through the votes of the newly-won masses."

B. Fair Play for Cuba Committee (FPCC)

The April 6, 1960 edition of the *New York Times* newspaper contains a full page advertisement captioned, "What Is Really Happening in Cuba," placed by the FPCC. This advertisement announced the formation of the FPCC in New York City, listed various sponsors of the Committee and declared the FPCC intended to promulgate "the truth about revolutionary Cuba" to neutralize the distorted American press on Cuban affairs.

The *New York Times* edition of January 11, 1961 reported that at a hearing conducted before the United States Senate Internal Security Subcommittee on January 10, 1961, Dr. CHARLES A. SANTOS-BUCH identified himself as one of the organizers of the FPCC. Also, Dr. SANTOS-BUCH identified ROBERT TABER as a co-organizer of the FPCC and said TABER drafted the aforementioned FPCC advertisement. Dr. SANTOS-BUCH further testified that he and TABER obtained $3,500 from the Cuban Government through the son of Cuba's Foreign Minister, which funds, along with about $1,100 collected from supporters of the FPCC, paid for the cost of aforementioned advertisement in the *New York Times*.

[BUREAU DELETION] advised that the Socialist Workers Party (SWP) in New York had become active in the FPCC, and that SWP members, in a recent FPCC election, had been able to remove several Communist Party members who were on the Executive Board of the FPCC and gain control of the organization. This source asserted that the SWP members believed that they had achieved a great influence in the course of the Cuban revolution through their control of the FPCC.

[BUREAU DELETION] advised that PHIL BART, National Organizational Secretary and member of the National Committee, CP, USA, had reportedly stated recently that the FPCC had been captured by the Trotskyites, but that the CP had not given up on the FPCC.

The SWP and the CP, USA, have been designated by the Attorney General of the United States pursuant to Executive Order 10450.

C. Freedomways Associates, Incorporated

The records of the New York Secretary of State, Albany, New York, show that the certificate of incorporation of Freedomways Associates, Incorporated, was filed on March 2, 1961.

The Spring, 1964, issue of *Freedomways* is self-described as "A Quarterly Review of the Negro Freedom Movement" published by Freedomways Associates, Incorporated, 799 Broadway, New York City.

On May 24, 1961, a source advised that a report was given on *Freedomways* at a meeting of the National Board, Communist Party, USA (CPUSA), held on May 24, 1961. It was stated that the original plan called for the publication to be openly Marxist, but that it was later decided it would not be avowedly a Marxist publication. Editorials are in the hands of a mixed group of Marxists and non-Marxists. It was stated that the central purpose of "Freedomways" is to develop a theory and positive criticism of currents in the Negro movement, as well as to raise the level of understanding and discussion taking place in Negro life today and to project a socialist and pro-Soviet orientation.

On May 25, 1961, another source advised that *Freedomways* was set up for the CPUSA by JAMES JACKSON, a member of the National Committee of the CPUSA.

D. Fruit of Islam

On May 8, 1964, a source advised that the Fruit of Islam (FOI) is a group within the Nation of Islam (NOI) composed of male members of the NOI. The purpose of the FOI is to protect officials and property of the NOI, assure compliance of members with NOI teachings and to prepare for the "War of Armageddon." Members of the FOI are required to participate in military drill and are afforded the opportunity to engage in judo training. The FOI is governed by a military system wherein the members are controlled by general orders similar to those issued by regular military organizations.

E. Independent Socialist Youth (ISY) AND Independent Socialist Club (ISC)

A source at various times from April to December, 1958, advised that the Independent Socialist Youth (ISY) was organized in March, 1958, at Detroit, Michigan, in part by efforts of members of the Socialist Workers Party (SWP). The ISY was referred to by SWP members as an "IBM" group (independent, broad, and militant). The ISY emphasized that it welcomed persons from all political tendencies who were interested in socialism. The ISY membership was comprised of individuals who belonged to the Communist Party (CP), SWP, Young Socialist Club of Wayne County (YSC), and independent socialists. The ISY had no definite program for political action; however, members of the YSC, who made up the majority of the ISY membership, tried to influence the ISY toward being a revolutionary socialist group. In an attempt to extend this influence, the YSC was officially dissolved on August 18, 1958, and the members urged to join the ISY.

By November, 1958, the SWP members in the ISY found they could not introduce the program for political action they wanted; therefore, they withdrew their support from the ISY, which caused it to become defunct. Part of the reasoning behind this action was the belief on the part of the SWP members that the ISY could not serve any useful purpose, but a similar-type group organized on the campus of Wayne State University, Detroit, could be of value in furthering the SWP youth movement.

An SWP member who was a student at Wayne State University was assigned to attempt to get a socialist youth group organized on the campus of that school. This member, together with assistance from a former member of the ISY and ISY contacts at the university, was successful in getting a group organized on the campus of Wayne State University in December, 1958, under the name Independent Socialist Club (ISC). The club was organized under the political science department of the university. Officers were elected and a new constitution was drawn up. Reportedly, with the exception of one SWP member, the ISC consists mostly of "independent socialists" or persons who are not socialists but are interested in learning the socialist viewpoint.

The SWP and the CP, USA have been designated pursuant to Executive Order 10450.

F. May 2 Movement (M2M) Formerly known as May 2 Committee

A source advised on March 3, 1965 as follows:

The M2M is the name now used by the May 2 Committee, which was organized on March 14, 1964, at New Haven, Connecticut, by a group of young people participating in a symposium, "Socialism in America," being held at Yale University. The original aim of the M2M was to plan and execute a demonstration in New York City on May 2, 1964, demanding withdrawal of United States troops from Viet Nam.

The M2M is dominated and controlled by the Progressive Labor Party (PLP) and has for its aim and purpose the embarrassment of the United States government by meetings, rallies, picketing demonstrations and formation of university level clubs at which a Marxist-Leninist oriented approach and analysis is taken of United States domestic and foreign policies.

This source advised on May 19, 1965, that the current headquarters of the M2M is 640 Broadway, New York City, Room 307.

G. Muhammad's Temple of Islam No. 11, Boston, Massachusetts, also referred to as the Nation of Islam (NOI)

On March 18, 1954, a source stated that the Nation of Islam (NOI) had become active in Boston, Massachusetts, and knew that it had held meetings as early as November, 1953.

On May 11, 1964, a second source stated that the Temple of Islam in Boston, Massachusetts, is known as Muhammad's Temple of Islam No. 11 or Muhammad's Mosque No. 11. It is located at 35 Intervale Street, Dorchester (Boston), Massachusetts, and is the local branch of Muhammad's Temple of Islam whose headquarters are in Chicago, Illinois.

————————. .————————

H. Muhammad's Temple of Islam No. 13, Springfield, Massachusetts, also referred to as the Nation of Islam (NOI)

On March 9, 1955, a source advised that the Nation of Islam (NOI) had, at that time, just opened a Temple in Springfield, Massachusetts.

On May 11, 1964, a second source advised that NOI Temple No. 13 is located on the corner of Oak and Tyler Streets, Springfield, Massachusetts. The membership refer to Temple No. 13 as either Muhammad's Temple of Islam No. 13 or Muhammad's Mosque No. 13. This source stated that Temple No. 13 is a part of the national organization which has its headquarters in Chicago, Illinois.

————————. .————————

I. Muhammad's Temple of Islam Hartford, Connecticut, Temple No. 14 aka Muslim Cult of Islam, Nation of Islam

The July 12, 1956 edition of the *Pittsburgh Courier,* New York edition, a weekly Negro newspaper published at Pittsburgh, Pennsylvania, contains an article reflecting that Temple No. 14 of the Muslim Cult of Islam was located at Hartford, Connecticut.

A source advised on May 19, 1961 that Muhammad's Temple of Islam, Hartford, Connecticut, Temple No. 14, also known as the Muslim Cult of Islam and Nation of Islam, is affiliated with the Headquarters of the Nation of Islam, Chicago, Illinois.

————————. .————————

J. Muslim Girls Training (MGT)

On May 19, 1960, a source advised that the Muslim Girls Training (MGT) is a group within the Nation of Islam and is composed of all female members of the NOI. The MGT is similar in structure to the Fruit of Islam, which is composed of all male members of the NOI, in that the MGT has officers, similar to military organizations, to whom other female members are accountable. MGT members receive instructions in homemaking, hygiene, calisthenics, and other subjects such as Muslim history and the English language. There also exists a Junior MGT which is composed of female members of the NOI who are between the ages of 15 and 19 and who are afforded military-type drill.

Since 1957 various officers and "sisters" of the MGT have, at meetings of the MGT, used the term MGT so that it also means General Civilization Class. General Civilization Class refers to classes conducted within the MGT.

The above refers to activities of the MGT at Muhammad's Temple of Islam No. 2, 5335 South Greenwood, Chicago, Illinois.

On May 16, 1960, another source advised that the MGT is a group within the NOI which is composed of all female members of the NOI. The MGT is similar in structure to the Fruit of Islam, which is composed of all male members of the NOI. In theory the MGT exists in all Temples of the NOI and is patterned after the MGT at Muhammad's Temple of Islam No. 2, Chicago. General Civilization Class refers to the collective group of classes held within the MGT.

K. Muslim Mosque, Incorporated (MMI)

The March 13, 1964 edition of the *New York Times,* a daily newspaper published in New York, New York, contained an article on page 20 which indicated that MALCOLM X (LITTLE), former national official of the Nation of Islam (NOI) who broke with the NOI on March 8, 1964, publicly announced in New York City on March 12, 1964, that he had formed the Muslim Mosque, Incorporated (MMI). The MMI, according to the article, would be a broadly based politically oriented black nationalist movement for Negroes only, financed by voluntary contributions. In this public statement, MALCOLM X urged Negroes to abandon the doctrine of non-violence when it is necessary to defend themselves in the civil rights struggle, and he also suggested that Negroes form rifle clubs to protect their lives and property in time of emergencies in areas where the government is unable or unwilling to protect them.

Incorporation papers of the MMI filed on March 16, 1964, with the Business Section, Clerk of Courts, New York County, New York, New York, reflect that the MMI was incorporated under the Religious Corporation Law of the State of New York to work for the imparting of the Islamic Faith and Islamic Religion in accordance with "accepted Islamic principles." The principal place of worship to be located in the Borough of Manhattan, New York, New York.

The May 23, 1964 edition of the *New York Amsterdam News,* a weekly Negro newspaper published in New York City, contained an article by columnist JAMES BOOKER in which he indicated that he had heard that the visit by MALCOLM X with Muslim leaders during his African tour has changed him to become more religious.

On October 6, 1964, a confidential source advised that the MMI is apparently affiliated with the true orthodox Islam religion through its affiliation with the Islamic Foundation (of New York), 1 Riverside Drive, New York City. The only teachings of the MMI are on the Islamic religion.

This confidential source advised on May 17, 1965, that the headquarters of the MMI are located in Suite 128, Hotel Theresa, 2090 Seventh Avenue, New York, New York, where they were established on March 16, 1964. These headquarters are shared with the Organization of Afro-American Unity (OAAU) which was also headed by MALCOLM X.

MALCOLM X was assassinated on February 21, 1965 while addressing an OAAU rally at the Audubon Ballroom, Broadway and 166th Street, New York City.

L. Nation of Islam, formerly referred to as the Muslim Cult of Islam, also known as Muhammad's Temples of Islam

In January, 1957, a source advised ELIJAH MUHAMMAD has described his organization on a nationwide basis as the "Nation of Islam" (NOI), and "Muhammad's Temples of Islam."

On May 8, 1964, a second source advised ELIJAH MUHAMMAD is the national leader of the NOI; Muhammad's Temple of Islam No. 2, 5335 South Greenwood Avenue, Chicago, Illinois, is the national headquarters of the NOI; and in mid-1960, MUHAMMAD and other NOI officials, when referring to MUHAMMAD's organization on a nationwide basis, commenced using either "Mosque" or "Temple" when mentioning one of "Muhammad's Temples of Islam."

The NOI is an all-Negro organization which was originally organized in 1930 in Detroit, Michigan. MUHAMMAD claims to have been selected by Allah, the Supreme Being, to lead the so-called Negro race out of slavery in the wilderness of North America by establishing an independent black nation in the United States. Members following MUHAMMAD's teachings and his interpretation of the Koran believe there is no such thing as a Negro; that the so-called Negroes are slaves of the white race, referred to as "white devils," in the United States; and that the white race, because of its exploitation of the so-called Negroes, must and will be destroyed in the approaching "War of Armageddon."

In the past, officials and members of the NOI, including MUHAMMAD, have refused to register under the provisions of the Selective Service Act and have declared that members owe no allegiance to the United States.

On May 5, 1958, the first source advised MUHAMMAD had, upon advice of legal counsel, tempered his personal statements and instructions to his ministers concerning the principles of his organization in order to avoid possible prosecution by the United

States Government; however, he did not indicate any fundamental changes in the teachings of his organization.

On May 7, 1964, a third source advised MUHAMMAD had, early in July, 1958, decided to de-emphasize the religious aspects of the teachings of Islam and to stress the economic benefits to be derived by those Negroes who joined the NOI. This policy change, according to MUHAMMAD, would help him acquire additional followers and create more interest in his programs.

M. Nation of Islam, Mosque No. 7

On May 3, 1965, a source advised that the Nation of Islam (NOI) affiliate in New York City is known as Mosque No. 7, and is also referred to as Temple No. 7. It is part of the national organization of the NOI headed by Elijah Muhammad with headquarters in Chicago, Illinois.

There are three branches of Mosque No. 7; one at 105-03 Northern Boulevard, Queens (known as Mosque No. 7B), another at 120 Madison Street, Brooklyn (known as Mosque No. 7C), and one at 878 Prospect Avenue, Bronx (known as Mosque No. 7D).

There is no branch in Manhattan, although plans are being made to obtain a location which will be the principal meeting place of the Mosque and will be known as Mosque No. 7.

The date Mosque No. 7 originated in New York City is unknown but in this connection it should be noted that in 1953, a second source advised that there was a Temple of the NOI (known to source then as the Muslim Cult of Islam) in New York City located at 135th Street and 7th Avenue, as far back as 1947.

N. Organization of Afro-American Unity, Incorporated (OAAU)

On June 28, 1964, MALCOLM X LITTLE, founder and leader of the Muslim Mosque, Incorporated (MMI), publicly announced the formation of a new, all Negro, militant civil rights action group to be known as the Organization of Afro-American

Unity (OAAU), with himself as chairman. This announcement was made at a public rally held by the MMI in the Audubon Ballroom, Broadway and 166th Street, New York City.

A printed and published statement of basic OAAU aims read by MALCOLM X at this meeting indicates that it shall include "all" people of African descent in the Western Hemisphere, as well as "our" brothers and sisters on the African continent. It is patterned after the "letter and spirit" of the Organization of African Unity established (by African heads of states) at Addis Ababa, Ethiopia, in May, 1963.

A recording of the remarks of MALCOLM X at this meeting indicates that the aim of the OAAU is to eliminate differences between Negroes so they can work together for "human rights," while the initial objective is to "internationalize" the American civil rights movement by taking it to the United Nations. LITTLE condemned the non-violent civil rights movement and claims that Negroes should be taught to protect themselves, when and if necessary. The OAAU will sponsor a program for Negroes of education, politics, culture, economics, and social reform.

On May 17, 1965, a confidential source advised that the headquarters of the OAAU are located in MMI headquarters, Suite 128, Hotel Theresa, 2090 7th Avenue, New York City.

MALCOLM X was assassinated on February 21, 1965, while addressing an OAAU rally at the Audubon Ballroom, New York City.

On April 13, 1965, a second confidential source advised that on March 26, 1965 the OAAU filed a Certificate of Incorporation with the Department of State, State of New York, Albany, New York, and henceforth the organization's true name will be Organization of Afro-American Unity, Incorporated.

O. Progressive Labor Party, Progressive Labor Movement, "Progressive Labor"

A source advised on July 2, 1962, that Progressive Labor groups held a conference in New York City on July 1, 1962, where MILTON ROSEN acted as chairman. He read a statement at this conference setting forth their intention to form a new Marxist-Leninist party in the United States. ROSEN stated that a more formal organization was necessary, one which would provide a framework for all who wanted to join in a united effort to build an American vanguard. The forces of this new organization are to consolidate all existing forces around Progressive Labor and organize additional forces; expand and improve political activities; win additional forces to an outlook of Marxism-Leninism and increase the open advocacy of socialism; develop a significant Marxist-Leninist program for the new party; and organize a collective organization of leaders and members.

The Worker, an East Coast Communist newspaper, issue of January 7, 1962, page 10, column 3, reported the expulsion of MILTON ROSEN, former Labor Secretary of the New York State Communist Party, from the Communist Party, United States of America.

A second and third source advised in February, 1963, that this new Marxist-Leninist party had not yet been organized on a formal basis, but that Progressive Labor groups had been formed in several localities in line with the proposals of MILTON ROSEN. The sources advised as of February, 1963, that the leaders of this group were referring to it as the Progressive Labor Movement.

A fourth source advised on March 15, 1964, that the Progressive Labor Movement follows, supports, and is politically oriented toward the Communist Party line of Red China rather than of the Soviet Union.

A fifth source advised on March 28, 1964, that at a Progressive Labor Movement meeting held in New York City on that date, it was announced that the Progressive Labor Movement would try to hold a national convention in New York City in September, 1964, to organize the Progressive Labor Movement on a more formal basis into a Progressive Labor Party.

The fifth source also advised that the Progressive Labor Movement published a monthly magazine called *Progressive Labor* and also a quarterly theoretical publication called the *Marxist-Lenin-*

ist Quarterly. The source also advised that starting June 1, 1964, the Progressive Labor Movement would start publishing a weekly newspaper in New York City.

The March, 1964, issue of *Progressive Labor* sets forth that it is published monthly by the Progressive Labor Company, General Post Office Box 808, Brooklyn 1, New York.

———————— . ————————

P. Provisional Organizing Committee for a Marxist-Leninist Communist Party (POC); also known as Provisional Organizing Committee for the Reconstitution of a Marxist-Leninist Party; Provisional Committee for the Reconstruction of the Marxist-Leninist Communist Party; Provisional Committee to Reconstitute the Communist Party, USA

The September, 1958, issue of *The Marxist-Leninist Vanguard,* which is self-identified as being published by the "Provisional Organizing Committee for a Marxist-Leninist Communist Party," contains an article on page 1 entitled "Communist Conference" which discloses that a conference was held in New York City, August 16 and 17, 1958, "to guarantee the survival of Marxism-Leninism in the USA." At this conference a call was issued for the formation of a "Provisional Organizing Committee for the Reconstitution of a Marxist-Leninist Party."

In the same issue of *The Marxist-Leninist Vanguard* there is contained "a declaration" which reads in part:

Therefore, we of the Marxist-Leninist caucus of the old Party, having met in a national conference on August 16th–17th, 1958, have constituted ourselves as a Provisional Committee for the Reconstitution of the Marxist-Leninist Communist Party.

The October, 1958, issue of *The Marxist-Leninist Vanguard* on page 1 contains an article entitled, "5 Questions," which stated, "our aim is to forge ahead in our movement, and later, join in a constitutional convention with any other movement which is fighting for the creation of a genuine Communist vanguard party."

[BUREAU DELETION] that the POC continues to function as an organization with most of the meetings being held in the residences of individual members. It has active groups in New York, New York; Chicago, Illinois; Cleveland, Ohio; Philadelphia, Pennsylvania; and Northern California. The organization is also known as the Provisional Committee to Reconstitute the Communist Party, USA.

Q. Revolutionary Action Movement (RAM)

On November 3, 1964, a source made available a document entitled "The Revolutionary Action Movement Manifesto," the document having been obtained by the source from an individual known to be a member of RAM.

This document stated, in part, that RAM was officially organized in the winter of 1963, by Afro-Americans who support the revolutionary objectives of ROBERT F. WILLIAMS, now residing in Cuba, and his concept of organized violence to achieve the liberation of the Afro-American people in the United States. This manifesto reflected that RAM had oriented its program to one of education and political revolution and the organization of a "black" political party with revolutionary objectives, having recognized the need for a "black revolution" that could and would seize power. RAM philosophy is described in this document as one of revolutionary nationalism, that is, one involving the struggles of the non-white races of the world against exploitation and enslavement by the white capitalist and imperialist nations.

Regarding WILLIAMS, above, it should be noted that on August 28, 1961, a Federal warrant was issued at Charlotte, North Carolina, charging him with Unlawful Flight to Avoid Prosecution for the Crime of Kidnapping. Subsequent to the issuance of this warrant, WILLIAMS fled the United States to Cuba, where he now publishes a monthly newsletter entitled *The Crusader,* from Havana.

On November 16, 1964, a second source advised that he

learned recently from a RAM member that the organization was begun in Detroit, Michigan, largely under the impetus of DON FREEMAN, Cleveland, Ohio, described as the "Father" of RAM and referred to as RAM's "Black Stalin." FREEMAN now serves as RAM Chairman, with MAXWELL STANFORD, Philadelphia, Pennsylvania, serving RAM as Field Chairman. This second source advised that there is no formal headquarters, as such, for RAM at present, but that headquarters are, in effect, with FREEMAN since he plays a dominant role in the leadership and directs the policies and activities of the organization.

This second source, in September, 1964, advised that RAM is dedicated to the overthrow of the capitalist system in the United States, by violence if necessary, and to its replacement by a socialistic system oriented toward the Chinese communist interpretation of Marxism-Leninism. RAM is entirely non-white in membership, clandestine in nature, and owes its primary allegiance to the "Bandung World," that is, the non-white races of the world, rather than any national entity, as such.

To date, according to the second source, in November, 1964, RAM has organized units and membership in several of the larger cities in the United States east of the Mississippi River, and the organization is currently active, attempting to recruit new members and expand its sphere of influence.

R. Socialist Workers Party-Los Angeles Local (SWP-LAL)

On [BUREAU DELETION] advised that the SWP-LAL has been in existence since the 1930s and continues to exist. The source further advised that the SWP-LAL is a local branch of the National SWP with aims and purposes identical to those of the National SWP.

The SWP has been designated by the Attorney General of the United States, pursuant to Executive Order 10450.

S. Socialist Workers Party-Philadelphia Branch

A source advised on May 25, 1964, that the Philadelphia Branch of the Socialist Workers Party (PBSWP) is an affiliate of the National SWP, which maintains headquarters at 116 University Place, New York, New York, and, as such, follows the aims and purposes of the National SWP. The source advised that the PBSWP, which has been an active organization in Philadelphia since 1940, does not have a headquarters at the present time but utilizes residences of various members for meetings and functions. The source added that the PBSWP utilizes the name "Militant Labor Forum" for public affairs and "Workers Party" as a ballot name when running candidates for public office.

T. Socialist Workers Party-New York Local

A source stated on August 25, 1960, that the Socialist Workers Party (SWP) New York Local (NYL) was founded in 1938 in New York City.

A second source stated on April 16, 1965, that the NYL was affiliated with and followed the aims and purposes of the National SWP.

The SWP has been designated pursuant to Executive Order 10450.

U. Socialist Workers Party-San Francisco Division

A source advised on August 1, 1960, that the San Francisco Branch of the Socialist Workers Party (SWP) was formed approximately in the early part of 1938 and the Oakland Branch of the SWP was formed in the latter part of 1938.

A second source advised on October 26, 1959, that the name of the Oakland Branch of the SWP was changed to the Oakland-Berkeley Branch of the SWP.

A third source advised on April 20, 1964, that the San Francisco Branch and the Oakland-Berkeley Branch of the SWP follow the policies and directives of the National SWP with which they are affiliated.

The SWP has been designated by the Attorney General of the United States pursuant to Executive Order 10450.

V. Socialist Workers Party-Seattle Branch

In May, 1961, a source advised that during the month of May, 1941, the Seattle Branch of the Socialist Workers Party (SWP) was reorganized and received official recognition as a branch of the Party from the national office of the SWP in New York, New York.

On May 6, 1964, another source advised that the Seattle Branch, SWP, with headquarters at 3815 5th Avenue Northeast, Seattle, Washington, is a present affiliate of the National SWP, following the aims and principles of the National SWP. According to source, membership in the Seattle Branch includes RICHARD FRASER, who is a member of the SWP National Committee, and his wife, CLARA FRASER, who is an alternate member of the SWP National Committee.

W. Workers World Party

On April 17, 1959, a confidential source advised that on February 12, 1959, a Socialist Workers Party (SWP) minority group, under the leadership of National Committee member SAM BALLAN, split from the SWP.

The source stated that this minority group, referred to as the Marcyites, after many years of program and policy differences on varied issues concerning tactics and interpretation of political events, split from the SWP on the grounds that the Party was liquidating itself by departing from the Marxist precepts of LEON TROTSKY and retreating from the fight for the world socialist revolution. The final issue which ultimately forced the split was the minority's opposition to the SWP regroupment policy which involved cooperation with the Communist Party (CP) periphery—individuals characterized by the minority as petit-petty bourgeois.

The minority program, according to the source, advocates unconditional defense of the Soviet Union and has as its goal the building of a revolutionary party with a complete proletarian orientation for the purpose of overthrowing capitalism in the United States and throughout the world.

On May 12, 1960, the source advised that this minority group had chosen the name Workers World Party.

On May 6, 1963, a second confidential source stated that the headquarters of the Workers World Party were located at 46 West 21st Street, New York, New York.

The SWP and the CP have been designated pursuant to Executive Order 10450.

X. Young Socialist Alliance

The May, 1960, issue of the *Young Socialist* (YS), page 1, column 3, disclosed that during April 15 through 17, 1960, a national organization entitled "The Young Socialist Alliance" (YSA) was formed by the nationwide supporter clubs of the publication *YS*.

The above issue, page 6, set forth the Founding Declaration of YSA. This declaration stated that the YSA recognized the Socialist Workers Party (SWP) as the only existing political leadership on class struggle principles, and that the supporters of the *YS* have come into basic political solidarity with the SWP on the principles of revolutionary socialism.

A source advised on May 7, 1965, that the original YSA was an organization formed during October, 1957, in New York City by youth of various left socialist tendencies, particularly members and followers of the SWP. The leaders of this group were the guiding forces in the establishment of the national organization.

The source further advised on May 7, 1965, that the YSA is dominated and controlled on a national basis by the SWP through having SWP members comprise exclusively the National Executive Committee (NEC) and through an official SWP representative at all YSA NEC meetings. The YSA, in reality, is the youth and training section of the SWP and the main source of new SWP members.

The headquarters of the YSA are located in Room 631, 41 Union Square West, New York City.

The SWP has been designated pursuant to Executive Order 10450.

Y. Young Socialist Club of Wayne County (YSC)
also known as Wayne University Young Socialist Club;
Wayne Young Socialist Club;
Young Socialist Club

A source advised in 1955, 1956 and 1957, that the Young Socialist Club of Wayne County, also known as Wayne University Young Socialist Club (YSC), was organized on the campus of the Wayne State University, Detroit, Michigan, in the fall of 1954, through the efforts of the Detroit Branch, Socialist Workers Party (SWP). As a result of the University's action in banning the YSC from campus in the spring of 1956, the YSC adopted the name Young Socialist Club of Wayne County and continued to function by using the facilities of the SWP for its headquarters.

This source advised that the YSC has been controlled and directed by members of the SWP from its inception to the present time. The purpose of the YSC was to afford the SWP an opportunity to make contacts, recruit members in the SWP, and spread propaganda among the students and other young people.

The constitution of the YSC states its purpose "shall be to unite young students, workers, and members of minority groups who wish to build and participate in an independent, militant, socialist group. It shall engage in a broad program of political, educational, and social activities, bringing socialist ideas to young people in an atmosphere of free and open discussion."

Another source advised on August 20, 1958, that the YSC was officially dissolved on August 18, 1958, as a tactical move by the youth faction of the Detroit Branch SWP.

The SWP has been designated pursuant to Executive Order 10450.

ACKNOWLEDGMENTS

This book benefited greatly from the research conducted by members of the Malcolm X seminar I taught at Stanford during the spring of 1991. I wish to thank Leslie Alexander, Kwame Anku, DoBee Ferrell, Michael Friedly, Elizabeth Haydel, Laurie McLean, Antoinette Rogers, Dionne Scott, and Eric Young. Seminar member Heidi Hess made a special contribution to this research effort by volunteering to continue work after the academic year.

I also appreciate the assistance and intellectual stimulation I received from Martin Luther King, Jr., Papers Project staff members and summer interns at Stanford. Andre Namphy of Harvard University worked closely with me as a research assistant during the final stages of manuscript preparation. I also received valuable assistance from King Project interns Brian Woods of Emory University, Holly Bass of Sarah Lawrence College, Theresa Napson of American University; Pamela Nadsen of Columbia University; Audia Wells of Emory University, and Michele Mitchell of Northwestern University. Finally, as always, I benefited from the stimulating comments, critical and supportive, of King Project staff members, namely Stewart Burns, Pete Holloran, Susan Carson, Karl Knapper, Megan Maxwell, and Virginia Shadron.

Index